# The Contested World Econo

The rapid growth of the field of international political economy since the 1970s has revived an older tradition of thought from the pre-1945 era. *The Contested World Economy* provides the first book-length analysis of these deep intellectual roots of the field, revealing how earlier debates about the world economy were more global and wide-ranging than usually recognized. Helleiner shows how pre-1945 pioneers of international political economy included thinkers from all parts of the world rather than just those from Europe and the United States featured in most textbooks. Their discussions also went beyond the much-studied debate between economic liberals, neomercantilists, and Marxists, and addressed wider topics, including many with contemporary relevance, such as environmental degradation, gender inequality, racial discrimination, religious worldviews, civilizational values, national self-sufficiency, and varieties of economic regionalism. This fascinating history of ideas sheds new light on current debates and the need for a global understanding of their antecedents.

Eric Helleiner is Professor and University Research Chair at the Department of Political Science and Balsillie School of International Affairs, University of Waterloo. His previous books include *The Neomercantilists* (2021), *Forgotten Foundations of Bretton Woods* (2014), *The Status Quo Crisis* (2014), and *States and the Reemergence of Global Finance* (1994). He is winner of the 2020 IPE Distinguished Scholar Award (International Studies Association) and the Francesco Guicciardini Prize for Best Book in Historical International Relations (2016).

# The Contested World Economy

## The Deep and Global Roots of International Political Economy

Eric Helleiner

*University of Waterloo, Ontario*

Shaftesbury Road, Cambridge CB2 8EA, United Kingdom

One Liberty Plaza, 20th Floor, New York, NY 10006, USA

477 Williamstown Road, Port Melbourne, VIC 3207, Australia

314–321, 3rd Floor, Plot 3, Splendor Forum, Jasola District Centre,
New Delhi – 110025, India

103 Penang Road, #05–06/07, Visioncrest Commercial, Singapore 238467

Cambridge University Press is part of Cambridge University Press & Assessment,
a department of the University of Cambridge.

We share the University's mission to contribute to society through the pursuit of
education, learning and research at the highest international levels of excellence.

www.cambridge.org
Information on this title: www.cambridge.org/9781009337502

DOI: 10.1017/9781009337489

First published 2023

*A catalogue record for this publication is available from the British Library.*

*A Cataloging-in-Publication data record for this book is available from the Library of
Congress.*

ISBN 978-1-009-33750-2 Hardback
ISBN 978-1-009-33752-6 Paperback

To Gerry

# Contents

# Preface

I have thought about writing this book for quite some time. Since I began teaching international political economy (IPE) over three decades ago, I have been struck by the absence of a volume that could help students understand the deep and global roots of this field in the pre-1945 years. Using the terminology of the historian Fernand Braudel, one could say that IPE has been missing a relatively succinct summary of its history from the standpoint of both the "longue durée" and "the perspective of the world". For many years, I have tried to fill this gap in various *ad hoc* ways for students while working on other research topics. About a decade ago, however, I decided that it was time to begin to try to fill this gap in the literature because I did not see anyone else taking up the task.

Initially, I thought I could write this book relatively quickly. How mistaken I was. Very early on in the project, I recognized many limitations in my own historical knowledge and the need to rectify them with much more extensive reading of primary and secondary literature than I had anticipated. The learning process has been both humbling and energizing, and I am more aware than ever of many enduring holes in my knowledge of various specific dimensions of this subject. Since my goal has been to produce a relatively succinct survey of this topic, however, I had to stop the research at some point. I have not been able to include in this book all the fascinating material I have learned. (Some additional analysis can be found in my 2021 book *The Neomercantilists* as well as various articles and chapters I have written.) But this wider reading has informed the choices that I have made about what to include and what to leave out of this book. I hope these choices have produced a book that is useful not just for the next generation of students but also for established scholars in the field. At the very least, I will be happy if readers find this history as interesting as it has been to me.

This project could not have been completed without the help of many others. To begin with, I am enormously grateful to the Killam Research Fellowship program of the Canada Council for the Arts for providing me with more time to conduct the research than I would normally have had. I also thank the Social Sciences and Humanities Research Council of Canada for the supporting this research project (grant number 435-2015-0571). Many thanks, too, to John Haslam for his interest in this project as well as to Toby Ginsberg for supporting the publication process. I am also grateful to Taarini Chopra for editing help and to the many students who have provided such useful insights and feedback on the material we were studying together over the years. I have also learned so much from many scholars around the world who have done important work on various dimensions of the history of political economy. I could not have written this book without their outstanding research. I am particularly indebted to those with language skills I do not have who made many thinkers and intellectual traditions understandable to me in ways that they would not otherwise have been.

I would also like to express my thanks to many anonymous reviewers who provided excellent comments on this manuscript and other related work I have written as well as to Derek Hall for some particularly helpful comments and conversations in the final stages of the project. I am also very grateful to many other people who gave me useful advice, comments, and/or research help along the way, including Rawi Abdelal, John Abraham, Jeremy Adelman, Andrew Baker, Cornel Ban, Fernando Barcellos, Rachel Beal, Judy Bennett, Nick Bernard, Andrea Bianculli, Ricardo Bielschosky, Matthew Bishop, David Blaney, Mark Blyth, Dorothee Bohle, Mauro Boianovsky, Gabriel Brasil, Mehmet Bulut, Ana Flávia Cardoso, Hyoung-kyu Chey, Greg Chin, Chris Clarke, Judy Clapp, Benjamin Cohen, Katharina Coleman, Peter Dauvergne, Robert Denemark, Vash Doshi, Nat Dyer, Sarah Eaton, Marc Flandeau, Jane Forgay, Marc-André Gagnon, Abel Gaiya, Andrew Gamble, Patti Goff, Ilene Grabel, Stephan Haggard, Elsbeth Heaman, John Hobson, Emma Huang, Onur Ulas Ince, Harold James, Jeremiah Johnson, Juliet Johnson, Miles Kahler, Yarlisan Kanagarajah, Saori Katada, Deniz Kilinçoğlu, Amy King, Jonathan Kirshner, Seçkin Köstem, Amitav Kutt, Genevieve Lebaron, Madison Lee, Mario Alfonso Lima, Stefan Link, Jane Lister, Joseph Love, Laura MacDonald, Mackenzie Macleod, Anton Malkin, Jamie Martin, Sarah Martin, Mauricio Metri, Mark Metzler, Olga Mikheeva, Rana Mitter, Mary Morgan, Manuela Moschella, Isabela Nogueira de Morais, Andreas Nölke, Raphael Padula, Şevket Pamuk, Rosario Patalano, Megan Pickup, Yuri Pines, German Prieto, Andrés Rivarola Puntigliano, Cintia Quiliconi, Vikram Raghavan, Syahirah Abdul Rahman, M. V. Ramana, Fabio Rambelli, Leonardo Ramos, Salim Rashid, John Ravenhill, Lena Rethel, Adrienne Roberts, Cristina Rojas, Ariel Ron, Antulio Rosales, Aditi Sahasrabuddhe, Eduardo Silva, Tim Sinclair, Quinn Slodobian, Irene Spagna, Glenda Sluga, Frances

Stewart, Maria Dyveke Styve, Lisa Sundstrom, Masayuki Tadokoro, Burak Tansel, Maria Antonieta Del Tedesco Lins, Yves Tibergen, Christy Thornton, Ernani Torres, Diana Tussie, Oscar Ugarteche, Erik van Ree, Ernesto Vivares, Andrew Walter, Hongying Wang, Mat Watson, Isabella Weber, Heather Whiteside, Sandra Whitworth, Guo Wu, Jeremy Yellen, Sandra Young, Ali Zaidi, and Shizhi Zhang.

I apologize to those I have forgotten and thank them too, including people who raised useful questions and comments during presentations I made at the Balsillie School of International Affairs, Bilkent Üniversitesi, Boston University, Brown University, Carleton University, Cornell University, Duke University, École Nationale d'Administration Publique, European University Institute, FLASCO Ecuador, Humboldt-Universität zu Berlin, Institut Barcelona D'Estudis Internacionals, Princeton University, Scuola Normale Superiore, Sheffield University, Texas A&M University, Tulane University, Universidad de Buenos Aires, Universidade de São Paolo, Universidade Federal do Rio de Janeiro, Université de Montréal, University of British Columbia, University of California, Santa Barbara, University College London, Université de Genève, University of Manchester, University of Melbourne, University of Oslo, and University of Southern California, as well as at meetings of the Canadian Political Science Association, History of Economics Society, and International Studies Association. Some parts of Chapter 8 appeared in "The return of national self-sufficiency?" *International Studies Review* 23(3)(2021): 933–57, published open access under the terms of the Creative Commons CC BY license (https://creativecommons.org/licenses/by/4.0/) at https://academic.oup.com/isr/article/23/3/933/6063510 with copyright @ 2021 Oxford University Press.

Jennifer deserves special thanks for her insights and for much else that would take pages to list. I also want to give special thanks to Gerry, to whom this book is dedicated. Had he been born in a different generation, he too might have studied IPE. No doubt, he must be part of the reason I have been drawn to the field (although he certainly never tried to steer me in that direction). But my thanks are not just for that. They are even more for his patience, understanding, sense of humour, commitment, compassion, optimism, and ability to recognize the important things in life. I am so lucky to have had his support and companionship on this and other journeys.

# Abbreviations

| | |
|---|---|
| AICW | Inter-American Commission of Women |
| APRA | Alianza Popular Revolucionaria Americana |
| CCP | Chinese Communist Party |
| GEACS | Greater East Asia Co-Prosperity Sphere |
| GMD | Guomindang |
| IAB | Inter-American Bank |
| IBRD | International Bank for Reconstruction and Development |
| ILO | International Labour Organization |
| IMF | International Monetary Fund |
| IPE | international political economy |
| ITUCNW | International Trade Union Committee of Negro Workers |
| LSI | Labour and Socialist International |
| NAACP | National Association for the Advancement of Colored People |
| PKI | Partai Komunis Indonesia |
| SI | Sareket Islam |
| UNIA | Universal Negro Improvement Association |
| US | United States |
| WILPF | Women's International League for Peace and Freedom |

# 1    Introduction and Overview

Scholars of international political economy (IPE) often locate the origins of their field in the contested nature of the world economy of the early 1970s. Interest in the subject was bolstered by dramatic developments such as the US government's ending of the official convertibility of US dollars into gold (1971), the massive hike of the oil price by major oil-producing states (1973), and the call for a New International Economic Order from a wide coalition of less industrialized countries (1974). Scholarship on these and other dimensions of international economic relations began to be described formally as "IPE", a subject which then soon had its own textbooks and university courses.[1]

Although the global upheavals of the early 1970s encouraged the growth of the formal field of IPE, many of its early proponents emphasized that their subject had much deeper roots. They drew important inspiration from earlier political economists who had an international focus, particularly those from the pre-1945 period. For example, Susan Strange, one of the key architects of the field during the 1970s, highlighted that IPE was "more a rebirth or revival than a birth".[2] A similar point was made by another important pioneer of IPE, Benjamin Cohen, in his widely cited history of the field's growth after 1970: "though we date the modern study of IPE only from the 1970s, the field's roots go much further back".[3]

Despite comments such as these, IPE's antecedents in the pre-1945 era remain understudied. Particularly striking has been the absence of a book that attempts to provide an overview of the field's pre-1945 roots. This situation contrasts sharply with closely related subjects, such as international relations, economics, or political theory, all of which have done a much better job at telling their respective deep histories. In the words of Helge Hveem, "contemporary IPE's lack of reflection of its

---

[1] Cohen 2008. See also Clift et al. 2022, 346 for how references to "international political economy" surged at this time.
[2] Strange 1985, 14.
[3] Cohen 2008, 17.

long history is striking".[4] In this book, I have tried to begin to fill this gap in existing literature.

I have taken up this task because of a belief that scholars and students of IPE would benefit from a better understanding of the pre-1945 intellectual roots of their field. In addition to being intrinsically interesting, analyses from this earlier era provide insights into many topics that remain highly relevant to IPE scholarship today (as well as to that in other fields of study with overlapping interests in the politics of the world economy). Knowledge of this history is also important because participants in contemporary political debates often invoke it. Indeed, even politicians and policymakers with little awareness of pre-1945 history are influenced by thinkers from that era. As the political economist John Maynard Keynes famously noted, "madmen in authority, who hear voices in the air, are distilling their frenzy from some academic scribbler of a few years back".[5] Many ideas developed during the pre-1945 years endure as "voices in the air" that continue to shape contemporary discussions about issues that interest IPE scholars.

This book has also been motivated by two specific frustrations with how IPE's pre-1945 history is conventionally depicted. When IPE textbooks refer to this deep history, they typically focus on leading thinkers from Europe and the United States who helped to pioneer the distinct perspectives of economic liberalism (such as Adam Smith and David Ricardo), neomercantilism (such as Alexander Hamilton and Friedrich List), and Marxism (Karl Marx and later Marxist theorists of imperialism such as Vladimir Lenin and Rosa Luxemburg).[6] Students certainly need to learn about these figures, not least because their ideas were prominent in the past and remain so in contemporary debates. But they should also be taught about pre-1945 thinkers from other parts of the world as well as about perspectives beyond these "three orthodoxies" that were influential before 1945.

This volume widens the deep history of IPE in both of these ways. First, it embraces a more *global* conception of the field's pre-1945 roots

---

[4] Hveem 2009, 371. See also Hobson 2019, 150. This volume focuses on the pre-1945 era, but important analyses were also developed between 1945 and the early 1970s (e.g. Cohen 2008, 20–21; Germain 2021; Hirschman 1945; Palma 2009; Tussie and Chagas-Bastos 2022; Weber 2015, 927–29). A full history of relevant analyses in that era has yet to be written.

[5] Keynes 1936, 383.

[6] I have included Russian thinkers such as Lenin in the "European" category in this book, but Russian intellectuals after 1917 increasingly depicted Russian identity as "Eurasian" (e.g. Tikhonov 2016, 388). I have tried not to use the terms "Western" and "non-Western" very frequently in the book because of the complications they raise (e.g. Tussie and Chagas-Bastos 2022) and because they were not commonly used before the late nineteenth century (Osterhammel 2014, 86).

by highlighting contributions made by thinkers not just from Europe and the United States but also from elsewhere.[7] Some of the latter thinkers adapted the three orthodoxies emerging from Europe and the United States in innovative ways. Others developed independent versions of those three perspectives. Still others developed perspectives with quite different content. In some cases, thinkers from these other parts of the world also influenced thinkers in Europe and the United States themselves.

Many of these contributions from beyond Europe and the United States – and the thinkers who made them – continue to be invoked in political discourse and contemporary IPE scholarship in the places where they lived (and beyond). This volume is designed to improve understanding of these contemporary references in ways that can both enrich analyses of contemporary political debates and help to build more "global conversations" among IPE scholars across the globe.[8] For those who are committed to the latter task, this book may also provide some inspiration by revealing extensive and multidirectional international flows of ideas among earlier political economists in the pre-1945 era.

Second, this book also seeks to widen the deep history of IPE by showing that discussions of the international dimensions of political economy before 1945 involved much more than a debate between the three perspectives of economic liberalism, neomercantilism, and Marxism. One limitation of this conventional focus is that it downplays important internal divisions *within* each of these perspectives. These divisions were often just as interesting and important as the ones that separated the three perspectives from each other. For example, one of the most important phenomena shaping the world economy in this era – imperialism – had supporters and opponents among each of the three perspectives.[9] In the process of featuring this and other internal divisions within each of the three orthodoxies, this volume highlights some thinkers who receive little attention in existing IPE textbooks but whose ideas were important in their time and have sometimes left lasting legacies into the current era.

---

[7] This approach complements recent IPE scholarship that presents more global conceptions of the history of the world economy itself (e.g. Hobson 2020) as well as recent work that provides a more global perspective on the history of the field of international relations (Acharya and Buzan 2020). Because some thinkers discussed in this volume moved around, the division between thinkers from Europe and the United States, and those from elsewhere is not always straightforward. Where this is relevant, I have tried to explain in footnotes why I have located people in one category or another.

[8] See, for example, Blyth 2009; Chin, Pearson, and Wang 2014; Deciancio and Quiliconi 2020; Tussie and Riggirozzi 2015.

[9] The word "imperialism" is usually used in this book to refer to the control of foreign territories by formal colonial rule, but two Peruvian thinkers discussed in the volume – José Carlos Mariátegui (Chapter 7) and Víctor Raúl Haya de la Torre (Chapter 13) – used it in a wider way to refer to control via economic domination.

An even more important limitation of the conventional focus on the three-way debate is that it overlooks many other relevant perspectives that were prominent in the pre-1945 period. Almost half of this volume is devoted to describing these other perspectives (as well as many divisions within them), including autarkism, environmentalism, feminism, Pan-Africanism, Pan-Islamism, Pan-Asianism, and some distinctive visions of economic regionalism.[10] The content of some of these perspectives sometimes overlapped with that of the three orthodoxies, but they each raised distinctive ideas that deserve more attention in IPE textbook accounts of pre-1945 debates. In telling this wider history, I demonstrate how these earlier debates covered many topics that are attracting growing attention in IPE scholarship, such as national self-sufficiency, environmental degradation, gender inequality, racism, religious worldviews, civilizational values, and varieties of economic regionalism. Scholars and students interested in these topics today can learn much from studying these earlier analyses.

In short, this book seeks not just to improve knowledge of the deep intellectual roots of the field of IPE but to do so through an approach that is wider – both in its geography and content – than the conventional one in the field's textbooks. It highlights the richness of pre-1945 debates on topics of interest to IPE scholars today, debates that involved more than just thinkers from Europe and the United States and more than just a debate between economic liberals, neomercantilists, and Marxists. Of course, the book does not claim to provide a fully comprehensive analysis of pre-1945 thought in this area. That task would require a much longer volume. Instead, I have restricted my focus to thinkers whose ideas became quite well known either in specific settings or more widely at the international level. Some readers will no doubt find this focus too narrow, but I ask them to recognize my goal of providing a relatively succinct introduction to these pre-1945 intellectual roots of IPE.

I have also imposed a temporal constraint on the analysis by starting with Adam Smith's publication of *The Wealth of Nations* in 1776. The decision to start with this European thinker might seem odd for a volume that aims to create a more global history of ideas. It is, however, linked to this very focus. The European economic liberal tradition that Smith helped to pioneer was the first perspective on political economy to achieve worldwide influence. A century after the publication

---

[10] Other perspectives could be mentioned, such as non-Marxist versions of socialism. Various chapters in this book identify thinkers who were non-Marxist socialists (either because they were sceptical of Marxism or because they were pre-Marxist socialists), but their ideas about the international dimensions of political economy were extremely disparate. The distinctiveness of each of their views related more to their connection to the other perspectives I have identified.

of *The Wealth of Nations*, thinkers as far away as in Japan noted the global impact of Smith's work, expressing amazement about how "the intellectual power of a single man can change the face of the entire world".[11] Half a century later, the prominent Indian scholar Benoy Kumar Sarkar also insisted that "modern civilization begins in 1776 with the publication of Adam Smith's *Wealth of Nations*".[12] Because Smith's book was the first to assume such a prominent place in debates about political economy across the world, it is a useful place to begin a globally oriented history of the deep roots of the field of IPE.

I hasten to add that my choice of this starting point is not meant to imply that pre-Smithian analyses of political economy are undeserving of attention. As I will show, many such analyses informed the perspectives discussed in this book in important ways. Smith himself was reacting against earlier European mercantilist works of political economy.[13] Pre-Smithian texts analyzing political economy from other parts of the world were also cited by various thinkers in the nineteenth and early twentieth centuries, including some that long predated European mercantilism, such as Ibn Khaldun's work from fourteenth-century North Africa or the much older *Arthashastra* in South Asia and the Chinese texts *Guanzi* and *The Book of Lord Shang*. Although some scholars have suggested the study of political economy was invented in early modern Europe, the thinkers who referenced such works believed that it had wider and earlier origins.

## The Story in Brief

The book's history begins with an analysis of the ideas not just of Smith but also of other European thinkers who developed international dimensions of the classical economic liberal tradition, including David Ricardo, Richard Cobden, John Stuart Mill, and Walter Bagehot. Chapter 2 highlights how these economic liberals shared the belief that free trade and free markets would foster global prosperity, international peace, and individual liberty. At the same time, they did not always concur about the precise ways in which these outcomes would be generated by the policies they favoured or even which of them was most important. They also disagreed about issues such as: the universal relevance of economic liberalism; how extensive international specialization should be; their willingness to endorse exceptions to free trade; their interest in economic

---

[11] Fukuzawa [1875]2009, 107.
[12] Sarkar 1922, 144.
[13] In the European context, the first use of the term "political economy" is usually credited to Antoine de Montchrétien in 1615 (Palatano 2016).

integration beyond free trade in goods; as well as the place of force, imperialism, civilizational discourse, and intergovernmental cooperation in the economic liberal project. In other words, I highlight how there were many varieties of European classical economic liberalism rather than just one.

The diversity within the economic liberal perspective grew further when its ideas attracted the attention of thinkers from other parts of the world in the nineteenth and early twentieth centuries. Chapter 3 shows how many non-European thinkers who were attracted to economic liberalism also adapted it in various ways to better fit their local contexts. I highlight adaptations made by various thinkers from the Americas (Carlos Calvo, Thomas Cooper, Harold Innis, José da Silva Lisboa, Manuel Pardo y Lavalle), South Asia (Dadabhai Naoroji, Rammohun Roy), Africa and the Ottoman Empire (Alexander Crummell, Hassuna D'Ghies, Olaudah Equiano), as well as East Asia (Taguchi Ukichi, Yan Fu). In addition, I demonstrate how the ideas of some of these figures found an audience in Europe, revealing how liberal ideas flowed not just from Europe to the rest of the world but also in the other direction. Further, some economic liberals outside Europe questioned the European origins of this perspective by claiming its independent roots in their own region. In the Chinese case, I also describe how a thinker living at roughly the same time as Adam Smith, Chen Hongmou, developed ideas that bore some similarities to aspects of European economic liberalism without knowledge of the latter.

The rest of the first section of the volume examines the two prominent reactions against classical economic liberalism that are featured in most IPE textbooks: neomercantilism and Marxism. Neomercantilists rejected the liberal advocacy of free trade, urging instead strategic trade protectionism and other forms of government economic activism in order to promote state wealth and power.[14] Their goals were similar to those of pre-Smithian mercantilist thinkers, but they defended their priorities in new ways by engaging critically with classical economic liberal thought. Chapter 4 describes the much-studied role of Hamilton and List in helping to pioneer neomercantilist thought, but it also features other thinkers who developed distinctive and influential versions of this perspective in Europe (William Ashley, Mihail Manoilescu, Gustav Schmoller, Sergei Witte) and the United States (Henry Carey). The ideas of these latter thinkers highlight how neomercantilism in Europe and United States had more diverse content than the common textbook depiction suggests.

---

[14] The "neomercantilist" perspective is sometimes referred to as an "economic nationalist" or "realist" one in IPE textbooks. I have discussed elsewhere why I think "neomercantilism" is the more useful label (Helleiner 2021a, 3–10).

Chapter 5 examines neomercantilist thinkers from outside Europe and the United States whose thought also became well known in various places during the nineteenth and early twentieth centuries. Some of them adapted ideas described in Chapter 4 in creative ways, including thinkers from Argentina (Alejandro Bunge), Australia (David Syme), China (Liang Qichao), Ethiopia (Gabrahiwot Baykadagn), India (Mahadev Govind Ranade, Benoy Kumar Sarkar), and Turkey (Ziya Gökalp). Others developed unique neomercantilist ideas without much, or any, reference to neomercantilist thought from Europe and the United States, including figures in Canada (John Rae), China (Sun Yat-sen, Zheng Guanying), Egypt (Muhammad Ali), Japan (Fukuzawa Yukichi, Ōkubo Toshimichi), and Korea (Yu Kil-chun). This second group of thinkers reveal how the ideas of Hamilton and List did not play the same kind of central role in the emergence of neomercantilist thought that Smith's did in the growth of economic liberalism. Taken together, all the thinkers described in this chapter reinforce the point that neomercantilist thought was characterized – like that of economic liberalism – by considerable diversity.

Marxists reacted against the core goals of classical economic liberalism in quite a different way. They sought to challenge capitalism in order to end class-based inequality and exploitation within the world economy. Chapter 6 analyzes Marx's ideas about global capitalism as well as those of some of his influential European (including Russian) followers. The latter included thinkers commonly discussed in IPE textbooks, such as Lenin and Luxemburg, but also other European thinkers who usually receive less attention (such as Carl Ballod, Rudolph Hilferding, Henry Hyndman, Karl Kautsky, Leon Trotsky, and Georg Vollmar). As with classical economic liberals and neomercantilists, I highlight important differences among the ideas of these various Marxist thinkers. The differences cut across a wide range of topics such as their views of free trade, imperialism, multilateral cooperation, strategies for challenging capitalism, the prospects for socialism in one country, and the relationship between capitalism and war.

Chapter 7 shows how Marxist thought diffused to other parts of the world, attracting support from many thinkers who made important and innovative contributions to this intellectual tradition. I focus on figures from a number of places, including Trinidad (C. L. R. James, George Padmore), China (Mao Zedong), India (Manabendra Nath Roy), Indonesia (Tan Malaka), Japan (Kōtoku Shusui, Takahashi Kamekichi, Sano Manabu), and Peru (José Carlos Mariátegui). Each of these figures became well known in specific contexts and, in some cases, in wider international Marxist networks. In addition to sometimes developing ideas that predated better-known European ones on the same subject, they often called attention to issues that received less attention in European Marxist debates, such as racial discrimination, Eurocentrism, the relationship between Marxism and Islam, the nature and impact of imperialism outside of Europe, and revolutionary politics in places subject to imperialism.

While the first section of the book attempts to broaden understandings of classical economic liberalism, neomercantilism, and Marxism, the second seeks to show that a focus on these three perspectives is too narrow. During the period examined in this book, political economy debates with an international focus went well beyond disagreements between and among thinkers holding these perspectives. They also involved thinkers committed to other perspectives with distinctive goals that had a high political profile in many contexts around the world.

The first of these was an autarkic perspective that prioritized the promotion of a state's economic self-sufficiency in order to enhance its autonomy from foreign influence.[15] This autarkic goal was rejected by classical economic liberals, neomercantilists, and most Marxists, and it is usually ignored in IPE textbooks. But Chapter 8 identifies influential autarkic ideas developed by a number of thinkers from places as diverse as Britain (John Maynard Keynes, just briefly in 1933), China (Chen Gongbo), Germany (Johann Fichte, Friedrich Zimmermann), Haiti (Edmund Paul), India (Mohandas Gandhi), Japan (Aizawa Seishisai, Shizuki Tadao), Korea (Lee Hang-ro), Paraguay (José Gaspar Rodríguez de Francia), Russia (Peter Kropotkin), Turkey (Sevket Süreyya Aydemir), and the West African colony of the Gold Coast (Kobina Sekyi). The chapter also highlights important disagreements amongst these thinkers, ranging from the specific reasons they prioritized state autonomy to their views of the relationship between autarky and peace.

Chapter 9 examines a perspective that is usually portrayed in IPE textbooks as one that has emerged only in more recent decades: environmentalism. I show how a number of thinkers in the pre-1945 period developed pioneering environmentalist ideas that gained considerable attention in their time. With differing degrees of commitment, these figures were united by their desire to curtail human-induced environmental degradation in the world economy in order to foster more sustainable ways of living. They disagreed, however, about the causes of, and solutions to, the environmental degradation they identified. Some combined their environmentalism with economic liberal views (Alexander von Humboldt, Stanley Jevons); others with neomercantilism (Henry Carey); still others with Marxism (Marx himself) and autarkism (Eve Balfour,

---

[15] Autarkic goals could also be applied to larger entities such as regions, as noted in Chapter 13.

Graham Vernon Jacks, Sada Kaiseki). Some also promoted environmentalist ideas that did not fit well into any of those categories, such as the Lakotan cosmology of Black Elk, the "Cartesian" approach of Frederick Soddy, and the decentralist visions of Richard Gregg, Radhakamal Mukerjee, Lewis Mumford, and John Ruskin.

Feminism is another perspective often depicted as a more recent one in IPE debates, but it too had important roots in the pre-1945 years. Chapter 10 highlights many thinkers from that era who challenged patriarchal practices and structures in order to end women's subordination within the world economy. Like pre-1945 environmentalists, there were many divisions among these thinkers that overlapped with other perspectives. The most prominent divide was between those who sought to promote feminist goals within an economic liberal framework (Jane Addams, Bertha Lutz, Chrystal Macmillan, Harriet Martineau) and those more drawn to socialism and Marxism (Williama Burroughs, Kamaladevi Chattopadhyaya, Aleksandra Kollontai, Paulina Luisi, Magda Portal, Clara Zetkin). Some other thinkers also linked feminist goals to other perspectives such as neomercantilism (once again, Henry Carey), Pan-Africanism (Amy Ashwood Garvey), and anarchism (He-Yin Zhen).

Chapter 11 analyzes a perspective – Pan-Africanism – that rarely is mentioned in IPE textbooks, despite the wide support it garnered in many parts of the world from the start of the twentieth century onwards. Many of its advocates were keenly interested in the international dimensions of political economy. Specifically, important Pan-African thinkers sought to cultivate the economic solidarity of Africans and the African diaspora in order to challenge their subordinate position in the world economy. While feminists highlighted the patriarchal nature of the world economy, Pan-Africanists challenged its racialized hierarchies. They included three thinkers who are discussed in earlier chapters: Amy Ashwood Garvey, C. L. R. James, and George Padmore. Chapter 11 focuses on three other prominent Pan-African thinkers who developed innovative ideas on this topic: W. E. B. Du Bois, Marcus Garvey, and Hubert Harrison. While sharing core Pan-African goals, these thinkers disagreed about a number of issues, ranging from their views of capitalism to the role of the African diaspora in Pan-African politics.

Also overlooked in most IPE textbooks are other "Pan" perspectives in the late nineteenth and early twentieth centuries that invoked different kinds of transnational identities. Chapter 12 focuses on two influential ones whose supporters developed innovative religious and civilizational perspectives on the international dimensions of political economy: Pan-Islamism and Pan-Asianism. These thinkers sought to cultivate the economic solidarity of a transnational community that was conceptualized in either religious (Pan-Islamism) or civilizational (Pan-Asianism) terms in order to promote its common interests and values within the world economy. The discussion of the Pan-Islamic movement focuses on three prominent figures: Jamal al-Din al-Afghani, the Ottoman sultan Abdulhamid II, and Sayyid Abul A'la Mawdudi. The key Pan-Asian thinker examined is Sun Yat-sen, who fused his neomercantilist ideas (discussed in Chapter 5) with a vision of Pan-Asian economic solidarity and of an international economic order inspired by Chinese tributary norms.

The final chapter of the second section of the book examines some distinctive ideas about economic regionalism that also receive little attention in IPE textbook accounts of pre-1945 thought. Some thinkers discussed in other chapters of this book endorsed the idea of regional free trade arrangements, but this chapter highlights quite different conceptions of economic regionalism that emerged during the interwar years and the early 1940s. Some arose in the context of Japanese debates about a Greater East Asia Co-Prosperity Sphere, of which the most sophisticated was Akamatsu Kaname's "Wild Geese Flying Pattern theory" of regional economic integration. Others were associated with post-1933 German designs for Europe's economy, including "Schachtian" managed bilateralism (Hjalmar Schacht), fascist multilateralism (Walther Funk), and visions of a "great-space economy" (Friedrich Zimmermann). The final example comes from Peru's Víctor Raúl Haya de la Torre, who advanced a distinctive anti-imperialist vision of regionalism initially through what he called "Indoamerican economic nationalism" within Latin America and then via a wider vision of "democratic Interamericanism without empire" that was inclusive of the United States.

The book's analysis ends at a place that many IPE courses begin: the 1944 Bretton Woods conference. Thanks to John Ruggie's, IPE scholars are very familiar with the "embedded liberal" perspective of the Anglo-American officials who helped to design the postwar global economic order at that meeting, particularly John Maynard Keynes (who had abandoned his brief interest in autarky by this time) and Harry Dexter White.[16] Chapter 14 describes how these thinkers reformulated classical economic liberalism by promoting a novel kind of institutionalized multilateralism that would make an open world economy compatible with active public management of the economy in order to boost global prosperity, international peace, and individual freedom. The chapter also goes beyond Ruggie's analysis by tracing some intellectual roots of this perspective earlier in the twentieth century, including

---

[16] Ruggie 1982.

through an examination of the ideas of thinkers such as Jehangir Coyajee and John Hobson. It also highlights how embedded liberals at Bretton Woods were interested in broader kinds of active public management of the economy than those emphasized by Ruggie.

The chapter also calls attention to another neglected issue in Ruggie's work (and most other literature on embedded liberalism): the relative silences of the Bretton Woods' architects concerning the perspectives discussed in the second section of this book. Although scholars rarely comment on these silences, they are noteworthy in light of the influence these perspectives had in other contexts during the lead-up to, and at the time of, the 1944 conference. The fact that they received little attention from the embedded liberals of Bretton Woods sheds important light on the latter's priorities. Those priorities, in turn, had important consequences for the trajectory of global economic governance in the post-1945 world. For this reason, the pre-1945 history told in this book is important even for students and scholars whose IPE courses begin with Bretton Woods. It sheds new light on that foundational moment in the historical evolution of global economic governance.

There are, thus, many reasons for widening the deep history of IPE. The concluding chapter summarizes the case for embracing this approach (beyond the fact that it provides a new perspective on the embedded liberalism of Bretton Woods). The chapter emphasizes the ways in which this wider approach provides a more comprehensive account of the field's deep history, bringing some neglected voices and debates more centrally into the story. It also highlights how this wider history can help strengthen efforts to foster more "global conversations" in the field of IPE today, improve analyses of contemporary political discourse, and contribute to the study of topics that are attracting growing interest within contemporary IPE scholarship.

### Some Final Comments

Before proceeding into the detailed history, I need to add some final comments. First, although this book seeks to widen IPE's deep history, I am very aware of many limitations in my coverage (and likely unaware of others). Two limitations have already been noted: the focus only on ideas that became quite well known and the temporal decision to begin with Smith's work. Some of the other limitations relate to my language skills and access to translations as well as weaknesses in my regional- and country-specific knowledge. Another limitation of all histories of this kind is their heavy dependence on texts that have been preserved. This dependence skews the analysis away from a focus on figures (often less powerful ones) who expressed their ideas through other means as well as on those whose texts have not been well preserved.

Second, some readers may think I have cast the net too narrowly by focusing on a history of ideas relating to "international political economy" rather than "global political economy". The former was the label chosen by the pioneers of the formal field in the early 1970s, but many scholars now prefer the term "global political economy" (GPE) in order to emphasize that they are focused on more than just economic relations between "nations" or states.[17] Some, for example, study the ways in which political economy at the domestic level interacts with that at the international or global level. Others are interested in analyzing the politics of the world economy as a whole. I am very sympathetic to these wider understandings of the focus of the field. Indeed, it should be evident already that many of the thinkers discussed in this book were concerned with much more than just international economic relations.

In this volume, however, I have decided to retain the label "international political economy" for two very practical reasons. First, it continues to be very widely used, even by those who have a wide view of the field's focus. Second, it has helped me to keep this project manageable by encouraging a focus on thinkers who said at least something about international economic relations (including the relations of imperial powers with colonized peoples as well as the engagement with economic issues by multilateral institutions). In other words, my criteria for selecting thinkers has had a minimum condition of meeting the narrow conception of the focus of the field, even though many of them had a much wider focus, including on the politics of the world economy as a whole. In this way, I hope this history will be of interest both to those who prefer the narrower conception of the field and to those with a broader view. I also hope it might be useful for many scholars and students in other fields – such as international relations, economics, history, geography, sociology, anthropology, business studies, and international law – who may not see themselves as part of the formal field of IPE/GPE but whose interests overlap with it in various ways.

Third, some readers may think this book is too narrow in another sense. Many intellectual historians have noted the difficulty of interpreting historical ideas without a detailed understanding of the context within which they were developed and the specific goals of those who developed them.[18] Once again, I am very sympathetic to this point. Given the spatial and

---

[17] The term "international" was coined by Adam Smith's contemporary, Jeremy Bentham, in the 1780s (Pitts 2018, 118; Suganami 1978).

[18] For discussion of this issue in the context of the history of international relations, see Ashworth 2019.

temporal scope of this volume, however, I do not have room to explore these issues in depth with respect to each of the various thinkers being discussed. Without getting too caught up in terminological issues, I have written this book more as a conventional "history of ideas" than as a work of "intellectual history" in the way this latter term is often used today.

Fourth, readers may be struck by the gender imbalance among the thinkers discussed. This imbalance relates to the broader male dominance in public debates about political economy – and many other academic subjects – in this period. Indeed, it is striking how some men even tried to claim the subject as a masculine one. For example, male readers of the first known political economy treatise published by a Japanese woman (the text appeared in 1817–18) described its author, Tadano Makuzu, as "thinking like a man" and having a "manly" mind.[19] Other anti-feminist views expressed by prominent political economists are described in Chapter 7. The relatively small number of women discussed in this volume, in other words, is linked to the wider patriarchal structures against which the feminists discussed in that chapter were fighting.

Fifth, some readers may question whether some of the perspectives I discuss include collections of thinkers whose views were too disparate to be usefully placed together under one umbrella. I certainly understand this concern, particularly since one of my objectives is to call attention to many divisions within these various perspectives. Still, I believe some core goals joined thinkers into the groupings I have identified. Summarizing the discussion above, I have consolidated these goals into very succinct descriptions in Table 1.1.

I need to emphasize that many thinkers advanced ideas that cut across these categories. For example, I have already noted how many environmentalists and feminists embraced other perspectives such as economic liberalism, neomercantilism, Marxism, autarkism, and Pan-Africanism. I have also highlighted how Marxists such as C. L. R. James and George Padmore endorsed Pan-Africanism, while Sun Yat-sen combined support for neomercantilism with Pan-Asianism. There are many other thinkers discussed in the book who mixed and matched perspectives in creative ways. Students and scholars who are wary of committing to one perspective should derive inspiration from these cases. They should also be encouraged by the fact that some famous thinkers changed their minds dramatically over time, such as Keynes, who shifted from endorsing free trade before the 1930s to autarkic ideas in 1933 and who then helped to pioneer the embedded liberalism of Bretton Woods in the early 1940s.

---

[19] Quoted in Gramlich-Oka 2006, 4, 177. She was one of the many advocates of "*kokueki* mercantilism", which is discussed briefly in Chapter 5.

Table 1.1 *Core goals of pre-1945 perspectives*

| Perspective | Core goals |
|---|---|
| Classical economic liberalism | Promote free trade and free markets in order to foster global prosperity, international peace, and individual freedom |
| Neomercantilism | Promote strategic trade protectionism and other forms of government economic activism in order to boost state wealth and power |
| Marxism | Challenge capitalism in order to end class-based inequality and exploitation within the world economy |
| Autarkism | Promote a state's economic self-sufficiency in order to enhance its autonomy from foreign influence |
| Environmentalism | Curtail human-induced degradation of the natural environment in the world economy in order to foster more sustainable ways of living |
| Feminism | Challenge patriarchal practices and structures in order to end women's subordination within the world economy |
| Pan-Africanism | Cultivate the economic solidarity of Africans and the African diaspora in order to end their subordination within the world economy |
| Pan-Islamism | Cultivate the economic solidarity of Muslims to promote their interests and values in the world economy |
| Pan-Asianism | Cultivate the economic solidarity of Asians to promote their interests and values in the world economy |
| Economic regionalisms | Prioritize regional economic integration in order to promote goals such as (in the cases examined in Chapter 13) Akamatsu's regional developmentalism, German power, or Indoamerican anti-imperialism |
| Embedded liberalism | Promote a form of institutionalized liberal multilateralism that makes an open world economy compatible with various kinds of active public management of the economy in order to boost global prosperity, international peace, and individual freedom |

It is also important to underline that I have distinguished these perspectives by their normative goals relating to the international dimensions of political economy. The international focus is central to the distinctiveness of some of the perspectives; that is, the thinkers associated with these perspectives would not necessarily be lumped together if the focus were on other dimensions of political economy. More generally, I also need to highlight that my focus on normative goals is not the only way that alternative perspectives in political economy can be classified. Political economists have different perspectives about a range of other issues. I have chosen to focus on distinctive normative goals as the organizing principle for the book because of their centrality to the political contestation of the world economy in this period. To be sure, some of the perspectives I analyze had a deeper analytical unity beyond the common normative goals outlined in Table 1.1, a unity that was often fostered by well-established intellectual networks and communities. But others did not. Indeed, I highlight how some of the perspectives identified in the book included thinkers who drew on very disparate analytical traditions and had little connection to, or even awareness of, each other.

Sixth, the choice to focus on normative goals has also influenced the kinds of figures I feature in this book. They include not just scholars but also political leaders, officials, public intellectuals, and activists. Many of those outside the scholarly world were more interested in advocacy than theorizing, and they made less effort than the scholars to back up their distinctive normative goals with sophisticated analyses of how the world works. I have included them because they contributed to political economy debates in their time in important ways. It is also important to recall that the professionalization of the study of political economy was much less advanced in the pre-1945 era than it is today. In that context, a wider range of people helped to advance debate on the subject than just professional scholars.

Finally, I should clarify that I have not written this book because I am trying to promote one or another side in the debates between (or within) these perspectives. My goal has been to improve understanding of diverse viewpoints rather than advocate for one or another of them. Of course, I have my biases that stem from many sources, including my positionality within the world economy. But I have tried to keep these biases – as much as I am aware of them – out of the analysis as much as possible and let readers evaluate these various ideas for themselves.

I have, however, been driven by an analytical bias. Some IPE scholars are sceptical that ideas have much impact on their subject of study. From their standpoint, the focus of IPE analyses should be on other factors such as material interests, the exercise of power, and/or the significance of institutional arrangements. Those factors are certainly important, but my own reading of history suggests that ideas – including those of political economists – also matter. As Keynes put it, "the ideas of economists and political philosophers, both when they are right and when they are wrong, are more powerful than is commonly understood". After this famous passage, Keynes added: "indeed, the world is ruled by little else".[20] In my view, that last point takes the argument too far.

[20] Keynes 1936, 383.

But one reason for studying the history of ideas is that they can have, and have had, important influence in shaping the dynamics and structures of international economic relations and the politics of the world economy more generally.[21]

The focus on ideas also provides a reminder that the study of IPE is tied up in broader questions about competing values. This point was often emphasized by Strange, who highlighted how the ideas of Adam Smith and other early scholars of political economy emerged from the study of moral philosophy whose focus was, in her words, on "fundamental values – how they could be reflected in the ordering of human society and how conflicts between them could be resolved". Strange urged IPE scholars to return to this foundation: "Sooner or later, it will be necessary to go back and start at the beginning if we are to achieve a genuine synthesis of political and economic activity".[22] In an era when much IPE scholarship has steered away from addressing what Benjamin Cohen calls "the Really Big Question of systemic transformation", I think it is useful to be reminded of the larger debates that helped to inspire the deep roots of the field.[23] After all, as Heloise Weber puts it, "the big questions continue to be as important as they have ever been".[24]

[21]  For a recent discussion, see Voeten 2021.
[22]  Strange 1995, 171.
[23]  Cohen 2008, 13.
[24]  Weber 2015, 916.

# Part I

# The Three Orthodoxies in a Global Context

# 2    The Rise of European Classical Economic Liberalism

As noted in the introductory chapter, classical economic liberalism was the first perspective on political economy to achieve worldwide influence.[1] I show in the next chapter how thinkers in various parts of the world claimed that some of its core ideas originated in their respective regions. But the version that became best known around the world was developed by European thinkers. The most famous of them was Adam Smith, whose 1776 book *The Wealth of Nations* (or more accurately, *An Inquiry into the Nature and Causes of the Wealth of Nations*) quickly gained a reputation as a foundational text for economic liberalism. By the early twentieth century, there were few places in the world where this work was not known in intellectual circles. As his title suggested, Smith himself also saw his ideas as having universal relevance.

In the nineteenth century, some other European political economists consolidated the international dimension of the classical economic liberal perspective by building on Smith's ideas. This chapter focuses on four such thinkers who developed important analyses and were prominent figures in liberal circles in this era: David Ricardo, Richard Cobden, John Stuart Mill, and Walter Bagehot. These and other European classical economic liberals were united in the belief that free trade and free markets would foster global prosperity, international peace, and individual freedom. Beyond this core message, however, there were some important disagreements among them about international issues that are often overlooked.

## Adam Smith's Famous Ideas

In contrast to many other thinkers discussed in this book, the man whose ideas became known around the world was a rather unassuming individual. Born in Scotland, Smith was educated at universities in Glasgow

---

[1] I follow the common practice of using the term "classical" economic liberalism to refer to European thinkers who advocated economic liberalism from Adam Smith up to John Stuart Mill.

and Oxford. By the time he published *The Wealth of Nations* at the age of fifty-three, he had spent many years as a teacher and earned a reputation as a classic absent-minded professor. Despite the subsequent global fame of his 1776 book, Smith did not promote it very actively, or even to respond publicly to critics after its publication. Two years after its publication, he was appointed to a lucrative position as a customs official, administering the very system of tariffs that he criticized.[2]

The originality of *The Wealth of Nations* should not be overstated. Smith drew on the ideas of many others, including French thinkers associated with a "physiocratic school" who had begun to advocate for free markets and free trade in the mid-eighteenth century. Indeed, historian David Todd notes that Smith was seen across Europe until the 1790s "as an advocate of 'French' ideas of political and economic liberty".[3] French thinkers also became major promoters and popularizers of Smith's message in the early 1800s, notably Jean Baptiste Say with his 1803 *Treatise on Political Economy*, which found a large international audience.

Like the physiocrats, Smith was very critical of those who supported what he called the "mercantile system" practiced by many European states during the seventeenth and eighteenth centuries. Historians have long debated whether Smith overstated the coherence – and even the existence – of what came to be known as a "mercantilist" school of thought in Europe in this period. To the extent that such a school existed, it was unified by the goal of boosting state power and wealth through protectionist trade policies and other kinds of government economic activism, such as the provision of export subsidies and support for trading monopolies.[4] Policies of this kind were certainly pervasive in Europe at the time that Smith was writing. Smith critiqued them, advocating for a "simple system of natural liberty" in which the government's role in the economy was much more limited and each individual was "left perfectly free to pursue his own interest his own way" in freely functioning markets and conditions of free trade.[5]

At the domestic level, Smith argued that an economy organized around this principle would enable individuals to conduct commerce as they saw fit, in keeping with humans' natural propensity to "truck, barter,

---

[2] For a recent biography (of which there are many) of Smith, see Norman 2018. For the initial reception of Smith's ideas in Britain and his reaction, see, for example, Teichgraeber 1987.
[3] Todd 2015, 6.
[4] See, for example, Magnusson 1994; Viner 1948.
[5] Smith 1776, IV.ix.51. Because there are so many editions of Smith's work, I have followed a common convention of citing passages with reference to the book number within the volume (in this case, IV), the numbers he assigned to sections (ix), and the paragraph number (51).

and exchange one thing for another".[6] It would also foster a wider and more productive division of labour that generated prosperity. Further, this kind of economy would automatically coordinate people's economic activities in an efficient, harmonious, and decentralized manner via incentives created by the price mechanism. In these ways, Smith argued that the pursuit of individual self-interest in freely functioning markets would benefit society as a whole, while maximizing individual freedom.

Of course, government was still needed to perform certain duties. Smith emphasized three: the protection of the society from violence and foreign invasion, the administration of justice, and the provision of "certain public works, and certain public institutions" that benefitted society but were unlikely to be created by individuals or small groups of people. But Smith argued that government should not try to take on more roles than these, not least because rulers were always "exposed to innumerable delusions" and because "no human wisdom or knowledge could ever be sufficient" to enable government direction of economic life to serve the interests of society successfully.[7] In the words of his most famous metaphor, he believed that an economy governed by the "invisible hand" of the market would generate greater social good than one actively managed by the government.[8]

### Smith's Case for Free Trade

For IPE scholars, Smith's case for free trade at the border was particularly important. To begin with, he argued that trade restrictions encouraged a poor allocation of resources because they gave a "monopoly of the home market" to firms in the protected sector, thereby raising their profits artificially and drawing capital to them in ways that depressed other "more valuable" sectors. Free trade policies, by contrast, would generate more efficient economic outcomes: "if a foreign country can supply us with a commodity cheaper than we ourselves can make it, better buy it of them with some part of the produce of our own industry, employed in a way in which we have some advantage". Smith also emphasized that free trade policies would ensure that the interests of consumers would no longer be "sacrificed" to those of inefficient and often monopolistic domestic producers that received trade protection.[9] More generally, Smith noted that international trade could provide an outlet for the surplus production of countries, enabling the use of resources that would otherwise be unemployed.

---

[6] Smith 1776, I.ii.1.
[7] Quotes from Smith 1776, IV.ix.51.
[8] Despite the fame of this metaphor, Smith used it only once in *The Wealth of Nations*. For his wider use of the term, see Harrison 2011; Rothschild 2001, ch. 5.
[9] Quotes from Smith 1776, IV.ix.25, 26; IV.ii.12; IV.viii.49.

Smith also emphasized some more dynamic economic benefits of free trade policies over time. In his view, they would boost countries' productivity as domestic producers faced greater competitive pressures and as they were able to sell to larger markets. Productivity improvements would also be fostered by the fact that free trade encouraged the transfer of technology and ideas between countries. As Smith put it, "extensive commerce from all countries to all countries" would generate "mutual communication of knowledge, and of all sorts of improvements". To highlight this point, he invoked the negative example of China, arguing that that its trade restrictions at the time prevented the country from learning "the art of using and constructing, themselves, all the different machines made use of in other countries, as well as the other improvements of art and industry which are practised in all the different parts of the world". Smith also pointed to the role of foreign commerce in introducing "a taste for the finer and more improved manufactures" from "more civilized nations", a change that encouraged production improvements domestically.[10]

In addition to linking free trade policies with economic prosperity, Smith argued that they contributed to individual freedom. In his view, trade protectionism was an "oppressive policy" that interfered with humans' natural liberty to interact and trade with each other.[11] This point built upon arguments made by earlier natural law philosophers such as Hugo Grotius, who had insisted in 1604 that "the right to engage in commerce pertains equally to all peoples" and who had revived an earlier European "universal economy" doctrine that saw the unequal distribution of resources across the globe as evidence of divine support for international commerce.[12]

The association Smith drew between free trade and individual liberty also related to his critique of protectionism for defending the monopoly privileges of powerful rent-seeking elites, while undermining the interests and freedoms of the rest of society. That critique applied to not just Europe but also elsewhere. For example, Smith argued that China's trade protectionism was part of a wider system in which "the oppression of the poor must establish the monopoly of the rich, who, by engrossing the whole trade to themselves, will be able to make very large profits".[13]

Smith also highlighted how the freedom of many peoples outside Europe was undermined by the mercantilist policies of European powers. For example, he argued that economic restrictions imposed by Britain on its American colonies represented "a manifest violation of the most sacred

---

[10]  Quotes from Smith 1776, IV.viii.c.80; IV.ix.41; III.iii.16, 15.
[11]  Smith 1776, IV.ix.26.
[12]  Quoted in Irwin 1996, 22–23.
[13]  Smith 1776. I.ix.15.

rights of mankind". Indeed, Smith's work suggested that British authorities should grant the troublesome and costly American colonies their independence and conduct commerce with them instead on the basis of "free trade" rather than via "the monopoly which she [Britain] at present enjoys".[14] This was a radical message to publish in 1776, just months before the American Declaration of Independence. Smith's ideas subsequently played a role in encouraging the British government to recognize the independence of the new American republic and to liberalize trade with it.[15]

Smith criticized European colonial policies elsewhere in the world as well. Among his targets were the East India Company and other trading monopolies sponsored by European powers in Asia, which he described as "destructive to those which have the misfortune to fall under their government". In addition to critiquing economic costs of colonialism, he condemned the broader cruelties and abuses conducted by European powers in their colonies and lamented how their behaviour had undermined the good that should have resulted from global economic integration. As he put it in discussing the European arrival in the Americas, "the savage injustice of the Europeans rendered an event, which might have been beneficial to all, ruinous and destructive to several of those unfortunate countries". He echoed the point in another passage about "East and West Indies" that critiqued Europeans for using superior force to "commit with impunity every sort of injustice in those remote countries".[16]

The final rationale Smith advanced for free trade was that it could be a force for international peace. Like his discussion of natural liberty, this argument had some roots in much older European thought that had linked commerce to international cooperation and friendship.[17] In Smith's own age, the French thinker Montesquieu's *Spirit of the Laws* (1748) had also popularized the idea that "the natural effect of commerce is to bring about peace" because trading countries "render themselves reciprocally dependent: if one has an interest in buying the other has an interest in selling; and all unions are based upon mutual needs". Montesquieu had further suggested that commerce was associated with the "ways of men" being "gentle", and that it "polishes and softens barbarian ways" and "brings with it the spirit of frugality, of economy, of moderation, of work, of wisdom, of tranquility, of order, and regularity".[18] Smith was sympathetic to these kinds of arguments, but he also warned of the enduring importance

[14] Quotes from Smith 1776, IV,vii.Part II.44; IV.vii.Part III.65.
[15] Morrison 2012.
[16] Quotes from Smith 1776, IV.vii.Part II.107; IV.i.32; IV.7.c.80.
[17] See, for example, Irwin 1996, ch. 1.
[18] Quotes in Hirschman 1945, 10fn19; 1977,60,70. Scholars often refer to this line of argument as the "doux commerce" thesis.

of inter-state rivalries on international economic relations. Citing the cases of England and France, he noted that "being neighbours, they are necessarily enemies, and the wealth and power of each becomes, upon that account, more formidable to the other". As he put it, "the wealth of neighbouring nations ... is certainly advantageous in trade", but it was "dangerous in war and politics" because "in a state of hostility, it may enable our enemies to maintain fleets and armies superior to our own".[19]

From this realist perspective, Smith suggested a very different reason than Montesquieu for why free trade might lead to a more peaceful world over the longer term. After discussing the fate of the peoples of the East and West Indies in the passage noted above, Smith speculated about a future day when "the natives of those countries may grow stronger, or those of Europe may grow weaker; and the inhabitants of all the different quarters of the world may arrive at the equality of courage and force which, by inspiring mutual fear, can alone overawe the injustice of independent nations into some sort of respect for the rights of one another". In the next sentence, he suggested that extensive worldwide trade was the best mechanism for creating this greater balance of power that was necessary for a peaceful world of mutual respect among states: "nothing seems more likely to establish this equality of force, than that mutual communication of knowledge, and of all sorts of improvements, which an extensive commerce from all countries to all countries naturally, or rather necessarily, carries along with it".[20]

### Smith's Caveats

Smith's various arguments linking free trade with prosperity, liberty, and peace set a foundation for nineteenth-century economic liberal thought. But it is important to recognize that Smith's endorsement of free trade was more cautious than that of many of his followers. To begin with, he thought it was politically unrealistic to push for pure free trade: "To expect, indeed, that the freedom of trade should ever be entirely restored in Great Britain, is as absurd as to expect that an Oceana or Utopia should ever be established in it. Not only the prejudices of the public, but, what is much more unconquerable, the private interests of many individuals, irresistibly oppose it".[21]

Smith also outlined some situations in which he thought protectionism might be justified. If a country's exports were being blocked by another country's trade restrictions, he suggested that retaliatory protectionism

---

[19] Quotes from Smtih 1776, IV. iii.c.13; IV.iii.b.11.
[20] Quotes from Smith 1776, IV.7.c.80. See also Muthu 2008.
[21] Smith 1776, IV.ii.43.

might be used against the latter (although only if there was a strong probability that this move would encourage those restrictions to be lifted). If a country had used protectionist policies for some time, Smith also cautioned against the sudden introduction of free trade because of the large job losses that might result: "humanity may in this case require that freedom of trade should be restored only by slow gradations, and with a good deal of reserve and circumspection".[22] Further, Smith argued that tariffs could be used to offset a competitive advantage accruing to imported goods that were taxed at a lower rate abroad than domestic producers were at home.

Finally, Smith insisted that protectionism could be justified to support national defense. As an example, Smith cited England's Navigation Acts, which had helped to build up England's naval capacity by requiring parts of the country's trade to be conducted via English ships. Although Smith was critical of some economic effects of this restriction, he defended the policy in this way: "As defence, however, is of much more importance than opulence, the act of navigation is, perhaps, the wisest of all the commercial regulations of England".[23] In a work otherwise known for its criticism of "mercantile system", this was a striking endorsement of one of the most notorious of England's mercantilist policies. It provides a reminder that Smith's critique of the "mercantile system", for all its radicalism at the time, did not go as far as that of some of his followers in the nineteenth century. Here and elsewhere in his work, Smith's arguments about trade policy were cautious and he highlighted the importance of evaluating that policy in light of the goal of boosting state wealth and power.[24]

One other important distinction needs to be made about Smith's views in relation to those of many of his nineteenth-century followers. Although he developed important arguments in favour of free trade, he did not emphasize the role of foreign trade in promoting the wealth of nations as much as many of them did. From his standpoint, the "home market", rather than the global one, was "the most important of all markets".[25] Smith also argued that capital was most efficiently employed in agriculture, then industry, and only last in commerce, including foreign commerce (and he prioritized the latter lower than domestic commerce).[26]

---

[22] Smith 1776, IV.ii.40.
[23] Smith 1776, IV.2.30. Smith also suggested the needs of national defence might justify Britain's "bounties upon the exportation of British made sail-cloth, and British made gunpowder" in order to support local production. As he put it, "If any particular manufacture was necessary, indeed, for the defence of the society, it might not always be prudent to depend upon our neighbours for the supply" (Smith 1776, IV.v.36).
[24] See also Earle 1986; Harlen 1999; Wyatt-Walter 1996.
[25] Smith 1776, IV.ix.48.
[26] See Smith 1776, II.v.19–31.

Similarly, he suggested that the "natural" development of nations involved a sequence associated with these priorities in which "the greater part of the capital of every growing society is, first, directed to agriculture, afterwards to manufactures, and, last of all, to foreign commerce".[27] One of Smith's criticisms of mercantilism was that it had unnaturally reversed these stages by promoting foreign trade before the others.[28]

This view was tied to his belief that all societies proceeded through stages of economic progress, starting with a focus on hunting, then shepherding, then agriculture, and culminating in a fully commercial society.[29] Smith associated the earlier stages with more "barbarous" societies and the latter ones with more "civilized" ones. The word "civilization" was a product of the European Enlightenment, having first been used in France in 1756 to refer to a society ruled by civil rather than military law as well as to a group of people who were virtuous, refined, and well-mannered.[30] As noted below, many economic liberals in the nineteenth century embraced a discourse of European civilizational superiority vis-à-vis the rest of the world. But Smith's use of the term was more nuanced. He praised some aspects of those societies that were closer to a "barbarous" state, while criticizing others associated with societies he described as more "civilized".[31] He also had no hesitation in noting that "China is a much richer country than any part of Europe". More generally, his stadial theory also did not blind him to the global context in which countries' economic development took place, including the disadvantages experienced by colonized societies and "the general advantages which Europe, considered as one great country, has derived from the discovery and colonization of America".[32]

## Important Nineteenth-Century Contributions

The international dimensions of economic liberalism were developed further by a number of thinkers in the nineteenth century. The first was David Ricardo, a banker and British politician whose best-known work was his 1817 *Principles of Political Economy*. For IPE scholars, the most important aspect of his work was his theory of comparative advantage, which focused on the economic benefits that could arise if free trade

---

[27] Smith 1776, III.i.8. See also IV.xi.22–25; II.v.19–31.
[28] Smith 1776, III.i.9.
[29] Smith's four-stage theory was not outlined explicitly in *The Wealth of Nations* but can be found in lectures he gave in the early 1760s.
[30] See, for example, Mazlish 2001, 293.
[31] See, for example, Williams 2014.
[32] Quotes from Smith 1776, I; XI.Part III.42; IV.vii.Part III.4.

enabled each country to specialize entirely in the production of different goods.

Ricardo demonstrated his theory mathematically by focusing on the trade in wine and cloth between Portugal and England. In his example, Portuguese workers produced wine more efficiently than cloth, while the opposite was true for Britain. If all Portuguese workers shifted into wine production and their British counterparts into cloth, Ricardo noted that the two countries could make more of what they were comparatively best at and then trade for the other product. Even if one country was more efficient at producing both products than the other country in an absolute sense (as Portugal was in his example), it was possible for free trade to produce mutual gains (especially if the terms of trade were favourable to both countries). He noted that the gains would be experienced not just by individuals and countries, but also by the "civilized world" as a whole:

Under a system of perfectly free commerce, each country naturally devotes its capital and labour to such employments as are most beneficial to each. This pursuit of individual advantage is admirably connected with the universal good of the whole. By stimulating industry, by rewarding ingenuity, and by using most efficaciously the peculiar powers bestowed by nature, it distributes labour most effectively and most economically: while, by increasing the general mass of productions, it diffuses general benefit, and binds together, by one common tie of interest and intercourse, the universal society of nations throughout the civilised world. It is this principle which determines that wine shall be made in France and Portugal, that corn shall be grown in America and Poland, and that hardware and other goods shall be manufactured in England.[33]

Ricardo's famous example of Britain exporting cloth in return for Portuguese wine is one that would have been very familiar to his British readers at the time. That trade pattern had emerged in the eighteenth century from a 1703 trade treaty that England had pressured Portugal into signing on terms that benefitted the former, resulting in regular trade surpluses with its trading partner. Matthew Watson has highlighted how Ricardo's analysis did not mention this political foundation of the trade relationship nor the power relations that generated the unequal terms of the treaty. As Watson points out, it also did not address another political condition that sustained the relationship on the Portuguese side: its ongoing trade deficits with England were paid for with gold from its Brazilian colony.[34] Rather than focus on these political issues, Ricardo sought to show in more abstract terms how international specialization emerged from market processes under conditions of free trade.

[33] Ricardo [1817]1908, 114.
[34] Watson 2017.

Ricardo's argument added an important new case for why free trade could boost prosperity. It was not just his focus on comparative – as opposed to absolute – advantage that was novel. Equally important was his focus on a world in which countries specialized completely in the production of specific products. To be sure, Smith had been interested in the economic benefits arising from an international division of labour. As countries moved through his four stages of economic progress, however, Smith anticipated that they would have increasingly *diversified* domestic economies rather more *specialized* ones.[35]

### The Views of Mill and Cobden

Ricardo's theory of comparative advantage took up just a few pages in his 1817 book, but it was popularized by others, including the prominent British intellectual John Stuart Mill in his widely read work *Principles of Political Economy*. First published in 1848 and then revised by Mill in many editions until his death in 1873, this work became the best-known synthesis of many classical economic liberal arguments. In it, Mill echoed Smith's points about a larger market enabling productivity improvements and the role of commerce in encouraging learning from abroad. Regarding the latter, he asserted that "commercial adventurers from more advanced countries have generally been the first civilizers of barbarians" and that commerce "between civilized nations" promoted communication that was "one of the primary sources of progress". In addition, he argued "the opening of a foreign trade" could encourage a people who were in "a quiescent, indolent, uncultivated state" to work harder and to save and accumulate capital because of its effect of "making them acquainted with new objects, or tempting them by the easier acquisition of things they had not previously thought attainable".[36]

Like Ricardo, Mill highlighted free trade's global economic benefits in generating a "more efficient employment of the productive forces of the world". He also placed strong emphasis on the argument that free trade would generate international peace, arguing that this political rationale for the policy was more important than any economic ones. Rather than repeat Smith's idea that worldwide trade would generate peace by creating more equal power among states over the long term, he focused on an argument closer to Montesquieu's emphasis on the mutual interests generated by economic interdependence. As he put it, commerce was

---

[35] See Schumacher 2020.
[36] Quotes from Mill [1871]1965, 581.

"rapidly rendering war obsolete, by strengthening and multiplying the personal interests which are in natural opposition to it".[37]

Mill did, however, follow Smith in acknowledging that protectionist policies such as Navigation Acts might be justified in the interests of national defense, although he referred to this as an "invidious exception to the general rule of free trade".[38] In one short passage, he also argued that trade barriers could be defensible if they were "imposed temporarily (especially in a young and rising nation) in hopes of naturalizing a foreign industry, in itself perfectly suitable to the circumstances of the country". This exception to free trade was justified, he argued, because "the superiority of one country over another in a branch of production often arises only from having begun it sooner".[39] Mill's ideas on this topic were influenced by a Canadian thinker, John Rae, whose ideas are discussed in Chapter 5. Smith had not mentioned this case for temporary infant-industry protection and many economic liberals were upset at Mill's willingness to endorse it.

Prominent among Mill's critics on this issue was the British textile merchant and politician Richard Cobden, who emerged as one of the best-known advocates of free trade both in Britain and abroad from the mid-1830s until his death in 1865. Cobden reportedly declared that Mill had "done more harm by his sentence about the fostering of infant industries, than he had done good by the whole of the rest of his writings". Mill himself also became increasingly frustrated by how his brief passage on this issue was being used by opponents of free trade to justify their ideas. He eventually concluded that subsidies were a better means for countries to support infant industries because they were "not nearly so likely to be continued indefinitely" (although the controversial passage remained in the last edition of his book that he updated in 1871).[40]

Cobden's views also deserve attention because he played a more important role than any other nineteenth-century thinker in popularizing the idea that free trade and peace were linked.[41] He reiterated the reason cited by Montesquieu and Mill: war would be inhibited by the mutual economic interdependence created by free trade. He also suggested that the material progress ushered in by free trade would reduce conflict. In addition, Cobden argued that free trade would undermine the power of

---

[37] Quotes from Mill [1871]1965, 578, 582.
[38] Mill [1871]1965, 920. Other British liberals such as Stanley Jevons (1865, 324–25) (see Chapter 9) went further to question whether Britain had really benefitted from the Navigation Acts.
[39] Mill [1871]1965, 922.
[40] Quotes of Mill from Helleiner 2021a, 301.
[41] For his influence, see, for example, Cain 1979.

aristocratic landowning elites that supported militarism and war. Echoing the older "universal economy" doctrine, Cobden suggested further that peace would be bolstered by the fact that free trade was related to a divine plan: "Free Trade is a Divine Law: if it were not, the world would have been differently created. One country has cotton, another wine, another coal, which is proof that, according to the Divine Order of things, men should fraternize and exchange their goods and thus further Peace and Goodwill on Earth".[42]

Even more ambitiously, Cobden argued that free trade was fostering a more cosmopolitan kind of identity by "drawing men together, thrusting aside the antagonism of race, and creed, and language, and uniting us in the bonds of eternal peace".[43] Adam Smith had been sceptical of the possibility of this kind of cosmopolitan identity, arguing that people were rarely capable of extending sympathy beyond their own country.[44] But Cobden's line of argument seemed more plausible for many liberals in an era when global trade and communication were expanding rapidly with the invention of steamships, railways and the telegraph. This argument, as well as the others that Cobden put forward, suggested that the national security case for protectionist policies endorsed by Smith (and Mill) might be unnecessary.

### Promoting Free Trade

Indeed, many European economic liberals promoted free trade with enormous passion in the middle decades of the nineteenth century when many countries across Europe and elsewhere liberalized trade. In their view, liberal political economy had the status of a universally valid, scientific truth for promoting global prosperity, international peace, and individual freedom. This sentiment was particularly strong in Britain, which unilaterally repealed its Navigation Acts in 1849 as well as its protectionist Corn Laws three years earlier (which had discouraged grain imports from outside its empire). As the first country to undergo the industrial revolution, Britain became the workshop of the world in this period, importing vast quantities of primary materials and exporting industrial goods. It thus had much to gain from policies of free trade both at home and abroad. Indeed, some British supporters of free trade emphasized these gains in ways that sat uncomfortably with more cosmopolitan liberal arguments. For example, one advocate of the abolition of the Corn

---

[42] Quoted in Cain 1979, 240.
[43] Cobden 1903, 187.
[44] See, for example, Forman-Barzilai 2000.

Laws highlighted in 1842 how free trade would mean "we might supply the whole world with manufactures, and have almost a monopoly of the trade of the world". Earlier in 1829, another praised how free trade in corn would "render all the world a tributary to us".[45]

As we shall see in later chapters of this book, the fact that Britain seemed to derive special benefits from free trade raised suspicions abroad from those who saw the policy simply as a British tool of domination rather than one serving the cause of global prosperity, peace, and freedom. Recognizing this resistance, the prominent British liberal Walter Bagehot urged his liberal colleagues at the 100th anniversary of the publication of *The Wealth of Nations* to recognize that "in many cases, the eagerness of England in the Free-trade cause only does that cause harm". Bagehot also went a step further to suggest that English free traders were mistaken when they argued that economic liberalism had universal relevance. In his view, economic liberalism was "a theory proved of, and applicable to, particular societies only", namely those with "grown-up competitive commerce" such as England and "lands populated by the Anglo-Saxon race".[46] For this reason, he referred to economic liberalism as "English political economy". This position contrasted with the tone of Smith's famous book, which had suggested that his ideas were relevant for cultivating the wealth of all nations. Bagehot's argument was also a much more modest claim than Cobden's suggestion that free trade was a "divine law" for the world as a whole.

Cobden himself also recognized the foreign resistance to British free trade ideas and the need for British advocates not to promote them too aggressively abroad. As he put it, "we came to the conclusion that the less we attempted to persuade foreigners to adopt our trade principles, the better; for we discovered so much suspicion of the motives of England, that it was lending an argument to the protectionists abroad to incite the popular feeling against free-traders".[47] In this context, Cobden emphasized the benefits of unilateral trade liberalization and he played a leading role in the successful campaign to repeal Britain's Corn Laws. Other classical economic liberals also backed unilateral trade liberalization, including Smith and Ricardo.[48]

Like many other economic liberals, Cobden also supported initiatives to liberalize trade through bilateral treaties among willing countries and even helped negotiate one of the most famous of these in the mid-nineteenth

---

[45] Quotes from Helleiner 2002, 320. In that article, I describe these kinds of thinkers as "liberal economic nationalists".
[46] Bagehot [1876]1885, 6, 31, 27, 9.
[47] Quoted in Bhagwati and Irwin, 1987, 114.
[48] See Bhagwati and Irwin, 1987, 198; Sally 1998, 54–56.

century: the 1860 "Cobden–Chevalier" treaty between Britain and France. Smith had warned against bilateral "treaties of commerce" that discriminated against countries that were not a party to them.[49] But Cobden's treaty included an unconditional "most-favored nation" clause that committed each country to grant to each other any privileges that they extended to other countries in future treaties. The clause reduced the discriminatory nature of bilateralism and even triggered a kind of "free trade epidemic", as many other European countries pursued similar treaties with such clauses in order to join in the "Cobden network".[50]

Some British policymakers also supported the use of military force to promote free trade, a practice that seemed to directly challenge the liberal equation of free trade with peace and freedom. One of the most famous examples involved the Opium Wars in which Britain forced open Chinese markets to foreign commerce in 1839–42 and again in 1856–60. Many British economic liberals supported this military action, arguing that it was needed to deal with what they perceived as a tyrannical foreign government that was preventing its own people from realizing the benefits of free trade. Many European liberals also associated free trade more generally with a mission to bring Christianity and European "civilization" to non-European regions of the world.[51]

The use of military force to promote free trade was contested, however, by other economic liberals, including Cobden. The latter did not disagree with the goal of spreading Christianity via commerce.[52] But he mobilized opposition to the Second Opium War, objecting to Britain's military action and challenging the idea that the Chinese were "barbarians". In his view, China had an advanced and civilized commercial society. Undermining the discourse of European civilizational superiority, he argued that it was Britain's use of force that represented the barbaric act.[53]

### Liberal Imperialism?

These disputes within economic liberal circles extended to debates about the role of British colonial rule as a tool for promoting liberal policies. Mill argued that it had an important role to play, a position no doubt influenced by the fact that he worked between 1823 and 1858 for the East India Company (the institution that ruled India on behalf of Britain in this

[49] Smith 1776, IV.vi.
[50] Quotes from the title of Lazer 1999 and from Accominotti and Flandreau, 2008, 151. See also Kindleberger 1975.
[51] See, for example, Phillips 2011; Spall 1988.
[52] See, for example, Spall 1988, 415.
[53] Cobden quote in Phillips 2010, 22.

period). Despite his general commitment to individual freedom and self-government, Mill argued that a colonial "despotism" could be justified on the paternalistic grounds that colonized peoples were not yet ready for a liberal form of rule because of their "barbarous" or "backward" nature. In contrast to the imperialism of the mercantilist era, Mill advocated a new liberal kind of imperial rule by specialized experts committed to bringing colonized societies to a more advanced stage of civilization, including through policies inspired by liberal political economy. As he put it in 1856, there were "conditions of society in which a vigorous despotism is in itself the best mode of government for training the people in what is specifically wanting to render them capable of a higher civilization".[54]

Mill's endorsement of this kind of liberal imperialism contrasted with the opinions of other British liberals of his era, including, once again, Cobden. The latter often – but not always – opposed imperialist policies, associating them with the mercantilist and militarist worldviews and policies that he opposed.[55] But Mill and other liberal imperialists could cite some of Smith's views in support of their cause. Although Smith had been very critical of colonial policies, he had also suggested that the British empire could be reformed in a liberal direction by creating an imperial federation in which free trade existed, defense costs were shared, and colonies had representation in an imperial parliament. Smith had also noted that colonies could provide larger export markets and that imperial powers could contribute to the advancement of colonized societies.[56] At the same time, the Eurocentric paternalism of Mill's views towards colonized peoples contrasted with Smith's less judgmental stance as well as with Smith's opinion that all societies could progress through developmental stages on their own.[57]

In Mill's view, the export of capital and labour from Britain was one of the advantages of colonization for colonized peoples. Drawing on the ideas of another British liberal Edward Wakefield from the 1830s, Mill argued that this export of capital would also benefit the imperial power, as profitable investments in the colony would help to stem declining profit rates at home.[58] In keeping with his liberal worldview, Mill also depicted these gains in cosmopolitan terms: "To appreciate the benefits of colonization,

---

[54] Mill quotes from Travers 2007, 6. See also Chatterjee 2012, 181–83; Mantena 2010, 30–39.

[55] For Cobden's views, see, for example, Ambirajan 1978; Cain 1979, 247; Hobson 2012, 36–40.

[56] For debates about Smith's views of colonies, see, for example, Williams 2014; Ince 2021; Hobson 2012, ch. 3.

[57] For Smith's "anti-paternalism", see Hobson 2012, 78–83.

[58] For Wakefield's views, see, for example, Semmel 1993.

it should be considered in its relation, not to a single country, but to the collective economical interests of the human race ... The exportation of labourers and capital from old to new countries, from a place where their productive power is less, to a place where it is greater, increases by so much the aggregate produce of the labour and capital of the world".[59]

The reference to "new" countries invoked settler colonies in places such as North America. When Mill trumpeted the benefits of the migration of labour to them, it is important to recognize that he was endorsing the colonization and dispossession of the Indigenous peoples who lived there. Mill glossed over this point by referring to the movement of population "from the overcrowded to the unoccupied parts of the earth's surface". When praising the imperial government's role in the process "of relieving one labour market and suppling another", he did not acknowledge the accompanying processes of violence and coercion towards Indigenous peoples in these "unoccupied" territories.[60]

He was not alone in overlooking this point. While condemning the violence and injustice committed by European imperial powers in many parts of the world, Adam Smith said little about the topic in the context of the settler colonies of North America. As Onur Ince argues, Smith suggested instead that these were only lightly populated territories inhabited by hunters or "savages" without a conception of property in land.[61] In that context, he suggested – like Mill – that Europeans were settling unowned or unoccupied lands and, thus, that no injustice was involved. As Smith put it in a remarkably vague phrase, the process of colonizing "thinly inhabited" countries was one in which "the natives easily give place to the new settlers".[62]

Mill's emphasis on the benefits of capital and labour mobility went beyond Smith and Ricardo, each of whom had focused primarily on the benefits of free trade in goods. For example, Smith said little about the international migration of workers in *The Wealth of Nations* and he

---

[59] Mill [1871] 1965, 970.

[60] Mill [1871] 1965, 970.

[61] Smith quoted in Ince 2021, 1089. As Ince (2021, 189) notes, Smith's classification of the Indigenous peoples of North America as "savages" within his stadial theory rested on an argument that their cultivation practices did not represent proper "agriculture". In the pre-1945 period, the kind of view that Smith advanced was challenged by Indigenous scholars such as Laura Cornelius Kellogg (co-founder of the American Indian Association in 1911), who argued in 1912 that some Indigenous peoples in the continent had, before Europeans arrived, already progressed through four key stages of human civilizational progress: (1) hunting/fishing, (2) pastoral, (3) agricultural, and (4) "horticultural". As she put it, "there is nothing more densely ignorant than the white man on these various stages of the American Indian's development" (Kellogg [1912]2011, 162). Recent work by agronomists shows that Iroquoian agriculture, for example, was highly productive between the sixteenth and eighteenth centuries (Mt. Pleasant and Burt 2010).

[62] Smith 1776, IV.vii.Part 2.1.

praised the tendency of people to invest in domestic, rather than foreign, industry.[63] Ricardo's theory of comparative advantage explicitly rested on an assumption that capital and labour were not mobile. Like Smith, he also explicitly expressed a preference that the wealthy invest within their own country rather than abroad.[64]

### What Role for Multilateral Cooperation?

In addition to these debates about unilateral trade liberalization, bilateral commercial treaties, and the use of force, what did classical economic liberals say about the role of wider multilateral cooperation among governments in supporting an integrated world economy? They showed little interest in the ambitious forms of multilateral economic governance that would later be endorsed at the 1944 Bretton Woods conference by embedded liberals (see Chapter 14). But some backed the creation of weak "public international unions" in the second half of the nineteenth century to encourage international cooperation on issues such as telegraphs, postal services, railways, the standardization of weights and measures, and the publication of customs tariffs. Some liberals also supported the creation of two multilateral regional "monetary unions" in the 1860s, under which coins from one country would be valid in others: the Latin Monetary Union and the Scandinavian Monetary Union. In that same decade, liberals such as Bagehot and Mill even supported an unsuccessful initiative to create a wider world monetary union of this kind that would foster global commerce, peace, and even cosmopolitan identities. As Bagehot put it in 1866, "if civilization could make all men of one money, it would do much to make them think they were of one blood".[65]

In general, however, multilateral intergovernmental cooperation and institutions had a much lower profile in the classical economic liberal project of the nineteenth century than they would assume in the twentieth century. They even played little role in the establishment of the international gold standard in late nineteenth century that facilitated cross-border economic flows in that era. This international monetary standard emerged not from a multiateral agreement but rather from numerous unilateral decisions of governments.[66] Many economic liberals also applauded how it seemed to help maintain international economic

---

[63] Indeed, it was in the context of the latter that Smith invoked his famous metaphor of the "invisible hand" (Smith 1776, IV.ii.9). Smith was sceptical of the prospects for large migration (e.g. Smith 1776, I.viii.31).

[64] Ricardo [1817]1908, 117.

[65] Quoted in Helleiner 2003, 130. See Helleiner 2003, ch. 6 for these initiatives.

[66] Gallarotti 1992.

equilibrium via market forces without the need for active intergovernmental cooperation or discretionary public management of the domestic
economy.[67]

## Conclusion

The next chapter highlights the diffusion of European classical economic
liberalism to other parts of the world. Its global reach was fitting given
its content. Classical economic liberals prioritized free trade that would
foster global economic integration. They also emphasized that free trade
and free markets would generate the cosmopolitan benefits of promoting global prosperity, international peace, and individual freedom. The
most famous exposition of these arguments came in Smith's *The Wealth
of Nations*, but other thinkers also made important contributions to
the development of this perspective in the nineteenth century, such as
Ricardo, Cobden, Mill, and Bagehot.

Although European economic liberals shared these core ideas, they
disagreed with each other on some important issues. For example, thinkers did not always concur about the precise mechanisms by which their
preferred polices would generate the outcomes they hoped for. They
even had differing opinions about which of these outcomes were most
important. They also disagreed about how extensive international specialization should be in a world of free trade as well as about the extent
to which exceptions to free trade should be allowed. Further, their thinking diverged vis-à-vis their interest in international economic integration
beyond free trade in goods as well as with respect to the place of force,
imperialism, civilizational discourse, and intergovernmental cooperation
in the economic liberal project. They even had contrasting views about
whether economic liberalism had universal relevance. In short, there
were many distinct versions of classical economic liberalism. When it
circulated to other parts of the world, even more versions appeared, as
we shall see in the next chapter.[68]

---

[67] Although analysts often associate nineteenth-century European economic liberalism
with support for the gold standard (e.g. Polanyi 1944), some European free traders
preferred a bimetallic monetary order in this period (e.g. Howe 1990).

[68] Further differences among economic liberal thinkers are discussed in Chapters 9 and 10
in the context of their engagement with environmentalist and feminist thought.

# 3 Economic Liberalism from Non-European Perspectives

The emergence of economic liberalism was much more than just a European story. Economic liberal ideas soon found supporters among thinkers from many other parts of the world. Their global diffusion was encouraged by the rapid growth of international trade, communication, and the movement of people during the nineteenth century. Expanding translation activity in this period also helped to spread the liberal message; indeed, Jürgen Osterhammel notes the works of Smith and Mill were "among the European authors most widely translated in other parts of the world".[1] As early as the 1820s, a kind of informal transnational network of liberal thinkers had come into existence that extended across Europe, parts of Asia, the Americas and Africa.[2] Later in the nineteenth century, an even more global intellectual network of this kind was fostered by the London-based Cobden Club, which was created after the British thinker's death in 1866 to actively promote his ideas.[3]

This chapter highlights some examples of non-European thinkers who embraced European liberal free trade thought around the world. But it also shows how these figures often adapted it in various ways in response to their local circumstances. These adaptations created new varieties of economic liberalism, thereby widening the diversity of its content that was already highlighted in the last chapter. In some cases, their views also found an audience in Europe itself. Non-European thinkers also questioned the European origins of economic liberalism, pointing to thinkers from their regions who had developed similar ideas. Some even suggested that Smith's ideas themselves had been influenced by non-European thought.

---

[1] Osterhammel 2014, 25.
[2] See, for example, Bayly 2012; Coller 2015.
[3] Palen 2016.

### Reception in the Americas

The United States was a place where Adam Smith's free trade message gained many early supporters, including prominent politicians such as Benjamin Franklin (who knew Smith from his travels to Europe) and Thomas Jefferson. Indeed, Smith's death in 1790 attracted more attention in the United States than in Britain itself.[4] This early interest in Smith's ideas was hardly surprising. Thinkers in the new American republic appreciated how *The Wealth of Nations* had attacked the same British colonial trade restrictions that many of the American revolutionaries had found so frustrating.

Some American supporters of free trade also subsequently modified Smith's views in various ways. Particularly striking were the ideas of a school of thinkers that emerged in the 1820s and 1830s in the agricultural-exporting American South, where free trade policies were very popular. The most prominent member of this school was Thomas Cooper, a professor at South Carolina College who was praised by Jefferson for being "the greatest man in America in the powers of the mind and in acquired information".[5] Although Cooper was a supporter of Smith's ideas, he rejected Smith's views on one important topic: slavery.

Smith had denounced slavery both on efficiency grounds and because it violated individual freedom.[6] Cooper, by contrast, forcefully defended the system of slavery on which the American South's cotton exports were based, including the constraints that system imposed on slaves' liberty. As he put it in 1835, "we talk a great deal of nonsense about the rights of man. We say that every man is born free, and equal to every other man. Nothing can be more untrue". To justify slavery, he turned to racist arguments about the "natural inferiority" of the slaves and asserted they "will not labor voluntarily" in the way that liberal economics expected.[7]

Cooper's views represented only one strand of American free trade thought. Other nineteenth-century free traders in the United States were strong supporters of the *abolition* of slavery. Indeed, by the mid-nineteenth century, there were strong links between the free trade and abolitionist movements, with many of the latter embracing the idealistic vision of global prosperity, peace, and liberty advanced by Cobden (who

---

[4] Liu 2018, 213. See also Irwin 2017, 68–70.

[5] Quoted in Carlander and Brownlee 2006, 390. See also Conkin 1980, 142. Because Cooper's early life was in England, he could be considered a "European" economic liberal, but I have placed him in this chapter because the analysis being discussed was developed in his new American context.

[6] For a discussion of Smith's views, see Shilliam 2021a.

[7] Quotes from Cooper 1835, 189, 192–93.

was also an abolitionist).[8] Within the Cobden Club, American members in fact soon outnumbered all other nationalities except for the British. In the late nineteenth century, many of these American free traders also opposed rising American imperialist sentiment.[9]

Distinctive strands of free trade thought also appeared in Latin America, another region where the ideas of European economic liberalism were embraced relatively quickly. As in the United States, trade restrictions imposed by Spanish and Portuguese colonial authorities served as an important trigger for Latin American demands for independence in the late eighteenth and early nineteenth centuries. In this context, many Latin American figures were attracted to Smith's free trade message and invoked it in support of the revolutionary cause. For example, one of the earliest Latin American calls for independence came in the late 1790s from Juan Pablo Viscardo y Guzmán, a Peruvian living in London who cited Smith's work to argue that prosperity was impossible without freedom from colonialism.[10] In the early nineteenth century, prominent revolutionary leaders such as Simón Bolívar were also influenced by British liberals such as Smith and Jeremy Bentham, and they associated free trade with the cause of throwing off oppressive colonial rule.[11]

The link drawn between liberty and free trade continued to appeal to many Latin Americans after their countries gained independence, including in the mid-nineteenth century when many Latin American governments followed European policymakers in embracing free trade policies. As the Mexican liberal politician and teacher of political economy, Guillermo Prieto, put it, 'The faith I have in free trade is the faith I have in all sublime manifestations of liberty".[12] Free trade also appealed for this reason to the important Chilean thinker Francisco Bilbao who led artisans in a 1851 revolt that fought for a "government of liberty" in which free trade would exist alongside popular sovereignty and universal education.[13]

Conservative elites in Colombia at this time also drew a link between free trade and liberty, but with a quite a different focus. They championed free trade as a policy that would guarantee their freedom to import European luxury goods that distinguished their class within the country.[14] Like many elites in the US South, they showed little interest in the liberty of workers in the agricultural exporting sector, as they backed

---

[8]  Meardon 2008; Palen 2015, 2016.
[9]  Palen 2016, 60, 251.
[10] Brading 1991, 535–40, 551–52, 559–60; Hale 1968, 250–53.
[11] Lynch 2006, 160–61; Cot 2014.
[12] Quoted in Salvucci 1996, 67.
[13] Gootenberg 1993, 138. See also Wood 2006.
[14] Gootenberg 1989, 84, 131; Rojas 2002, 111–16.

coercive labour regimes. The same was true of the first prominent supporter of Smith's free trade ideas in Brazil, José da Silva Lisboa, who helped to draft a more liberal trade policy for Brazil in 1808 and who supervised the first Portuguese translation (by his son) of *The Wealth of Nations* in 1811–12. A supporter of the landed classes, he defended slavery on the grounds that the general principles of political economy did not apply to countries specializing in tropical agriculture, for whom more particular principles were needed.[15]

Thinkers in Latin America were also attracted to liberal economic arguments because they helped to justify their region's commodity-exporting role in the world economy. In colonial times, this position of the region within the international division of labour was a product of imperial preferences and power. After independence, however, many Latin Americans defended their region's enduring commodity-exporting role by using liberal ideas that emphasized the need for countries to specialize in what they were best at producing. Pointing to their countries' natural endowments, they argued that an economic strategy centered on export-oriented agriculture and/or mining was entirely justified. As the Argentine thinker (and later president) Domingo Sarmiento argued in 1845: "We are neither industrialists nor navigators, so, for centuries to come, Europe will supply us with manufactures in exchange for our primary commodities; and we will both profit from such an exchange".[16]

Others were less inclined to see their role as commodity exporters as this kind of near-permanent condition in the way that David Ricardo's theory of comparative advantage suggested (as noted in the last chapter). For advocates of this more developmental strand of liberalism, free trade policies would generate dynamic economic gains that would enable the rise of a more diversified economy with industry over time, following through the stages that Adam Smith had suggested (see previous chapter). In addition to noting the benefits of free trade outlined by Smith, these figures often suggested that rising living standards would attract immigrants whose skills and capital would contribute to the creation of a more diverse and complex economy. Politically, they also saw free trade policies as a tool of state-building when those policies helped to foster the growth of domestic markets that tied disparate parts of the country together.[17]

Many of these Latin American developmental liberals combined their support of free trade with endorsements of a more activist economic role

[15] Coutinho 2016; Mendes Cunha and Suprinyak 2017, 22; Vernengo 2007.
[16] Quoted in Salvatore 1999, 34.
[17] Jacobsen 2005, 135; Gootenberg 1989, 98, 141, 144; 1993, 27–9, 141; Sowell 1996; Weiner 2004, 21–22.

for the state than their European counterparts.[18] For example, Peruvian free traders in the mid-nineteenth century supported a state monopoly for their country's key export – guano – that promoted local entrepreneurs as managers and traders of the resource. A key supporter of the monopoly was the prominent Peruvian merchant and politician Manuel Pardo y Lavalle, who had studied political economy in Europe and wrote extensively on the topic. Soon after he became Peru's first civilian president in 1872, Pardo also established a national monopoly in the growing nitrate sector. Earlier, at the height of the guano boom in 1860, he had advanced an ambitious proposal to use guano revenue to build railroads that integrated the nation and supported the growth of domestic agriculture and industrialization. In his view, this domestic state activism was needed to foster the country's economic diversification away from its dependence on guano, supplies of which would soon be depleted.[19]

Innovative ideas about the governance of a liberal global economy also emerged from Latin America. Particularly important was the "Calvo doctrine" developed in the 1860s by an Argentine lawyer, Carlos Calvo, who was a colleague of Sarmiento. A strong advocate of free trade and the need for Latin American countries to attract foreign investment and migration, Calvo was also very critical of how European powers intervened in Latin America to defend the economic interests of their citizens and firms, including with military force. Calvo proposed that all disputes over economic contracts be resolved in the legal system of the country where the contract took effect, thereby ensuring that Europeans and their firms would be forced to accept the primacy of the laws of the Latin American countries in which they operated. This defense of Latin American sovereignty challenged European discourses that justified intervention on the grounds that Latin American societies were not advanced enough to ensure proper legal processes.[20] At a deeper level, Calvo also suggested that imperialist protection of European interests undermined the liberal order in his region by distorting domestic markets and the rule of law. The anti-imperialist Calvo doctrine was rejected by European governments at the time, but it began to be incorporated in many international agreements among Latin American states in the late nineteenth century.[21]

---

[18] In Eastern Europe, this combination of support for free trade and domestic state activism was also common. See, for example, the views of the prominent Polish thinker Wawrzyniec Surowiecki in 1810 (Jedlicki 1999, 58–63).

[19] Gootenberg 1993.

[20] Davis (2018; 2021, 44) notes, however, that Calvo did not fully reject European civilizational discourse and accepted the need for foreign intervention when states were unable to protect property and the rule of law.

[21] See Davis 2018; 2021 and Dawson 1981, 51. When European warships threatened Venezuela after it stopped servicing external debts in 1902, another Argentine lawyer,

Important adaptations of European economic liberalism emerged in the Americas not just from the United States and Latin America, but also from Canada. Like their Latin American counterparts, Canadian liberal admirers of Adam Smith debated the extent to which their country's dependence on commodity exporting could lead to a more diversified economy capable of generating sustainable growth over time. In the interwar years, optimists such as W. A. Macintosh argued that this was possible, but Harold Innis – a dominant figure in Canadian political economy at this time – was more pessimistic. Through detailed historical work, he showed how Canadian economic development had been shaped by exports to more industrialized countries of successive "staple" products from fish to fur to minerals, lumber, and wheat. With its development so dependent on changing foreign demand, Innis argued that Canada experienced unstable boom and bust cycles as well as painful adjustment costs associated with the rise and fall of each staple and its distinctive features, such as its technologies, its infrastructures (often government-financed), its forward and backward linkages to the rest of the economy, and its broader institutional arrangements.[22]

In contrast to Ricardo's optimism about the benefits of international trade for commodity exporters, Innis suggested that Canada thus suffered from a dependent and unstable externally oriented model of development characterized by economic disequilibria and rigidities. This model was very different from the Smithian vision of decentralized, smoothly functioning markets and more self-generating growth that Innis found so attractive. Innis' staples approach was part of his broader effort to develop economic analysis appropriate to Canada's distinctive context and needs rather than those of Europe. As he put it in 1929, "A new country presents certain definite problems which appear to be more or less insoluble from the standpoint of the application of economic theory as worked out in the older highly industrialized countries". Indeed, he went further in his critique of those who believed in the universal relevance of European theory, arguing that "the application of the economic theories of old countries to the problems of new countries results in a new form of exploitation with dangerous consequences".[23]

---

Luis María Drago, proposed a more radical doctrine that would prohibit the European use of force to compel Latin America governments to repay their public debts to foreigners. Calvo opposed Drago's idea that challenged liberal norms of debt repayment. In Teresa Davis' (2018, 138) words, he and others viewed it "as a fundamental threat to the world of legally regulated circulation that international law was meant to bring into existence".

[22] See, for example, Neill 1972.
[23] Innis [1929]1956, 3.

## Adaptations in South Asia

South Asia was another place where European economic liberalism found early supporters and was modified in interesting ways. The most important South Asian thinker in the early nineteenth century to embrace its ideas was Rammohun Roy, who worked for British colonial officials in Bengal between 1803 and 1815 and then became a private financier and public intellectual. Roy's writings circulated not just in Bengal but also in Europe and North America, providing an early example of the multi-directional flow of liberal ideas. Indeed, Lynn Zastoupil notes that "by 1820 he was famous on both sides of the Atlantic".[24] In the early 1830s, he also travelled to Britain and became actively involved in British political debates, including by supporting local free traders who were criticizing the East India Company's monopolistic practices.[25]

Like critics of colonial trade restrictions in the Americas, Roy's frustrations with the East India Company's control of local trade help to explain why he and other Indians were drawn to economic liberal thought. Also similar to some thinkers in the Americas, Roy's economic liberalism had a strong developmental orientation. He saw the promotion of free trade, private enterprise, and property rights as a way for India to boost its living standards and compete more effectively with Europe. Because the quality of India's manufacturing had been equal to, or better than, Europe's in the recent past, Roy argued that India certainly had the capacity to catch up economically with Europe. His developmental orientation was also evident in the concerns he expressed about whether free trade in India might simply benefit commodity traders and landlords unless it was accompanied by active efforts to modernize industry and agriculture with the help of European capital, technology, and knowledge. As he put it, what was needed was the "diffusion of knowledge of European arts and sciences, in the interest of *national improvement*".[26]

Although Roy was sympathetic to liberal nationalist movements in Latin America and elsewhere, he did not call for the political independence of India. Instead, he hoped that British imperialism could be a progressive force in India and that Indians could become equal subjects in a multiethnic and liberal British empire. He was particularly hopeful that a liberal British empire would enable British capital and skilled labour to flow to South Asia in ways that helped advance its economic development. Roy insisted, however, that European settlers should be

---

[24] Zastoupil 2010, 5. When Spanish liberals reissued a constitution in 1820, they even dedicated it to him (Bayly 2012, 47).

[25] Zastoupil 2010; Ganguli 1977, 41, 56; Bayly 2012, 49, 83.

[26] Quoted in Ganguli 1977, 88. See also pp. 36–38; Bayly 2012; Chatterjee 2012.

limited just to educated Europeans "of character and capital" to minimize the danger that they might "assume an ascendency over the aborigi-
nal inhabitants, and aim at enjoying exclusive rights and privileges, to
the depression of the larger, but less favoured class".[27] His views on
this issue disappointed some British economic liberals who opposed all
restrictions on European settlement at the time, but some of their specific ideas may help to explain Roy's position. For example, when calling for unrestricted settlement in 1824, James Silk Buckingham, who
worked closely with Roy, praised how Islam and Hinduism "would be
made to disappear more rapidly" by this policy.[28]

A second key Indian thinker who engaged with European economic
liberal ideas was Dadabhai Naoroji. Raised in a relatively poor Parsi family, Naoroji studied and then taught at a British-run school in Bombay
before moving to Britain in 1855, where he lived until 1907 while often
traveling back and forth to India. In Britain, he became a well-known
figure and was even elected to the British parliament in the early 1890s
(the first Indian to achieve this feat). He was also one of the pioneers
of the Indian nationalist movement, assuming leadership roles in the
Indian National Congress (the first significant nationalist organization
in the colony) after its creation in 1885.[29] As we shall see in Chapter 6,
Naoroji's ideas about British imperialism also had broader influence,
including in European Marxist circles.

Naoroji's interest in economic liberalism was evident from the fact that
he joined the Cobden Club, and even served on its executive committee.[30]
His best-known contribution to political economy was his "drain theory",
which he first advanced in an 1867 paper and then developed further in
subsequent publications, including his 1901 book *Poverty and Un-British
Rule in India*. The theory provided one of the first detailed economic
critiques of European colonialism from the standpoint of a colonized
subject.[31] Drawing on extensive statistical work, Naoroji argued that
British colonial rule was draining wealth from India through a number
of channels, such as the remittances of European employees of the colonial government and payments by that government to Britain for various services (including interest payments on public debt). This drain, he
argued, was a direct cause of the "extreme impoverishment" of India both
in an immediate sense and over time (by causing a shortage of capital

---

[27] Quoted in Zastoupil 2010, 116; Chatterjee 2012, 151. See also Ganguli 1977, 38–41.
[28] Quoted in Chatterjee 2012, 144.
[29] Patel 2020.
[30] Singh 1975, 30.
[31] Earlier broader critiques of European colonialism from the perspective of the colonized
included *The Colonial System* by the Haitian writer Jean Louis Vastey ([1814]2014).

that undermined the prospects for India's economic development).[32] He depicted India's poverty caused by the drain as a distortion of natural market processes: "it is the pitiless perversion of economic laws by the sad bleeding to which India is subjected, that is destroying India".[33]

Naoroji was not the first thinker to suggest that British rule was draining India's wealth. Adam Smith himself had referred to the early British rulers as "plunderers of India".[34] In the early 1830s, Roy had also complained about a "tribute" that Britain extracted from India in the form of the colonial government's spending in Britain as well as the export of savings by its European employees.[35] Some Indian thinkers in the 1840s had also begun to develop economic critiques of British colonialism that Naoroji noted when he first proposed his theory in 1867. But Naoroji's arguments were much more detailed and sophisticated than these earlier analyses. He also combined them with broader criticism of European racism.[36]

Although Naoroji was critical of British rule, he sought – like Roy – to reform it rather than reject it at the time he was developing his drain theory (he called for self-rule later in his life). As he put it in 1870, "the salvation of India, its future prosperity, its civilization, and its political elevation, all depend on the continuance of the British rule".[37] He urged British authorities to reduce the drain by measures such as raising public debt in India, increasing local purchasing, and employing more Indians in the colonial civil services (which would also retain skills and knowledge locally). He also tried to appeal to British interests by noting that a more prosperous India would be a richer market for British goods and by arguing that the drain of India's wealth had not helped the average British citizen because it had gone "into the pockets of the capitalists".[38]

Like Roy, Naoroji was engaging sympathetically with liberal imperialist ideas but from the perspective of the colonized. Indeed, Naoroji drew on the ideas of the most famous liberal imperialist of his age in the field of political economy, John Stuart Mill, in support of some of his ideas. For example, he quoted the latter's comment that "industry is limited by capital" in order to make the point that the drain of capital from India was inhibiting Indian industrialization. He also noted that the colonial government was not pursuing the kinds of policies that Mill deemed necessary for cultivating an "effective desire for accumulation", such as

---

[32] Quoted in Masani 1939, 429.
[33] Quoted in Patel 2020, 9.
[34] Smith 1776, V.1.Part III.47.
[35] Quoted in Ganguli 1977, 129.
[36] Masani 1939, 98–99, 408; Naoroji 1887, 1, 23, 33; Patel 2020, 131–34.
[37] Quoted in Masani 1939, 124–25. See also p. 356 and Naoroji 1887, 333.
[38] Quoted in Masani 1939, 420. See also pp. 407–9.

moderate taxation and expanded public education. Despite his membership in the free trading Cobden Club, Naoroji also cited Mill's endorsement of infant industry protection, arguing that the drain of wealth had
left India unable to compete in a world of free trade: "I like free trade,
but ... free trade between England and India in a matter like this is something like a race between a starving, exhausting invalid and a strong man
with a horse to ride on. ... Young colonies, says Mill, may need protection. India needs it in a far larger degree ...Let India have its present
drain brought within reasonable limits, and India will be quite prepared
for any free trade".[39]

In these ways, Naoroji used the ideas of this prominent British
thinker to highlight how Britain was not upholding liberal imperialist
ideals. In Christopher Bayly's words, he employed a rhetorical style of
"counter-preaching", which was "designed to subvert the contemporary
self-confidence of colonial elites by emphasizing their moral failure as
colonial rulers".[40] In the same vein, he argued that it was the "duty" of
the British to promote India's economic development not just by reducing the drain but also through activist policies. In addition to calling for
"vast public works of a productive character", he suggested that colonial
authorities could borrow from abroad to support Indian industrialization via new state-owned companies. This strategy, he argued, would
minimize problems associated with foreign private investment such as
exploitation, foreign control, and the export of profits.[41]

### African and Ottoman Interest

European economic liberalism also attracted early interest among some
figures in Africa or with African roots. Among the latter was Olaudah
Equiano, an ex-slave (who was born in the Kingdom of Benin) who
emerged as a leading opponent of the slave trade in London in the 1780s
and who helped create an abolitionist society titled "Sons of Africa". In
1789, he published a book describing the horrors of slavery and the
slave trade that attracted enormous attention. Published in nine English
editions and translated into Dutch, German and Russian, the volume
helped to build support in Britain and elsewhere for ending the slave
trade. Equiano's arguments were important not just for their critique
but also for their solution. He suggested that the slave trade should
be replaced by a "free trade" system in which Africa was encouraged

---

[39] Quotes in Ganguli 1965, 136; Naoroji 1887, 104, 217.
[40] Bayly 2012, 105.
[41] Quotes from Naoroji 1887, 39, 41.

to grow crops such as cotton and indigo to be exchanged for British manufactured goods.[42]

Building on economic liberal ideas, Equiano argued this reform would provide mutual economic gains for both Africans and Britain. Africans would gain freedom from slavery as well as an advance in "civilization" from the economic development that would be generated by this arrangement. Britain would acquire a new and growing market for its manufacturers as well as new sources of resources for their operations. The only losers from this arrangement, he argued, would be "those persons concerned in manufacturing neck-yokes, collars, chains, hand-cuffs, leg-bolts, drags, thumbscrews, iron muzzles, and coffins; cats, scourges, and other instruments of torture used in the slave-trade"[43]. In Equiano's formulation, free trade could, thus, contribute directly to dismantling the system of slavery that Smith critiqued. Replacing the slave trade with "legitimate commerce" with Africa in this way became a key goal of British abolitionists and liberals in the nineteenth century (as well as those in the United States).[44]

After the slave trade from West Africa diminished, intellectuals in that region continued to support free trade. A prominent example was Alexander Crummell in Liberia. Born in the United States, Crummell was the son of an ex-slave from Sierra Leone. When racial discrimination prevented him from earning a university education in the United States, he pursued a degree in Britain at Cambridge, supported by abolitionists. After graduating in 1853, he moved to Liberia (which became independent in 1847) and emerged as a strong advocate for free trade. He described the latter as "a new evangel to men", which ensured that "in every land the masses of the population are being made more comfortable, and are becoming blessed". Indeed, Crummell argued that Liberia, as a "rising Christian state", had a duty through free trade to be contributing "to the world's well-being and civilization".[45]

---

[42] Equiano did not use the phrase "free trade" in his proposal in the book, but he did in the same year in a letter to Lord Hawkesbury as part of published evidence for committee hearings into the slave trade (quote in Edwards [1969]2001, 332). The argument that Africa could be a large market for British exports was made two years earlier in a 1787 text by another ex-slave Quobna Ottobah Cugoano (Gunn 2010, 650–51). Although Equiano was living in London, I have placed him in this chapter because he emphasized his African identity.

[43] Quotes from Equiano [1789]2001, 177–78.

[44] Hopkins 1995; Pella 2015, 99–102.

[45] Crummell 1855, 82, 58. Despite his US roots, I have placed Crummell in this section because I am quoting from his writings while he was in Liberia and committed to building up the Liberia state. His commitment subsequently waned and he returned to the United States in the early 1870s.

Crummell acknowledged the devastating role of international commerce in Africa in the past: "For nigh 3 centuries, commerce, on the coast of Africa, was divested of every feature, humane, generous, and gracious. Commerce then was a robber; commerce was a marauder; commerce was a devastator; a thief; a murderer!". But in the new free trade era, he argued that commerce had now become a force for economic progress and "good-will" as well as "the handmaid of religion" and a conveyer of "civilization".[46] In addition to praising Liberia's trade with countries outside Africa, Crummell argued in 1870 that Liberia should expand commerce with the African interior. Indeed, invoking a kind of intra-African liberal imperialism, he argued that Liberia had a national obligation to "train, educate, civilize and regulate, the heathen tribes around us" and that "force, that is authority, *must* be used in the exercise of guardianship over heathen tribes". He backed up this advice by citing Mill's comment that "barbarians have no rights as a *nation*, except a right to such treatment as may, at the earliest possible period, fit them for becoming one".[47]

Like developmental liberals in Latin America, Crummell combined his support for free trade with advocacy of domestic government economic activism in order to ensure that Liberia gained as much as possible from its role as an agricultural exporter. He lamented how Liberia's resources seemed to be enriching British and other foreign merchants rather than Liberians. To increase gains for the latter, he called for the Liberian government to support road construction, commerce, and agricultural production, including with the use of subsidies to encourage the growth of cotton exports that could compete more effectively with cotton from the US South. As he put it, Liberian producers could be "competing with the oppressors of our race in the ports of Liverpool and Glasgow, and beating down their ill-gotten gains!"[48]

European economic liberalism also found an early supporter in North Africa, Hassuna D'Ghies, who came from a prominent family in Tripoli (a city-state that was under nominal Ottoman sovereignty at the time). After receiving a traditional Islamic education, D'Ghies travelled to France in 1813 and then to London in 1822, where he was quickly drawn into liberal intellectual circles. He became a disciple of Bentham, supporting

---

[46] Quotes from Crummell [1855]1862, 110, 72, 110–11, 72. In the neighbouring British colony of Sierra Leone, James African Horton ([1868]1969, 175–76) was more sceptical about the inherent civilizing role of trade, noting that "civilized merchants in a savage country, without the influence of a civilized Government to correct their action, rather retard than encourage civilization". He cited the example of an English trader in West Africa who flogged Africans and traded "by brute force".
[47] Quotes from Crummell [1870]1892, 171, 185, 185fn.
[48] Crummell [1855]1862, 85.

liberal ideas of free trade, liberty, and constitutional rule. But he also insisted that European liberals needed to better understand and respect the local circumstances and culture of his homeland, including its Islamic values. While agreeing with the need to abolish slavery, he was critical of British abolitionists for their "dictatorial tone" and for failing to recognize the need to support African economic development as a substitute and the importance of compensating slave owners (of which his family was one).[49]

When France invaded Algiers in 1830, he joined an Algerian thinker from Bentham's circle, Hamdan Khodja, in condemning the invasion in French public debates on liberal grounds. In the face of the French aggression and growing European power in North Africa, D'Ghies began to see a reformed Ottoman Empire – rather than an independent African nation-state – as the best entity for promoting liberal goals in his region. Because the Ottoman Empire seemed to be the one state in the region able to resist European power, he joined those committed to its modernization, assuming the editorship of the empire's official newspaper in 1836. The latter had already been promoting liberal ideas since its creation in 1831, reflecting the growing influence of these ideas within Ottoman ruling circles. Around this same time, D'Ghies also began to support the Ottoman Empire's restoration of control over his home state, thereby embracing a more imperial style of liberalism.[50]

Although D'Ghies died a few months after assuming his editorship, his ideas influenced some prominent European liberals such as David Urquhart, who had met him in the early 1820s and would later become a prominent liberal European defender of the Ottoman Empire as well as an advocate for the defense of its values and culture.[51] D'Ghies hoped that the Ottoman Empire would become an agent of liberal reform was also realized soon after his death. During the Tanzimat era (1839–76), Ottoman policymakers embraced free trade and domestic market-oriented reforms. Indeed, its policies were seen as a model by some British economic liberals, such as Nassau William Senior, who praised Ottoman officials in the late 1850s for being "the best free traders in the world". He added: "I wish you could give some lessons to France". Ottoman authorities also supported the work of local thinkers who imported European economic liberalism and even promoted the latter through the school system and other means by the 1860s.[52]

Like D'Ghies' version, the new Ottoman economic liberalism was often combined with appeals to Islamic values. For example, the 1839

---

[49] Quoted in Coller 2015, 536.
[50] Coller 2015, 2016; Kilinçoğlu 2015, 23–24; Pitts 2009.
[51] Coller 2016, 102.
[52] Quote in Özveren 2002, 134. See also Kilinçoğlu 2015, 28; Özgur and Genc 2011.

edict that inaugurated the Tanzimat era legitimized its reforms with reference to principles of Islamic law.[53] The prominent Ottoman thinker and statesman Ahmed Cevdet Pasha in this period also argued that earlier writers from the region, including the famous fourteenth-century scholar Ibn Khaldun, had pioneered some liberal economic ideas before European thinkers did.[54] As Cemil Aydin notes, Ottoman thinkers also linked European notions of civilizational advancement to "classical Islamic notions of civility, chivalry, and social ethics".[55] In this way, thinkers such as Cevdet argued that civilization was a product of not just Europe but of all parts of the world.

### East Asian Perspectives

East Asia was a region where interest in European economic liberalism appeared relatively late. In the Japanese case, the delay resulted from the government's tight control over the inflow of foreign ideas before the 1850s. After the country was forcibly opened by the United States in 1853–54, however, many Japanese thinkers became interested in European economic liberalism, which they often associated with the wider embrace of "civilization and enlightenment". Like Ottoman thinkers, some Japanese scholars translated the European concept of civilization in a way that was compatible with their own intellectual tradition: in this case, the Confucian goal of improving human character and social life through learning and morality.[56]

Prominent Japanese economic liberals such as Taguchi Ukichi also echoed their Ottoman counterparts in arguing that there were deep local roots of economic liberal thought. The leading Japanese advocate of free trade ideas after the 1870s (and sponsor of the first full Japan translation of *The Wealth of Nations* between 1882 and 1888), Taguchi argued that liberal economic principles could be found in the Confucian classics: "The ancient sages made inaction the foundation of the way of government. Their words may appear simple, but in fact they contain the true principle of wise economics". This line of argument led Taguchi to suggest that the Japanese needed to learn modern liberal economics not because it had been discovered in the West but because it was a "universal truth".[57]

Chinese thinkers did not show much interest in European economic liberalism until even later than this interest emerged in Japan. The lack of interest did not reflect a lack of exposure. Two Chinese scholars were,

---

[53] Anscombe 2010.
[54] Kilinçoğlu 2015, 29, 53–58, 90; 2017, 238.
[55] Aydin 2007, 23.
[56] Aydin 2007.
[57] Quotes in Morris-Suzuki 1989, 47; Blacker 1964, 147fn17.

in fact, the target audience for an important French treatise that anticipated many of Smith's arguments: Anne-Robert-Jacques Turgot's 1766
*Reflections on the Formation and Distribution of Wealth*. Turgot wrote this
text for Gao Leisi and Yang Dewang, who had been brought to France
in 1752 as young men for religious training with the Jesuits, and who
returned to China in 1766 with a pension from the French king in return
for reporting information about their homeland. Turgot wrote *Reflections*
as a background document to some questions he sent them about China,
but his work appears to have attracted little attention in China.[58]

During the 1830s, more extensive exposure to European economic liberalism came when British merchants sponsored what Chen Songchuan
calls a massive "information war" to try to convince the Chinese people
of the virtues of free trade and liberal economics in advance of the first
Opium War. This propaganda initiative involved the publication of the
first Chinese-language works that promoted European liberal economics, including books in 1838 and 1840 written by a German Protestant
missionary Karl Gützlaff. But these works generated little interest among
the conservative and inward-looking Chinese intellectual class. Even the
scholars who expressed an interest in learning from Europe at this time,
such as Wei Yuan (see Chapters 4 and 12), cited the works only for their
information about the outside world rather than their free trade message.[59]

Interest in foreign literature about political economy began to increase
after the second Opium War when a few British liberal economic texts
were translated into Chinese. But it was not until after the country's
humiliating defeat to Japan in 1895 that this interest grew significantly,
particularly after an influential Chinese translation of *The Wealth of
Nations* was published in 1901. The translator, Yan Fu, was a prominent Chinese scholar who had first become interested in Smith's thought
when he had the opportunity – very unusual for a Chinese scholar at
the time – to study in Britain between 1877 and 1879. His translation
included a strong message for China: Smith's ideas were a key source of
British wealth and power.[60]

Yan argued that Smith's advocacy of individual economic liberty
unleashed the energy of the British people in ways that were channeled
to national collective ends by a strong sense of public spirit. For China to
survive in the conflictual world of the early twentieth century, he argued,
it needed to embrace this combination of economic individualism and
national collective purpose. For Yan, liberal economic policies were thus a

---

[58] Groenewegen 1977, xvii–xix; Nguyen and Malbranque 2014.
[59] Quote from Chen 2012, 1706. See also Lutz 2008, 69, 85, 182–84, 191–92, 199–210.
[60] Schwartz 1964.

means to serve the end of boosting China's wealth and power.[61] Although Yan Fu endorsed free trade policies, he believed that China needed a more interventionist state domestically than Smith suggested in order to address its economic difficulties and avoid excessive inequality within the country.[62] Yan also insisted that foreign investment take place in a manner that did not undermine Chinese control over the country's resources.[63]

Like Ahmed Cevdet and Taguchi Ukichi, Yan suggested that some aspects of European economic liberalism had been developed earlier by thinkers from his own country. He acknowledged that "there was no such systematic development of economic discourse as in the West", but he highlighted how "in Chinese economic history, one can easily find famous administrators in different dynasties who wrote treatises about market supply and demand".[64] Other Chinese scholars soon made a similar point, such as Chen Huan-Chang, whose PhD in economics from Columbia University examined the history of Chinese economic thought. In the 1911 published version, he highlighted – as Taguchi had – that ancient Chinese classics had endorsed market-oriented policies. He also noted early Chinese thinkers who had endorsed free trade, including Confucius, who Chen described as an "extreme free trader, in regard to both internal and foreign trade". He concluded: "Confucianism did not make China weak. She is weak not because she followed the teachings of Confucius, but precisely because she did not truly follow his teachings".[65]

Tang Qingzeng took this point further in his 1936 book titled *History of Chinese Economic Thought*. A graduate of Harvard and a fan of Adam Smith, Tang argued that the Scottish thinker himself had been influenced by Chinese thought via the ideas of the French physiocrats, particularly François Quesnay. He noted a work of Quesnay's from 1767 that depicted China as a model of a prosperous and harmonious agrarain society that was governed by natural law and with minimal government interference in the economy. Tang argued that this model stemmed back to the ideas of Confucius, a figure that Quesnay also cited as an inspiration.[66]

Although Tang was right to note Smith's interest in Quesnay's work, the influence of the latter on Smith's *The Wealth of Nations* should not be overstated. Smith had already outlined many of his core ideas before

[61] Schwartz 1964.
[62] Zanasi 2020, 153.
[63] Liu 2016, 59.
[64] Yan [1902]2000, 28.
[65] Quotes from Chen 1911, 683, 720.
[66] Borokh 2013.

engaging deeply with French physiocratic thought.[67] *The Wealth of Nations* also rejects some of the ideas of the physiocrats, such as their view that agriculture was the only productive economic activity. In addition, Smith was less enamored of Chinese policies than Quesnay was, including the fact that "the Chinese have little respect for foreign trade".[68] Quesnay, by contrast, argued "foreign trade probably did more harm than good to the prosperity of the country".[69] But Tang's broader argument was a significant one: that the birth of European economic liberalism took place in a context where some European thinkers such as Quesnay drew inspiration from Chinese intellectual tradition.

It is also important to recognize the point made by Tang and others that Chinese thinkers independently developed ideas that were similar to some of those associated with European economic liberalism. These thinkers included not just those from ancient China but also some eighteenth-century Chinese contemporaries of Quesnay and Smith. In the context of Japan's rapid commercialization and urbanization in the eighteenth century, similar ideas were emerging in that country, too.[70] As William Rowe notes, there was "there was clearly in eighteenth-century China, as in contemporaneous Japan, an emerging discourse of political economy" in which "comprehension of the operation of the market was quite sophisticated, arguably no less so than in the contemporaneous West".[71]

As an example, Rowe focuses on the ideas of Chen Hongmou, an influential Qing official until his death in 1771 (just before *The Wealth of Nations* was published). Although Chen was not a theorist like Smith, Rowe notes how Chen argued that markets were "governed by rationally inferable laws of economic behavior" and that profit maximization, self-interest, and market dynamics could be socially beneficial and encouraged to work for the public good.[72] According to Rowe, he was also a "consistent champion" of trade liberalization, arguing that it would generate economic gains for both China and foreigners as well as boost international peace. Rowe notes that he was also interested in the (China-centric) civilizational rationale that trade could bring "non-Chinese into closer touch with the Qing's civilized social model".[73] In addition, Rowe

---

[67] Chiu and Yeh 1999; Hont 2005, ch. 5.
[68] Quote from Smith 1776, IV.ix.40.
[69] Quoted in Ta 2014, 95. See also Jacobsen 2013.
[70] Metzler and Smits 2010, 15; Najita 1987.
[71] Rowe 1993, 31, 32.
[72] Rowe 1997, 18.
[73] Rowe 2001, 421–42. For the broader support for trade liberalization in Chen Hongmou's era, see Zhang 2021.

refers to Helen Dustan's analysis of broader Chinese thought at this time, which concluded that "a rudimentary form of economic liberalism did exist in eighteenth-century China and that it was indigenous".[74]

I have seen no evidence that the specific ideas of Chen Hongmou and other similar Chinese thinkers at the time were known in Europe, despite Quesnay's interest in China's political economy and the fact that Turgot corresponded with the two Jesuit-trained Chinese scholars.[75] When economic liberal ideas achieved global prominence in the nineteenth and early twentieth centuries, it was the European version that became known. But the attraction of these European ideas for some Chinese thinkers was heightened by the fact that European economic liberalism resonated with intellectual traditions from their country's own past, just as it did with some traditions elsewhere, such as those in Japan and the Islamic world.[76]

## Conclusion

European classical economic liberalism was the first perspective on political economy to reach a worldwide audience. As we shall see in subsequent chapters, thinkers around the world reacted against it in various ways. In this chapter, we have examined thinkers from outside Europe who were attracted to its ideas. Many of them also adapted European classical economic liberalism in various ways, thereby creating even more varieties of economic liberalism than those already identified within the European context in the previous chapter.

As we have seen, adaptations of European economic liberalism took many forms and raised issues that were less prominent in European liberal thought. For example, Equiano advanced new ideas about how free trade could end slavery, and thinkers such as Naoroji directly challenged European racism (while others such as Cooper endorsed racist views and saw slavery and free trade as compatible). Naoroji also advanced innovative economic critiques of imperialism and proposed new policies for colonial officials to pursue in support of liberal imperialist goals. Some thinkers also challenged Eurocentric civilizational discourses by linking ideas of civilizational progress to their own societies' intellectual

[74] Dunstan 1996: 327. See also Zanasi 2020.
[75] For European knowledge of China's political economy, see Millar 2017. Young (1996) speculates about whether Ho and Yang may have transmitted Chinese ideas about political economy to Turgot during discussions leading up to his 1866 book. But I have seen no evidence that Turgot (or Smith) ever interacted with them before they left for China or that they were interested in Chinese political economy debates.
[76] Trescott 2007.

traditions and accomplishments. A number of figures also combined their support of free trade with calls for various kinds of government economic activism domestically designed to promote national developmental goals. Their interest in government economic activism to serve developmental goals overlapped with that of neomercantilist thinkers described in the next two chapters.

Some of the internal disagreements between European economic liberals noted in the last chapter also surfaced amongst economic liberals outside Europe. For example, some opposed imperialism, while others accepted liberal conceptions of empire (including the empires of non-European states). Disagreements also existed on the question of the universal relevance of economic liberalism, with Taguchi fully endorsing this idea while Innis and D'Ghies were more sceptical. Thinkers such as Naoroji and Yan were also more wary of foreign investment than a figure such as Roy. Sarmiento's acceptance of a Ricardian vision of international specialization also contrasted with Innis' concerns about its implications for commodity exporters and with the more Smithian preferences for an increasingly diversified domestic economy over time of Pardo, Innis, and Mackintosh.

In addition to highlighting adaptations of European thought and internal disagreements within the liberal camp, this chapter showed how the global dimension of the emergence of economic liberalism involved much more than just the worldwide diffusion and adaptation of European ideas. As we have seen, ideas also flowed in the other direction, as in the example of Quesnay's interest in Confucian thought and the participation of thinkers from outside Europe in European liberal circles. Further, thinkers beyond Europe pointed to pre-Smithian thinkers in their own regions who developed ideas similar to some dimensions of European economic liberalism, suggesting that economic liberal ideas outside Europe had independent local roots rather than being merely branches of European thought.

# 4    Neomercantilist Reactions in Europe and the United States

This chapter and the next analyze neomercantilist reactions against classical economic liberalism. As noted in Chapter 2, Adam Smith contrasted his views with the ideas of earlier European mercantilist thinkers who had supported protectionist trade policies and other forms of government economic activism in order to boost state wealth and power. Neomercantilists echoed many of the policy preferences and objectives of those earlier mercantilist thinkers, but they advanced new intellectual defenses for them in the context of reacting against the new promotion of free trade and free markets by Smith and his followers. They put particular emphasis on the need for strategic trade protectionism that was designed to support specific domestic economic sectors, especially industry. The latter was deemed critically important to state wealth and power in the new industrial age that emerged during the nineteenth century.

IPE textbooks usually identify the key pioneers of neomercantilist thought to have been Alexander Hamilton and Friedrich List. After describing their views, I turn to examine some other thinkers in Europe and the United States who are less familiar but deserving of attention. Many of these thinkers were inspired by List but adapted his ideas in some interesting ways, such as Gustav Schmoller, Sergei Witte, Mihail Manoilescu, and William Ashley. The other, Henry Carey, was more inspired by Hamilton than List, but developed an important version of neomercantilist thought that was very distinctive from both of theirs. With these examples, I highlight how neomercantilism in Europe and the United States had more diverse content than the common textbook depiction suggests.[1]

## Hamilton's Pioneering Ideas

Alexander Hamilton's remarkable life is well known to many. After immigrating to the United States from the Caribbean at a young age, he

---

[1] For a more detailed discussion of the thinkers analyzed in this and the next chapter (as well as other neomercantilist thinkers), see Helleiner 2021a.

soon became an aide-de-camp to George Washington and then wrote many of the Federalist Papers published in the late 1780s in support of the ratification of the US Constitution. After the latter came into force in 1789, Hamilton became the first US Treasury Secretary while still in his thirties. For scholars of IPE, Hamilton has also long attracted attention because of a lengthy document he authored in that position in 1791 titled *Report on Manufactures*.

The report argued that the US government needed to actively promote the growth of American manufacturing in order to boost the power and wealth of the newly independent country. In Hamilton's view, industrialization was key for the "independence and security" of the United States. He also noted that many economic benefits that would be generated by the growth of domestic manufacturing. For example, it would boost America's wealth by increasing productivity, creating new job opportunities for under- and unemployed Americans, and generating "greater scope for the diversity of talents and dispositions which discriminate men from each other". Further, farmers would be able to sell more to domestic markets, thereby reducing their dependence on unreliable foreign ones as well as on poor terms of trade arising from the "unsteadiness" of foreign demand for agricultural exports. More generally, Hamilton suggested that a more diversified national economy would encourage "the spirit of enterprise", increase the domestic division of labour, reduce transportation costs, and create new opportunities for local firms to increase exports and attract foreign buyers.[2]

To realize these many benefits, Hamilton insisted that the US government needed to take an active role in cultivating local manufacturing. This argument directly challenged the liberal economic advice of Adam Smith's *The Wealth of Nations*, which had already gained a wide audience in the United States (as noted in Chapter 2). Hamilton contested Smith's view by noting that entrepreneurs were easily discouraged from building new industries on their own by the "intrinsic difficulties" of competing with existing firms, "the fear of want of success in untried enterprises", and "the strong influence of habit and the spirit of imitation". He also argued they would be disadvantaged by the fact that foreign governments supported firms from their own countries with "bounties premiums, and other artificial encouragements". In this context, Hamilton urged US legislators to recognize the need for policies such as trade protectionism that encouraged local entrepreneurs to set up new manufacturing operations and that also might prompt European industrialists to consider the "transfer of himself and his Capital

---

[2] Quotes from Hamilton [1791]1964, 161, 128, 159, 133.

to the United States".[3] He also discussed other forms of government economic activism such as temporary direct subsidies, public procurement policies, and the encouragement of invention through financial benefits or exclusive privileges.

Hamilton's arguments built on his knowledge of earlier European mercantilist thought and practice. But he also respected Smith's ideas, a respect that was evident in the cautious nature of his neomercantilist recommendations. He went out of his way to highlight that government support for manufacturing only made sense "in certain cases, and under certain reasonable limitations".[4] Moreover, he endorsed only quite moderate tariffs and targeted bans on imports, and insisted that these measures should be implemented only if there was no risk of a domestic monopoly emerging. He also acknowledged the economic cost that protection would bring in the short-term in the form of higher import prices (while suggesting that those prices would reduce over time with growing local competition and lower transportation costs). Indeed, he suggested that direct subsidies of manufacturing might be a better policy than protectionism because they would avoid this cost as well as the risk of scarcity and smuggling (in addition to encouraging exports more directly).[5]

## List's More Ambitious Neomercantilism

Hamilton's ideas helped to generate support for the introduction of new US tariffs in 1792 and they influenced later neomercantilists, including Friedrich List, whose 1841 book *The National System of Political Economy* presented a more detailed and ambitious neomercantilist line of argument. Born in the German-speaking Duchy of Württemburg, List lived a quite cosmopolitan life before completing his book, spending some years in both United States and France. For many contemporary IPE scholars, List's *National System* holds the same kind of foundational place in neomercantilist thought that *The Wealth of Nations* has in economic liberal thought. As we shall see, this view overstates List's influence over neomercantilist thought as a whole. But it is certainly the case that List's book was a widely read neomercantilist text in the pre-1945 years.

List's work included a much stronger attack on free trade than Hamilton's report had advanced. In a context where Britain was the dominant economic power, List argued that a world of free trade would enable "the English manufactures to monopolise the markets of all nations".

---

[3] Quotes from Hamilton [1791]1964, 140–41, 149.
[4] Quote from Hamilton [1791]1964, 118.
[5] Helleiner 2021a, 40.

He suggested that British free traders were well aware of this fact and he criticized them for discouraging other countries from pursuing protectionist policies that Britain itself had used to build up its wealth and power in the past. As he put it in a famous passage, "it is a very common device that when anyone has attained the summit of greatness, he kicks away the ladder by which he has climbed up, in order to deprive others of the means of climbing up after him".[6]

List shared many of Hamilton's views about how industrialization would boost a country's power and wealth. But he went further to note that the resulting national power would help not just to defend a country's sovereignty (as Hamilton had emphasized) but also to project influence abroad, including through imperialist policies. Indeed, List was a strong advocate of the latter, even suggesting that "Europe will sooner or later find herself under the necessity of taking the whole of Asia under her care and tutelage, as already India has been so taken in charge by England". His rationale for calling for the colonization of all of Asia reflected a deep Eurocentrism in his thought: "a regeneration of Asia [is] only possible by means of an infusion of European vital power, by the general introduction of the Christian religion and of European moral laws and order, by European immigration, and the introduction of European systems of government".[7]

List also went beyond Hamilton in arguing that industrialization "forms a fundamental condition of all higher advances in civilisation". He associated it with the growth of individual political liberty (of which he approved as a political liberal) as well as intellectual and socio-cultural progress. Particularly central to his argument was the idea that industrialization boosted what he called the deep "productive power" of a country, which derived "from mental and physical powers of the individuals; from their social, municipal, and political conditions and institutions; from the natural resources placed at its disposal, or from the instruments it possesses as the material products of former mental and bodily exertions (material, agricultural, manufacturing, and commercial capital)". In his view, Adam Smith's analysis – with its focus on "exchangeable value" and "material capital" – had overlooked the importance of this broad foundation of the wealth of nations. As he put it, "*the power of producing wealth* is ... infinitely more important than *wealth itself*".[8]

List noted briefly that governments could support the growth of local industry with measures such as subsidies, special privileges, or the creation

---

[6] Quotes from List [1841]1909a, 297, 295.
[7] Quotes from List [1841]1909a, 336.
[8] Quotes from List [1841]1909a, 117, 181, 108.

of state-sponsored firms. But his 1841 book was focused much more centrally on the need for strategic trade protectionism. Like Hamilton, he hoped that protectionist policies would not just foster national firms but also "stimulate foreigners to come over to our side with their productive powers".[9] Further, he shared Hamilton's view that, without government support, new industrial enterprises would have great difficulty competing with established foreign manufacturers, particularly English ones (which were also supported by their own government). List criticized the Smithian school for focusing on the immediate economic costs of trade restrictions, while ignoring the larger gains to be derived from these policies for the country's productive power over time. He also questioned free traders' assumption that countries' position in the international division of labour was simply a product of natural conditions. While that might be true for agriculture, he argued that it did not apply to manufacturing where countries could cultivate a competitive advantage over time with government policies, as England's history demonstrated.

While List endorsed protectionism more strongly than Hamilton, he was also critical of earlier mercantilist thinkers for their advocacy of "prohibitory" trade restrictions instead of "moderate" ones. He warned against "excessively high import duties, which entirely cut off foreign competition, injure the country which imposes them, since its manufacturers are not forced to compete with foreigners, and indolence is fostered".[10] He insisted, too, that protectionist measures should be only temporarily imposed "until that manufacturing power is strong enough no longer to have any reason to fear foreign competition". In addition, List criticized earlier mercantilist thinkers for failing to recognize the benefits of free trade in raw materials and agricultural products, which helped both local industry and "the prosperity and progress of the whole human race".[11] This latter position led List to support the abolition of Britain's Corn Laws, one of the highest profile free trade initiatives of his era (see Chapter 2).[12]

List also controversially argued that strategic protectionism should be implemented only by countries with a "temperate" climate. In his view, countries in the "tropics" were "unfitted by nature for such a course" and should thus focus only exporting primary products in exchange for manufactures from temperate countries under conditions of free trade or within imperial empires. They were, in his words, destined to

---

[9] List [1841]1909a, 135.
[10] Quotes from List [1841]1909a, 272; [1841]1909b, 312–13.
[11] Quotes from List [1841]1909a, 144, 152.
[12] Helleiner, 2021a, 64.

be in "a state of dependence" vis-à-vis temperate countries (although he suggested that the industrialization of a growing number of temperate countries might prevent any one of these countries "from misusing their power over the weaker nations of the tropics").[13] Even within the temperate regions of the world, List suggested that industrial protectionism should only be implemented by countries facing competition from a more advanced manufacturing power and those which had "an extensive and compact territory, large population, possession of natural resources, far advanced agriculture, [and] a high degree of civilisation and political development". He further suggested that German states would benefit by lowering trade barriers amongst themselves and that consideration should be given to the idea of a wider "Continental alliance against the British supremacy" involving trade treaties.[14]

One final feature of List's neomercantilist thought deserves attention: the emphasis he placed on the idea of "*nationality*, as the intermediate interest between those of *individualism* and of *entire humanity*". List criticized liberals for embracing what he called a "boundless *cosmopolitanism*" and "dead *materialism*" that depicted "individuals as mere producers and consumers, not citizens of states or members of nations". For List, nationality needed to be placed at the center of the study of political economy because of the distinct needs of each nation as well as the persistence of international rivalry and conflict between them. He also emphasized that "the unity of the nation forms the fundamental condition of lasting national prosperity". As he put it, the successful cultivation of a country's productive powers could only take place with a strong "national spirit" in which "the interest of individuals has been subordinated to those of the nation, and where successive generations have striven for one and the same object".[15]

Despite List's criticism of the "boundless cosmopolitanism" of liberals, he did not reject cosmopolitan goals altogether. Indeed, he criticized earlier mercantilist thinkers for failing to recognize "the future union of all nations, the establishment of perpetual peace, and of universal freedom of trade, as the goal towards which all nations have to strive, and more and more to approach". He even depicted his neomercantilist advice for late industrializing countries as a step towards this long-term goal. In his view, a worldwide "universal republic" could "only be realised if a large number of nationalities attain to as nearly the same degree as possible of industry and civilisation, political cultivation, and power".

[13] Quotes from List [1841]1909b, 309.
[14] Quotes from List [1841]1909a, 247, 340.
[15] Quotes from List [1841]1909a, xliii, 141, 140, 132, 156, 132.

He suggested that neomercantilist policies were "the only means of plac-
ing those nations which are far behind in civilisation on equal terms with
the one predominating nation". For this reason, he argued that "the system of protection ... appears to be the most efficient means of furthering
the final union of nations, and hence also of promoting true freedom of
trade".[16] In this way, List suggested that his neomercantilist views were
compatible with the goal of building a long-term liberal cosmopolitan
future. Few other neomercantilists shared List's views on this issue.

## Some Adaptations of List's Ideas

List's book quickly attracted attention in the German-speaking world,
where it was invoked by protectionists who found themselves on the political defensive in the 1850s and 1860s. After German unification in 1871, the
neomercantilist cause then won an important convert when the new country's leader, Otto von Bismarck, backed the raising of tariffs in 1879. This
rejection of free trade by a powerful European country was an important
challenge to the prestige of free trade ideas at the time. Bismarck explained
his new support for trade protectionism using language that sounded quite
Listian: "Free trade is the weapon of the strongest nation".[17]

Whether Bismarck was in fact influenced by List's ideas is unclear. But
some prominent German thinkers who supported Bismarck's tariffs cited
List's work, including Gustav Schmoller, who had emerged as the leader
of a prominent "German historical school" of political economy at the
time. Schmoller shared List's concern that free trade threatened German
wealth and power, but he modified the earlier German thinker's ideas in
ways that created a distinctive version of neomercantilist thought. Particularly important was his interest in free trade's consequences for domestic
distributional issues (a topic about which List's 1841 book said very little).
Schmoller had emerged as an influential advocate of policies to support
workers, including the kinds of social programs that Bismarck introduced
in the 1880s. He expressed concerns that free trade generated international competitive pressures that undermined not just German industry
but also initiatives to introduce worker-friendly factory laws. Unlike List
(but similar to Bismarck), he also backed agricultural protectionism as a
tool to help farmers adjust to new import competition in ways that prevented rising rural poverty and German dependence on imported food.[18]

---

[16] Quotes from List [1841]1909a, 272, 103.
[17] Quoted in Helleiner 2021a, 172.
[18] Helleiner 2021a, 81–85. For the lack of clarity on List's influence on Bismarck, see pp.
169–73.

Schmoller's ideas went beyond those of List in other ways. For example, he endorsed a notion that List had not discussed: that protectionist policies could serve as "international weapons" to gain the upper hand in negotiating trade treaties with foreign countries.[19] He also made an important contribution to neomercantilist thought by reinterpreting earlier European mercantilist ideas and practices in a more positive light than Smith had portrayed them. In his 1884 book *Studies on the Political Economy of Frederick the Great* (partially translated into English as *The Mercantile System and Its Historical Significance*), Schmoller praised earlier mercantilists for their "state-making and national-economy making" goals that had created "a new division of labour, a new prosperity, and which liberated a thousand forces of progress" in early modern Europe.[20] In his view, mercantilists had responded logically to the context of intense inter-state rivalry of their era, a context that he argued Germany faced, too, at the time he was writing. For these reasons, Schmoller embraced the label "neomercantilism" as a description for the policy program he backed (in contrast to List, who did not use this term). Like List, he also saw imperialism as a legitimate policy for states to pursue in order to boost their wealth and power.[21]

List's ideas also attracted attention, and were adapted, outside Germany by opponents of free trade. One important example was Sergei Witte who implemented an ambitious program of state-led industrialization inspired by List's ideas (and Bismarck's example) when he served as Russia's finance minister between 1892 and 1903. Like Schmoller (and Bismarck), Witte departed from List in backing agricultural protectionism (in this case to support the growth of a local cotton sector). As a conservative supporter of Russian autocracy, Witte also chose to overlook List's argument that industrial progress would go hand-in-hand with growing individual political liberties. List's 1841 book had, in fact, emphasized the importance of this point in the Russian context, arguing that the country's "further industrial and commercial progress" required liberal political reforms.[22] Witte simply ignored this advice.

Another thinker who modified List's ideas in interesting ways was Mihail Manoilescu, a Romanian who published in 1929 the most prominent neomercantilist book of the interwar years: *The Theory of Protectionism and International Trade*. Manoilescu subsequently held prominent political positions in his country and his economic ideas were invoked by policymakers elsewhere in Eastern Europe and Latin America.

---

[19]  Schomoller quoted in Ashley 1904, 130.
[20]  Quoted in Schmoller [1884]1910, 50–51.
[21]  Helleiner 2021a, 83–84.
[22]  List [1841]1909a, 75. For Witte, see Von Laue 1951.

Manoilescu praised List's work, but argued that protectionism had "a much wider extension than List believed". His reasoning was that successful economic development depended on shifting workers from low productivity sectors (such as agriculture) to ones with higher productivity (such as industry). For this reason, he argued that any protectionist policy was justified if it encouraged the growth of sectors whose "productivity surpasses the average productivity of the country", even if those sectors never became internationally competitive. In contrast to List, he also insisted "there is no *a priori* limit for the degree of protection" and that the protectionist policies he recommended were appropriate for any country and need not be only temporary.[23]

Further, Manoilescu creatively placed his neomercantilist advice in a multilateral context, suggesting that the League of Nations should recognize the right of countries to use protectionist policies as "reasonable and legitimate".[24] Manoilescu was likely unaware that List himself had outlined some vague ideas on this topic in an unpublished 1837 manuscript, where he proposed a "world trade congress" that "should consider the varied interests of regions and societies at different stages of economic development".[25] This issue was much more central in Manoilescu's thought. He argued that the League's support for protectionist policies in less industrialized regions would boost standards of living in those places in ways that reduced international inequality, created new export markets for already-industrialized countries, and promoted international peace. If industrialized countries could be encouraged to export capital to support industrialization elsewhere, he argued that these trends would be reinforced further. As he put it, "real solidarity does not mean to let rich countries live on the poverty of poor countries, but the enrichment of poor countries and incidentally also of rich ones".[26]

One final example of a European adaptation of List's ideas came from the country that had triggered much of List's criticism: Britain. During the first few years of the twentieth century, a major debate broke out in that country about the desirability of its longstanding free trade policies in the context of growing foreign competitive pressures. Some of those favouring new protectionist measures, such as William Ashley, invoked List's general criticisms of free trade (as well as those of Schmoller and earlier English mercantilists). But Ashley's use of List in the British context went beyond the ideas of the German thinker who had argued that

---

[23] Quotes from Manoilescu 1931, 240, xi, 137.
[24] Manoilescu 1931, 222.
[25] Quotes from List [1837]1983, 126.
[26] Manoilescu 1931, 218.

a country with "the highest degree of wealth and power" such as Britain should adopt unilateral free trade policies, not protectionist policies. List's reasoning was that free trade would ensure that "their agriculturists, manufacturers, and merchants may be preserved from indolence, and stimulated to retain the supremacy which they have acquired".[27]

In his 1841 book, List did note briefly how protectionist policies could be used to defend *established* industries when they suffered a temporary loss of competitiveness. But he had in mind situations where the latter was caused by imports from a dominant industrial power that was trying to monopolize global markets by declaring "a war of extermination against the manufacturers of all other countries".[28] British neomercantists such as Ashley argued, however, that this kind of unfair commercial war was being fought by *rising* powers such as Germany against British firms. In particular, they argued that local industries and workers needed to be defended against German practices of dumping excess goods on foreign markets at prices below the cost of production. Although Ashley and his protectionist colleagues lost the day in British policy debates at the time, they highlighted how List's protectionist ideas could be adapted to the circumstances of a declining industrial power.[29]

## The Distinctive Ideas of Carey

While List's ideas attracted the attention of free trade opponents across the world, many neomercantilist thinkers developed their ideas more independently of his. In addition to the examples provided in the next chapter, the most important neomercantilist thinker in the United States in the second half of the nineteenth century – Henry Carey – was in this category. Carey was aware of List's work, but he did not show much interest in it. He was more inspired by Hamilton's 1791 report, which he praised as "one of the most remarkable of its kind in existence".[30] But he developed a version of neomercantilist thought that was quite different from both Hamilton's and List's in a number of publications after the late 1840s, of which the most important was his three-volume book *Principles of Social Sciences*, published in 1858–59.

Carey is less well known than Hamilton and List in the early twenty-first century, but his ideas were very influential in the pre-1945 era. Carey was one of the founders of the US Republican Party in the 1850s

---

[27] Quotes from List [1841]1909a, 93.
[28] List [1841]1909a, 240.
[29] Helleiner 2021a, 103–7.
[30] Carey 1858b, 183fn. For his view of List, See Helleiner 2021a, 145–47.

and his ideas provided the intellectual justification for its support of American trade protectionism well into the early twentieth century. He was also an advisor to Abraham Lincoln, who strengthened American protectionism after being elected US president in 1860. Carey's work also played an important role in building support for the new protectionist policies introduced in Germany in 1879 and in many other countries, including some beyond Europe and United States (as noted in the next chapter). Another sign of the prominence of Carey's thought in the nineteenth century was the fact that leading advocates of other perspectives, such as John Stuart Mill and Karl Marx, also engaged with and critiqued it.[31]

Carey shared the general view of Hamilton and List that industrialization behind tariff walls would boost national wealth and independence. Like List, Carey also critiqued free trade policies for enabling Britain to become "the tyrant of the world". But he also expressed a distinctive concern that free trade was empowering a social group of "traders" in all countries to become rich and powerful at the expense of other domestic groups such as workers and farmers.[32] In his view, these traders manipulated prices and monopolized trade, while workers and farmers were left exploited, dependent, and subject to international competitive pressures that drove down their wages and the prices they were paid for their produce. For this reason, Carey described the world of free trade as a kind of "slavery", with "the foundation of the system … being found in the idea of cheapening labor, and all other raw materials of manufacture".[33]

Protectionist policies, Carey argued, would undermine the power of traders and encourage a "harmony of interests" to be re-established domestically, as industry prospered, workers' wages grew, and farmers gained new local markets for more diverse kinds of agricultural production. As farmers and manufacturers worked side-by-side in "local centres of attraction", more diversified national economies would flourish and extensive "association" between people would be cultivated in ways that benefited them economically and developed their "individuality". As part of this vision, Carey endorsed political decentralization, which he argued would foster greater political participation as well as economic and intellectual vibrancy. He also predicted that the greater domestic social harmony fostered by protectionist policies would contribute to

---

[31] For Carey's ideas and influence in the United States and abroad, see Helleiner 2021a, chs. 5–6.

[32] Quotes from Carey 1858a, 392. Carey also noted the costs of free trade for the environment and women, as noted in Chapters 9 and 10 of this book.

[33] Quotes from Carey 1859, 382.

a "harmony of nations" that would be reinforced by the reduced influence of traders who Carey depicted as warmongers.[34]

Carey's social concerns did not extend to support for the kinds of state welfare programs or labour legislation that Schmoller endorsed. He saw protectionism at the border as the key government policy needed to address domestic social inequality and conflict. In his *Principles of Social Sciences*, Carey also devoted very little attention to activist policies that a government might undertake *within* its borders to promote industrialization. At the domestic level, Carey favoured a liberal economy made up of small independent farmers and firms participating in decentralized free markets, with the state playing a very limited role.[35]

While he said little about domestic government economic activism, Carey endorsed stronger protectionism at the border than did Hamilton and List. His *Principles* did not include the kind of cautions they each made against excessive or long-lasting trade barriers. He also did not restrict his protectionist advice to the manufacturing sector. Further, whereas Hamilton's 1791 report focussed only on the United States and List advocated neomercantilist policies only for some temperate zone countries, Carey argued that protectionism should be embraced by all countries. He even included Britain in this advice, arguing that it was suffering from the same social inequality arising from free trade as other countries were. Carey also urged that protectionist policies be introduced in tropical places such as India that were colonized. As he put it, "the Hindoo was as capable of applying the machinery of Arkwright as the Englishman". Indeed, Carey criticized not just Britain's free trade policies in its Indian colony but also its extraction of wealth, Its colonial monopolies, and the centralized power of colonial administration. Carey suggested that India would "grow rich, and rapidly grow" only when it became "independent" and was able to pursue neomercantilist policies.[36]

Carey was a strong critic of imperialism more generally (and of his own country's aggressive policies, including its destruction and oppression of local "native tribes"). While List (and others such as Schmoller and Ashley) backed colonization, Carey argued that this policy was "based upon the idea of cheapening labor, land, and raw materials of every kind – thus extending slavery throughout the earth". He also criticized the kind of Eurocentric civilizational discourse that List and many others (including the liberals discussed in Chapter 2) used to justify imperialism, arguing that Britain had often brought "barbarism" rather than civilization to

---

[34] Quotes from Carey 1858a, v, 45, 53; 1859, 153.
[35] Helleiner 2021a, ch. 5.
[36] Quotes from Carey 1858a, 363; Carey [1847]1889, 407.

its colonies. Rather than blaming the poverty of the colonized on their "uncivilized" character, Carey argued that it was better to blame free trade: "There lies the difficulty, and not in the character of the people".[37] He also invoked non-European societies as models, including the decentralized self-governing villages of pre-colonial India, and he engaged with thinkers from beyond Europe and United States, such as Japan's Tomita Tetsunosuke, who visited Carey and was advised by him to be wary of Western countries.[38]

Carey's anti-imperialism was part of his broader commitment to a defensive kind of neomercantilism that sought power for the "self-protection" of a country rather than for the offensive projection of power internationally.[39] As part of this focus, he argued that countries might need to protect themselves not just from British exports but also from the influence of British finance by establishing monetary systems that were independent of a metallic standard. Indeed, he became a supporter of the introduction of a currency of this kind in his own country during the US civil war. Carey also showed no interest in List's long-term goal of a "union of all nations". In yet one more contrast with List, his long-term utopia was a world of independent states with diverse national economies that traded with each other – perhaps even in conditions of free trade – in a manner that respected each other's sovereignty.[40]

## Conclusion

Reacting against classical economic liberalism, neomercantilist thinkers in Europe and the United States advocated strategic protectionist policies and other forms of government activism in order to cultivate state wealth and power. It is important, however, not to overstate the differences between neomercantilists and economic liberals. As we have seen, some economic liberals such as Smith and Mill endorsed protectionist measures that were needed for national defense, such as Britain's Navigation Acts. Mill also expressed some sympathy for infant-industry protection (although he was fiercely criticized by other liberals for this position and eventually abandoned it). From the other side, List depicted neomercantilism as a strategy that might enable a liberal world of "universal freedom of trade" to be created over the longer term. Henry Carey, too, signaled some openness to the possibility of a world of free trade in the distant future.

---

[37] Quotes from Carey 1858a, 372; 1859, 335; 1858a, 367, 374, 375.
[38] Helleiner 2021a, ch. 5, 177–78.
[39] Carey 1859, 468.
[40] Helleiner 2021a, 160–63.

As in the case of classical economic liberalism, neomercantilist thought also had considerable diversity. Its advocates disagreed over many issues, such as the specific purposes of protectionism, the level of their interest in domestic social issues, their views of industrialization and imperialism, the degree of their Eurocentrism, their broader political orientation, the universal relevance of neomercantilist policies, and their long-term aspirations. Even in their policy recommendations, neomercantilists differed over the kinds of protection they endorsed, the desirability of other kinds of government economic activism, and the degree of their interest in multilateral institutions. When we examine neomercantilist thought beyond Europe and the United States, the diversity of its content widens even further.

# 5     Neomercantilist Reactions Elsewhere

Neomercantilist reactions against classical economic liberalism were not confined to Europe and the United States. As European liberal ideas diffused around the world, similar reactions emerged elsewhere. Some of those who endorsed neomercantilist policies for bolstering their state's wealth and power were policymakers. Others were thinkers who hoped to shape government action. Although existing IPE textbooks devote very little attention to these figures, their ideas attracted attention in various contexts around the world.

Neomercantilists outside Europe and the United States sometimes drew upon the ideas of their counterparts in those two places while also adapting those foreign ideas in innovative ways. In other cases, versions of neomercantilist thought emerged more independently. This chapter provides examples of both of these phenomena.[1] Although all of the thinkers discussed in this chapter shared core neomercantilist beliefs, they each developed distinctive versions of this worldview, reinforcing the point made in the last chapter about the diversity of its content in the pre-1945 period.

## Local Roots of Japanese Neomercantilism

The best-known case of a country beyond Europe and United States where neomercantilist ideas were prominent in the pre-1945 years was Japan. Its 1868 Meiji Restoration famously brought to power many figures who were devoted to a strategy of state-led industrialization and development which could boost Japan's wealth and power to address the new external threat it faced at the time from the United States and European powers. That strategy could not initially include trade protectionism because of provisions in the trade treaties that Japan was forced to sign by those foreign powers. But the Meiji leadership signalled its

---

[1] Further examples (and more detail on the cases discussed here) can be found in Helleiner 2021a.

frustrations with these constraints and then succeeded by 1911 in recovering their country's full tariff policy autonomy, after which Japan's tariffs rose rapidly.

The writings of foreign neomercantilists had some influence in Meiji Japan. Carey's ideas were cited as early as 1871 in Japanese government circles. List's work became known soon thereafter and was invoked by Matsukata Masayoshi, a powerful figure in Japanese economic policy-making throughout the 1880s and 1890s. In the first two decades of the twentieth century, many Japanese officials were also inspired by Schmoller's thought.[2] But Japanese neomercantilists drew inspiration from much more than just these foreign ideas. In the early Meiji years, the most important influence on their thought was a local intellectual tradition that had emerged in the country during the Tokugawa period (1603–1867) and bore some similarities to European mercantilism.

For most of the Tokugawa period, Japan had a relatively closed economy (see Chapter 8). This local mercantilist tradition was developed in a context of *internal* economic competition between relatively autonomous local lords who shared authority with the central shogunate. As Japan's domestic economy became increasingly commercialized in the eighteenth and early nineteenth centuries, many of these lords began to try to maximize the wealth and power of their respective domains through policies designed to promote exports to, and discourage imports from, central markets in Osaka and Edo. These policies included the creation of government firms and trading monopolies, the importation of skilled labour from other jurisdictions, and the provision of various kinds of support to local farmers, merchants, and manufacturers.[3]

The thinkers who recommended these mercantilist policies advised local authorities that the pursuit of *kokueki* ("prosperity of the country") was part of their Confucian duty to "order the realm and save the people" (*keisei saimin*) by enriching the state and its inhabitants.[4] This logic helped to legitimize policies that risked being criticized by more conservative Confucian thinkers who were sceptical of merchants and the pursuit of commerce and private profit. Advocates of this *kokueki* mercantilism also invoked the phrase *fukoku kyōhei* ("rich state, strong army") that came from a famous ancient Chinese text from the era of that country's Warring States (453–221 BCE). The text was *The Book of Lord Shang* and it described the views of Shang Yang, who was part of a Legalist school of thought that stressed the need to cultivate state power.

[2] Helleiner 2021a, 85–90, 173–80.
[3] Helleiner 2021a, 202–4.
[4] Quotes from Roberts 1998, 1; Sagers 2006, 25.

Shang emphasized the connection between state wealth and power, and helped launch economic reforms in the state of Qin that boosted its power in ways that contributed to its eventual victory over other Chinese states at the time. Supporters of *kokueki* mercantilism drew parallels between the inter-state competition of Shang's era in China and that amongst the local authorities in Tokugawa Japan.[5]

This rich history of local mercantilist thought was very well known to policymakers in early Meiji Japan, many of whom transferred its insights to the pursuit of Japan's wealth and power as a whole vis-à-vis the outside world. In the 1870s, the most important example was Ōkubo Toshimichi, whose 1874 *Memorandum on the Promotion of Production and Encouragement of Industry* initiated the country's path of state-led industrialization and development. In his role as a government minister until his assassination in 1878, Ōkubo became famous for promoting Japan's manufacturing, shipping, trade, and agriculture through the creation of state-owned firms and with financial support to private companies. From the historical evidence, it is not entirely clear whether Ōkubo was familiar with the ideas of foreign neomercantilist thinkers such as Carey and List. What is certain, however, is that his advocacy of state-led development (which included a desire to revise the trade treaties signed with foreign powers) drew its main inspiration from earlier Japanese mercantilist thought.[6]

Like many other early Meiji leaders, Ōkubo came from the Satsuma domain, which had pursued particularly ambitious local mercantilist initiatives to boost its wealth and power after 1830. He had worked for, and was influenced by, one of the Satsuma leaders who was deeply committed to these initiatives. He had also studied the writing of Satō Nobuhiro, who was credited with designing Satsuma's initial mercantilist policies. As early as 1865, Ōkubo urged the pursuit of the goal of *fukoku kyōhei* for all of Japan (a position that Satō had also endorsed in some earlier writing). In the early 1870s, the influence of Ōkubo's Satsuma intellectual roots was also evident when he encouraged his officials to read one of Satō's works.

When justifying his activist policies, Ōkubo insisted in his famous 1874 memorandum that "a country's strength is dependent upon the prosperity of its people" and that the promotion of manufacturing was key to "strengthen the foundations of national wealth and power". He also noted that it was "the duty of state officials, wholeheartedly and skillfully on the basis of actual conditions, to encourage industry and increase production

[5] Helleiner 2021a, 202–9. The famous passage from *The Book of Lord Shang* reads: "He who rules the state well consolidates force to attain a rich state and a strong army" (Shang 2017, 174).
[6] Helleiner 2021a, 209–16.

and thus secure the foundation of wealth and strength without delay". When highlighting the need for government activism, he called attention not just to Japan's limited capital and industrial experience but also to the "weakness of spirit" of its people and their enduring dependence "on the strength of the guidance and encouragement provided by governments and administrators".[7] This language repeated the Confucian rationales of *kokueki* thinkers, as did the central role that Ōkubo gave to his government factories of acting as models for private firms to follow. The history of *kokueki* mercantilism was also evident in Ōkubo's proposal for a government trading company to take greater control of Japan's external trade.

Although Ōkubo drew inspiration from *kokueki* mercantilism, he deserves to be described as Japan's first prominent *neo*mercantilist because he was forced to respond to the ideas of European economic liberalism in ways that earlier Japanese mercantilists were not. As noted in Chapter 3, Smithian liberalism began to be introduced into Japan after the country's forced opening in the 1850s and it gained considerable authority in the early Meiji years. In this new intellectual context, Ōkubo's creation of government-owned industries was challenged by supporters of economic liberalism, prompting him to argue defensively that "these industries are absolutely necessary even though they go against the laws of political economy".[8] This intellectual context also helps to explain why Ōkubo endorsed a more limited role for the state in promoting economic development than that endorsed by the earlier Satsuma leadership and Satō.

Many other Japanese neomercantilist thinkers in the early Meiji years were also inspired by the local history of *kokueki* mercantilism, including even those who were very interested in European and American thought, such as the powerful Matsukata who also came from Satsuma. Another important example was Fukuzawa Yukichi, who became the best-known public intellectual in Japan in that era. Fukuzawa helped introduce Adam Smith's ideas to Japan, but he believed that strategic protectionism was more appropriate for Japan than Smith's free trade advice. Rather than invoke the ideas of foreign neomercantilists to defend this point, he echoed the arguments of *kokueki* thinkers, including the need to prioritize *fukoko kyohei*.[9] In his 1875 book *An Outline of a Theory of Civilization*, Fukuzawa also suggested creatively that the pursuit of wealth and power would only need to be a short-term strategy. He held out hope that "a point will be reached where men do not fight for land and do not covet wealth … People in the world will be surrounded by an atmosphere of

---

[7] Quotes in Iwata 1964, 236; Brown 1962, 194; Marshall 1967, 16; Crawcour 1997, 73.
[8] Quoted in Sagers 2006, 95.
[9] Helleiner 2021a, 216–24.

courtesy and mutual deference; they will bathe, as it were, in a sea of morality".[10] Fukuzawa's depiction of this future utopia had strong Confucian undertones. He depicted it as a more advanced stage of "civilization" than that existing anywhere at the time.

Fukuzawa's ideas were influential not just in Japan but also in neighbouring Korea among a group of thinkers who emerged as leading advocates of neomercantilist ideas in that country after its forced economic opening from the mid-1870s onwards. These *Gaehwa* (enlightenment) thinkers challenged the autarkic policies that their country had long pursued (see Chapter 8), arguing for the pursuit of state wealth and power via activist policies in the context of an open world economy. In their view, those policies were the only ones that could preserve Korea's sovereignty in the face of the new foreign challenges it was facing at the time. They had some influence on government policies before Korea was formally colonized by Japan in 1910 (after which the Korean economy was restructured to serve Japanese needs).[11]

The best-known of the *Gaehwa* thinkers was Yu Kil-chun, who studied with Fukuzawa in Japan. Like his teacher, Yu was interested in economic liberalism, but insisted that local commercial and industrial firms needed government support in many sectors because they "could not compete at first" in international commerce, which he depicted as a war-like activity.[12] Although Yu and other *Gaehwa* thinkers were familiar with European and American thought, neomercantilist ideas from those regions do not appear to have had much, if any, impact on them. In addition to being influenced by Fukuzawa, Yu and other *Gaehwa* thinkers built on a local Korean tradition of thought from the late eighteenth century that had challenged the dominant autarkic mindset and called for the pursuit of Korea's wealth and power through the promotion of commerce and industry. The *Gaehwa* thinkers also followed Japanese neomercantilists in citing ancient Chinese legalist thought and the precedent of the Warring States period in China.[13]

## Neomercantilist Thought in China

Those ancient ideas and history were also invoked by thinkers who pioneered neomercantilist ideas in China itself in the nineteenth century. These figures were associated with the "self-strengthening" movement that gained influence in the wake of the Second Opium War (1856–60).

[10] Fukuzawa [1875]2009, 149–50.
[11] Helleiner 2021a, 269–79.
[12] Quoted in Lee 2000, 59.
[13] Helleiner 2021a, 269–79.

China's military defeat in that war was more humiliating than that in the First Opium War (1839–42), and it triggered new interest in economic reforms that would help China to match the wealth and power of European countries and the United States. Rather than embrace the advice of foreign texts promoting economic liberalism that were beginning to be translated in China at the time (see Chapter 3), many in the self-strengthening movement called for a more state-led economic development strategy to cultivate *fuqiang* (wealth and power). The latter term was a shortened version of the phrase *fuguo qiangbing* ("rich state, strong army") that had first appeared in *The Book of Lord Shang*.[14]

The most important of these thinkers was Zheng Guanying, who authored a number of widely read publications between the early 1870s and early 1890s, the most famous of which was his 1893 *Words of Warning in a Flourishing Age*. A leading merchant in Shanghai, Zheng urged Chinese authorities to recognize that their empire was suffering defeat in a new kind of worldwide "commercial warfare" where states were fighting each other economically for profit shares. Zheng drew direct parallels between the ancient age of the Warring States and the conflictual international system that China faced in his era. Zheng's phrase "commercial warfare" also drew inspiration from that ancient history; Zheng borrowed it from another Chinese reformer in the 1860s who had been interested in Shang's writing about "agricultural warfare".[15]

Zheng argued that China's losing position in the worldwide commercial war was "draining" its wealth and eroding its "right to profits". Citing British practices elsewhere, he warned that further economic losses would result in military conquest: "trade was the means used by the British to expand their territory. The occupation of America, India and Burma and intercourse with China were all accomplished by her merchants serving as the vanguard". Because of China's military weakness, Zheng argued that China needed to boost its capacity to win commercial war, "fighting with wealth rather than force".[16] This strategy, he argued, required ambitious economic reforms, ranging from the promotion of modern industry, shipping, mining, and agriculture to the fostering of commerce and improvements to infrastructure, education and finance.

As part of this strategy, Zheng also endorsed the use of higher tariffs to support local industry. The latter challenged the constraints on China's tariff autonomy embodied in the trade treaties that foreign powers had imposed (as in Japan) after the Opium Wars. Zheng also

---

[14] Helleiner 2021a, ch. 8.
[15] Helleiner 2021a, 241.
[16] Quotes in Wu 2010, 132; Gerth 2003, 60; Halsey 2015, 75; Hu 1988, 539.

objected to those treaties' provisions that gave foreigners extraterritorial privileges in his country (as did many Japanese neomercantilists vis-à-vis similar provisions in the trade treaties their country had been forced to accept). He suggested that foreigners could invest and reside instead in Chinese "multinational public business zones" located near its border regions and under its control. In addition, he urged the creation of state-sponsored firms, and the use of military force to support Chinese merchants abroad. Like neomercantilists elsewhere, Zheng emphasized the interdependence of state wealth and power, arguing "strength can not be achieved without wealth, and wealth can not be secured without strength". Zheng was also interested in the cultivation of nationalism, arguing that it had contributed to Europe's wealth and power.[17]

Zheng placed his recommendations in a stadial theory of progress, arguing that China had passed through an ancient stage (lasting until 221 BCE), a medieval one, and then a modern era beginning with the Opium Wars. In the latter, he insisted that China needed to focus on boosting its wealth and power, but he also predicted – like Fukuzawa – one more stage in the distant future when this focus would no longer be necessary. In that future era, the world would be unified and Confucianism would be embraced everywhere. A similar but more detailed theory of this kind was popularized in the 1890s (and endorsed by Zheng) by another advocate of neomercantilist policies, Kang Youwei, who argued that the world was evolving through three ages of Disorder, Approaching Peace, and then Great Harmony. While the second stage required the pursuit of state wealth and power, Kang anticipated that the last would usher in the Confucian ideal of a universal moral empire.[18]

Zheng and others in the self-strengthening movement developed their neomercantilist ideas without engagement with foreign neomercantilist thought (which did not attract attention in China until the early twentieth century). Instead, they drew inspiration from China's own intellectual history, including the ancient Legalist tradition, which included not just Shang but also other famous texts such as *Guanzi*, whose economic content was, in the words of Richard von Glahn, "decidedly mercantilist".[19] That tradition had also influenced a Chinese "statecraft" school that gained prominence in the early nineteenth century for its advocacy of the cultivation of wealth and power through the promotion of commerce. A key figure in that school was Wei Yuan, who urged Chinese authorities in the 1840s to respond to the first Opium War by building a

[17] Quotes in Wu 2010, 189. For Zheng's ideas, see Helleiner 2021a, 238–45.
[18] Helleiner 2021a, 245.
[19] Von Glahn 2016, 77. See also pp. 120–21.

new arsenal and shipyard with foreign technology and by supporting an expansion of China's external trade. The ideas of Wei and the statecraft school became a key reference point for the self-strengthening move-ment after the Second Opium War.[20]

Zheng's writings and those of other self-strengthening thinkers found an audience not just in China but also in Japan and Korea (as did those of Wei). They also found a sympathetic ear among reform-minded Chi-nese officials such as Li Hongzhang, who created some state-supported firms in the 1870s and 1880s to promote economic modernization (one of which employed Zheng briefly).[21] But these Chinese reforms were much less ambitious and successful than those pursued by the Meiji leadership in Japan. The divergent economic paths of the two East Asian countries became particularly evident when Japan defeated China mili-tarily in 1895. That defeat was a shock to the Chinese elite and it encour-aged some further reforms before the country's 1911 revolution ushered in a new generation of leaders, some of whom were committed to imple-menting neomercantilist ideas more seriously.

For the history of neomercantilist thought, the most important of this new generation was Sun Yat-sen, who served briefly as the new Chinese republic's first provisional president and then remained a prominent figure in China's turbulent politics until his death in 1925. Sun's neo-mercantilist writings became extremely influential in the country during the interwar years, including his 1920 book *International Development of China* and lectures he gave in China in 1924 on the topic of *The Three Principles of the People*. Sun was heavily inspired by the self-strengthening movement, and especially by Zheng, with whom he had developed a close friendship.[22]

Sun reiterated Zheng's concerns about the existence of a worldwide trade war as well as the drain of China's wealth and erosion of its right to profits. He also warned that China had become the "poorest and weak-est state in the world" and one that was subject to foreign "economic domination" that could "spell the loss of our country as well as the anni-hilation of our race". This economic domination, Sun argued, stemmed from the leading position of foreign companies and banks in China as well as from the unequal treaties that imposed free trade (leading to an "invasion" of foreign goods) and the treaty ports (where foreigners held special privileges). Sun argued that China's economic oppression was reinforced by the political and military power of Western countries,

---

[20] Helleiner 2021a, 233–42.
[21] Helleiner 2021a, 238–40, 245.
[22] Sun [1920]1922, 1928. For his ideas, see Helleiner 2021a, 245–59.

noting that "the way their political power cooperates with their economic power is like the way in which the left arm helps the right arm".[23]

Like Zheng, Sun argued that a nationalist strategy of state-led industrialization and economic development was the key to ending this foreign domination and to boosting China's living standards. But his strategy was even more ambitious than that of Zheng. In addition to backing high tariffs to allow "native industries a chance to develop", Sun suggested that Chinese authorities should establish state-owned industrial firms, undertake massive infrastructural projects, and promote large-scale agricultural and resource development schemes. He also wanted the state to support the "people's livelihood" and reduce domestic inequality, a preference stemming from his interest in socialist (but not Marxist) thought.[24]

Sun also argued forcefully that China needed foreign capital to help finance his ambitious economic plans. As he put it, "Europe and America are a hundred years ahead of us in industrial development; so in order to catch up in a very short time, we have to use their capital". But he insisted that foreign capital needed to be carefully managed by the Chinese state in order to ensure that it served the Chinese people. In his 1920 book, he went further, proposing that foreign capital be channeled through a new kind of multilateral financial institution established by the League of Nations. Under his plan, the Chinese government would contract with this "International Development Organization" (IDO) to support a wide range of Chinese development projects. In this way, Chinese sovereignty would be better protected, while the lending countries would gain an outlet for their "surplus capital" and new export markets for their goods. More generally, Sun argued that his proposed IDO would foster international peace by containing inter-imperialist rivalries. He later acknowledged that his proposal had been inspired partly by a hope that Kang Youwei's Great Harmony Age soon might be at hand.[25]

Sun was much more familiar with works of foreign political economy than Zheng was, but he did not cite any of the foreign neomercantilist thinkers discussed in the previous chapter. He did praise the protectionist policies of Germany, the United States, and Japan as well as some of their domestic economic practices. But his broad neomercantilist vision had its roots in Chinese intellectual tradition, including not just the self-strengthening movement and the statecraft school but also older currents of Chinese thought, including *Guanzi*, which Sun argued had, in fact, established the study of economics itself.[26]

[23]  Quotes from Sun 1928, 12, 53, 41, 88.
[24]  Quotes from Sun 1928, 41, 270.
[25]  Quotes from Sun [1920]1922, 198, 227, 8.
[26]  Helleiner 2021a, 245–59.

As in Japan, even those Chinese thinkers who became interested in European neomercantilist thought in the early twentieth century continued to take strong inspiration from this local intellectual tradition. The leading figure to introduce European neomercantilist ideas to China was Sun's political rival before the 1911 revolution, Liang Qichao, who studied the ideas of the German historical school (see previous chapter) after fleeing into exile in Japan in 1898. In his writing (which had a very high profile in China during the first decade of the twentieth century), Liang praised that school's advocacy of neomercantilist policies while also adapting its advice in various ways, including by critiquing China's treaty ports and expressing strong concerns (stronger than Sun's) about private foreign investment in his country. Liang also embraced the German historical school's support for imperialism and even suggested to Chinese that "if as the largest race on this planet we are able to build a country fit for evolution, then who will be able to usurp from us the title of the Number One Imperialist Nation on Earth?" At the same time that Liang was inspired by foreign ideas, however, his neomercantilist thought was also heavily influenced by the ideas of the self-strengthening movement, the statecraft school, Shang Yang, and *Guanzi*.[27]

## Neomercantilists in Upper Canada and Egypt

Neomercantilist ideas in other places also sometimes emerged without much, if any, engagement with the neomercantilist thought of Europe and the United States. One example came from the British colony of Upper Canada, where a Scottish-born immigrant, John Rae, authored a sophisticated critique of Smith's ideas in his 1834 book *Statement of Some New Principles on the Subject of Political Economy*. The historian Joseph Spengler describes Rae as "possibly as brilliant an economist as nineteenth century North America was to produce" and his ideas were later invoked by Canadian politicians who introduced the country's protectionist National Policy of 1879 (as well as by neomercantilists as far away as Turkey, as noted below).[28] Despite his strong criticism of Adam Smith, Rae's work was even praised by John Stuart Mill, whose endorsement of infant-industry protectionism (see Chapter 2) drew directly on Rae's ideas.[29]

Rae's book contained no reference to List (who had already begun to publish criticisms of free trade by this time) and List did not reference Rae. The Canadian thinker did make one brief reference to Hamilton's

---

[27] Liang quote from Pusey 1983, 312. See also Helleiner 2021a, 262–69.
[28] Spengler 1959, 393. The ideas of List and Carey were also invoked at that time (Helleiner 2019a).
[29] Helleiner 2021a, 299–301.

1791 report, but Rae's main inspiration appears to have come from his practical Canadian experiences. Criticizing Smith's free trade views directly, Rae argued that protectionist policies were needed to cultivate local manufacturing in commodity-exporting countries in order to promote their independence and wealth. Rae highlighted the economic benefits of industrialization mentioned by other neomercantilists such as reduced transportation costs and import dependence, greater economic diversity, new job opportunities, and local markets for farmers. But he was most interested in how the wealth of nations was tied to the "power of invention" associated with manufacturing and its productivity gains.[30]

In Rae's view, Smith did not give enough attention to the fact that a country's manufacturing capabilities could be "acquired" through protectionist policies that fostered local firms as well as the "transfer" of industries from abroad via investment and the movement of skilled labour. Although protectionism would create costs in the short term, he argued that it would boost national wealth – if applied "cautiously" – over the long term. To realize these long-term gains, Rae argued that countries required a high "effective desire of accumulation", by which he meant a willingness "to sacrifice a certain amount of present good, to obtain another greater amount of good, at some future period". He suggested that the strength of this "desire" could be augmented by factors such as strong property rights, stable government, good laws, security, and educational initiatives to raise the "general intelligence and morality of the society".[31]

In contrast to many other neomercantilist thinkers, Rae acknowledged that governments could not always be trusted "to act for the good of the society". But he suggested that they were more likely to do so when policies concerned "the wealth of the community". This was even true, he argued, of despotic governments because "there the legislator looks on the wealth of the people as his own". In contrast to List's view that neomercantilist policies should be pursued only by countries with advanced liberal "political development", Rae argued that even such despotic governments should try to pursue them. Their higher risk of making mistakes, he suggested, was offset by larger potential economic gains because they usually ruled countries with less "inventive power", less "advance in science and arts", and greater "addiction to luxury". As he put it, "the power of the legislator to effect beneficial change is so great, that even his most blundering efforts are seldom altogether successless. A fruitful soil yields large returns, even to a very unskillful husbandman".[32]

---

[30] Rae [1834]1964, 15.
[31] Quotes from Rae [1834]1964, 71, 258, 37, 109, 119, 362.
[32] Quotes of Rae from Rae [1834]1964, 377–79.

Much more ambitious neomercantilist ideas were developed independently by one of Rae's contemporaries: Muhammad Ali, the ruler of Egypt between 1805 and 1848.[33] Formally a vassal of the Ottoman sultan, Ali was determined to boost Egypt's wealth and power through extensive reforms that included the establishment of state-owned manufacturing factories, the importation of foreign technology and expertise, and the launching of large-scale infrastructure projects to build canals, roads, and improved irrigation. Ali also took control of all land and turned Egypt into a major cotton exporter, with his government as the monopoly buyer domestically. Although Ottoman policy prevented the raising of tariffs in his subimperial jursidiction, Ali controlled Egypt's exports and imports by state trading monopolies. He also rejected foreign investment and loans, favouring internal sources of finance to support his initiatives.

In their scale and ambition, Ali's policies went well beyond the kinds of cautious neomercantilist recommendations made by his European and North American contemporaries such as Hamilton, List, Rae, and Carey. His policies were, in fact, the most dramatic neomercantilist ones pursued anywhere in the world at this time. In the 1830s, Ali also increasingly projected military power beyond Egypt into Western Arabia, Syria, and Sudan in ways that threatened other powerful interests in the region, including the Ottoman sultan and the British. Reacting to this threat and to Ali's declaration of independence in 1838, a combined Ottoman and British military operation constrained him in 1840 and forced him to abolish his monopolies and reduce his military, resulting in the unraveling of both his power and the industries he had built up.

Ali never wrote a detailed treatise on political economy, but he explained the neomercantilist vision behind his initiatives in a number of contexts, including when defending them against criticisms from European liberal supporters of free trade who visited Egypt. When the latter argued that Egypt's place in the international division of labour was agricultural exporting, he insisted that any country could use government economic activism to become a commercial and industrial power, just as the leading European countries had done. He acknowledged the short-term costs involved in building up Egypt's wealth and power, but argued he was making his country more "productive" over the long term. He also justified his extensive state control of the economy by arguing that "we cannot apply the same rules to Egypt as to England: centuries have

---

[33] Because Ali was Albanian-born (and came to Egypt as an Ottoman mercenary soldier), he could be classified as a European thinker, but I have placed him in this chapter because his initiatives and ideas emerged in the Egyptian context. For more details on Ali, see Helleiner 2021a, 304–11.

been required to bring you to your present state; I have only had a few years".[34] When making these kinds of arguments, Ali did not cite any specific European or American neomercantilist thinkers.

The fact that his policies were so different from List's recommendations may help to explain why the German thinker made no reference to Ali's important initiatives in his 1841 book (despite the fact that the latter was being written at the very time of the dramatic Anglo-Ottoman invasion). Instead, List simply cited Egypt as one of the many countries that he thought would be "foolish" to try to industrialize (see previous chapter).[35] Other foreign thinkers took more note, however, including Rae. The Canadian thinker acknowledged that "unmitigated slavery and despotism" prevailed in Egypt, but he approved of what Ali was trying to do: "errors, no doubt, may have been, and may be committed, but the good assuredly overbalances the evil".[36] Later in the nineteenth century, Ali's initiatives were also cited positively by neomercantilists elsewhere, including in the Ottoman Empire and as far away as in Japan and China.[37]

### Adapting Carey and List

Other neomercantilists outside Europe and the United States engaged much more with the works of neomercantilists from those two places, often adapting their ideas in innovative ways. For example, the leading Australian advocate of neomercantilist ideas during the last third of the nineteenth century, David Syme, invoked the work of Hamilton and Carey, but also added some novel arguments for protectionism that reflected his local circumstances in the colony of Victoria. Syme argued that if local manufacturers could be fostered, Victorians would no longer be vulnerable to long delays in obtaining foreign goods and parts or to the risk of fraudulent imported goods. Industrial firms could also, he argued, provide more steady employment for the many immigrants who had been drawn to Victoria's gold-mining boom in the 1850s but who subsequently became destitute. In addition to building support for protectionist policies in Victoria, Syme's writings attracted attention beyond Australia in both Europe and the United States (where they were praised by supporters of Carey's ideas).[38]

Carey's work was also cited by the leading Ethiopian advocate of state-led industrialization in the early twentieth century, Gabrahiwot Baykadagn. Gabrahiwot's most important work of political economy,

---

[34] Ali quotes from Marsot 1984, 189; Tagher 1950, 21.
[35] List [1841] 1909a, 152.
[36] Rae [1834] 1964, 379.
[37] Helleiner 2021a, 310–11.
[38] Helleiner 2021a, 185–89.

*Government and Public Administration,* was published in Amharic five years after his 1919 death with the financial support of Haile Selassie, the country's crown price (and soon to be emperor). While drawing heavily on Carey's ideas as a strategy for strengthening Ethiopia's "power and wealth", Gabrahiwot also adapted them in important ways to the distinctive context of his country.[39] For example, he rejected Carey's enthusiasm for political decentralization, arguing that a strong centralized state was needed to tackle "banditry and war", which were a huge "impediment to progress" in Ethiopia.[40] He also urged the government to take a more active domestic economic role than Carey discussed, pursuing initiatives such as land reform and ambitious strengthening of education and infrastructure. Further, Gabrahiwot urged opposition to the foreign-owned Bank of Abyssinia, which monopolized the country's banking system, arguing that it was distrusted by Ethiopians and was undermining national development by lending primarily to foreigners whose companies simply exported their profits from the country.[41]

At around the same time, List's ideas were adapted by the Turkish thinker Ziya Gökalp, who helped to shape the economic debates in his newly independent country during the early 1920s. In his 1923 book *The Principles of Turkism* and other writings, Gökalp rejected the free trade advice of "English political economy", arguing that "a national economy and large-scale industry can be achieved only through a protectionist policy". He praised List's (and Rae's) defense of protectionist policies in support of industrialization as well as the German thinker's emphasis on the importance of nationality. At the same time, he chose to overlook the fact that List did not think a country like Turkey should industrialize (see previous chapter). Gökalp's "economic patriotism" also called for a much more ambitious kind of government economic activism than List (or Rae) had endorsed, including national economic planning and the creation of some state-owned enterprises. This "state capitalism" was needed, Gökalp argued, because the Turkish people did not always have the necessary skills and "spirit of enterprise", and they expected "the state to take the initiative in everything new and progressive". It would also prevent "the rise of a new class of speculators" and the imperialist influence of "insatiable and predatory capitalists" from Europe, while enabling the profits of industry to be socialized in order to "ensure the prosperity of the people and put an end to all kinds of misery".[42]

---

[39] Gabrahiwot [1924]1995, 136.
[40] Gabrahiwot [1924]1995, 71.
[41] For Gabrahiwot's ideas see Helleiner 2021a, 189–94.
[42] Quotes from Gökalp 1959, 307, 313, 306, 310–12.

List's ideas also attracted attention in Latin America, including from the prominent Argentine thinker Alejandro Bunge in the early twentieth century. Bunge saw industrialization as key for cultivating Argentina's wealth and power and ending its subordinate role as an agricultural exporter to Britain. He also shared List's interest in regional trade agreements that lowered tariffs among subordinate countries, arguing for such an arrangement between his country and many of its neighbours. Like Gökalp, however, he ignored List's scepticism about the relevance of neomercantilist policies to his country. He also went beyond List in highlighting the poor terms of trade that agricultural exporters faced in international markets, a phenomenon that he attributed to the market power of industrial countries. They were able to use this power, he argued, to lower the prices of their resource imports while keeping that of their industrial exports high.[43]

Another example of a thinker who adapted List's ideas in interesting ways was Mahadev Govind Ranade, a prominent scholar in colonial India in the late nineteenth century and founding member of the Indian National Congress in 1885.[44] While praising List's advocacy of industrial protectionism and his emphasis on productive powers and nationality, Ranade rejected the German thinker's idea that industrialization should be pursued only in temperate regions. Instead of simply ignoring List's views on this topic (as Gökalp and Bunge did), he confronted them directly. Recalling India's history of exporting manufactured goods to Europe, he attacked those who "assign to the backward Torrid Zone Regions of Asia the duty of producing Raw Materials, and claim for the advanced European Temperate Zone Countries, the work of transport and manufactures". He also highlighted various costs to India of its agricultural exporting role, including the fact that "the Agricultural Industry in the Torrid Regions has to work under the disadvantage of an uncertain rainfall, and suffer from famine visitations, which, when they come, paralyze Production, and condemn millions to violent or slow death". Industrialization would, he argued, create a more diversified economy that could act as "a permanent National Insurance against recurrent dangers".[45]

Ranade also departed from List's praise for British colonial rule of India by developing some strong economic critiques of its colonial policies. Through the imposition of free trade and other policies, colonial authorities had, he argued, undermined India's indigenous manufacturing and encouraged a "ruralization" of India. Like his colleague Naoroji (see Chapter 3), Ranade argued that Britain was also draining India's capital

---

[43] Helleiner 2021a, 97–99.
[44] Goswami 2004.
[45] Quotes from Ranade 1906, 25–28.

in various ways. In his view, India's wealth and economic independence had been further undermined by the monopolization of India's domestic and international commerce by Britain. He concluded that "this Dependency has come to be regarded as a Plantation, growing raw produce to be shipped by British Agents in British Ships, to be worked in Fabrics by British skill and capital, and to be re-exported to the Dependency by British merchants to their corresponding British Firms in India and elsewhere".[46]

Although Ranade was very critical of British colonial rule, he sought to reform rather than reject it. He urged British colonial authorities to support Indian industrialization by protectionist policies as well as by measures such as government procurement, spending on infrastructure and education, government borrowing abroad for funds to be lent to local firms at low rates, and the "pioneering", "guaranteeing", or "subsidizing" of new firms.[47] Ranade was also an early promoter of the Indian *swadeshi* ("own country") movement that called on Indians themselves to use their consumption choices to support Indian industrialization by purchasing goods made by local manufacturing firms. Ranade backed up these various ideas with a broader attack on the claim of economic liberals that their ideas had universal relevance. Invoking Bagehot's description of economic liberalism as "English political economy" (see Chapter 2), he urged the development of an "Indian political economy" that corresponded to its distinct context, in keeping with what he called "the Law of Relativity and Correspondence".[48]

Ranade's ideas were cited by later Indian nationalist politicians, including Jawaharlal Nehru. They also inspired subsequent Indian neomercantilist thinkers such as Benoy Kumar Sarkar, who produced the first full Bengali translation of List's *National System* in 1932 and who has been described as "the most prominent social scientist in interwar colonial India".[49] After the mid-1920s, Sarkar went beyond both List and Ranade in endorsing new conceptions of national economic planning as tools to serve neomercantilist goals. He also drew connections between Indian neomercantilist thought and the ideas contained in an ancient South Asian text, the *Arthashastra* (Science of Wealth), whose initial author, Kautilya, lived in the third and fourth centuries BCE and had urged the promotion of state wealth and power through activist economic and trade policies.[50]

---

[46] Quotes from Ranade 1906, 28–29, 106.
[47] Quotes from Ranade 1906, 203, 34.
[48] Ranade 1906, 1–2. See p. 11 for his invocation of Bagehot. Ranade's interest in relativism appears to have been influenced partly by Henry Maine's comparative studies of Asia and Europe (Adams 1971, 82). See also Helleiner 2021a, 118.
[49] Quote from Goswami 2012, 1464. For his influence on Nehru, see Helleiner 2021a, 349n10.
[50] Sarkar [1926]1938, x. For Sarkar's ideas, see Helleiner 2021a, 120–23.

## Conclusion

Thinkers outside Europe and the United States contributed to neomercantilist thought both by adapting the ideas of neomercantilists from those places and by developing their own versions of this perspective more independently. In both cases, these thinkers widened the diversity of neomercantilist thought beyond that already noted in the previous chapter. For example, they identified new kinds of policies to serve neomercantilist goals, such as higher degrees of state activism in the domestic economy, state trading companies, "multinational public business zones", challenges to foreign banking monopolies, public management of foreign capital, the construction of multilateral financial institutions, and consumer-based initiatives. In terms of political orientation, Sun developed a more left-wing version of neomercantilism than those described in the last chapter. In East Asia, thinkers also introduced distinct ideas such as "commercial warfare" and visions of a Confucian-inspired long-term future.[51] Finally, many thinkers were forced to develop distinctive strategies to pursue neomercantilist goals in more constrained political circumstances than those faced by their counterparts in Europe and the United States, such as the colonial context of Ranade and contexts where tariffs could not be raised, as in East Asia or subimperial Egypt.

The fact that many versions of neomercantilist thought were developed quite independently from those in Europe and the United States highlights the relatively decentralized emergence of this perspective. There was no single figure in the neomercantilist camp who inspired all thinkers in the way that Smith did for classical economic liberals (or Marx did for Marxists, as we shall see in the next two chapters). Neomercantilists around the world also drew on distinctive older intellectual traditions. Many referenced European mercantilist thought, but Sarkar also invoked the ancient text *Arthashastra*, while many East Asian thinkers were inspired by earlier intellectual traditions in Japan, Korea, and China (including some that dated back to the era of the Warring States in China). The distinctiveness of many East Asian conceptions of neomercantilism was also reinforced by the intra-regional circulation of ideas among these three countries.[52]

---

[51] Regarding the latter, this chapter noted the ideas of Fukuzawa, Zheng, and Kang on this topic. Chapter 12 notes Sun's ideas as well.

[52] I have developed the themes in this paragraph in more detail in Helleiner 2021a.

Between the mid-nineteenth and early twentieth centuries, Marxism emerged as a major rival to both economic liberalism and neomercantilism in debates about political economy around the world. Marxists prioritized very different goals from those of supporters of the other two perspectives. They were focused on challenging capitalism in order to end class-based inequality and exploitation within the world economy. This distinct perspective was, of course, pioneered by Karl Marx himself, but some of the best-known Marxist ideas about the international dimensions of political economy were developed by later Marxists.

This chapter examines Marx's ideas about the world economy as well as those of a number of his European (including Russian) followers. Like the discussion of economic liberalism and neomercantilism in previous chapters, I highlight many disagreements that existed among Marxists. Some of these disagreements are featured in contemporary IPE textbooks, but others are less well known. Chapter 7 then broadens the picture to examine a number of Marxist thinkers from other parts of the world whose ideas became influential within, and in some cases beyond, their regions. Their ideas adapted European Marxism in ways that contributed further to the internal diversity of this worldview before 1945.

### Marx and Globalizing Capitalism

The pioneer of Marxism was born into a middle-class German family and studied law and philosophy at university, earning a PhD in 1841. Marx's interest in political economy appears to have been stimulated by a brief stint as a newspaper editor in 1842–43, after which he began to write extensively on the subject. He combined this writing with involvement in political activism in a number of locations where he lived, including in London, which became his base from 1849 until his death in 1883.[1]

---

[1] There are many biographies of Marx; for a recent example, see Sperber 2014. For Marx's early interest in political economy, see, for example, Szporluk 1988, 20–21.

For his followers around the world in the pre-1945 period, Marx's most famous work was *The Communist Manifesto*, published in 1848 as an expression of the founding principles of a "Communist League" that he had helped to create with some others the year before. A short text, *The Manifesto* was co-authored with Friedrich Engels, the son of a German textile manufacturer. Also widely read in pre-1945 Marxist circles was his much more theoretical and lengthy *Capital*, whose first volume appeared in 1867. Three other volumes of this work were published after his death in 1884, 1895, and 1905–10.

In *The Communist Manifesto*, Marx and Engels differentiated their views from other socialists who had, since the early nineteenth century, criticized the individualism, competition, and inequality of capitalist societies. They were critical of some socialists for romanticizing the precapitalist world, while others were condemned for favouring only a reform, rather than an overthrow, of capitalism. Still others, such as England's Robert Owen and France's Charles Fourier, were criticized for their "utopian" focus on cultivating small-scale socialist communities rather than a wider social revolution led by the proletariat.[2] To distinguish their position from these others, Marx and Engels embraced the term "communist" that had begun to be used in Europe in the 1840s to refer to socialist critics of private property who called for greater public control of productive resources.[3]

From early on, Marx showed a keen interest in the international dimensions of capitalism, arguing that capitalist forms of production led by a bourgeois class had generated an increasingly globalized economy. As he and Engels put it in *The Communist Manifesto*, "the need for a constantly expanding market for its products chases the bourgeoisie over the whole surface of the globe. ... The bourgeoisie has through its exploitation of the world market given a cosmopolitan character to production and consumption of all countries". In another famous passage, they elaborated on this point:

The bourgeoisie, by the rapid improvement of all instruments of production, by the immensely facilitated means of communication, draws all nations, even the most barbarian, into civilization. The cheap prices of its commodities are the heavy artillery with which it batters down all Chinese walls, with which it forces the barbarians' most entrenched hatred of foreigners to capitulate. It compels all nations, if they are not to be overwhelmed, to adopt the bourgeois mode of production; it compels them to introduce what it calls civilisation into their midst, i.e., to become bourgeois themselves. In one word, it creates a world after its own image.[4]

---

[2] Quote from Marx and Engels [1848]2004, 92.
[3] See, for example, Herres 2015; Leopold 2015.
[4] Marx and Engels [1848]2004, 65–66.

Marx's perspective on the globalizing economy of his era was very different from that of economic liberals who saw free trade ushering in a harmonious world of prosperity, peace, and individual freedom. From Marx's perspective, capitalist society was characterized by deep class conflict between a dominant bourgeoisie and an exploited proletarian class of workers from whom a surplus was extracted. Free trade simply extended this class conflict and exploitation on a wider scale. For this reason, he was very critical of liberals who saw the free trade policies of his era as ushering in a kind of "brotherhood" amongst all nations. As he put it in a speech in 1848, "To call cosmopolitan exploitation universal brotherhood is an idea that could only be engendered in the brain of the bourgeoisie. All the destructive phenomena which unlimited competition gives rise to within one country are reproduced in more gigantic proportions on the world market".[5]

Marx also advanced criticisms of neomercantilist views, including those outlined in List's 1841 book, which was among the first works of political economy that Marx read.[6] In Marx's view, List's focus on Britain's domination of the world through free trade overlooked the class-based nature of oppression by the bourgeoisie in the increasingly global capitalist system. As Marx put it in the mid-1840s, List's advocacy of German strategic protectionism would simply allow the German bourgeoisie "to *exploit* his *fellow countrymen*, indeed exploit them even *more* than they were exploited from abroad".[7] Marx subsequently made similar points about the views of Carey (with whom he corresponded), criticizing him for representing "the industrial bourgeoisie of America" and for his focus on "harmony within bourgeois society".[8]

To end class exploitation, Marx argued, that the capitalist system needed to be challenged and overthrown via a revolution of the proletariat. Revolutionary conditions would emerge as the expansion of capitalism reached its limits, declining profits set in, and immiseration and discontent grew among the workers. Marx focused mostly on the prospects for revolution in Europe where industrial capitalism was most developed. In the first edition of volume 1 of *Capital*, he suggested that the rest of the world simply would follow Europe's economic path: "the country that is more developed industrially only shows, to the less developed, the image of its own future".[9] Late in his life, however, Marx became interested in how

---

[5] Quoted in Went 2002, 26–27.
[6] Marx was familiar with List for another reason: the newspaper editorship he assumed in 1842 had initially been offered to List (who had turned it down); Szporluk 1988, 20–21,
[7] Quoted in Szpolruk 1988, 36.
[8] Quotes from McLellan 1973, 285; Marx [1857–61]1973, 805.
[9] Marx [1867]1976, 91.

capitalist development in Russia was not following the European example, suggesting in 1882 that a revolution led by Russian peasants, rather than industrial workers, could bypass capitalism by using their traditional common land ownership as "the starting point for a communist development". He added that such a revolution could become "the signal for a proletarian revolution in the West, so that both complement each other".[10]

Indeed, international solidarity was important to Marx's view of revolution. He and Engels had famously ended *The Communist Manifesto* with the words "Proletarians of all lands unite!" Although they acknowledged that the proletariat "must first acquire political supremacy" as a "national class", Marx and Engels insisted that "the workers have no fatherland". Like many economic liberals at the time, they argued more generally that "national differences and antagonisms between peoples are daily vanishing more and more with the development of the bourgeoisie, with freedom of trade, the world market, uniformity in industrial production and in the corresponding conditions of existence".[11] To foster proletarian internationalism, Marx supported the International Workingmen's Association – later known as the First International – which brought together many European left-wing groups (Marxist and non-Marxist) between 1864 and 1876, until internal tensions led to its dissolution.

To accelerate the prospects of revolution, Marx also backed some policies that sometimes surprise contemporary IPE students. For example, he supported free trade in a speech in 1848, although for very different reasons than economic liberals: "Generally speaking, the Protective system in these days is conservative, while the Free Trade system works destructively. It breaks up old nationalities and carries antagonism of proletariat and bourgeoisie to the uttermost point. In a word, the Free Trade system hastens the Social Revolution. In this revolutionary sense alone, gentlemen, I am in favor of Free Trade".[12] At other moments in the 1860s and 1870s, however, he endorsed limited trade protectionism in the German context on the grounds that it would better promote the growth of local industrial capitalism, thereby more effectively setting the stage for a revolution.[13]

In some contexts, Marx also suggested that European colonialism had an important role to play in accelerating the global spread of capitalism. For example, in one 1853 passage (that he intended as a criticism of Carey's views on the subject), Marx argued that British colonial rule in India

---

[10] Quoted in Szporluk 1988, 180.
[11] Quotes from Marx and Engels [1848]2004, 94, 79.
[12] Quoted in Szporluk 1988, 41
[13] Larrain 1991, 233; Szporluk 1988, 37, 178. He also endorsed industrial protectionism for a future independent Ireland on the same grounds in 1867.

was causing a "social revolution" that undermined "Oriental despotism" and the "undignified, stagnatory, and vegetative life" of pre-colonial India. He added: "England has to fulfil a double mission in India: one destructive; the other regenerating – the annihilation of old Asiatic society, and the laying of the material foundations of Western society in Asia".[14] While acknowledging the brutal nature of this process, Marx depicted it as a necessary step before a "great social revolution" ushered in a post-capitalist future: "The bourgeois period of history has to create the material basis of the new world – on the one hand universal intercourse founded upon the mutual dependency of mankind, and the means of that intercourse; on the other hand, the development of the productive powers of man and the transformation of material production into a scientific dominance of natural agencies".[15] In this passage, Marx also highlighted his view that a future post-capitalist society would be able to take advantage of the impressive material achievements of the "bourgeois period". As he put it earlier with Engels in *The Communist Manifesto*, "The bourgeoisie, during its rule of scarce one hundred years, has created more massive and more colossal productive forces than have all preceding generations together".[16]

Like his views on free trade, however, Marx's views on colonialism were also mixed. While noting the important "double mission" of British rule in India, he also suggested that Indian independence would enable Indians to "reap the fruits of the new elements of society scattered among them by the British bourgeoisie" and he later supported the 1857 Indian rebellion against the British.[17] In other writings, Marx also decried Britain's plundering of India's wealth and noted how the destruction of Indian handicraft production had forced it into a problematic role of commodity exporter serving Britain's needs.[18] In addition, Marx backed anti-colonial struggles elsewhere in the world and depicted British imperial rule as a barrier to modern industrialization in Ireland.[19]

## Marxist Theories of Imperialism

The significance of imperialism for capitalism's evolution became a central preoccupation of many European thinkers who developed Marxist theory further after Marx's death in 1883. They were particularly

[14] Quote from Marx 2019, 641, 654. For the link to Carey, see Larrain 1991; Perelman 2008.
[15] Quotes from Marx 2019, 658–59.
[16] Marx and Engels [1848]2004, 66.
[17] Quote from Marx 2019, 657. For his support of the mutiny, Pradella 2017, 581.
[18] Chandra 1965, 132; Kumar 1992, 499.
[19] For Ireland, see Larrain 1991. For his support of anti-colonial struggles, see, for example, Pradella 2017.

interested in the dramatic expansion of European (and US and Japanese) imperial rule across the world in the late nineteenth and early twentieth centuries.[20] European Marxists explained this phenomenon with reference to the evolution of capitalism.

### Lenin and Luxemburg

The best known of these Marxist theories of imperialism was outlined by Vladimir Lenin in his work *Imperialism: The Highest Stage of Capitalism,* which was published one year before he played a leading role in the 1917 Russian revolution. Lenin openly acknowledged that his analysis built upon a 1902 book titled *Imperialism* by the British liberal thinker John Hobson (whose views are discussed more in Chapter 14 of this book). Hobson had attributed the growth of imperialism to "capitalist-imperialist forces", including powerful private financial capitalists who sought to protect their growing investments abroad and secure safe locations for new investments.[21] These capitalists' interest in foreign investment, Hobson argued, stemmed from declining investment opportunities at home, as growing domestic inequality prevented the masses from being able to purchase all the goods that capitalist factories produced.

Lenin developed Hobson's analysis further within a Marxist analytical framework and set of goals. He argued that capitalism had evolved from a stage of "capitalist free competition" centred around industrial capital and free trade to a "monopoly stage of capitalism" dominated by "financial capital" and policies of protectionism and imperial expansion. Like Hobson, Lenin linked imperial expansion to growing exports of European capital to what he called "backward countries" As Lenin put it, "The need to export capital arises from the fact that in a few countries capitalism has become 'overripe" and (owing to the backward state of agriculture and the impoverished state of the masses) capital cannot find a field for 'profitable' investment". In the new colonies, he noted that European capitalists could earn high profits because "capital is scarce, the price of land is relatively low, wages are low, raw materials are cheap".[22]

Lenin argued that imperialism also helped to secure a stable supply of raw materials that was needed for capitalism's growth in its latest stage. As he put it, "The more capitalism is developed, the more strongly the

---

[20] As noted in the next chapter, Japanese imperialism was examined more closely by Japanese Marxists. Much less attention was paid by these Marxist theorists of imperialism to the expansion of settler colonialism in places such as North America, Australia, and New Zealand in this period.

[21] Quote from Hobson 1902, 102.

[22] Quotes from Lenin [1916]1970, 85, 45, 61.

shortage of raw materials is felt, the more intense the competition and the hunt for sources of raw materials throughout the whole world, the more desperate the struggle for the acquisition of colonies". In addition, he suggested that the profits earned in the colonies enabled capitalists to "bribe certain sections of the workers" in Europe in ways that blunted revolutionary sentiment. To support this point, he quoted one of the most famous imperialists of the period, Cecil Rhodes, as stating that "if you want to avoid civil war, you must become imperialists".[23]

Although Lenin's analysis drew on Hobson's work, he did not share the latter's view of what needed to be done. To counteract the trends he identified, Hobson had called for reforms to reduce domestic inequality such as taxation and social reform (as well as free trade policies to constrain the oligopolistic power of capitalists). Lenin argued capitalists would never agree to redistributive reforms of the kind Hobson called for: "as long as capital remains what it is, surplus capital will be utilised not for the purpose of raising the standard of living of the masses in a given country, for this would mean a decline in profits for the capitalists".[24] Instead of reforming capitalism, Lenin argued that its overthrow was necessary.

Indeed, Lenin argued that revolution was around the corner because imperialism was what he called the "highest stage" of capitalism. In his view, the imperialist stage of capitalism inevitably generated conflicts between the major imperial powers, as evidenced by the outbreak of World War I, which he depicted as "a war for the division of the world, for the partition and repartition of colonies and spheres of influence of finance capital, etc". Inter-imperialist war, in turn, created revolutionary conditions because workers, when faced with its barbarism, would recognize the better option of overthrowing the capitalist system that created it. For this reason, he argued that "Imperialism is the eve of the social revolution of the proletariat".[25]

Another Marxist who developed a prominent analysis of imperialism in the early twentieth century was the Polish-born Rosa Luxemburg, whose key work *The Accumulation of Capital* was published three years before Lenin's *Imperialism*. After completing a PhD in political economy in 1897, Luxemburg became a well-known figure in German Marxist circles as well as within the leading transnational socialist organization at this time, the Second International (created in 1889 and lasting until 1916). Like Lenin, Luxemburg appealed to European workers during World War I not to fight in inter-imperialist wars, arguing that they faced

---

[23] Quotes from Lenin [1916]1970, 80, 120, 76.
[24] Lenin [1916]1970, 61.
[25] Quotes from Lenin [1916]1970, 9–10, 14 (from Lenin's 1920 preface).

a choice between socialism or a kind of "barbarism" involving "depopulation, desolation, degeneration, a vast cemetery".[26] Luxemburg was jailed during most of World War I for her anti-war activism and then was murdered in 1919 by right-wing forces in the wake of a failed revolutionary uprising in Germany.

Although Luxemburg's opposition to the war echoed Lenin's, her explanation of imperialism differed somewhat from his. She agreed that imperialism was linked to capital exports and the securing of raw materials, but her main analysis was centered on its role in securing foreign markets for goods that could not be absorbed at home because of the poverty of the workers. In her words, imperialist expansion helped to resolve "the inherent contradiction between the unlimited expansive capacity of the productive forces and the limited expansive capacity of social consumption under conditions of capitalist distribution". Luxemburg also pointed to the role of imperialism in finding new labour to exploit in foreign lands, arguing that capital "must be able to mobilise world labour power without restriction in order to utilise all productive forces of the globe". Echoing Marx, Luxemburg argued that capitalism was driven to expand geographically to incorporate all non-capitalist societies. As she put it, capitalism "tends to engulf the whole globe and to stamp out all other economies, tolerating no rival at its side".[27]

Despite her somewhat different analysis of the causes of imperialism, Luxemburg shared Lenin's view that imperialism was the "final stage" of capitalism. One reason was that capital accumulation could not continue when there were no new non-capitalist regions left to incorporate. But Luxemburg also argued that capitalism would be undermined even before these geographical limits were reached by imperialism's growing "lawlessness and violence, both in aggression against the non-capitalist world and in ever more serious conflict among the competing capitalist countries". As she put it, "the more violently, ruthlessly and thoroughly imperialism brings about the decline of non-capitalist civilisations, the more rapidly it cuts the very ground from under the feet of capitalist accumulation. Though imperialism is the historical method for prolonging the career of capitalism, it is also a sure means of bringing it to a swift conclusion".[28] For this reason, Luxemburg anticipated that a revolution of "the international working class" would take place "long before" the geographical limits of capitalist expansion were actually reached.[29]

---

[26] Quoted in O'Brien 2021, 67.
[27] Quotes from Luxemburg [1913]1963, 343, 362, 467.
[28] Quotes from Luxemburg [1913]1963, 417, 446.
[29] Quoted in Hudis 2018, 80. See also Luxemburg [1913]1963, 467.

Luxemburg also devoted extensive attention to imperial powers' use of force and violence when expanding into the non-capitalist world to secure investments, markets, resources, and labour. She was very critical of how liberal arguments about the peaceful nature of trade and competition completely neglected this "blustering violence" of capital.[30] In keeping with these arguments, Luxemburg condemned colonialism strongly and expressed her deep sympathy for the colonized, including "the poor victims on the rubber plantations of Putumayo" and "the Blacks in Africa with whose corpses the Europeans play catch".[31] She was deeply critical of the ideology of imperialism as a civilizing mission and argued that pre-capitalist societies were in some ways more stable, resilient, and advanced than capitalist ones.

Lenin was also critical of colonialism, but showed much less interest in its impact on colonized people in his 1916 *Imperialism*. To be sure, he called attention in one passage to "the imperialist oppression and exploitation of most of the countries and nations of the world, for the capitalist parasitism of a handful of wealthy states". He also noted that the export of capital "greatly accelerates the development of capitalism in those countries to which it is exported", a point that seemed to echo Marx's earlier view that colonialism might have an important role to play in encouraging capitalist development in colonized territories.[32] Particularly absent from Lenin's 1916 work, however, was any detailed analysis of the issues of violence and exploitation in colonial territories that Luxemburg highlighted. Indeed, he even seemed to dismiss Luxemburg's moral concerns about the issue, responding to her work on one occasion with the following comment: "The description of the torture of negroes in South Africa is noisy, colourful and meaningless. Above all it is 'non-Marxist'".[33]

At the same time, Lenin was more willing to assign revolutionary agency to the colonized, an issue that Luxemburg addressed much less. Although Luxemburg called for "international solidarity embracing all parts of the world, all races and peoples", she did not try to cultivate links with people in colonized regions.[34] Her revolutionary advice was focused on workers in Europe. She was even very critical of movements that sought national self-determination (including in her native Poland), arguing that they were reactionary diversions from the international class struggle.[35] By contrast, Lenin showed more interest in these

---

[30] Luxemburg [1913]1963, 452.
[31] Quoted in Hudis 2018, 74.
[32] Lenin [1916]1970, 62, 63.
[33] Quoted in O'Brien 2021, 65.
[34] Quoted in Virdee 2017, 2400. See also O'Brien 2021; Hudis 2018.
[35] Singh 2018, 136.

movements and their potential to be anti-imperialist forces.[36] As noted below, this issue would become even more prominent in his thinking after the Russian revolution.

### Hyndman and Kautsky

A Marxist thinker who did more than both Lenin and Luxemburg to build ties with colonized peoples in the pre-1914 era was Britain's Henry Hyndman. Initially a pro-empire conservative, Hyndman converted to Marxism after reading Marx's work in 1880. Although much less well known than Lenin and Luxemburg to IPE scholars today, he popularized Marx's ideas in English, participated actively in the Second International, and created Britain's first socialist party (the Social Democratic Federation). Well before Lenin and Luxemburg published their analyses, Hyndman argued in the early 1900s that imperialism was driven by capitalism's need for new markets and resources and that it was delaying the collapse of capitalism. His party was also the only British socialist group to support colonial labour movements and to establish branches in places such as South Africa and India.[37]

Unlike most European Marxists, Hyndman also engaged with critics of imperialism from colonized regions, most notably Naoroji, whose drain theory (discussed in Chapter 3 of this book) he embraced in the late 1870s even before reading Marx. Hyndman struck up a friendship with Naoroji and cited his work. He also promoted it to others, including Marx in 1881 (whose ideas about Britain's drain of wealth may have been influenced partly by it).[38] Hyndman also tried unsuccessfully to convince the liberal Naoroji to back more radical politics in India, arguing that revolutionary movements in both India and Britain would reinforce each other. He did, however, convince Naoroji to speak to the 1904 meeting of the Second International, where the Indian thinker was one of the few non-Europeans in attendance and where he received an ovation for his criticism of Britain's treatment of India as a form of "barbarism".[39] Hyndman and other members of his party were, in fact, among the most prominent critics of colonialism within the Second International. According to Sunit Sarvraj Singh, the party was also "alone within the

---

[36] See, for example, d'Encausse and Schram,1969, 21–23; Hoston 1994, 24, 31–32; Singh 2018, 136; Szporluk 1988, 187.

[37] Morris 2014; Singh 2018, 108.

[38] See Goswami 2004, 227, 337fn34; Masani 1939, 19, 235; Morris 2014, 297; Patel 2020, 84–85; Singh 2018, 107, 110, 134.

[39] Quoted in Masani 1939: 432. See also pp. 398–400, 429–31; Mehrotra and Patel 2016, 243, 250–51; Patel 2020, 223–25, 236.

Socialist International in going so far as to argue that the task of quash-
ing the vampirism of British rule in India was as important, if not more
important, than achieving socialism in Western Europe".[40]

It is important to note that the opposition of Lenin, Luxemburg, and
Hyndman to imperialism was not universally shared among Marxists at
the time. Like liberals and neomercantilists, European Marxists were
split on the issue, with some well-known figures such as Germany's Eduard Bernstein arguing that imperialism deserved support on the grounds
that "savages must be subjugated and made to conform to the rules
of higher civilisation".[41] Prominent non-Marxist socialists such as the
British Fabians were also supportive of imperialism. Indeed, the issue
was the subject of heated debate within the Second International before
World War I.[42]

Before turning to post-1917 Marxist thought, it is important to mention one other prominent thinker, Karl Kautsky, who developed distinctive ideas about imperialism before 1917. Born in Prague, Kautsky
studied in Vienna before moving to Germany and becoming actively
involved with the German Social Democrats, who were the largest
socialist party in the world before World War I. He also lived in London
from 1885 to 1890, when he became close to Engels, who gave him
the task of editing volume 4 of Marx's *Capital*. After returning to Germany, he soon became what Lenin described as "the principal Marxist
theoretician of the epoch of the so-called Second International", known
particularly for his advocacy of a gradualist, parliamentary route to
socialism instead of the more revolutionary strategy favoured by Lenin
and Luxemburg.[43]

Like Lenin and Hyndman, Kautsky assigned greater agency in the
anti-imperialist struggle to colonized peoples than Luxemburg did. In a
prominent 1914 article (published just after the start of World War I),
he noted "the awakening of Eastern Asia and Indians well as of the Pan-
Islamic movement in the Near East and North Africa" and argued that
their growing opposition to imperialism "threatens not just one or other
of the imperialist States, but all of them together". He was also very
critical of how imperial powers forced colonies "to restrict themselves
entirely to agricultural production", arguing that agrarian regions "must
aspire to become industrial countries, in the interests of their own prosperity or even autonomy". Within the Second International, he also

---

[40] Singh 2018, 109. See also pp. 108, 136; Morris 2014.
[41] Quoted in Virdee 2017, 2399.
[42] See, for example, d'Encausse and Schram 1969, 15–16; Manjapra 2014, 173–74; Singh 2018, 144.
[43] Lenin [1916]1970, 87.

opposed advocates of the idea of socialist colonialism, arguing that the phrase was a "complete logical contradiction".[44]

Particularly interesting was Kautsky's distinctive view that imperialism was not necessary for capitalism's expansion or an inevitable phase in its development. Indeed, Kautsky argued that inter-imperialist rivalries were increasingly dysfunctional to capitalism because the rising financial costs of military spending and colonial expansion were imposing unpopular tax burdens on the proletariat and absorbing capital that could otherwise be invested abroad. As capitalist elites recognized these drawbacks, Kautsky predicted that they would begin to ally together to dominate and exploit the world cooperatively in a new phase of capitalism that he called "ultra-imperialism". As he put it, "the capitalist economy is seriously threatened precisely by the contradictions between its States. Every far-sighted capitalist today must call on his fellows: capitalists of all countries, unite!"[45]

Not surprisingly, this argument of Kautsky provoked strong opposition, particularly from Lenin. Indeed, Lenin's *Imperialism* was essentially a long rebuttal of it. As Lenin noted, Kautsky's case was not new. Hobson had also suggested that inter-imperialist war might become a thing of the past as capitalists from different imperialist powers increasingly cooperated with each other in creating a kind of "inter-Imperialism".[46] It is easy to understand why Lenin found Kautsky's line of argument so frustrating. It directly challenged his case that World War I was an inevitable product of capitalism and that imperialism was the "highest stage" of capitalism. It also undermined his efforts to convince workers that only a socialist revolution could end the war. In Lenin's words, it was "a most reactionary method of consoling the masses with hopes of permanent peace being possible under capitalism".[47]

To counter this case, Lenin argued that peace between capitalist states could never be more than just a temporary "truce" because of the uneven development of capitalism.[48] As one country grew more quickly than another, tension and rivalry would inevitably grow and lead to war. Lenin also extended his critique of Kautsky to include how the latter had not initially taken a stronger position against World War I. When the German parliament had voted to approve war credits at the start of the conflict, Kautsky had urged the Social Democrats to abstain but then accepted the majority position in favour of approval. Indeed, almost all socialist parties of the Second International backed their governments

---

[44] Quotes from Kautsky [1914]1970, 45, 44; Guettel 2012, 467.
[45] Kautsky [1914]1970, 46, 44–45.
[46] Hobson 1902, 351. See also 311–12.
[47] Lenin [1916]1970, 113.
[48] Lenin [1916]1970, 114.

in war, thereby undermining international working-class solidarity and inhibiting the kind of revolutionary moment that Lenin (and Luxemburg) believed had been created by the war. Lenin saw his 1916 work *Imperialism* as "a monument exposing to the full the shameful bankruptcy and treachery of the heroes of the Second International", in whose company he assigned Kautsky a prominent place.[49]

## Some Marxist Debates after 1917

After becoming the leader of post-revolutionary Russia in 1917, Lenin quickly created a new organization called the Comintern (Communist International) – often known as the Third International – which met for the first time in 1919. In contrast to the Second International's loose cooperation among national socialist parties, the Comintern was a centralized organization designed to direct Communist parties around the world from its Moscow headquarters. Its purpose was also more ambitious: to foster worldwide anti-capitalist revolution. As Lenin explained, "the greatest difficulty of the Russian revolution" was the need "to effect the transition from our strictly national revolution to the world revolution".[50]

Initially, Lenin hoped the Russian revolution would spur revolutions in European countries such as Germany. When those revolutions failed to materialize in 1918–19, however, he shifted his attention to give more emphasis to the task of supporting anti-colonial movements elsewhere. This shift was easily justified within Lenin's theoretical framework. If capitalism relied on imperialism, anti-colonial struggles would not just liberate colonized peoples but also weaken the economic systems of capitalist states and spark revolutions there. As part of this shift, the chair of the Comintern, Grigory Zinoviev, contrasted his organization with the European-focused Second International, arguing in racialized terms that the Comintern did not "only want to be an International of the toilers of the white race but also an International of the toilers of the black and yellow races, an International of the toilers of the whole world".[51] The Second International had not engaged in much depth with radical political movements beyond Europe, such as anti-colonial activists or those associated with China's 1911 revolution or with that beginning in Mexico the previous year.[52]

---

[49] Lenin [1916]1970, 12. For Kautsky's position, see, for example, Noonan 2017, 19.
[50] Quoted in Cheng and Yang 2020, 1338.
[51] Quoted in Makalani 2011, 81.
[52] See, for example, Colás 1994, 522.

Lenin urged Marxists to be open to supporting all anti-colonial move-ments even if they had a "bourgeois-democratic" character. In his view, anti-colonial movements of any kind would help to weaken global capi-talism. He also argued that countries with feudal conditions needed to go through a bourgeois revolution first in order to lay the conditions for a later proletarian-led socialist revolution. As we shall see in the next chapter, Lenin's endorsement of this two-step revolutionary path was challenged by many Marxists elsewhere in the world. It also became increasingly controversial in Moscow when non-Marxist leaders sup-ported by the Comintern repressed local Communists in places such as Turkey in the early 1920s and China in 1927. In 1928, the Comin-tern declared an end to its support for bourgeois-nationalist movements, although that position was softened after 1935, when the Soviet Union's leadership sought wider allies to fight fascism.[53]

When it became clear that the Russian revolution was not triggering worldwide revolutions any time soon, the Soviet leadership was forced to confront another controversial issue: the nature of their country's engagement with the capitalist world economy. Marx did not provide much guidance on this issue since he had assumed revolutions would be contagious and that socialism would exist in the context of a federation of leading socialist countries.[54] There were, however, some thinkers who before 1917 had discussed the issue of how individual socialist states might operate within global capitalism.

One was Georg Vollmar, a German socialist interested in Marx's ideas, whose 1879 book *The Isolated Socialist State* suggested that a socialist revolution in one country was more likely to occur than simul-taneous revolutions across many. In that scenario, Vollmar suggested that a socialist state could flourish within global capitalism because of its superior economic efficiency arising from domestic planning and a state monopoly of foreign trade. He seemed to anticipate this socialist state pursuing neomercantilist policies in ways that made it "the *securest* trading firm in the world" with "the most favourable position conceiv-able on the world market". In a prediction perhaps relevant to the place of communist China in the global economy of the early twentieth-first century, he even argued that it would have "a much greater influence on the world market than [the world market] on it".[55]

Others argued that socialism in one state would need more autarkic policies, such as Carl Ballod, a prominent Latvian scholar in Germany

[53] See, for example, Fowkes and Gökay 2009; Hoston 1994, 35–36.
[54] van Ree 2010.
[55] Quotes in van Ree 2010, 148. See also the earlier views of the German socialist Ferdinand Lassalle (van Ree 2010, 147).

who was also influenced by Marx. In his 1898 book *A Look into the Future State*, Ballod argued – like Vollmar – that it was "completely unthinkable that the whole earth will turn socialist in one blow". In contrast to Vollmar, however, he argued that a single socialist state would need to be a "closed state, which produces all it requires on its own territory", a territory that would have to include colonies in the case of Germany.[56] Kautsky wrote a forward for the book and it was widely read and republished in subsequent editions in 1919, 1920, and 1927. Among its readers was Lenin who, according to Nicholas Balabkins, "knew this work well and made copious notes on it".[57]

### Socialism in One Country?

In the first few years after the revolution, the Russian leadership seemed inclined towards a relatively autarkic economic strategy as it repudiated foreign debts, introduced a more centrally planned economy with tight controls on foreign trade, and faced an external blockade. In the early 1920s, however, it normalized economic relations with capitalist powers and began to import capital and technology from them to help modernize the Soviet economy. That new policy continued even after Joseph Stalin came to power in 1924 and declared his commitment to "socialism in one country". The phrase endorsed the idea the Soviet Union could thrive as a single socialist state, but it did not necessarily mean a commitment to new autarkic goals. Indeed, Stalin's government continued, and even expanded, its imports of capital, technology, and machinery, paid for by increased exports of grain and other primary goods. Even in the depths of the Great Depression when Soviet trade collapsed (as did that of most countries), Soviet authorities signed many new agreements with foreign companies and emphasized in 1932 that their country's industrialization was "not designed to reduce imports in general, and imports of machinery and installations in particular".[58] Indeed, Oscar Sanchez-Sibony notes that Soviet trade declined less than that of most other countries in the early 1930s.[59]

Stalin's commitment to the idea of "socialism in one country" was controversial in Marxist circles. Its most prominent critic was Leon Trotsky, who had been a key figure in the 1917 revolution but who was exiled by Stalin in 1928 and murdered by the latter's agents in 1940. One of Trotsky's concerns was whether Soviet socialism could survive in a context where

---

[56] Quotes in van Ree 2010, 152.
[57] Balabkins 1973, 115.
[58] Quote in Dohan 1976, 634. See also Link 2020; Sanchez-Sibony 2014a.
[59] Sanchez-Sibony 2014b, ch. 1 (especially p. 54).

capitalist powers were militarily and economically superior. He also worried that the "productive forces" of socialism would be held back by the failure to create a wider international economic space of socialist societies. Further, Trotsky had long argued that rule by the Russian proletariat was unlikely to last in the face of peasant resistance without support from European socialist states. As he put it in 1906: "Without the direct State support of the European proletariat the working class of Russia cannot remain in power and convert its temporary domination into a lasting socialistic dictatorship".[60]

Trotsky's arguments drew on a larger theoretical framework he developed to challenge the idea that industrial capitalism developed in each country in a linear manner following Europe's path. In his view, each country's trajectory was influenced instead by the "uneven and combined development" of global capitalism as a whole. By "uneven", he meant that the initial emergence of capitalism in Western Europe had transformed the conditions in which capitalism subsequently grew elsewhere. By "combined", he referred to the fact that distinct modes of production could co-exist within one country in this context. In the Russian case, he noted that its industrialization had been promoted by elites to address economic and geopolitical competition from Western Europe and that it had been made possible with imports of capital and technology from the latter. That global context for the emergence of Russian capitalism had, he argued, generated a modern proletariat with revolutionary socialist views that co-existed with a large peasant population in a semi-feudal state.[61]

With this theoretical framework, Trotsky justified a proletarian revolution in Russia despite the fact that its context was very different from that of Western European countries. But his framework also highlighted how that revolution took place in a global context that would constrain it via the international nature of capitalist production as well as the hostility and power of dominant capitalist states. The revolution would survive, he argued, only if it provoked socialist revolutions abroad. At the same time, he held out hope for that outcome since it would be consistent with the interconnected ways in which societies evolved in the global capitalist system. In 1935, he called for the creation of a Fourth International devoted to this kind of revolutionary internationalism, which he argued Stalin had betrayed with his focus on "socialism in one country". By 1938, a small body of this kind had been created that brought together Trotsky's followers.[62]

Although Marxists were unsuccessful in triggering socialist revolutions beyond Russia before 1945, what kind of international economic relations

---

[60] Quoted in van Ree 1998, 110, 88.
[61] For Trotsky's ideas, see, for example, Rosenberg 2020.
[62] See, for example, Høgsbjerg 2017.

did they hope to construct among a future collectivity of socialist states? Although Marx said little about this issue, he seemed to anticipate an integrated socialist world economy. As noted above, he argued that capitalism had created "the material basis of the new world", which included "universal intercourse founded upon the mutual dependency of mankind, and the means of that intercourse". Others echoed this general idea, such as Luxemburg, who ended her 1913 book with the statement that socialism sought to develop "the productive forces of the entire globe" and was thus a "universal system of economy".[63] In 1920, the Comintern also clearly anticipated an integrated global socialist economy and one that was subject to centralized planning: "All state barriers which tend to subdivide the entire system of production, must be removed. The Supreme Economic Council of the Imperialists of the Entente must be replaced by the Supreme Economic Council of the world proletariat, to effect a centralized exploitation of all the economic resources of mankind".[64]

The idea that an integrated global economy could be actively planned and managed by governments to serve socialist goals also appealed to some Marxists who refused to support the Comintern. For example, it was backed by the Labour and Socialist International (LSI), a loosely organized body created in 1923 to bring together Marxists (including Kautsky) and non-Marxist socialists who were opposed to the Comintern. Like the Second International, this body was dominated by Europeans and especially by the German Social Democratic Party.[65] Its 1925 congress rejected the dichotomy between "protectionism" and "anarchic free-trade", calling instead for "organised trade" under the control of the League of Nations as well as a "Collective International Economic Council" that would "regulate consumption, international production, currency and transport relations, [and] raw material distribution".[66]

Prominent within LSI debates was Rudolf Hilferding, an Austrian thinker whose 1910 work *Finance Capital* had contributed to Marxist theories of imperialism.[67] After the Russian revolution, he became very critical of the Soviet regime and emerged as the leading economic thinker in the German Social Democratic Party (serving twice as the country's finance minister, in 1923 and 1928). Hilferding endorsed free trade as a force for peace, but he also argued in 1925 that "economic competition between nations for conquest of markets must be replaced by cooperation". In 1931, he reiterated this point, calling for both "the removal

[63] Luxemburg [1913]1963, 467.
[64] Communist International 1920, 13.
[65] Imlay 2016, 232.
[66] Quoted in Shaev 2018, 266–67.
[67] Hilferding [1910]1981.

of unhealthy protectionism" and "*international cooperation* under the leadership of the League of Nations and the International Labour Organization ... to replace the chaos wrought by economic nationalism with a well-planned order of world-wide exchange".[68] Hilferding's reference to the International Labour Organization, which had been created in 1919 as part of the League of Nations, highlighted its important role in non-Soviet socialist visions of a more managed world economy, including through its support for international labour standards. The latter had been a key topic of discussion in the Second International and even among much earlier socialists such as Robert Owen.[69]

## Conclusion

With their focus on ending class inequality and exploitation by challenging capitalism, Marxists presented a distinctive perspective on the international dimensions of political economy that prioritized goals very different from those of economic liberals and neomercantilists in the pre-1945 years. As with the other two perspectives, there were many disagreements among European Marxists, including over the question that divided economic liberals from neomercantilists: the merits of free trade. As we have seen, Marx himself came down on both sides of the issue at different times in his life.[70] Other intra-Marxist disputes related to issues that caused division within both liberal and neomercantilist circles such as the desirability of imperialism or of multilateral cooperation.

Many of the quarrels among European Marxists, however, concerned issues distinctive to the content of their worldview, such as strategies for challenging capitalism, the prospects for socialism in one country, and the relationship between capitalism and war. These disagreements also highlighted some important policy prescriptions that got little attention from the liberal and neomercantilist thinkers discussed in previous chapters. One was the idea of autarky, a policy that found wider support among some quite different thinkers who will be discussed in Chapter 8. A second was the idea of international economic planning, a policy that also generated interest (in a less ambitious way) among the embedded liberal thinkers discussed in Chapter 14.

---

[68] Quotes in Shaev 2018, 265, 266, emphasis in original. See also Noonan 2017, 39–40; Smaldone 1988.

[69] Murphy 1994, 74–75.

[70] Lenin also changed his mind on the issue (Palen 2021). Disagreements over free trade were also apparent among non-Marxist socialists (e.g. Trentmann 1997).

The Global Diffusion of Marxist Thought

European Marxism diffused widely to other parts of the world in the late nineteenth and early twentieth centuries. Its content encouraged this diffusion since *The Communist Manifesto* had appealed to workers "of all lands" to unite in a common struggle against capitalism.[1] The success of the Russian revolution was particularly important in encouraging the spread of Marxist thought across the world. Not only did it raise the profile of Marxism among radical thinkers around the globe, but it also brought to power a regime devoted to cultivating revolutionary sentiment worldwide through the Third International.

Previous chapters have shown how the international circulation of classical economic liberalism and neomercantilism was accompanied by extensive adaptation of those worldviews. The same was true of Marxism when it was embraced outside of the European context. This chapter examines adaptations made by Marxist thinkers in a number of places, including Japan, India, China, Indonesia, Peru, and the Caribbean. Each of these figures made important contributions to Marxist debates that found wide audiences both in various local contexts and sometimes in wider international Marxist circles.

## Marxism Comes to Japan

One place where Marxist thought gained early supporters beyond Europe was in Japan. The early Japanese interest was somewhat ironic given that Marx himself showed little interest in the country. European Marxist theories of imperialism in the early twentieth century also did not devote extensive attention to Japan's acquisition of colonies in Taiwan (1895) and Korea (1910). The task of analyzing the causes and consequences of this non-European imperialism from a Marxist perspective was largely left to Japanese thinkers themselves.

---

[1] Marx and Engels [1848]2004, 94.

The key intellectual innovator on this topic was Kōtoku Shūsui, a journalist and political activist who emerged as the leading socialist thinker in Japan in the early twentieth century and who helped translate *The Communist Manifesto*. In 1901, Kōtoku published *Imperialism: Monster of the Twentieth Century* which criticized not just European imperial expansion but also Japan's annexation of Taiwan and its military participation in the repression of China's Boxer rebellion in 1900 by foreign powers. His book attracted extensive attention in Japan and was quickly translated into Chinese and Korean. It was later banned by the Japanese government after Kōtoku was executed in 1911 at the age of forty for an alleged plot to kill the emperor.[2]

In his 1901 book, Kōtoku argued that European and American imperialism was driven not just by "the military caste and the politicians who feed their vanity by such exploits", but also by capitalists who sought foreign markets to make up for domestic "overproduction". That overproduction, he argued, resulted from "the lack of purchasing power of the majority of the population, the unjust distribution of income, and the growing divide between the rich and the poor" in Europe and the United States. In his view, the establishment of "a socialist system" would be a much better model for them to pursue: "the economic problems in the countries of Europe and the United States today will not be solved by oppressing the population of underdeveloped societies and making them buy their manufactured products, but rather by greatly boosting the purchasing power of the vast majority of people in their own countries".[3]

Kōtoku suggested Japan's acquisition of colonies was even more foolish. He noted that "the Japanese people do not have a surplus of capital to invest in these new territories or an abundance of manufactured products to sell to these new markets". Rather than responding to economic pressures, Japanese imperial expansion was being undertaken primarily "to raise the prestige of the nation, to project its power, and to decorate the chests of our military officers with ribbons and medals".[4] He predicted that the financial costs to Japan of military expansion and colonial rule would bankrupt the country and lead to widening domestic inequality as elites benefitted while the masses became poorer.

Well before Lenin, Kōtoku also warned that economic rivalry between imperialist powers would lead to worldwide war: "how will they manage to keep their frantic competition within bounds when they run out of lands and new markets to capture?" In addition, he was very critical of the impact of imperialism on the colonized, arguing that imperialism

---

[2] See Notehelfer 1971; Tierney 2015.
[3] Quotes from Kōtoku [1901]2015, 203, 196–97.
[4] Quotes from Kōtoku [1901]2015, 199, 204.

did "not signify the implanting of civilization overseas but rather the destruction of other civilizations" and the plundering of their "wealth and resources". Kōtoku argued that imperialism and war could only be ended by "a revolutionary movement worldwide in scope" that ushered in a world "where the common people rule themselves" and "in which the workers own all in common".[5] Like Luxemburg, he was also sceptical of anti-colonial movements driven by nationalism, a sentiment which he saw as a kind of false consciousness undermining the drive for what he called (in another publication) "worldwide socialism" and the prospects for a world government in the future.[6]

Robert Tierney highlights how some of Kōtoku's ideas about the causes of imperialism were strongly influenced by the British liberal thinker John MacKinnon Robertson, whose 1898 book *Patriotism and Empire* developed arguments that were similar to many of Hobson's (discussed in the previous chapter of this book).[7] But Kōtoku's arguments about the distinctiveness of Japanese imperialism were his own and they challenged the Eurocentric focus of well-known European analyses of imperialism at the time. Kōtuko also went beyond Robertson when arguing that capitalist imperialism would lead to war and especially when linking his theory of imperialism to the Marxist goal of worldwide revolution. Well before Lenin added a Marxist spin to Hobson's liberal analysis, Kōtoku did the same with Robertson's.

Marxism became much more influential in Japan in the 1920s, with Lenin's work attracting particular attention. Much debate centered around the applicability of Lenin's theory of imperialism to Japan's situation. Particularly prominent was an analysis in 1927 by Takahashi Kamekichi, a journalist who had already published a prominent Marxist interpretation of Japan's economic development. In his 1927 work, Takahashi insisted that Lenin's theory did not explain Japan's distinctive kind of "petty bourgeois imperialism".[8] According to Takahashi, instead of representing the highest stage of capitalism, Japan's imperialism responded to the country's unique status as a late industrializing country needing resources in a global context where dominant powers had abandoned free trade for spheres of influence. Further challenging Lenin's ideas (and closer to those of Kautsky), Takahashi argued that the status quo imperial powers had decided that they had more to gain by dividing up the world in this way than by fighting.[9]

---

[5] Quotes from Kōtoku [1901]2015, 197–98, 202, 187, 206.
[6] Quoted in Tierney 2015, 63.
[7] Tierney 2015. See Robertson 1899.
[8] Quoted in Hoston 1986, 48.
[9] Hoston 1984, 12fn27.

By highlighting the distinctive external constraints facing late industrializers such as Japan, Takahashi also challenged Marx's argument in *Capital* (see previous chapter) that "the country that is more developed industrially only shows, to the less developed, the image of its own future".[10] As Takahashi put it, "the path of historical development in backward countries occurs under conditions that differ substantially from those in advanced countries".[11] This analysis also led Takahashi to an opposite normative stance from that of Kōtoku (and most other Japanese Marxists at the time as well as the Comintern): one of supporting Japanese imperialism. In his view, Japan's style of imperialism was fully justified to enable the country's capitalist development in the global economic order that was dominated by Europe and the United States. Capitalist development would then foster the growth of Japan's proletariat, laying the foundation for a socialist revolution.[12]

Takahashi added one more controversial argument: Japan's "petty bourgeois imperialism" could liberate the rest of Asia from outside powers. As he put it, "just as the interests of the petite bourgeoisie coincide with those of the proletariat and are not one with the interests of the grande bourgeoisie, the interests of petty imperialist countries coincide more with those of countries subject to imperialism than with those of large imperialist countries". He also added a racial element to this analysis, arguing that Japan would lead Asia in fighting against "exploitation" by the "white races" from America and Europe.[13] Takahashi subsequently became a consultant to Japan's colonial administration in Taiwan and Manchukuo, and was increasingly linked to pro-imperialist right-wing nationalist groups after Japan's invasion of China in 1937.

Another Japanese Marxist who deserves brief mention is Sano Manabu. Sano was a teacher of economics at Waseda University who helped to establish the Japanese Communist Party in 1922. After being arrested in 1929, he became a leading figure in the "tenkō" movement in 1933 in which hundreds of communists renounced their membership in the Communist Party. He was provoked by the Comintern's intense criticism of Japanese imperialism and its strong attacks on the Japanese emperor system, a system Sano believed was an "expression of national unity which lessened the brutality of domestic class opposition, brought equilibrium to social life and facilitated change as society underwent reforms".[14]

---

[10]  Marx [1867]1976, 91.
[11]  Quoted in Hoston 1984, 24.
[12]  Hoston 1994, 235.
[13]  Takahashi quotes from Hoston 1986, 81; 1984, 21.
[14]  Quoted in Wagner 1978, 100. See also Hoston 1983, 113; 1994.

After this point, Sano remained committed to Marxism, but argued that Japan needed its own distinctive version that fit its national identity and broader "Oriental" values that were less materialist. He was also inspired by Stalin's idea of socialism in one country, but interpreted it creatively to mean that communists "would not have to become defenders of the Soviet Union". He also widened the idea to argue that Japan should be part of a regional "enlarged one-state socialist bloc" including other East Asian peoples who shared a common cultural tradition. As he put it, "the formation of a socialist league of Japan, China, and Korea first, rather than vague internationalism, is possible, and furthermore, a necessary aim".[15]

## Mariátegui's Peruvian Marxism

Latin America was another region that attracted little attention from Marx and the subsequent European theorists of imperialism. Even the Comintern itself developed no formal theory about the region before 1928. Latin American Marxists themselves, however, developed some innovative ideas about how Marxist thought might be adapted to their region. The most important and influential of them was José Carlos Mariátegui, a Peruvian became attracted to Marxism while living in Italy briefly between 1919 and 1923. Mariátegui became a well-known figure across Latin America because of his editing of a journal (*Amauta*) that circulated widely across the region as well as because of his writing (especially his 1928 book *Seven Interpretative Essays on Peruvian Reality*) and his political activities (which included founding the Socialist Party of Peru in 1928). Like Kōtoku, he died young, but in this case from health difficulties in 1930 at the age of thirty-five.[16]

Mariátegui was very interested in how Marxist analyses of imperialism could be applied to his region. While most countries in the region were not formally colonized when he was writing, Mariátegui insisted they "function economically as colonies of European and North American industry and finance" because "all of them are, more or less, producers of raw materials and foodstuffs that they sent to Europe and the United States, from which they receive machinery, manufactured goods, etc". In the case of his own country, Mariátegui argued that its reliance on commodity exporting – and the prices of those commodities set in London and New York – left it in a position of "economic dependency". He also noted that commodity production was dominated by foreign firms that made little contribution to the local economy and exploited Indigenous peoples

---

[15] Sano quotes from Hoston 1994, 351; Wagner 1978, 99, 103; Hoston 1994, 352.
[16] Helleiner and Rosales 2017.

"to the extreme" and "with the assistance of the national bourgeoisies". Indeed, Mariátegui was sceptical more generally about the impact of foreign investment, noting that "the profits from mining, commerce, transportation and such do not stay in Peru" but left the nation "in the form of dividends, interest, etc".[17] His views contrasted with Lenin's suggestion (noted in the last chapter) that foreign investment "greatly accelerates the development of capitalism in those countries to which it is exported".[18]

Mariátegui did not think that Latin American capitalist economies could escape their *de facto* colonial status: "The Latin American countries came late to capitalist competition. The inside lanes had already been assigned. The destiny of these countries in the capitalist order is that of being simple colonies". He also argued that their subordinate status was likely to intensify with further capitalist growth: "the economic condition of these republics is undoubtedly semi-colonial, and this characteristic of their economies tends to be accentuated as capitalism, and therefore imperialist penetration, develops". For these reasons, he insisted on the need for a socialist revolution. But he also noted, without much explanation, that "the task of socialism, when it comes to power in the country, depending on the hour and the historical compass to which it must adjust, will to a great degree be the realization of capitalism, or better, the realization of the historical possibilities that capitalism still contains, in the sense that this serves the interests of social progress".[19]

Mariátegui also did not provide much detail about the kinds of policies that might be needed to reduce Latin American dependency in the future. Indeed, he acknowledged that the task of ending Peru's commodity exporting role would be a difficult one: "Because of its disadvantageous position in terms of geography, human resources, and technology, Peru cannot dream of becoming a manufacturing country in the near future. For many years it will have to continue its role in the world economy as exporter of primary products, foodstuffs, et cetera". At the same time, he called for "Peruvianizing, nationalizing, emancipating our economy". He also praised free trade on the following grounds: "Free trade as an idea and as practice was a step toward internationalism in which the proletariat will recognize one of its desired ends, one of its ideals. Economic borders are weakened. This event strengthened the hope of a day to come when political borders no longer exist".[20]

---

[17]   Quotes in Helleiner and Rosales 2017, 679.

[18]   Lenin [1916]1970, 63.

[19]   Quotes in Pearlman 1996, 89, 130, 83–4.

[20]   Quotes in Helleiner and Rosales 2017, 680. Other Latin American socialists also cited this reason for supporting free trade, such as Juan Baustista Justo, founder of the Argentine Socialist Party in 1896 (Helleiner and Rosales 2017, 680n9).

Mariátegui became particularly well known for his distinctive ideas about the politics of revolutionary struggle. Although he agreed with Lenin that nationalism was a "revolutionary" force in regions subject to imperialism, he challenged the idea that Marxists in Latin America should join with bourgeois forces in a united front. He insisted that "only the socialist revolution can stand as a definitive and real barrier to the advance of imperialism". He also did not think bourgeois forces could be trusted to join a nationalist cause because they were too closely allied with imperialist forces and because of the distinctive racial politics of Latin America. As he put it, race "keeps the question of the struggle for national independence in those American countries with a large percentage of indigenous people from paralleling the same problem in Asia or Africa". He elaborated: "The feudal or bourgeois elements in our countries feel the same contempt for Indians, as well as for Blacks and mulattos, as do the white imperialists. This racist sentiment among the dominant class acts in a way absolutely favorable to imperialist penetration ... The solidarity of racism and prejudice joins class solidarity in making the national bourgeoisies the docile instruments of Yankee or British imperialism".[21]

Mariátegui also insisted that a Peruvian revolutionary movement needed to be inclusive of Indigenous peoples. Because the Peruvian people were "four-fifths Indian", he noted that "our socialism would not be Peruvian – nor would it be socialism – if it did not establish its solidarity principally with the Indian's vindications". He also argued that "we have inherited instinctively the idea of socialism" from the Inkans, who he described as having had "the most advanced primitive communist organization that history has known". In this way, Mariátegui linked Indigenous values to the worldwide socialist ideals, while also highlighting the distinctiveness of Latin American socialism. Regarding the latter, he noted that "we certainly do not wish socialism in America to be a copy and imitation. ... We must give life to an Indo-American socialism reflecting our own reality and in our own language".[22]

As part of his emphasis on the uniqueness of Latin American socialism, Mariátegui kept his distance from the Comintern, naming his political party a "socialist" one in 1928 instead of a "communist" one. That choice was strongly criticized by the Comintern, which declared his thought "no more advanced than the ideas of old-fashioned *petit bourgeois* socialism". Earlier in 1923, however, Mariátegui applauded the Third International for recognizing that "the social revolution must not be a European revolution, but a world revolution", while criticizing the

---

[21] Quotes in Helleiner and Rosales 2017, 681, 683, 682.
[22] Quotes in Vanden and Becker 2011, 52; Helleiner and Rosales 2017, 683–84.

Second International for its indifference to "the fate of Asian and African workers" and for promoting a form of internationalism that "ended at the borders of the West, at the boundaries of Western civilization". In 1929, he also emphasized the principle of solidarity with European revolutionaries, arguing that "in our struggle against foreign imperialism we are fulfilling our duty of solidarity with the revolutionary masses of Europe".[23]

## Indian and Chinese Contributions

The Comintern's orthodoxy was also challenged by the Indian thinker and activist Manabendra Nath Roy, but in a more direct way within the Comintern itself. Growing up in Bengal, Roy was active in the *swadeshi* movement in 1905 (see Chapter 5) and then more radical anti-colonial activism before leaving India in 1915 and traveling in Asia, the United States, and Mexico. While in the latter, he converted to Marxism in 1919 and helped to establish the Mexican Communist Party. He then represented that party at the Second World Congress of the Comintern, which took place in Moscow the next year.[24]

At that meeting, Roy challenged European Marxists who believed that imperialism was a progressive economic force in colonized regions (just as Mariátegui would soon do in Latin America):

Foreign imperialism, imposed on the Eastern peoples prevented them from developing, socially and economically, side by side with their fellows in Europe and America. Owing to the imperialist policy of preventing industrial development in the colonies, a proletarian class, in the strict sense of the word, could not come into existence there until recently. Skilled craft industries were destroyed to make room for the products of the centralized industries in the imperialist countries; consequently a majority of the population was driven to the land to produce food grains and raw materials for export to foreign lands.[25]

Roy also disagreed very publicly with Lenin about the relative importance of anti-colonial movements in the overall anti-capitalist struggle. Pointing to the economic significance of colonies – particularly in Asia – as sources of resources and income for global capitalism, he argued that the revolutionary movements in the East would determine the fate of their European counterparts.[26] Roy further challenged Lenin's draft policy for the 1920 conference, which suggested that the Comintern should back "bourgeois-democratic liberation" movements in colonized

---

[23] Quotes from Helleiner and Rosales 2017, 682, 678.
[24] Roy 1997, ch. 1; Spenser 2008.
[25] Quoted in d'Encausse and Schram 1969, 161.
[26] d'Encausse and Schram 1969, 151–52.

regions that opposed imperialism. Roy objected on the grounds that the bourgeoisie in colonies with relatively advanced economies could not be trusted because they were often allied with imperialist forces and held reactionary views. He urged the Comintern to focus instead on organizing peasants and workers and supporting communist parties in colonized regions. His general view bore some similarities to that of Mariátegui, but it was also informed more specifically by the Indian context. Roy was particularly worried that Lenin's draft policy would lead the Comintern to support Mohandas Gandhi (see Chapter 8), a figure who impressed Lenin but who was seen by Roy as a social reactionary.[27]

Lenin agreed to modify his draft on this latter point, but insisted that cooperation with bourgeois movements should not be ruled out. The resolution approved by the Comintern reflected this compromise by urging support for the more ambiguously labelled "revolutionary-liberation" movements.[28] In this way, Roy's intervention had an important influence in shaping the Comintern's formal policy towards colonized regions. In practice, however, Lenin's preferences subsequently drove the Comintern's policy in this area in the early 1920s, as the Comintern backed non-Communist movements such as the Kemalists in Turkey and Sun Yat-sen's Guomindang (GMD) in China.[29]

But the issue remained a controversial one within the Comintern, particularly after Sun's successor, Chiang Kai-shek, massacred local communists in 1927. The Comintern had urged the Chinese Communist Party (CCP), after its founding in 1921, to ally with the GMD in a united anti-imperialist front. This forced cooperation was made easier by the fact that leading Chinese Marxists agreed on the initial need to prioritize nationalism over class struggle and found Lenin's theory of imperialism attractive.[30] The developments of 1927, however, encouraged the Comintern to shift towards Roy's 1920 position of being more sceptical of bourgeois nationalist movements (at least until 1935, when the threat of fascism prompted a new interest in broad-based anti-fascist alliances).[31]

Ironically, Roy himself found his position within the Comintern dramatically undermined by these same events in China. After rising within the Comintern hierarchy since 1920, Roy had been sent by the organization to try to help reconcile the GMD and CCP in 1927. When he failed, Roy rapidly lost influence, culminating in his expulsion from the Comintern

---

[27] Derrick 2008, 111; Chowduri 2007, 34, 53–54.
[28] Quoted in d'Encausse and Schram,1969, 153.
[29] d'Encausse and Schram 1969, 29; North and Eubin 1963.
[30] For these views, see d'Encausse and Schram,1969, 54; Hoston 1994, 279–83; Zanasi 2020, 191–92.
[31] Fowkes and Gökay 2009.

in 1929.[32] He then returned to India, where he was jailed. When he was released, he turned his back on communism, joined Gandhi's Indian National Congress, and embraced what he called a "radical humanism".[33]

Chinese Marxism was also influenced by these events. They encouraged Chinese communists to consider interpretations of Marxism that were different from those of the Comintern and of foreigners more generally. Particularly important were the views of Mao Zedong who, after consolidating his leadership of the CCP in the mid-1930s, challenged the universal pretentions of European Marxist thought by calling in 1938 for a "Sinification of Marxism". He defined this process as making Marxism "exhibit a Chinese character in all its manifestations, that is to say, applying it in accordance with China's characteristics".[34] He elaborated on this idea in 1940 when arguing that the bourgeois-nationalist stage in China's development (that preceded the move to a socialist society) should be a "new democracy" governed by a coalition of all revolutionary classes, including workers, peasants, and national capitalists. He also suggested that industrialization was key and that Sun's ideas should form the basis for policy in this stage.[35]

### Tan Malaka's Indonesian Marxism

Another interesting adaptation of European Marxism came from the colony of the Dutch East Indies (which became Indonesia at independence), where one of the first communist parties outside Russia – the Partai Komunis Indonesia (PKI) – was created in 1920. Although the PKI quickly affiliated with the Comintern, Indonesian Marxists soon challenged the latter's ideas, particularly on the issue of the relationship between Marxism and Islam. The issue arose because the Comintern called in 1920 on communists everywhere "to struggle against Pan-Islamism", a statement reflecting the Soviet leadership's concern about growing resistance to their rule from Muslims in central Asia (for a discussion of Pan-Islamism, see Chapter 12).[36] The Comintern statement was not made with the Indonesian context in mind, but it triggered strong opposition from many Indonesian Marxists.

At the time, many of them had joined a nationalist Islamic group, Sareket Islam (SI), which was colony's largest mass organization. They

---

[32] Chowduri 2007, 77; North and Eubin 1963; Wu 1969.
[33] Quote in Goebel 2014, 489.
[34] Quotes in Wylie 1979, 472.
[35] Mao quote from Gregor and Chang 1989, 119. See also Gregor 2000, 75; Hoston 374, 385; Jiang 2012, 154–55.
[36] Quoted in d'Encausse and Schram,1969, 153.

sought to push the SI in more radical anti-capitalist directions by citing Koranic text expressing concern for poorer people and critiquing
inequality and greed. But the 1920 Comintern statement dramatically
undermined their efforts to emphasize the compatibility between Marxism and Islam. It also empowered conservatives within the SI to portray
Marxists as enemies of Islam. By 1921, SI conservatives had successfully
pushed for a policy to eject all PKI members.[37]

In this context, it is not surprising that PKI members urged the Comintern to reconsider its opposition to Pan-Islamism. Particularly prominent in this role was Tan Malaka, a young PKI activist who emerged as
the leading Indonesian Marxist thinker in the interwar years. Initially
from West Sumatra, Tan Malaka had first encountered Marxism when
studying in Holland between 1913 and 1919 to become a teacher. After
returning to Indonesia, he had taught workers on a Sumatran rubber
plantation, an experience that encouraged a deep opposition to Dutch
colonialism and a desire to help the Indonesian working class. He conceptualized that help in Marxist terms, calling in his first article for a
communist publication in 1920 for "the organisation and education of
the proletariat, the organisation of class struggle for the achievement of
the objective of the overthrow of the capitalist system and the introduction of planned production on the basis of communist principles".[38]

After securing a teaching position at a PKI school in Java in 1921, Tan
Malaka quickly rose in the party to become its chair by the end of that
year. In that role, he urged the SI to see the benefits of cooperating with
the PKI, arguing that Muslims and communists were natural allies in the
anti-imperialist struggle. Tan Malaka's interest in this issue was not just
tactical. He had been born into a devout Muslim family and continued to
value Islam highly after his conversion to Marxism. As he noted later in his
life, "even though the events of 1917 stirred up a flooding wave of passion
in my pemuda heart, carrying me away and sweeping me along down-
stream to the present day, my interest in Islam has always continued".[39]

After being expelled from Indonesia in early 1922, Tan Malaka was
welcomed by the Dutch communist party in Holland, where he spoke
out against Dutch colonialism and encouraged the party to include the
liberation of Indonesia in its 1922 election platform. Like Naoroji in
Britain (see Chapter 3), he even ran for office in that election (unsuccessfully), becoming the first Indonesian ever to do so. He then ended
up in Moscow at the 1922 Comintern congress, where he appealed

---

[37] See, for example, Cribb 1985; Fowkes and Gokay 2009; Landau 1990, ch. 3; McVey 1965.
[38] Quoted in Jarvis 1987, 42.
[39] Quoted in Mrázek 1972, 29. See also p. 32; Jarvis 1987; McVey 1965, 103, 116–18.

directly to the delegates to reverse the Comintern's 1920 condemnation of Pan-Islamism. He explained how the Comintern's stance on this issue had been used against the PKI and he criticized communists outside Asia for trying to influence the region without adequate knowledge of it. Supported by a delegate from Tunis, he urged the Comintern to recognize the benefits of an alliance between communism and Islam to fight imperialism: "At present Pan-Islamism is a national-liberation struggle, because Islam for the Moslems is everything: not only religion, but also the state, the economic system, the food, in fact everything. ... This fraternity is called the liberation struggle against the British, French, and Italian capitalists, consequently against world capitalism". The Congress responded by approving an alliance of the PKI and SI, while reiterating its broader criticism of Pan-Islamism.[40]

The issue of the PKI's relationship with SI was linked to the broader theoretical debate between Roy and Lenin over the question of whether communist parties in colonial regions should be working with non-communist nationalist movements. Indeed, at the 1922 Congress, Tan Malaka opposed the stance of Roy (who had also expressed his scepticism of Pan-Islamism). But the PKI also rejected the idea that Indonesia first needed a bourgeois revolution to set the conditions for socialism. Instead, Indonesian Marxists were united in the belief – closer to Roy's – that the anti-imperialist struggle should lead directly to the establishment of a socialist state. When colonial authorities became increasingly repressive, the PKI attempted to start a revolution in late 1926, but with disastrous results that set back the communist cause for the rest of the colonial period.[41]

Tan Malaka opposed the PKI's decision from abroad, arguing that the PKI did not yet have enough support among the people. The events then prompted him to end his relationship with the PKI as well as with the Comintern, which had cited the revolution positively as evidence of the advanced nature of revolutionary sentiment in Asia. He created a new party that was explicitly independent from outside forces and whose 1929 Manifesto was highly critical of Stalin and the Comintern: "It would be in the interests of imperialism and not of the Indies if Stalin were to make himself master of an eventual revolutionary movement in the Netherlands Indies ... the Moscow leadership is good only for Russia. ... The entire Third International is built up in the Russian interest". Tan Malaka did not return to Indonesia until 1942, when he continued his anti-imperialist work by countering Japanese propaganda during its rule of the territory.[42]

---

[40] Quoted in McVey 1965, 162. See also pp. 163, 236–38, 420fn24.
[41] Jarvis 1987; McVey 1965, 65–66, 129, 160.
[42] Quote in Jarvis 1987, 48–49. See also McVey 1965, 316–17, 330, 350–51; Mrázek 1972.

## Caribbean Marxists

Two final examples of thinkers who modified Marxism in interesting ways in the pre-1945 years both came from the Caribbean island of Trinidad. The first was George Padmore, who became interested in Marxism after leaving the island in 1924 to study in the United States. Attracted by its anti-colonial message, he formally joined the Communist Party in 1927 and then became involved with the International Trade Union Committee of Negro Workers (ITUCNW), which had been created by the Comintern in 1929. In that role, he encouraged Marxists to devote more attention to what he called "race chauvinism".[43]

The relationship between racism and capitalism was not tackled theoretically in Marx's writings. Indeed, Erik van Ree notes that Marx and Engels often "racialized skin-colour groups, ethnicities, nations and social classes, while endowing them with innate superior and inferior character traits".[44] The Second International also did not address the issue in any depth. Indeed, as noted in the previous chapter, some of its members embraced ideologies of imperialism, which were often infused with racism. The Comintern showed more interest in tackling the subject, critiquing those who drew "a line of distinction between races and colors in the matter of human rights" at its 1920 meeting and announcing its commitment to "fight for race equality of the Negro with the white people" in 1922.[45] Although the Comintern initially focused heavily on racism in the United States, it increasingly embraced a more global outlook on the issue, including through the creation of the ITUCNW.[46]

Padmore played an important role in encouraging this more global outlook through his work for the ITUCNW. After organizing a 1930 conference in Hamburg that formally launched the body, he became its leader in late 1931 based in that German city. In that same year, he published *The Life and Struggles of Negro Toilers*, which provided detailed evidence from across the globe to support his view that "the Negro workers are the most exploited, the most oppressed in the world". He called on them to "join forces with their white brothers against the common enemy – World Capitalism". Because he also attributed their exploitation and oppression to "white chauvinism", however, he argued that these workers needed not just to challenge capitalism, but also to wage

---

[43] Padmore [1931]1971, 122. See also Matera 2015, ch. 6.
[44] van Ree 2019, 54 (abstract).
[45] Quotes from Communist International 1920, 25; Turner 2005, 104.
[46] Adi 2013; Weiss 2019.

"the struggle against race chauvinism, against all colour bars, for uniting the workers of all races and nations".[47]

While emphasizing the need for solidarity among these workers, Padmore was very critical of Pan-African movements such as Garveyism (discussed in Chapter 10) that sought to boost solidarity only among Africans and the African diaspora around the world in support of the establishment of an independent African state. In his view, Garveyites overlooked the centrality of class exploitation and used "racial and national consciousness for the purpose of promoting the class interests of the black bourgeoisie and landlords". He accused them of "merely trying to mobilise the Negro workers and peasants to support them in establishing a Negro Republic in Africa, where they would be able to set themselves up as the rulers in order to continue the exploitation of the toilers of their race, free from white imperialist competition". Instead, he insisted that "they must realise that the only way in which they can win their freedom and emancipation is by organising their forces millions strong, and in alliance with the class-conscious white workers in the imperialist countries, as well as the oppressed masses of China, India, Latin America and other colonial and semi-colonial countries, deliver a final blow to world imperialism".[48]

When the Nazis came to power in Germany in 1933, Padmore was deported to London, where he became increasingly critical of the Comintern and then was formally expelled from that organization in 1934. To counter the fascist threat, the Soviet Union had begun to withdraw its support for anti-imperialist activities in order to cultivate better relations with Britain, France, and the United States. Padmore and others were deeply frustrated by this shift in Soviet and Comtinern policy, a frustration that grew deeper when Moscow refused to support Ethiopia against Italy's invasion in 1935.[49] From his new London base, Padmore began to work closely with supporters of the Pan-African movement who were also deeply engaged in the Ethiopian cause (see Chapter 11). In works he published in the late 1930s, Padmore continued to challenge racism associated with colonial rule and now drew parallels to the racism of German fascism at the time. At the same time, he retained his commitment to Marxist ideas. In addition to attributing imperialism to capitalism, he urged Africans to throw off colonial rule as a step towards creating a world socialist federation.[50]

---

[47] Quotes from Padmore 1931, 122, 7.
[48] Quotes from Padmore 1931, 126.
[49] Esedebe 1994, 98–100; Høgsbjerg 2014, 102; Hooker 1967, 31; Weiss 2019.
[50] Derrick 2008, 409–10, 434; Hooker 1967, 58; James 2015, 11, 37–38; Schwarz 2003, 141.

One of the figures Padmore encountered in London was a childhood friend from Trinidad, C. L. R. James, who had arrived in 1932. Already a critic of colonialism, James was soon attracted to Marxist thought, particularly the views of Trotsky. He joined the Troskyite movement in 1934 and was elected to the International Executive Committee of the Fourth International at its founding meeting in 1938.[51] The year before, he also published *World Revolution: The Rise and Fall of the Communist International*, which sought to popularize Trotsky's criticisms of Stalin and the Comintern.

Among other things, the book attacked Stalin's "theory of Socialism in a single country" for turning "the main business of the Communist International" into "the defence of the USSR" rather than international revolution. It also chastised Stalin and the Comintern for encouraging communists worldwide to get ready to fight a war against Germany and Japan when they should have been fostering solidarity among "the working-class movement and the colonial peoples" to "put an end to imperialist barbarity" and "build international socialism". Like Padmore, James was also very critical of the Soviet response to the Italian invasion of Ethiopia. If Stalin had defended Ethiopia, James argued, the invasion could have been checked and "the mass feeling that had been aroused all over the world would have been directed into a single channel under the direction of the Third International".[52]

Like Padmore, James became involved with the Pan-African movement in London and published two important books in 1938 that highlighted the revolutionary agency of the peoples of Africa and the African diaspora. *A History of Negro Revolt* provided an overview of various uprisings from the Haitian revolution to African American struggles for justice and anti-colonial movements in Africa and the Caribbean.[53] His better-known book of that year, *The Black Jacobins*, provided a detailed analysis of the Haitian revolution. In James' Marxist interpretation, Haitian slaves were responding to the imperialist expansion of capitalism by leading the first anti-colonial revolution. He emphasized the key role of race in the story, while also insisting – like Padmore – on the centrality of class dynamics: "The race question is subsidiary to the class question in politics, and to think of imperialism in terms of race is disastrous. But to neglect the racial factor as incidental is an error only less grave than to make it fundamental".[54] At the time he was writing this book,

---

[51] Høgsbjerg 2017; Robinson 1983, ch. 10.
[52] Quotes from James [1937]2017, 222, 400, 373. See also Makalani 2011, 212–21; Matera 2015, ch. 2.
[53] James [1938]2012.
[54] James [1938]1989, 283.

James was close to another Trinidadian, Eric Williams, whose 1938 PhD dissertation at Oxford also highlighted the importance of slavery and the slave trade to the growth of European capitalism (as well as British industrialization more specifically). In his subsequent 1944 book titled *Capitalism and Slavery*, Williams (who had earlier been James' student in Trinidad) argued that "the commercial capitalism of the eighteenth century developed the wealth of Europe by means of slavery and monopoly" and that slavery in the Caribbean had been "basically an economic phenomenon". Williams added that "slavery was not born of racism: rather, racism was the consequence of slavery".[55]

James noted many decades later that his historical analysis of the Haitian revolution was driven by concerns of his day: "I had in mind writing about the San Domingo Revolution as the preparation for the revolution that George Padmore and all of us were interested in, that is, the revolution in Africa".[56] In case readers missed the relevance of the book, James noted near its end that "the blacks of Africa are more advanced, nearer ready than were the slaves of San Domingo".[57] *The Black Jacobins* was also interesting from an IPE standpoint because its very last paragraph highlighted James' rejection of autarkic visions of post-revolutionary Africa: "Nor will success [of a revolution] result in the isolation of Africa. The blacks will demand skilled workmen and teachers. International socialism will need the products of a free Africa far more than the French bourgeoisie needed slavery and the slave-trade".[58] In *World Revolution*, he had also upheld Trotsky's view that socialism needed to embrace the productivity of an integrated world economy, a view that James argued was compatible with the analyses of Marx and Engels:

For thousands of years educated men had solaced themselves with dreams of a Communist society, but the realistic conceptions of scientific Socialism could only arise when the international forces of production had made possible the abundance of commodities. For Marx and Engels, therefore, basing their whole structure on the economic interdependence of the modern world and the consequent political ties, the mere idea of a national Socialism would have been a pernicious absurdity ... "Proletarians of all lands, unite" was no idealistic slogan, but the political expression of economic need. They would not have raised it otherwise.[59]

---

[55]  Williams 1944, 210, 7. For the links between Williams and James, see Matera 2015, ch. 6; Høbsbjerg 2014, 174–77.
[56]  Quoted in Makalani 2011, 222.
[57]  James [1938]1989, 376.
[58]  James [1938]1989, 377.
[59]  James [1937]2017, 81.

## Conclusion

The ideas of European Marxists diffused widely across the world in the pre-1945 era, particularly after the Russian revolution. But many thinkers who were attracted to these ideas also made important contributions to Marxist thought about the international dimensions of political economy. For example, Kōtoku's arguments about the relationship between imperialism, war, and revolution pre-dated the better known ideas of Lenin and Luxemburg on this subject. These thinkers also called attention to issues that received less attention in European Marxist debates, such as the distinctiveness of Japanese imperialism (Kōtoku, Takahashi), external constraints impeding national capitalist development in less powerful regions (Takahashi, Mariátegui, Roy), the significance of race and racism (Takahashi, Mariátegui, Padmore, James), the relationship between Marxism and Islam (Tan Malaka), and the broader Eurocentrism of much Marxist thought (all of the thinkers discussed in this chapter in various ways).

Many of these thinkers also developed innovative ideas about revolutionary politics in places subject to imperialism. Some directly challenged Lenin's ideas about the need for broad-based anti-imperialist alliances (Mariátegui, Roy). Others agreed with Lenin on that point but endorsed different kinds of alliances (Tan Malaka, Mao). Thinkers outside Europe also gave more emphasis to the revolutionary agency of groups such as Indigenous peoples (Mariátegui) and workers in Africa or of African descent (Padmore, James). More generally, most of the thinkers discussed in this chapter were – or became – sceptical of the Comintern's efforts to control Marxist revolutionary movements beyond the Soviet Union. Many were also sceptical of the universal claims of European Marxism, insisting on the need for theory to be adapted to local circumstances and contexts.

*Part II*

Beyond the Three Orthodoxies

# 8    Autarkic Visions of Economic Self-Sufficiency

The first part of this book has explored the three perspectives that have received the most attention in IPE textbook discussions of pre-1945 thought: economic liberalism, neomercantilism, and Marxism. In many countries between the late eighteenth century and 1944, however, debates about international dimensions of political economy involved perspectives with different, although sometimes overlapping, content. These other perspectives deserve more attention, not least because they were sometimes more influential in many specific political contexts than were the three orthodox ones that have received so much attention. They are the subject of the second part of this book.

The first such perspective was an autarkic one. Proponents of economic autarky sought to promote the economic self-sufficiency of their state in order to enhance its autonomy from foreign influence. Autarkists rarely called for complete economic closure (in the same way that few economic liberals endorsed completely free movement of labour, capital, goods, and services across borders). But they highlighted the benefits of cultivating a high degree of economic self-sufficiency for a state as an ideal. This ideal was diametrically opposed to liberal visions of an integrated world economy. It also diverged from the goals of neomercantilists who favoured only strategically targeted forms of protectionism in the context of an open world economy. Chapter 6 noted some Marxist interest in the idea of autarkic socialist states, but autarkism was also not the dominant preference of pre-1945 Marxist thinkers. This chapter focuses on a number of other thinkers who developed this distinctive autarkic goal for their respective countries.[1]

---

[1] Chapter 13 also highlights some autarkic visions for larger regional economic blocs in the 1930s. This chapter uses some material I have previously published in Helleiner 2021b, which provides further details on the autarkic thinkers discussed in this chapter. That article was published open access under the terms of the Creative Commons CC BY license (https://creativecommons.org/licenses/by/4.0/) at https://academic.oup.com/isr/article/23/3/933/6063510 with copyright ©2021 Oxford University Press.

## Fichte's Closed Commercial State

When contemporary IPE scholars neglect autarkic thought, they follow in the footsteps of Adam Smith's *The Wealth of Nations*. In that work, Smith contrasted his views with other "systems of political economy", but did not mention autarkism.[2] Defenders of autarkic policies were, however, prominent within European political economy debates in which Smith was engaged. For example, just before *The Wealth of Nations* was published, the French thinker Jean-Jacques Rousseau – whose work was well known to Smith – backed an autarkic economic vision in two works on practical state-building: *Constitution Project for Corsica* (1765) and *Considerations on the Government of Poland* (1772). In contrast to both mercantilist thought and Smith's liberal vision, Rousseau favoured autarkic policies in order to defend his distinctive vision of a decentralized, egalitarian, frugal, agrarian-based economy in which money played a minimal role and in which a democratic republican form of government could flourish.[3] Smith was also familiar with the work of earlier thinkers who called for autarkic policies for other reasons, such as Sweden's Carl Linnaeus who sought to reduce his country's dependence on foreigners and curtail the export of its precious metals.[4]

In the post-Smithian era that is the focus of this book, the most famous European defense of autarky before the 1930s was developed by a German follower of Rousseau: Johann Fichte. Well known for his republican ideas in the wake of the French revolution, Fichte's autarkic views were outlined in his 1800 book *The Closed Commercial State* that was addressed to a Prussian minister at the time. Like Rousseau, Fichte was critical of commercial societies, but he rejected the French thinker's preference for decentralized agrarian-based economies, arguing that they would only result in "a miserable nation, still half-left-behind in barbarism". Instead, he endorsed a more sophisticated domestic economic structure with industry and an extensive division of labour. Within this structure, he called for a republican state to regulate wages, prices, and employment in ways that promoted egalitarian goals by guaranteeing citizens the right to work and to live "as agreeably as possible".[5] He insisted that this project could work only if it was supported by autarkic policies.

Fichte's main reason for insisting on a "closed" economy was that the government's ability to regulate the domestic economy risked being

---

[2] Quote from the title of Book IV of Smith 1776. Smith discussed the "mercantile system" and the "agricultural systems" of the French physiocrats who emphasized agriculture as the principal source of a country's wealth.

[3] For Rousseau's views, see Helleiner 2021b, 938.

[4] See, for example, Jonsson 2010.

[5] Fichte quotes from Nakhimovsky 2011, 112, 150.

undermined by foreign economic influences, including uncertainties associated with selling to international markets. In his view, all private economic exchanges between national citizens and foreigners needed to be prevented for this reason. To strengthen the government's economic control of the border and the nation's money supply, Fichte also insisted that citizens be forced to convert all gold and silver within the country into a new national currency that was valid only domestically and that comprised the sole money allowed within the country. That reform would also generate funds that could be invested in initiatives to create domestic substitutes for those foreign products that had contributed to citizens' well-being. After a transition period, Fichte argued that the only approved trade would consist of bilateral inter-governmental barter exchanges of produce that compensated for natural climatic differences. Travel abroad would also be controlled, although Fichte made an exception for scholars and artists whose sharing of ideas and culture across borders should continue to be supported because they benefitted the country and humanity.

Fichte also argued that autarky would curtail the exploitative nature of international commerce. Like Smith, Fichte critiqued Europe's "common exploitation of the rest of the world" and the mercantilist policies, including the creation of colonies, that were associated with that phenomenon.[6] While Smith saw free trade as a solution, Fichte argued that autarky was a better alternative. In addition to curtailing international exploitation and conflict, autarkic policies would address the problem that commerce between rich and poor countries was, in Fichte's view, inevitably unfavourable to the latter. He argued that rich countries benefited from positive trade balances, inflows of specie, and higher tax revenue that reinforced their wealth and power (including military power), while poor countries experienced the opposite, resulting in population loss and the gradual erosion of their independence. Fichte acknowledged that mercantilist policies might enable a poor country to become more wealthy and powerful, but he argued that the success of this strategy could not last if every other state employed it. Insulating one's country from international commercial competition altogether was, in Fichte's view, the better solution. Indeed, Fichte argued that once one country embraced autarky, others would quickly follow when they saw the advantages it generated.

Fichte also tied autarky to international peace, thus challenging one of the key liberal rationales for free trade. He argued that inter-state trade rivalries were a key cause of wars, while autarkic policies would end such rivalries and ensure that countries no longer had reason to oppress each other (because each was self-sufficient). Fichte also directly challenged

[6] Quoted in Nakhimovsky 2011, 73.

the view that international commerce could foster more cosmopolitan identities, arguing that "through our striving to be everything, and to be at home everywhere, we have become nothing, and find ourselves at home nowhere". Indeed, because international trade encouraged inter-state competition, he suggested that it fostered unhealthy nationalist rivalries. By contrast, autarky would encourage the development of a healthier "national character" that could lay the groundwork for improved international understanding based not on commerce but on the exchange of ideas and culture via scholars and artists.[7]

Fichte's views about the relationship between autarky and peace had one important caveat. In the transition period to autarky, Fichte argued that a country such as Prussia might need to annex nearby territories in order to create what he called "natural frontiers" that were more compatible with economic self-sufficiency.[8] This caveat highlighted how not all countries were perfectly suited for autarky. Fichte saw the redrawing of borders by force as a solution to this problem. He also noted that the gold and silver acquired from a country's domestic monetary transformation could be used to purchase military equipment and hire soldiers for this operation. After this military action, however, Fichte insisted that the "closed commercial state" should renounce any further aggression or acquisition of colonies.

### Northeast Asian Autarkists

At almost exactly the same moment that Ficthe's book was published, another important case for autarky was advanced halfway around the world in Japan. Japanese foreign economic policy had been moving in an autarkic direction since the 1630s, when authorities banned Japanese people from traveling abroad and restricted all trade with Europe, except that involving Dutch merchants in Nagasaki under highly controlled conditions. When British and Russian merchants increased their presence in Japanese waters in the late eighteenth century, the government responded by tightening autarkic policies. The turn towards greater autarky was then defended in 1801 by the Japanese scholar Shizuki Tadao, who coined the phrase *sakoku* (national isolation) to describe the policy.

Noting the growing foreign threat, Shizuki praised *sakoku*'s role in defending the country's autonomy, arguing that it protected Japan from "having our customs disturbed and our fortunes plundered by foreigners".[9]

---

[7] Fichte quotes from Nakhimovsky 2011, 83.
[8] Quoted in Nakhimovsky 2011, 110.
[9] Quoted in Hiroshi 2006, 20.

The goal of preventing disruption of local customs contrasted with Fichte's preference for preserving an international exchange of ideas and culture. But it had been a central rationale for Japan's initial tightening of external controls in the 1630s when authorities had feared foreign subversion associated with growing European promotion of Christianity in the country. The reference to foreign plundering also evoked earlier Japanese concerns that foreigners were robbing the country of its wealth by selling them useless goods in exchange for gold and silver from Japanese mines that could never be replenished.[10]

Shizuki's defense of autarky was outlined in a preface to a translation he made of part of a 1727 book titled *The History of Japan* written by a German scholar, Englebert Kaempfer, who had lived in the Dutch settlement in Nagasaki between 1690 and 1692. Kaempfer's book had gained a wide audience in Europe and then found its way to Japan in the 1770s, where it attracted attention in elite circles because it praised Japan's autarkic policies. Japanese authorities then asked Shizuki to translate the portion of the book with this praise in order to support their policy preference.[11] To the best of my knowledge, Kaempfer's text was the first European work addressing political economy to be translated into Japanese (and many decades before translations of *The Wealth of Nations* and List's *The National System of Political Economy* first appeared).

Kaempfer's work no doubt appealed to Japanese officials because it echoed arguments in favour of autarky that had long been made in Japan itself. The book argued that autarky provided Japanese rulers with autonomy "to do what they thought fit" and protected the Japanese people against the "covetousness, deceits, wars, treachery" and "vices" of foreign countries. Kaempfer also noted that Japan had no need for foreign goods and questioned the purpose of European missionary activity in the country, arguing that "in the practice of virtue, in purity of life, and outward devotion, they [the Japanese] far out-do the Christians".[12] These arguments very likely drew directly on Japanese thought since Kaempfer had been allowed to travel extensively beyond Nagasaki during his time in Japan, including spending several weeks in Edo.[13] To the extent that Kaempfer did borrow from Japanese thought, the Japanese translation of his work represented a remarkable example of how autarkic thought flowed from East to West and back again at this early

---

[10] See especially the views of Confucian scholar and official Arai Hakuseki, who tightened trade controls in 1709–16 (e.g. Nakai 1988, 107–13). For the tightening in the 1630s, see Laver 2011.
[11] Mervart 2015. For Kaempfer's book, see Kaempfer [1692]1906; Mervart 2009.
[12] Quotes from Kaempfer [1692]1906, 335, 305, 318.
[13] Goodman 2005, 364.

moment, displaying greater cosmopolitanism – despite its content – than that of other political economy perspectives in this era.

One of Shizuki's themes was developed in more detail in an 1825 work titled *New Theses* by the Japanese scholar Aizawa Seishisai. Shizuki had noted that the growing foreign threat to Japan at the time could play a useful role of "stiffening the most urgent resolve for defense against external threats and harmony at home".[14] This idea was at the center of Aizawa's work, which defended a government order in 1825 calling for the use of force to repel foreign ships attempting to land in Japan. Aizawa praised how the government's new policy might provoke a conflict with foreigners that would "unify the will of the people" through a reassertion of traditional Confucian values in ways that could enable Japan to fend off foreigners.[15] While Fichte saw autarky as a force for peace (at least in the long term), Aizawa hoped it might provoke war.

Aizawa advanced three other arguments in support of autarky. First, he repeated past Japanese concerns about foreign political and cultural influences, noting that international trade would enable foreigners to promote Christianity in ways that undermined the loyalty of the Japanese to their country and might serve as a prelude to annexation. Second, he echoed longstanding Japanese criticism of the exploitative nature of international commerce, arguing that "foreign trade is largely a frittering away of our precious metals for useless commodities". Finally, he saw autarky as a way to challenge the growing commercialization and decadence of Japanese society and to restore Japan's traditional agrarian-focused economy. For Aizawa, imports were largely "luxury items", while exports encouraged cash crop agriculture that undermined traditional Japanese farming and domestic food needs.[16] Aizawa's desire to protect Japanese society from foreign commercial pressures bore some similarities to Rousseau's ideas (which he did not know), but his goal of building a society around what Bob Wakabayashi calls a kind of "muscular Confucianism" was obviously very different.[17]

The works of Shizuki and Aizawa initially circulated only privately in Japanese intellectual circles, but both were finally published in the 1850s in the context of heated Japanese debates about the country's forced economic opening at the time (see Chapter 3). Shizuki's term *sakoku* quickly became widely used to describe Japan's past foreign economic policy, while Aizawa's text became "a virtual bible" to activists who were

[14] Quoted in Hiroshi 2006, 20.
[15] Quoted in Hiroshi 2006, 23.
[16] Quotes from Aizawa [1825]1986, 239.
[17] Wakabayashi 1986, 6.

committed to expelling foreigners from Japan.[18] While local mercantilist and neomercantilist ideas (described in Chapter 5) inspired many Japanese to back reforms designed to promote Japan's power and wealth in an open world economy, the texts of Shizuki and Aizawa were used by those opposing economic opening. Aizawa himself, however, had decided by this time that Japan needed to accept economic opening via treaties with the foreign powers in order to avoid invasion and colonization.[19]

Autarkic ideas were also prominent in neighbouring Korea, which refused economic opening until the mid-1870s. Dating back to the seventeenth century, Korea had maintained a policy of seclusion vis-à-vis European traders that was often stricter than that of Japan. As external pressure for economic opening grew after the mid-nineteenth century (including from Japan by the 1870s), however, some Koreans began to urge the adoption of a more outward-oriented, neomercantilist economic strategy to address the new external challenge (as noted in Chapter 5). In this context, supporters of the traditional autarkic policy were increasingly forced to justify their preference more explicitly.

They were led by the prominent scholar Lee Hang-ro, who had been recruited by the government to devise policies for dealing with foreign powers. One of Lee's rationales for retaining autarkic policies was a desire to preserve the autonomy of Korea's neo-Confucian culture. In his view, international trade would encourage profit-seeking behaviour and an inflow of foreign materialist ideas and consumer goods that threatened the country's Confucian values such as frugality and modesty. Economic openness, he argued, would contaminate the minds of the Korean people by unleashing a "flood" of unhealthy "human desires" that reduced them to "barbarians and beasts".[20] Lee's concern was summed up in his warning phrase "exchange of commodities, exchange of immorality", which became a dominant theme of opponents of economic opening in the late nineteenth century.[21]

Lee also outlined some political and economic reasons for preserving the country's longstanding autarkic policy. Politically, Lee argued that the policy would continue to insulate Korea from dangerous subversion by foreigners. Economically, traditional Korean producers would not be undermined by new foreign competition. Lee also suggested that international commerce would be exploitative because Korea would be exporting resources whose supply was limited in exchange for foreign manufactured goods that could be produced "without restriction".[22]

[18] Quote from Wakabayashi 1986, ix.
[19] Wakabayashi 1986, 24, 135–37.
[20] Quoted in Chung 1995, 126–27.
[21] Quoted in McNamara 1996, 62.
[22] Quoted in Chung 1995, 208.

## Pre-1930s Autarkic Thought Elsewhere

Prominent advocates of autarky existed in other regions of the world as well. Some were inspired by European thinkers. For example, Rousseau's ideas inspired the best-known autarkist in nineteenth-century Latin America: José Gaspar Rodríguez de Francia. Ruler of Paraguay from 1814 until his death in 1840, Francia became interested in Rousseau's thought during his university education that culminated in a PhD in theology from Argentina's University of Córdoba. In addition to emphasizing the need for an agrarian-based economy, Francia promoted Rousseau-inspired goals such as frugality, egalitarianism, patriotism, and especially the protection of his country's sovereignty. As part of the latter, Francia committed to creating what he called a "self-sustaining" economy in which the country's external trade was channeled through just two locations and restricted to some limited barter exchanges of the country's surplus commodities for goods Paraguay could not produce. In his view, this "system of non-intercourse" with other countries protected Paraguay from foreign political influence and economic "dependency".[23]

A few decades later, a prominent advocate of autarky in Haiti – Edmund Paul – drew on Fichte's ideas. Described as "one of the most significant political thinkers in nineteenth-century Haiti", Paul published an analysis in the early 1860s suggesting that his country work towards Fichte's closed commercial state as a long-term goal.[24] By promoting local industry through tariffs and other forms of government support, Paul argued that the country could achieve economic sovereignty to match the political independence it had gained through its earlier slave rebellion. To avoid the influence of foreign capital, Paul also argued that Haiti's economic development should be financed as much as possible by local funds, and he criticized the lack of patriotism of Haitians who exported their money to Europe. In addition, he endorsed a ban on foreign ownership of land that dated back to the country's 1805 post-revolutionary constitution, arguing that it protected the small local landholders against an influx of white investors in ways that upheld the country's ideals: "To accord the right of property to whites while color prejudice is still prevalent, would be to renounce the end which the nation pursues".[25]

Later in the nineteenth century, the Russian thinker Peter Kropotkin developed a more distinctive strand of autarkic thought that was linked to his anarchist views. Critical of both Marxist state planning and parliamentary roads to socialism, Kropotkin urged people to take direct control

---

[23] Francia's quotes from Williams 1979, 78; White 1978, 137.
[24] Quote from Nicholls 1996, 102.
[25] Quoted in Nicholls 1996, 103.

of land and factories in order to establish self-governing communes and cooperatives. For his radicalism, Kropotkin was soon imprisoned in 1877. After escaping and fleeing the country, he returned to Russia in 1917, after which he quickly became disillusioned with the consequences of the Russian revolution before his death in 1921. Kropotkin's books such as *The Conquest of Bread* (1892) and *Fields, Factories and Workshops* (1898) were widely read around the world in the late nineteenth and early twentieth centuries.[26] Even some who disagreed with Kropotkin's anarchist politics were attracted to his ideas about autarky, such as the prominent British Labour politician Philip Snowden in the immediate pre–World War I period.[27]

Kropotkin's autarkist views were related to a critical analysis of imperialism he developed in the 1890s (well before the better-known Marxist theories on this subject discussed in Chapter 4). Kropotkin attributed imperialism to the capitalist need to find external markets in a context where "the working people cannot purchase with their wages the wealth which they have produced".[28] He also highlighted how capital was being exported from leading powers to colonies and other agricultural regions in search of higher profits. Those investments, he argued, encouraged industrialization in those regions in ways that undermined the ability of leading countries to find new markets for their surplus goods. As competition for external markets intensified, he predicted war, a development that would only worsen the economic situation and help trigger social revolution.[29]

Kropotkin argued that autarkic policies were needed in postrevolutionary societies because "when the Revolution comes we must depend on foreign countries as little as possible". He also suggested that autarky would prevent foreign capitalists from having influence in the country and that the international division of labour simply "enriched a number of capitalists" and involved transportation that was "a waste of time and money".[30] When countries became more self-sufficient, he argued further, their people became involved in more diverse activities that encouraged innovation and generated progress. In his vision, postrevolutionary governments could still allow some trade but he recommended limiting it "to the exchange of what really *must* be exchanged, and, at the same time, immensely to increase the exchange of novelties, produce of local or national art, new discoveries and inventions,

---

[26] For the global influence of anarchist thought more generally in this period, see Anderson 2005; Khuri-Makdisi 2010.
[27] Trentmann 1997, 79–80.
[28] Kropotkin [1892]1906, 12.
[29] Kropotkin [1892]1906, 12, 242–43; 1898, 5–11, 27–39.
[30] Quotes from Kropotkin [1892]1906, 97, 260, 261. See also p. 264.

knowledge and ideas".[31] His interest in ongoing cultural and knowledge exchange was much closer to Fichte's version of autarky than that of the Japanese and Korean thinkers.

The views of the Northeast Asians on that issue found a stronger parallel in a strand of African autarkism developed independently in the early twentieth century by Kobina Sekyi. According to J. Ayodele Langley, Sekyi was "one of the most outstanding intellectuals in West Africa, and indeed in colonial Africa in general".[32] Born in the British colony of the Gold Coast, Seyki studied philosophy at the University of London, after which he became a prominent conservative anti-colonial nationalist. Sekyi was particularly critical of European imperialism for "denationalising" the peoples it conquered and he urged Africans to insulate their cultures and nationalities from European civilization. He argued that "the civilization of the West is based on commerce or trade" in ways that undermined natural social ties, generated inequality and greed, and resulted in "over-luxurious", "diseased" societies.[33]

In Sekyi's view, Africans needed to pursue development strategies that reflected their own culture: "Let each social group develop along the lines marked out for them by their unwesternised and therefore undemoralised ancestors, accepting from the West only such institutions as can be adapted to, and not such as cannot but alter, their national life". To meet those goals, Seyki argued that future independent African countries needed to embrace economic autarky, engaging in international trade only by barter when necessary. The pursuit of this strategy would, he argued, also contribute to world peace because the alternative strategy of following Europe's model would lead Africa to "ever creating new wants to supply an insatiable desire for conquest, ever oppressing others to further this conquest, and [was] bound to end by consuming all that has been acquired by such conquest in universal holocaust kindled by the demon of Greed".[34]

In South Asia, the most famous advocate of autarky was Mohandas Gandhi. Although Gandhi is best known for his lead role in the Indian independence struggle, he combined his anti-imperialist politics with a vision of economic self-sufficiency for India that he first outlined in detail in his 1909 work *Hind Swaraj* (Indian Home Rule). Gandhi wanted to see his country build upon its ancient tradition of self-governing villages whose economies were focused on localized artisan and agrarian activities.

---

[31] Kropotkin [1898]1901, 121. See also pp. 4–5, 259–61.
[32] Langley 1979, 44.
[33] Quotes from Sekyi [1917]1979, 244, 248, 243.
[34] Quotes from Sekyi [1917]1979, 250, 244–45.

He invoked the idea of *swadeshi* that had already become popular in Indian nationalist circles (see Chapter 5). But his vision contrasted with the views of Indian nationalists such as Ranade and Jawaharlal Nehru who favoured a neomercantilist, state-led industrialization strategy to catch up to the wealth and power of dominant industrial countries. In Gandhi's view, that strategy overlooked the drawbacks of modern industrial Western civilization with its extreme inequalities, exploitation, and violence that were incompatible with individual freedom and democratic life.

For this economic vision to be realized, Gandhi recognized the need to insulate India from foreign market pressures, including imports of European manufactured goods that would undermine traditional Indian producers, as they had in the colonial period. He argued that "it is certainly our right and duty to discard everything foreign that is superfluous and even everything foreign that is *necessary* if we can produce or manufacture it in our country". If his goals were implemented, Gandhi suggested, "every village of India will almost be a self-supporting and self-contained unit exchanging only such necessary commodities with other villages where they are not locally producible".[35] In addition, Gandhi argued that Indian producers would not feel any need to export because local consumers would provide a stable market for their goods.

When outlining this vision, Gandhi sometimes engaged directly with liberal arguments for free trade. For example, when liberal critics noted that homespun goods would be more expensive, Gandhi replied that economics was not just about economic efficiency and material progress but also about ethics and spirituality. He insisted that the kind of material economic progress valued by Western civilization was "antagonistic to real progress" of a moral kind. He called on Indians to resist "the monster-god of materialism" and instead to become a "truly spiritual nation" by building on ancient religious ideals. As he put it in 1916, "I venture to think that the scriptures of the world are far safer and sounder treaties on laws of economics than many of the modern textbooks". Gandhi also challenged the link between free trade and peace, arguing that Western industrial civilization generated excess production that encouraged the pursuit of export markets and free trade, including through war. If his country emulated Western civilization, Gandhi argued that it would become a threat to world peace. As he put it, "an exploiting England is a danger to the world, but if that is so, how much more so would be an exploiting India, if she took to machinery and produced cloth many times in excess of its requirements".[36]

---

[35] Quotes from Gandhi 1971, 262; Gupta 1968, 143.
[36] Quotes in Gandhi 1997, 160, 162, 158–59; 1971, 47.

## Autarkism's Popularity during the 1930s

It was in the 1930s that autarkic thought achieved its greatest political influence across the globe during the period examined in this book. The trigger for this development was the Great Depression of 1929–33 and the associated collapse of cross-border trade, foreign lending, and the international gold standard. As international economic relationships unravelled, many countries reinforced the de-globalization trend by defaulting on international debts and tightening controls on cross-border economic activity as a way of coping with the economic shock. This turn to more autarkic policies was supported and reinforced by a number of thinkers.

The most famous of these was British economist John Maynard Keynes in an essay published in 1933 under the title "National Self-Sufficiency". Trained at Britain's top schools, Keynes had first become an international celebrity after World War I with his sharp critique of the economic consequences of the postwar peace settlement. At that time, Keynes was still a devotee of the economic liberal and free trade thought that he had been taught. But he became increasingly interested in a more regulated form of domestic capitalism in the 1920s. His 1933 essay (based on a lecture he gave in Dublin) then signalled a particularly dramatic repudiation of his earlier support for free trade. Because of his prominence, the essay attracted enormous attention and was published in outlets in Britain, Ireland, the United States, and Germany in that year alone.[37] It remains the best-known autarkic tract of the twentieth century.

In it, Keynes declared: "I sympathise ... with those who would minimise, rather than with those who would maximize, economic entanglement among nations". Outlining a similar conception of self-sufficiency as Fichte, Keynes continued: "Ideas, knowledge, art, hospitality, travel – these are the things which should of their nature be international. But let goods be homespun whenever it is reasonably and conveniently possible; and, above all, let finance be primarily national". Keynes' core case for autarky also bore some similarities to the earlier German thinker's emphasis on the need for policy autonomy to pursue domestic economic activism. In Keynes' view, governments needed to be freed from external market constraints in order to try new kinds of economic policies to address the economic crisis: "we all need to be as free as possible of interference from economic changes elsewhere, in order to make our own favourite experiments towards the ideal social republic of the future". Keynes himself favoured activist macroeconomic policies aimed at promoting full employment. For these policies to be

---

[37] Nolan 2013. I have quoted from the version published in Britain in July.

effective, he noted that controls on cross-border financial movements were needed to prevent capital flight from undermining national efforts to boost "material prosperity" through lower domestic interest rates.[38]

As part of this vision, Keynes criticized the kind of "decadent international but individualistic capitalism" in place during the 1920s: "It is not intelligent, it is not beautiful, it is not just, it is not virtuous – and it doesn't deliver the goods". He also attacked the nineteenth-century liberal focus on "financial results" at the expense of other values, including equity and environmental goals:

The whole conduct of life was made into a sort of parody of an accountant's nightmare. Instead of using their vastly increased material and technical resources to build a wonder-city, the men of the nineteenth century built slums; and they thought it right and advisable to build slums because slums, on the test of private enterprise, "paid" ... We destroy the beauty of the countryside because the unappropriated splendours of nature have no economic value. We are capable of shutting off the sun and the stars because they do not pay a dividend.[39]

But Keynes also made clear that he had no sympathy for the kinds of activist economic policies being pursued in places such as Adolf Hitler's Germany or Joseph Stalin's Soviet Union. In keeping with his enduring sympathy for liberal political and economic values, Keynes insisted that autarky should never coexist with "Intolerance and the stifling of instructed criticism" and he highlighted his own preference for a domestic economic order that retained "as much private judgment and initiative and enterprise as possible". Keynes also suggested that his preference for national self-sufficiency might be just temporary, lasting only "so long as the present transitional, experimental phase endures".[40] As we shall see in Chapter 14, Keynes did indeed soon change his mind and became a key advocate in the early 1940s of the restoration of economic internationalism, albeit of a new kind.

In his 1933 essay, Keynes also noted that a policy of national self-sufficiency might be too costly for small countries such as Ireland that would lose the economic benefits of international trade. For larger countries, however, Keynes thought those benefits were overstated because non-tradeable goods and services were making up an increasing share of the economy and because "most modern mass-production processes can be performed in most countries and climates with almost equal efficiency". The costs of abandoning free trade would also be more than offset, he argued, by the economic gains arising from domestic economic activism

---

[38] Quotes from Keynes [1933]1982, 236, 241.
[39] Quotes from Keynes [1933]1982, 239, 241–42.
[40] Quotes from Keynes [1933]1982, 245, 240.

made possible by autarkism. Like some other autarkic thinkers, Keynes also questioned the liberal equation of free trade with peace, suggesting that economic interdependence might generate more, rather than fewer, reasons to go to war: "The protection of a country's existing foreign interests, the capture of new markets, the progress of economic imperialism – these are a scarcely avoidable part of a scheme of things which aims at the maximum of international specialisation and at the maximum geographical diffusion of capital wherever its seat of ownership".[41]

Although Keynes presented the best-known case for national autarky during the early 1930s, this policy also had high-profile advocates in other contexts. One was German Nazi supporter Friedrich Zimmermann (aka Ferdinand Fried), whose works such as *The End of Capitalism* (1931) and *Autarky* (1932) were influential in Nazi circles. In sharp contrast to Keynes, Zimmermann urged a "total renunciation of capitalism and liberalism". In his view, that shift required "giving up the idea of the world economy and the isolation of individual national economic spheres". In addition to enabling new kinds of national economic planning, autarky would, he argued, help to insulate Germany from external political influence. It would also allow a repudiation of the country's enormous external debts because "the entire compulsion of international debt and interest payments holds sway only as long as individual countries are compelled to be members of the global economy".[42]

Another autarkic vision was advanced in the Chinese context by Chen Gongbo, who had been one of the founders of the Chinese Communist Party in 1921 but then quit the party, joined the nationalist Guomindang, and emerged as one of its top economic theoreticians. In the early 1930s. Chen highlighted the growing support for autarky across the world and urged China to promote this goal too via economic planning and control to ensure the "survival" of the Chinese nation. He emphasized that this policy would insulate China from foreign political interference and strengthen the country's ability to resist Japanese imperialism. As he put it, "Let's just look at the fact that we depend on foreign people for clothes, food, housing, and consumption ... How can a nationality support its life in such a situation?"[43] Autarky would also boost the nation's internal political and economic cohesion, he argued, by forcing the industrializing coastal regions to reorient inwardly to sell to the rural economy and draw resources from it.

[41] Quotes from Keynes [1933]1982, 238, 236.
[42] Zimmermann quotes from Szejnmann 2013, 363; Link 2018, 359. See also the Nazi interest in wider visions of regional autarky in Chapter 13 of this book.
[43] Chen quotes from Zanasi 2006, 47, 39.

One final example of a case made for a high degree of national economic self-sufficiency originated from a prominent group of left-wing Turkish thinkers led by Sevket Süreyya Aydemir in the early 1930s. Like Chen, these thinkers advanced a kind of "anti-imperialist developmentalism".[44] Concerned about the domination and exploitation of poorer regions of the world by richer ones, Aydemir argued in 1932 that the "abnormal concentration of industry and capital in some countries [was] at the expense of the underdevelopment of others". In the context of a collapsing liberal international economic order and the growing prominence of autarkic thought elsewhere, Aydemir and his collagues saw an opportunity for Turkey to embrace a high degree of national self-sufficiency that would end its position as one of the exploited, agricultural-producing "semi-colonies".[45] While allowing for some trade (including imports of technology paid for by commodity exports), they urged a reorientation of production towards internal markets as well as state economic planning to promote ambitious industrialization goals. In this way, they argued, the country could gain real economic independence to match the political independence it had acquired in the early 1920s. After initially supporting the development of the ideas of this group, the Turkish government shut down a journal they ran in 1934 because of its radicalism.[46]

## Conclusion

Although autarkic thought has not received much attention from IPE scholars, there is a rich history of thinkers (including Ballod, as noted in Chapter 6) who prioritized their state's economic self-sufficiency in order to enhance its autonomy from foreign influence. Most were interested in autonomy from foreign economic influences, such as international market pressures and economic exploitation by foreigners. Some were also concerned about protecting their state from foreign cultural and political influences arising from international economic relationships. During the period examined in this book, this autarkic perspective had at least as important a place in political debates in some contexts as other ones that are better studied. Like other perspectives, some strands of autarkic thought also circulated internationally in the pre-1945 era, such as the ideas of Fichte, Kropotkin, and Keynes (as well as the ideas of earlier thinkers such as Rousseau and Kaempfer).

[44] Özveren and Özgur 2021, 912.
[45] Aydemir quoted in Gülap 1998, 954; Barlas 1998, 49.
[46] Barlas 1998, 47–50; Hanioğlu 2011, 188–91.

Also similar to the other perspectives analyzed in the first part of this book, considerable disagreements existed within the autarkic camp. Thinkers could not find common ground on the issue of whether autarky might be a force for peace (Sekyi, Gandhi, Keynes) or a policy to provoke war (Aizawa). Some insisted that autarkic policies should not restrict the international movement of ideas and culture between countries (Fichte, Kropotkin, Keynes), while others saw this as a core goal (especially Shizuki, Aizawa, Lee, Sekyi). The anti-imperialism of thinkers such as Aydemir, Chen, Gandhi, Kropotkin, and Sekyi also sat uncomfortably alongside Fichte's endorsement of annexation policies (and Ballod's endorsement of imperialism, as noted in the Chapter 6).

The domestic goals that autarkic thinkers sought to achieve with the country's greater autonomy were also enormously diverse. In Europe alone, these goals ranged from Fichte's ambitious republican economic planning to Kropotkin's anarchism and Keynes' managed liberalism to Zimmerman's Nazism. Beyond Europe, the goals associated with autarkic thought were even more varied, including the Confucian agrarianism of Aizawa and Lee, Francia's Rousseauan vision, Paul's industrial developmentalism, Sekyi's anti-colonial African nationalism, Gandhi's village-centered decentralism, Chen's nation-building goals, and Aydemir's left-wing industrial planning. The diversity of the goals of autarkists expands further if we add in Ballod's socialist goals from Chapter 6 as well as the views of some environmentally oriented autarkist thinkers discussed in the next chapter.

# 9    Environmentalist Calls for a More Sustainable Economic Order

When IPE textbooks identify environmentalism as an important perspective in the field, it is usually portrayed as a relatively new one that has emerged only within the last few decades. In fact, environmentalist perspectives about the international dimensions of political economy have a deep history in the pre-1945 era. In that period, many thinkers outlined their desire to curtail human-induced degradation of the natural environment in the world economy in order to foster more sustainable ways of living. This broad commitment is similar to that of modern environmentalists, even if the term "environmentalism" was not used in this way until at least the 1960s.[1]

Like environmentalism in the contemporary age, there were many versions of this perspective in the pre-1945 era. Some were concerned about environmental degradation only because of its implications for human society. Others moved beyond this anthropocentric approach to express a more "ecocentric" style of environmentalism that valued the natural environment for its own sake.[2] The specific ideas of environmentalists about the causes of, and solutions, to human-induced environmental degradation also varied considerably. In some cases, these variations intersected with other perspectives already examined in book, such as economic liberalism, neomercantilism, Marxism, and autarkism. In others, their views went beyond these perspectives in distinctive ways.

## Environmentalism and Classical Economic Liberalism

Let us begin with some environmentalists whose ideas were informed by an economic liberal intellectual framework. Many historians have dated the rise of modern ideas of environmental sustainability to the very time period – between the late eighteenth and mid-nineteenth centuries – when European economic liberalism first became popular. Influenced by

---

[1] See, for example, Falkner 2021, 45fn1.
[2] For this distinction in the broader environmental movement, see Falkner 2021, 58, 76.

advances in natural science and the decline of providentialist thinking, promoters of these ideas expressed concerns about the impact of modern economic growth on the natural environment. Some focussed on issues such as soil exhaustion and erosion, pollution, and the loss of species and wilderness. Others highlighted how intensified harvesting of forests was reducing timber supplies as well as causing flooding and changes to local climates that led to desertification. Fears were also expressed about depletion of non-renewable resources, including energy supplies such as coal.[3]

By the mid-nineteenth century, warnings were even being made about the risks to the human species as a whole arising from human-induced environmental degradation. As the American conservationist George Marsh put it in his influential 1864 book *Man and Nature*, "the earth is fast becoming an unfit home for its noblest inhabitant, and another era of equal human crime and human improvidence ... would reduce it to such a condition of impoverished productiveness, of shattered surface, of climatic excess, as to threaten the depravation, barbarism, and perhaps even extinction of the species".[4] Fears also began to be expressed as early as 1858 about the risk of human extinction arising from transformations in the composition of the earth's atmosphere that might cause climate change.[5]

Despite these growing environmental concerns, many of the key pioneers of classical economic liberalism said little about environmental degradation, including Adam Smith. To be sure, Smith highlighted how the human economy was rooted in the natural environment, noting how in agriculture "nature labours along with man; and though her labour costs no expense, its produce has its value".[6] He also used analogies from the natural world to describe the self-regulating nature of a market economy. In *The Wealth of Nations*, Smith even cited a 1768 book by Pierre Poivre that helped to pioneer European environmentalism by highlighting environmental problems in the French colony of Mauritius. But Smith did not echo Poivre's concerns about environmental degradation, nor those of others, including his contemporaries in Scotland who critiqued deforestation at the very time he was writing his 1776 book. For Smith, deforestation was a positive sign that a society was progressing through his stage theory of development towards a more agricultural society.[7]

---

[3] See, for example, Grove 1995; Guha 2000, Jonsson 2013; Radkau 2014; Warde 2018.

[4] Marsh 1864, 44.

[5] Grove 1995, 469–70. Grove notes, how, a few decades later, in 1896, the Swedish scientist Svante Arrhenius put forward his famous prediction that rising carbon dioxide levels in the atmosphere resulting from burning of fossil fuels could cause global warming.

[6] Smith 1776, II.v.12.

[7] Jonsson 2014. For Smith's views, see, for example, Jonsson 2010, 2013, 2014; Shabas 2005; Warde 2018, 236, 245, 283–38. For Poivre's work, see Grove 1995.

Smith did note that the production of a country would eventually reach limits imposed by natural factors such as the scarcity of productive agricultural land. But he saw that "stationary" state coming only in the distant future and depicted its eventual approach in economic terms rather than with reference to environmental degradation.[8] His focus was on the task of managing nature to boost human wealth, a task that he argued was best left to market mechanisms, which would generate price incentives to encourage effective resource management and technological improvement. At the international level, Smith also highlighted how countries could overcome the natural constraints of their land by importing food, as Holland did in his age.[9]

There were, however, some thinkers who combined an interest in economic liberal ideas with stronger concerns about environmental degradation. The most important early example was the German thinker Alexander von Humboldt, who fully embraced liberal political and economic ideals but was also one of key pioneers of modern environmentalism. Humboldt first became well known in Europe and the Americas for writing about his travels in Latin America between 1799 and 1804. His fame only grew with many other publications, culminating with his multi-volume work *Cosmos* published between 1845 and 1858 to widespread acclaim. Many later environmentalists were deeply influenced by Humboldt's ideas, including Marsh.[10]

In his various writings, Humboldt made major contributions to the study of the natural environment ranging from plant geography to geology and climatology. He also wrote eloquently about deep and dynamic interconnections between humans and nature and the need to see both as part of an integrated web of life on earth within a wider cosmos.[11] In addition, Humboldt was deeply critical of human-generated environmental degradation, including that caused by European colonialism in Latin America. He condemned European settlers in that region who had destroyed forests "with careless haste", causing wood shortages, hillside soil erosion, and local climate change that reduced rainfall. He noted that this reckless deforestation had often been associated with settlers' efforts to expand plantations growing monocrops such as sugarcane, indigo, and cotton that were designed simply to serve imperial needs.[12]

If Latin America could reject exploitative European colonialism, Humboldt hoped it could avoid these environmental problems and

---

[8] Quote from Smith 1776, I.viii.38.
[9] Smith 1776, IV.ix.37.
[10] See, for example, Walls 2009, 297; Wulf 2015, ch. 21.
[11] See, for example, Walls 2009.
[12] Humboldt quote from Rupke 2018, 76. See also Walls 2009, 9–10.

embrace new liberal commitments and improved scientific knowledge that enabled more sustainable ways of living.[13] As part of his liberal worldview, Humboldt also urged independent Latin American states to adopt free trade. In his view, international commerce conducted on this basis was important not just for individual freedom, but also for civilizational advancement and technical progress. Global economic integration would encourage the sharing of knowledge, including scientific knowledge, as well as international cooperation and the building of a common human consciousness that could help to address environmental problems. By contrast, he argued, economic isolation led to stagnation and missed opportunities to learn from others.[14]

Another prominent liberal thinker with a more cautious view of the relationship between free trade and environmental issues was Stanley Jevons. His 1865 book *The Coal Question* highlighted how British prosperity had come to be based on the non-renewal energy source of coal. Because coal was "limited in quantity", Jevons argued that it placed much more serious limits on Britain's future prosperity than the limits to agricultural growth noted by Smith.[15] Jevons' concern for the sustainability of British growth did not extend to the kind of wider environmental themes that Humboldt outlined. Instead, he was primarily focused on its consequences for Britain's dynamism and power (including its imperial power, which he praised).

Jevons was critical of those who believed that coal consumption would be reduced with more efficient steam engines. In what came to be known as the Jevons paradox, he argued that higher efficiency would only accelerate coal depletion through mechanisms such as boosting consumer demand, attracting more capital to the sector, and encouraging wider coal-using inventions. He argued that British policymakers needed instead to consider deliberate policy initiatives to reduce coal use in order to slow down its depletion. He rejected the idea of a general domestic tax on coal because it would be difficult to impose (given the many varieties of coal) and because it would interfere with the domestic "industrial freedom" that had brought Britain so much economic success. Instead, his policy discussion focused on the "less burdensome" policy of restricting coal exports.[16]

Jevons' willingness to consider export restrictions was striking given his strong liberal belief in the virtues of free trade in general (which even

---

[13] See, for example, Rupke 2018; Wulf 2015, ch. 4; Walls 2009 pp. 9–10, 123. See also late eighteenth and early nineteenth century Brazilian critiques of the deforestation and soil erosion caused by their colonial economy (Padua 2000).
[14] von Brescius 2012.
[15] Jevons 1865, 153.
[16] Quotes from Jevons 1865, 338.

included criticism of Mill's endorsement of infant-industry protection).[17] Despite this belief, Jevons emphasized the negative impact of Britain's free trade policy in accelerating the depletion of coal reserves on which his country's prosperity was so heavily dependent. He showed how the repeal of the country's export taxes on coal in the mid-1840s had led to a dramatic increase in coal exports. Coal exports were also boosted by Britain's broader free trade policies, he argued, because ships bringing growing resources to Britain from around the world used coal as ballast for their outgoing voyages. More generally, Jevons highlighted how increased domestic coal production also helped to pay for Britain's growing raw material imports both directly (as coal exports) and indirectly in the form of "manufactures which represent a greater or less quantity of coal consumed in the steam-engine, or the smelting furnace".[18]

These arguments did not lead him to recommend a reversal of Britain's broad free trade stance (although he noted that resisting the abolition of the Corn Laws "might have been far more efficient in preventing the exhaustion of our coal-mines than any measures we are now likely to adopt"). Instead, he urged consideration of the more targeted measure of reintroducing the duty on coal exports in order to be "sparing the fuel which makes our welfare and supports our influence upon the nations of the world". This policy, he acknowledged, would involve "subordinating commerce to purposes of a higher nature". As part of this advice, Jevons also suggested scrapping what he described as a "very unusual clause" in the 1860 Cobden–Chevalier trade treaty (see Chapter 2) that specifically prevented Britain from reimposing the export duty. In other words, Jevons was suggesting that free trade treaties should have exceptions for the purpose of conserving natural resources. As he put it more generally, he was raising the issue of whether free trade principles should be applied to "our own resources" only "last and most cautiously".[19]

Other prominent economic liberals found Jevons' analysis compelling, including John Stuart Mill, who mentioned Jevons' book in British Parliament and urged investigation of the issues he raised.[20] Interestingly, Mill had a more positive view of an eventual stationary state than Jevons, expressing elsewhere some broader concerns about the environmental consequences of economic growth (but without linking them to international issues). For example, he noted that a country's rapidly growing

[17] Jevons 1865, 304. See also pp. 306–9.
[18] Jevons 1865, 251.
[19] Quotes from Jevons 1865, 332–33, xviii, x, 344–45. Jevons rejected the idea that Britain could import coal from abroad because the cost of imported coal would undermine the competitiveness of Britain's manufacturing (Jevons 1865, 220–55).
[20] Jonsson 2020, 126.

population might deprive its people from experiencing "solitude in the presence of natural beauty and grandeur", which he argued was "the cradle of thoughts and aspirations which are not only good for the individual, but which society could ill do without". He also made a much broader environmental case for not just embracing a stationary state but even accelerating the move towards it:

Nor is there much satisfaction in contemplating the world with nothing left to the spontaneous activity of nature; with every rood of land brought into cultivation, which is capable of growing food for human beings; every flowery waste or natural pasture ploughed up, all quadrupeds or birds which are not domesticated for man's use exterminated as his rivals for food, every hedgerow or superfluous tree rooted out, and scarcely a place left where a wild shrub or flower could grow without being eradicated as a weed in the name of improved agriculture. If the earth must lose that great portion of its pleasantness which it owes to things that the unlimited increase of wealth and population would extirpate from it, for the mere purpose of enabling it to support a larger, but not a better or a happier population, I sincerely hope, for the sake of posterity, that they will be content to be stationary, long before necessity compels them to it.[21]

The issue of creating exemptions from free trade rules for conservation purposes also earned support in broader liberal circles later within the League of Nations. When the League hosted the world's first large-scale multilateral trade negotiation, the resulting 1927 treaty (which was never ratified) allowed for the maintenance of trade restrictions for "the protection of animals or plants against disease, insects and harmful parasites". The text noted that this exemption had "been admitted through long-established practice ... to be indispensable and compatible with the principle of freedom of trade".[22] This invocation of "long-established" practice probably referred to the creation of some international conservation treaties since 1900 that had also endorsed trade restrictions.[23]

## Neomercantilist and Marxist Environmentalism

Environmentalist perspectives were also advanced by some thinkers working in the neomercantilist intellectual tradition. Many neomercantilists showed little interest in the environmental consequences of the state-led development and industrialization strategies they backed. For them, nature was to be exploited and conquered to a maximum extent to serve neomercantilist ends. But some showed more concern for the

---

[21] Mill [1871]1965, 750–51.
[22] Quoted in Charnovitz 1991, 41.
[23] See Charnovitz 1991.

problem of human-induced environmental degradation and the need to promote more sustainable patterns of economic development.

The most important was Henry Carey, whose neomercantilist criticism of free trade was discussed in Chapter 4. Like Jevons, Carey had an anthropocentric perspective towards the natural environment rather than the more ecocentric one of Humboldt. In his view, the earth was "a great machine given to man to be fashioned to his purpose". But he was very concerned about one kind of environmental degradation – soil exhaustion – that he believed was exacerbated by free trade policies. In Carey's view, free trade had transformed many regions of the world into monocrop agricultural exporting zones in which soil nutrients were depleted without adequate replenishment. As he put it, "The farmers were everywhere invited to impoverish their soil by sending its products to England to be consumed".[24] The degradation of soils, in turn, forced farmers to abandon their lands in places as diverse as Brazil, India, Ireland, Jamaica, Mexico, Portugal, Turkey, Virginia, and the Carolinas.

Carey was very critical of free traders for neglecting this environmental issue: "It is singular that modern political economy should so entirely have overlooked the fact that man is a mere borrower from the earth, and that when he does not pay his debts, she does as do all other creditors – expelling him from his holding".[25] Indeed, the author of the liberal theory of comparative advantage, David Ricardo, had written about "original and indestructible powers of the soil".[26] Carey saw soil as more vulnerable to human abuse and he argued that protectionist policies would enable healthier soils to be restored. The growth of local manufacturing would benefit farmers who would be able to replenish nutrients to their soils by using human waste from nearby industrial towns. It would also boost local markets in ways that allowed them to shift away from monocrop agriculture towards more diverse kinds of farming that were better for soils and would enable cattle manure to be used to boost soil fertility.

Carey's ideas on this subject were inspired by the prominent German chemist Justus von Liebig. An acquaintance and follower of Humboldt, Liebig shared his German colleague's interest in the study of nature, arguing that "we consider Nature as one Whole, and all phenomena cohering like the knots in a net of rope".[27] Beginning in the 1840s, Liebig challenged dominant humus theories of plant nutrition that had identified soil fertility with the recycling of organic material. In his view,

---

[24] Quotes from Carey 1858a, 183, 329.
[25] Quotes from Carey 1858a, 336.
[26] Ricardo [1817]1908, 44.
[27] Quoted in Warde 2018, 330.

those theories overlooked the importance of the supply of inorganic mineral nutrients that plants needed to absorb. When crops were sold to distant locations (both within and between countries), he warned that the nutrients embodied in them were not recycled back to the original soil through the waste of humans and animals that ate the produce. In his view, centralized industrialization was contributing to this depletion of the nutrients of local soils because growing urban populations were increasingly separated geographically from the regions – both domestic and foreign – that grew their food. Liebig also lamented how the invention of toilets and modern sewer systems in the industrial age flushed human waste to the sea rather than recycling it back to the land.[28]

Liebig acknowledged that soil fertility could be improved by artificial chemical fertilizers as well as by fertilizers such as Peruvian guano that began to be imported to Europe and North America on a large scale in the 1840s. But he became increasingly pessimistic about their roles, including, in the case of guano, because of its limited and unreliable supply. As he put it in 1859, "no sensible man would entertain the idea of making the production of an entire country dependent on the supply of a foreign manure".[29] In the early 1860s, he also critiqued England for importing bones from abroad to grind up for phosphate fertilizer to sustain its soil fertility in ways that undermined other countries' stores of this resource: "Great Britain deprives all countries of the conditions of their fertility. It has raked up the battle-fields of Leipsic, Waterloo, and the Crimea; it has consumed the bones of many generations accumulated in the catacombs of Sicily ... Like a vampire it hangs on the breast of Europe, and even the world, sucking its lifeblood".[30] In Liebig's view, the best solution was to reform agriculture around smaller operations that served local markets in ways that allowed the easy recycling of nutrients.[31] In the absence of reform, he argued apocalyptically in the early 1860s that many societies risked collapse in the context of declining soil fertility, following the experience of previous civilizations that had experienced soil exhaustion.

Carey was one of the first political economists to pick up on the significance of Liebig's arguments for debates about international economic relations.[32] Liebig also began to cite Carey's work after the two began to correspond in 1856 and then met together during trips Carey made

---

[28] For Liebig's ideas, see Warde 2018.
[29] Liebig 1859, 269.
[30] Quoted in Brock 2002, 178.
[31] Liebig 1859, 229–31, 280.
[32] List was also interested in Liebig's ideas (who he knew personally) but drew on them simply to support his optimism about the prospects for increasing agricultural productivity via chemical fertilizer (List [1841]1909a, 104; Wendler 2015, 188).

to Europe in 1857 and 1859.[33] Many of Carey's followers in the United States and elsewhere also repeated the argument that free trade would generate soil exhaustion by encouraging agricultural exports. For example, the leading promoter of Carey's ideas in the British colony of Upper Canada, Isaac Buchanan, insisted in 1864 that "the argument against Free Trade, or a system of exporting the raw materials of a country, which is to be found in the exhaustion of her soil, has not been paid sufficient attention to. ... We are accustomed to take too little account of what is due to the earth".[34] A few years later, the first Japanese thinker to cite Carey's ideas, Wakayama Norikazu, also called on his government in 1871 "to prohibit the export of agricultural products and thereby to recover the fertility of the soil".[35]

Marx was another political economist who was influenced by Liebig's environmental warnings. Marx is often criticized by contemporary environmentalists for endorsing the human domination of nature in passages where he praised the progress of the productive forces of capitalism. But recent analyses of Marx's work (including many of his unpublished writings) highlight how his views about environmental issues were more complex. In some of Marx's earliest writing about political economy in 1844, for example, he identified the distortion of the relationship between humans and nature as a key aspect of modern alienation in capitalist societies and he argued that communism would involve "the genuine resolution of the conflict between man and nature".[36]

Marx began to express more specific environmental concerns about capitalism after reading Liebig's work in 1865–66, which prompted him to incorporate a discussion of soil exhaustion in the first volume of *Capital* published the next year. In the first German edition, he not only reiterated Liebig's arguments but praised them effusively, noting that Liebig's comments on the "history of agriculture, although not free from gross errors, contains more flashes of insight than all the works of modern political economists put together".[37] In contrast to Carey, who blamed soil exhaustion on free trade, Marx located its cause in broader capitalist forms of production:

Capitalist production collects the population together in great centres, and causes the urban population to achieve an ever-increasing preponderance ... it disturbs the metabolic interaction between man and the earth, i.e. it prevents the return

---

[33] Elder 1880, 21; Liebig 1859; Warde 2018, 348.
[34] Buchanan 1864, 75fn.
[35] Quoted in Sugiyama 1994, 8.
[36] Quoted in Smith 2018, 117. See also Foster 2000; Saito 2017.
[37] Quoted in Saito 2017, 218. He toned down this praise in subsequent editions.

to the soil of its constituent elements consumed by man in the form of food and clothing; hence it hinders the operation of the eternal natural condition for the lasting fertility of the soil ... All progress in capitalist agriculture is a progress in the art, not only of robbing the worker, but of robbing the soil.[38]

Like Carey, Marx was also interested in Liebig's idea that British imports were undermining what he called the "metabolic interaction between man and the earth" in other countries. But he did not share Carey's optimism that protectionism could address the problem. Although that policy might encourage better soil management by bringing town and country together, it would not address the deeper problem of the capitalist nature of modern agriculture. Marx's environmental concerns subsequently widened after reading the work of German scientist Karl Fraas, who argued that deforestation generated higher local temperatures and drier air that, in turn, contributed to desertification and declining soil productivity. This argument led Marx to become interested in how capitalist demand for timber was causing unsustainable and climate-changing deforestation.[39] In his writing about these various ideas, however, Marx never advanced a fully developed environmentalist critique of the international dimensions of capitalism. Neither did his followers in the pre-1945 era.

### Autarkic Environmentalists

The autarkic tradition of thought produced more thinkers who expressed concerns about human-induced environmental degradation when justifying their preferred approach to foreign economic policy. One example was Sada Kaiseki, a prominent Buddhist public intellectual in early Meiji Japan who emerged as the leading opponent of his country's growing economic openness. In the 1870s and early 1880s, Kaiseki led boycotts across the country of foreign products, such as kerosene lamps, umbrellas, hats, railways, steamboats, soap, milk, wine, and even Western calendars. Like many of the thinkers described in Chapter 8, Kaiseki argued that his country needed to be protected from foreign economic and cultural influences in order to pursue policies that were better suited to its distinctive needs. But his criticism of economic openness and his specific vision for Japanese economic policy included some strong environmental content.[40]

Kaiseki argued, for example, that new export-oriented monocrop production was causing soil exhaustion and deforestation that threatened

---

[38] Marx [1867]1976, 637–38.
[39] Saito 2017, ch. 5–6.
[40] Rambelli 2011, 2017.

to undermine the country's long-term prosperity.[41] He also worried that cheap and attractive machine-produced foreign imports were undermining local artisan producers whose operations were more in tune with nature. As Fabio Rambelli puts it, Kaiseki argued that "natural products and artisanal artifacts follow the natural rhythm of the seasons and are less exploitative of natural resources, and that human beings are more in control of the production process than in the case of mechanically mass-produced goods". His environmentalism was further evident in his opposition to foreign products that relied on fossil fuels such as petrol and carbon whose supply was finite and caused pollution. In Rambelli's words, Kaiseki wrote that "carbon 'is not recreated' once it's finished; furthermore, because of its very essence it 'burns things' and as a result 'where carbon is … neither crops nor plants grow'".[42]

Instead of European-style industrialization and export promotion being embraced by his country's leaders at the time, Kaiseki advocated a more autarkic economic strategy that centered on promoting "natural products" of the traditional agricultural and artisan sectors.[43] Kaiseki was not opposed to economic progress and the promotion of rising material welfare, but he insisted that these goals could be achieved without following foreign economic models. He acknowledged that his strategy might result in some economic inefficiencies, but argued that "inconvenience must be esteemed".[44] He also recognized that the rising prosperity of the country via his strategy would require Japanese producers to have a larger domestic market because Japanese products could "only be consumed internally and there is no way to expand their consumption elsewhere". As a result, he argued that "the only way to enrich the country is to expand consumption", including through educational, recreational, and leisure activities (especially for the wealthy) fostered by public spaces such as shrines, temples, amusement parks, tourist places, and marketplaces.[45]

Environmentalist arguments were also evident among some supporters of autarkic policies during the 1930s. Chapter 8 noted how Keynes' famous 1933 case for national economic self-sufficiency included a brief critique of liberals' focus on financial results at the expense of environmental goals: "We destroy the beauty of the countryside because the

---

[41] In the pre-Meiji era, Japanese forest and soil conservation practices had already become very sophisticated in the context of rapid economic and population growth and what Totman (1989, 184) calls the emergence of a well-established "conservation ethic" in the country (see also Grove 1995, 61–62; Marcon 2015; McMullen 2021).

[42] Quotes from Rambelli 2011, 121–22.

[43] Quote in Rambelli 2011, 121.

[44] Quoted in Sugiyama 1994, 1.

[45] Quoted in Rambelli 2011, 119.

unappropriated splendours of nature have no economic value. We are capable of shutting off the sun and the stars because they do not pay a dividend".[46] Keynes' comment implied that an autarkic policy would allow governments to give greater priority to these environmental values.

That general point was made much more directly and in more detail vis-à-vis soil issues by the British scientist Graham Vernon Jacks in a 1939 book he co-authored with Robert Orr Whyte titled *The Rape of the Earth: A World Survey of Soil Erosion*. The chapters written by Jacks warned of a threat to "the whole future of the human race" because the "destruction" of the soil was "proceeding at a rate and on a scale unparalleled in history". Chemical fertilizers did not provide a solution, he argued, because the problem included the erosion of soil stability, as witnessed during the massive US dust bowl of 1930s. He blamed the US experience and other instances of soil erosion squarely on human economic practices such as overgrazing, monocrop agriculture, and deforestation, arguing that "erosion is the modern symptom of maladjustment between human society and its environment".[47] Although he was a strong supporter of Britain's colonial role, he included colonial policies of these kinds among those he criticized.

Jacks emphasized that these poor human economic practices had international economic causes. He noted how "the immediate needs of the rapidly increasing European population in the nineteenth century necessitated an unrestrainable exploitation of new virgin lands without regard to ultimate consequences". In addition to blaming European demand for foreign commodities, he was particularly critical of how European capital had accelerated the development of foreign lands and then been repaid through commodity exports that destroyed those lands' soils. As he put it, "The main economic cause of recent accelerated erosion has been the transfer of capital across regional or political boundaries and its repayment with soil fertility". The problems were then compounded between 1914 and 1934 by a cycle of economic boom and bust, both of which encouraged overexploitation of the land: "In widely separated parts of the world the combined effect of boom, slump and drought produced a catastrophic biological and physical deterioration of whole regions, culminating in dust storms and floods".[48]

Summing up, Jacks was very critical of "what appears to be the one ultimate economic goal of mankind – the conversion of all soil fertility into less messy and more easily consumable forms of wealth". What was needed instead was "re-building human society in a frame whose

---

[46] Keynes 1933, 763–64.
[47] Quotes from Jacks and Whyte 1939, 27, 18, 26.
[48] Quotes from Jacks and Whyte 1939, 28, 211, 213.

shape is determined by the intrinsic nature of the soil and is independent of immediate economic and political considerations". This rebuilding would require the embrace of "human ecology" or "the art of living together with animals, insects and plants" and a rejection of beliefs such as the following: "what is good for the individual is good for everybody; that an owner may do with his property as he likes; that expanding markets will continue indefinitely; that free competition coordinates industry and agriculture". More specifically, he called for more careful grazing and forest preservation practices and argued that "the economic efficiency of large-scale monoculture and plantation agriculture which form the basis of international trade in food must be superseded by mixed farming, rotational agriculture, 'conservation cropping' and suchlike practices which cost more in money, labour and thought than monocultural systems". Although less economically efficient in the short term, he noted most "conservation systems of land utilization ... should ultimately be more productive than are exploitative systems".[49]

He warned, however, that competitive pressures in a "free world economy" inhibited the implementation of these reforms. For this reason, he applauded the widespread turn to more autarkic "economic nationalism" during the 1930s because it was "accomplishing the seemingly impossible task of inducing the human race to put the needs of the land before its own immediate material welfare". In his view, a return to free trade would threaten the progress being made: "if the nations could once more trade with each other without let or hindrance, all the well-laid plans for rebuilding the exhausted earth would be shelved and forgotten overnight". At the same time, Jacks allowed for the possibility of a return to economic internationalism in the future after healthier soils had been restored: "the present period of intense nationalism is only the first phase of the process of building up a new symbiotic relationship between civilization and the land".[50] The argument was reminiscent of Keynes' 1933 case that countries needed to be freed from external market pressures to experiment with new policies, while at the same time leaving open the door to a restoration of an open world economy in the future.

Jacks and Whyte's book became a seminal text for an emerging British movement promoting organic agriculture as a reaction against growing mechanization and use of chemical fertilizers and pesticides in industrial farming.[51] Its case for transforming agriculture was popularized by Eve Balfour's 1943 book *The Living Soil*, which included many quotes from

---

[49] Quotes from Jacks and Whyte 1939, 217, 38, 292, 216.
[50] Quotes from Jacks and Whyte 1939, 218, 216, 284.
[51] Conford 2001, 178.

Jacks and Whyte's publication and which became a bestseller in Britain and beyond. Loyal to the Conservative Party throughout her life, Balfour had taken up farming at a young age and then became an advocate of organic agriculture in 1938. Endorsing the "law of return", she argued that soil fertility would be bolstered if everything taken from the soil was returned to it in the form of wastes that generated humus.[52] She also emphasized the nutritional benefits of organic farming and was an advocate for greater public control of food production and distribution, arguing that the private profit motive and competitive pressures encouraged exploitation of the soil.

As part of this vision, Balfour argued that food must be grown "as near as possible to the sources of consumption", adding that "if this involves fewer imports and consequent repercussions on exports, then it is industry that must be readjusted to the needs of food". To those opposed to greater national economic self-sufficiency, she argued that they needed to recognize that this policy would be forced on Britain anyway as traditional exporters of food to Britain turned inward to avoid the problems of declining soil fertility that Jacks identified. Those countries' need for imports of British manufactures would also diminish as they industrialized. Summing up, she noted: "we shall no longer be able to look to these distant lands for supplies of 'cheap food' in return for manufactured goods. For this we should be profoundly thankful since it may well be the indirect means of restoring our own soil fertility".[53]

Balfour saw her book as contributing directly to British debates at the time concerning plans for the postwar international economic order (see Chapter 14). She urged the planners to recognize the centrality of healthy soils in these discussions: "If we destroy our soil – and it is not indestructible – mankind will vanish from the earth as surely as has the dinosaurs".[54] She also cited Jacks and Whyte's call for a change in attitudes and embrace of "human ecology", but went further to tie her environmentalist vision to the anti-fascist wartime cause:

We are fond of extolling the achievements of man and are apt to talk with pride of his "conquest of nature". This is at present of the same order as the Nazi conquest of Europe. As Europe is in revolt against the tyrant, so is nature in revolt against the exploitation of man. When man preys upon man it is form of cannibalism. When man sets out to "conquer" nature by exploitation, it is no less a form of cannibalism, for man is a part of nature. If he is to survive, he must learn to co-operate with the forces which govern nature as well as with his fellow man.

---

[52] Quote from Balfour 1943, 19.
[53] Quotes from Balfour 1943, 174, 177–78.
[54] Balfour 1943, 13.

If he refuses to learn this lesson, nature will hit back and exterminate him no less surely than the oppressed masses of tortured Europe will someday hit back and exterminate the tyranny that now rules them.[55]

## Other Versions of Environmentalism

Not all environmentalist perspectives in the pre-1945 period related clearly to the liberal, neomercantilist, Marxist, and autarkist worldviews examined in this book so far. Take, for example, environmentalist views expressed by Indigenous peoples in North America during the period being studied. The expansion of European settler colonialism in this region not only drove Indigenous peoples from their traditional lands but also generated massive ecological upheaval. Settlers' economic activities entirely transformed ecological systems and landscapes across the continent through activities such as the importation of new plants and animals, the introduction of new patterns of land use, the damming of rivers, the draining of wetlands, and the extensive clear-cutting of forests and other forms of resource extraction.[56]

When resisting settler colonialism, the costs of this "colonial ecological violence" – to use Jules Bacon's phrase – were often highlighted by Indigenous peoples.[57] An important example is Black Elk, a Lakota thinker who fought against the growing incursion of settlers during the late nineteenth century, including at the Wounded Knee Massacre in 1890. His views were outlined in a 1932 book titled *Black Elk Speaks* (based on recordings of him) that became very influential among the Lakota and wider Indigenous circles across the continent. As J. Baird Callicott notes, Black Elk's teachings drew on Lakotan cosmology to express a "powerful environment ethic".[58]

In the original recordings for the book, Black Elk outlined his view of how the Lakota had lived in a sustainable way in the pre-colonial period:

The four-leggeds and the wings of the air and the mother earth were supposed to be relative-like and all three of us lived together on mother earth ... We roamed

[55] Quotes from Balfour 1943, 193, 13. While Balfour opposed fascism, others in the British organic agriculture movement, such as Jorian Jenks, were more drawn to it (Bramwell 1989, 166–68; Conford 2001, 146–47; Gill 2010, 62–63).

[56] See, for example, Bacon 2019; David and Todd 2017; Whyte 2018.

[57] Quote from the title of Bacon 2019. These costs were also noted by some settlers themselves, such as John Rae (see Chapter 5), who commented on how "the white man robs their [Indigenous peoples'] woods and waters of the stores with which nature had replenished them" (Rae [1834]1964, 131).

[58] Callicott. 2018, 148. For broader discussions of the relationship between environmentalism and Indigenous worldviews in North America, see, for example, Borrows 2018; Leddy 2017; Watts 2013.

the wild countries and in them there was plenty and we were never in want ... we were outside in the fresh air, because it was this way that the Great Spirit wanted us to live. He also had also given us a way of religion. According to the four quarters and the four-legged animals – through them we send up our voices and get help from the Great Spirit. It was his intention at that time to put us together so that we would be relatives-like. We got powers from the four-leggeds and the wings of the air.[59]

Black Elk contrasted this world with the one ushered in during the nineteenth century when "the white man would come on us just like floods of water, covering every bit of land we had ... We were always leaving our lands and the flood devours the four-leggeds as they flee". He lamented how the new settlers "slaughtered all the relatives-like we had" and added: "From them we had our power and when we lost them we lost our power. Right now, they [the whites] get their power from the Thunder-beings [electricity] and we have no more power today that we can fall back on. They take everything we have just gradually until we won't have anything left. The first thing an Indian learns is to love each other and that they should be relative-like to the four-leggeds".[60]

A very different example of a thinker whose views did not relate clearly to the other perspectives outlined in this book so far is the British scientist Frederick Soddy. Well known for earning the Nobel prize in chemistry in 1921, Soddy wrote widely on political economy issues during the interwar years. He sought to develop what he called a new "Cartesian" approach to the subject that emphasized the constraints imposed on human economic activity by the first and second laws of thermodynamics.[61] Soddy insisted that "the flow of energy should be the primary concern of economics" and criticized economists for overlooking how the production of wealth depended entirely on "a continuous supply of fresh energy" from the sun which was then convertible into a useable form by plants".[62]

Soddy noted that the modern use of fossil fuels such as coal had generated a "flamboyant era" of capitalist growth because "for the first time in history, men began to tap a large *capital* store of energy and ceased to be entirely dependent on the *revenue* of sunshine". Like Jevons, however, Soddy warned that coal-fueled economic growth would reach limits because "you cannot burn it and still have it". He noted how this period had also "*indirectly* augmented the revenue of sunshine" by widening "the area under cultivation" around the world to provide food to Britain

[59] De Mallie 1984, 288–89.
[60] De Mallie 1984, 289.
[61] Soddy 1922, 4. Put briefly, the first and second laws state that the total energy of the universe is constant and that its transformation is accompanied by entropic dissipation.
[62] Quotes from Soddy 1926, 56, 294.

and other industrial countries in return for their manufactured exports. But the prosperity that Britain derived from this arrangement was also "destined to be short-lived" because growing populations in newly developed agricultural regions would soon absorb their own produce and build their own industries. Soddy argued "imperialism" marked the "final bid for survival" of this unsustainable model of growth:

The fiercest international rivalry for markets ensues, and to industrialised nations armaments are, as products of machino-facture, the one thing that can be turned out in almost limitless abundance. But armaments and war do not produce food. They merely determine the distribution as between competing nations, and tend to destroy food-producing power to an extent that makes even the victors actual losers.[63]

With this ecologically-oriented theory of growth and imperialism, Soddy urged recognition of the physical limits to human economic activity (although he believed humans could find new ways of using flows of solar energy and existing stores such as atomic energy). He was particularly critical of liberal economists who thought growth could be based on debt, which he argued only created "virtual wealth" and "power over men" by wealthy creditors rather than "power over Nature". In his view, exploitation by private creditors pushed down domestic wages and generated surplus wealth that needed an international outlet, thereby contributing further to the pressure for war. He called for an end to private bankers' ability to create money and for governments to use their monetary monopoly to maintain price stability, while protecting their policy autonomy with a flexible exchange rate and "direct national supervision" of foreign exchange transactions.[64] Soddy's views on these topics were partly informed by his interest in socialist thought before the late 1920s. But he increasingly associated with the political right, including prominent British fascists, who shared his interest in monetary reform.[65] The difficulty of classifying his ideas is compounded by the fact that they did not resonate with neomercantilist or autarkic perspectives because he was a strong supporter of free trade.[66]

Although his views are not easy to pigeon-hole, Soddy himself consistently praised the political economy ideas of John Ruskin, an Oxford professor of fine arts who had emerged in the 1860s as a prominent opponent of liberal political economy. Beginning with his 1862 text *Unto*

---

[63] Quotes from Soddy 1926, 29–30; 1922, 11–12, 31–32.
[64] Quotes from Soddy 1926, 100; 1934, 133.
[65] Merricks 1996b, ch. 6.
[66] See, for example, Soddy 1926, 285. For the difficulties involved in classifying Soddy into traditional schools of thought, see also Merricks 1996a, 62–63.

*This Last*, Ruskin criticized the modern, urban, consumer-oriented, industrial society that economic liberals of his day endorsed. In addition to attacking its immoral focus on self-interest and the degradation of work through specialized factory labour, Ruskin highlighted environmental problems associated with modern industrialism, such as excessive resource use, landscape destruction, and industrial pollution (including atmospheric pollution that he depicted in increasingly global terms). Although inspired by Humboldt's work, Ruskin's arguments stemmed from distinctive "Tory radical" position. As Albritton and Jonsson put it, he was "a conservative who treated urban bourgeois life with contempt but would not lift a finger in favor of social revolution".[67]

Ruskin's solution to the problems he identified was also very different than Soddy's. He advocated a return to a simpler and more sustainable, decentralized way of living that valued handicraft production, small-scale agriculture, artistic achievement, renewable energy, and the bonds of family and community. In the 1870s, he relocated to England's Lake District to embrace and promote this lifestyle with colleagues and others in the region, including factory workers via a guild he organized and funded. Through these initiatives, Albritton and Jonsson highlight how Ruskin and his followers "sought a way to exit the fossil fuel economy and consumer society" through social experiments that were designed to offer "a taste of the postindustrial future". Indeed, these two authors suggest that Ruskin saw his initiatives as showing how Britain could live in a future stationary state when Jevons' predictions of an exhausted Britain's coal supply came to pass.[68]

Ruskin's ideas inspired many, including Gandhi, who cited *Unto This Last* as a key influence on his thinking.[69] But there was one aspect of Ruskin's work that contrasted sharply with Gandhi's. The latter argued that national autarkic policies were needed to protect India's local village self-reliance against foreign competition. By contrast, Ruskin described himself in *Unto This Last* as "an utterly fearless and unscrupulous free-trader", despite his fierce criticism of the laissez faire ideas of classical economic liberals. In his view, free trade did not "imply enlarged competition" but rather "an end to all competition". Here was his logic:

When trade is entirely free, no country can be competed with in the articles for the production of which it is naturally calculated; nor can it compete with any other, in the production of articles for which it is not naturally calculated. Tuscany, for

---

[67] Quotes from Albritton and Jonsson 2016, 47. For his interest in Humboldt's work, see Grove 1995, 372.
[68] Quotes from Albritton and Jonsson 2016, 12, 23. See also p. 174.
[69] Parel 2006.

instance, cannot compete with England in steel, nor England with Tuscany in oil. They must exchange their steel and oil … Competition, indeed, arises at first, and sharply, in order to prove which is the strongest in any given manufacture possible to both; this point once ascertained, competition is at an end.[70]

Gandhi himself made only occasional comments about environmental degradation, such as the depletion of natural resources and soils.[71] But this topic received much more attention from Radhakamal Mukerjee, whose 1916 book *The Foundations of Indian Economics* was praised by Gandhi. A well-known Indian professor of economics who became active in the Indian independence movement, Mukerjee critiqued "Western industrialism" in this book, while supporting India's cottage-based industries and decentralized village-based economy (and citing Ruskin's ideas).[72] During the 1920s and 1930s, Mukerjee increasingly emphasized the need for the human economy to be in balance with the natural environment in regional ecological settings. As he put it in his 1938 book *The Regional Balance of Man,* "the permanence of civilization depends chiefly on man's intimate understanding of and co-operation with the totality of the region's forces, including not merely climate, soil, and topography, but also the associated vegetable and animal life". In his detailed studies of the Indian context, Mukerjee became very critical of how humans had caused a "loss of ecologic balance" in regional settings such as the Ganges valley, where the expansion of agriculture, overgrazing, deforestation, and "the indiscriminate extermination of grassland" had caused soil exhaustion and erosion as well as local climatic change that increased floods and droughts.[73]

Mukerjee also placed his environmental concerns in a global economic setting, noting that "many of the industrial countries of the West have adopted a scale of social and industrial living, which has little reference to the resources and possibilities of the regions themselves". He highlighted how this "unstable balance between man's demands and the region's yields" was only maintained by the West's "improvident use of resources in men and materials in other parts of the world". Mukerjee called for regional "social ecological planning" within a wider context of "interzonal ecologic co-operation on the earth". He argued that the latter would need to lay bare "the danger spots in human space distribution

[70] Ruskin [1862]1923, 75–76n1.
[71] See, for example, Guha 2000; Guha and Martinez-Alier 1997.
[72] Quote from Mukerjee, 1916, xix. Ruskin is referenced on p. 467. The key popularizer of Gandhian economic ideas in India, Joseph Kumarappa, also gave more attention to environmental issues, but his key work on this topic, *Economy of Permanence*, was published in 1945, just after the pre-1945 focus of this volume (Kumarappa 1945).
[73] Quotes from Mukerjee 1938, 3; 1934, 161.

and exploitation of the earth" in ways that avoided relationships "based on one-sided parasitism" and that focused on "the conservation and development of regional resources from the standpoint of its original or permanent residents rather than from that of the intrusive and immigrant non-residents". In the context of the large ecological problems of his age, he argued that "the problem of achieving a working balance of the world forces, and the balance of the nations and the regions in a new economy, is the supreme challenge for civilisation to-day".[74]

Mukerjee's ideas were cited by Richard Gregg, who emerged as a well-known American pacifist and environmentalist after he travelled to India in the mid-1920s and then promoted Gandhi's ideas in books such as *Economics of Khaddar* (1928) and *The Power of Non-Violence* (1935).[75] Gregg highlighted not just economic and social benefits of Gandhi's decentralist economic vision but also environmental ones. Quoting Soddy's ideas about wealth stemming from solar energy, he noted the "great numbers of unemployed Indians" who were "in effect, engines kept running by fuel (food), but not attached to any machines or devices for producing goods". He continued: "Mr Gandhi proposes to hitch them to charkhas [spinning wheels] and thus save a vast existing waste of solar energy". Gregg went further to argue – drawing once again on Soddy – that this "food-man-charkha combination is actually more efficient than the coal-steam-engine-textile-mill when the total consumption of solar energy units is considered". Indeed, he suggested that Europe and America had "much to learn" environmentally from this and other traditional economic practices in Asia: "It may well be that the great stability of the civilizations of China and India has rested upon their closer approximation to such a balance of energy resources or to a symbiosis with Nature than there was or is in the case of other civilizations".[76]

Although Gregg built upon Gandhi's ideas, he did not fully endorse the latter's autarkic ideas. To be sure, he praised how an economy centered on handicraft production would boost national "economic independence" and enable "greater freedom from foreign financial and commercial interests and control". Like Gandhi, he also argued that an economy centered on "small-scale, decentralized production and distribution" would be less tempted to engage in imperialism. But Gregg suggested further that this economic strategy would also helpfully generate "a revival of world trade" by boosting the purchasing power of Indians

[74] Quotes from Mukerjee 1938, 6, 311, 310.
[75] For his life, see Kosek 2005. For his reference to Mukerjee, see, for example, Gregg 1928, 74. He also popularized the phrase "voluntary simplicity" in a 1936 article published in an Indian journal (Gregg 1936[1974]).
[76] Quotes from Gregg 1928, 19, 27, 217.

and thus their ability to buy other countries' goods.[77] While noting that every nation should try to "produce its own essential food and clothing", he argued that "beyond and above that let trade proceed as merrily as it can, but with a minimum of exploitation". As an example of the latter, he was deeply opposed to how the "white man" in Europe and the United States exploited tropical countries by forcing them to specialize in mono-crop plantation agriculture in ways that was "reducing their prosperity, depleting their soil, ultimately decreasing their productivity, increasing their losses from plant disease and insects, and market depressions".[78]

Another prominent American environmentalist who cited Mukerjee's ideas (as well as those of Ruskin) was Lewis Mumford.[79] In his *Technics and Civilization* (1934) and *The Culture of Cities* (1938), Mumford retold Western history from an ecological standpoint, highlighting the transition from an "eotechnic" phase (centered on water and wood) to a "paleotechnic" phase (centered on coal and iron). While the former was environmentally sustainable, the latter "was marked throughout the Western World by the widespread perversion and destruction of environment", including "a reckless waste of resources", widespread pollution of the air and water, and exhausted soils.[80] Looking forward, Mumford anticipated an emerging "neotechnic" phrase that drew on less environmentally damaging sources of energy (including hydroelectricity) and better conservation of resources and soils associated with improved chemical and biological knowledge.[81]

As part of this shift, he called – like Mukerjee – for a turn towards decentralized economies organized around bioregional zones. In his vision, economic activity in these zones would be based on a region's natural endowments and centered on small-scale industry and farming that used renewable energy sources and encouraged a move away from the "dogma of increasing wants". Close links between town and country would also reduce transportation costs, enable recycling of human waste to the soil,

---

[77] Quotes from Gregg 1935, 235; 1928, 82, 79, 71.
[78] Quotes from Gregg 1935, 133–34. Gregg's interest in anti-racist politics was also evident in his correspondence with W. E. B. Du Bois (Slate 2012, 97).
[79] For Mukerjee, see, for example, Mumford 1934, 377. For Ruskin, see Mumford 1944, 415. Both Mumford and Mukerjee were influenced by Patrick Geddes, a Scottish biologist and sociologist who himself was deeply inspired by Ruskin (Geddes 1884; Guha and Martinez-Alier 1997; Manjapra 2014, 155–60; Scott and Bromley 2013). Geddes also praised Jevons' ideas and his calls for a "physical economics" in 1884 anticipated some of Soddy's later ideas (Geddes 1884, 28; see also p. 27; Merrick 1996b, 109–11). Geddes also inspired others who went on to play a role in the British organic agriculture movement (Conford 2001, 164–66). I have not discussed Geddes' ideas because I could not find international economic issues addressed in his work.
[80] Mumford 1934, 169, 255.
[81] Mumford 1934, 255–59.

and create stable local markets that avoided "the speculative fluctuations of the world market". In his 1944 book *The Condition of Man*, Mumford presented this vision of a regional "balanced economy" as a response to "the end of the Era of Expansion" and he invoked Mill's positive comments about the stationary state. Like Mukerjee and Ruskin, he also emphasized that his decentralist vision was not an autarkist one. In addition to praising the global flow of "ideas, values, and symbols", he highlighted the benefits of some inter-regional exchange of surplus goods or of "special materials and skills ... not universally found or developed throughout the world".[82]

Like Mukerjee, Mumford also combined his decentralist vision with an interest in international economic cooperation. In his 1941 book *The Faith of Living*, he called on wealthier nations to "make the major act of sharing and giving, for the benefits of the rest of mankind" in order to address the unjust distribution of natural resources in the world. As he put it, "international justice demands the creation of a world-wide authority for the allocation and distribution of power and raw materials. ... Such an authority would iron out inequalities; even fix quantities in advance of production ... This is the economic basis for that human brotherhood". Mumford's proposal for this kind of global authority sat uncomfortably with his 1944 insistence that "the task for our age is to decentralize power in all its manifestations". But he emphasized how different his proposal was from visions of international economic cooperation that sought to boost economic integration (such as that of the Bretton Woods conference taking place in the same year, as noted in Chapter 14):

Those naïve souls who conceive world co-operation in terms of vast armadas of airplanes plying back and forth across the continents and seas, are secretly thinking of making the standards of Paris and Hollywood, New York and Moscow, prevail throughout the planet...Such mechanical intercourse would merely continue the irrational and irregional [sic] expansion of the past: a blind automatism that must result in a final destruction of the civilization that thus seeks to perpetuate a moribund self.[83]

## Conclusion

Environmentalist perspectives on international dimensions of political economy have a much deeper history than the last few decades. The ideas of pre-1945 environmentalists were also not marginal to political

---

[82] Quotes from Mumford 1934, 391, 382; 1944, 408, 398, 403; 1934, 388. For his citing of Mill, see Mumford 1944, 400, 411. For his rejection of autarky, see Mumford 1938, 345; 1941, 242.
[83] Quotes from Mumford 1941, 244, 245; 1944, 419, 403.

debates in their time. They attracted considerable attention in various
political contexts around the world. Environmentalists linked analyses of
international economic relations and the world economy to a wide range
of human-induced kinds of environmental degradation, including deforestation, the depletion of other renewable and non-renewable resources,
soil erosion and exhaustion, loss of species and landscapes, industrial
pollution, and climate change.

Like other perspectives discussed in previous chapters, there were also
many distinct versions of environmentalism. While many of the thinkers
discussed in this chapter were concerned about environmental degradation only for anthropocentric reasons, some (particularly Humboldt
and Black Elk) promoted a more ecocentric version of environmentalism that valued the natural environment for its own sake. They also disagreed on important issues such as their support (e.g. Jevons, Jacks) or
opposition (e.g. Humboldt, Black Elk, Mukerjee, Gregg) to imperialism.
Particularly important was the fact that environmentalists were divided
according to whether they mixed their environmentalism with other perspectives such as liberalism, neomercantilism, Marxism, or autarkism,
or whether they developed distinct versions such as those of Black Elk,
Soddy, and the decentralism of Ruskin, Mukerjee, Gregg, and Mumford. Many of these divisions persist in the current age, although the
range of debate within contemporary environmentalist writing in the IPE
field often appears narrower than it was in the pre-1945 years.

# 10    Feminist Critiques of a Patriarchal World Economy

In the last few decades, a vibrant tradition of feminist thought has emerged within the field of IPE. Like environmentalism, feminism is often portrayed as a relatively new perspective in IPE, but it, too, has precursors in ideas put forward by prominent thinkers in the pre-1945 era. The term "feminism" has a deeper history than "environmentalism", being coined as early as 1837 by the French thinker Charles Fourier, who asserted that "the degree of feminine emancipation is a natural measure of the general emancipation".[1] When the term began to be used more widely in the late nineteenth century and after, its meaning was often contested and many of thinkers discussed in this chapter did not use it to describe their views.[2] They did, however, all share – with varying levels of commitment – a broad normative goal that has echoes in contemporary feminist IPE literature: that of challenging patriarchal practices and structures in order to end women's subordination within the world economy.

Like other perspectives examined in this book, early feminist thought came in many varieties (as it is still does in the current age).[3] Some thinkers worked within the economic liberal tradition, widening its focus to be inclusive of feminist goals. Others argued that economic liberalism was not compatible with the feminist cause and sought instead to merge feminist goals with socialist goals, both Marxist and non-Marxist. There were also important disagreements among liberal feminists as well as among socialist feminists. Although these debates involving liberal and socialist feminists "had a high profile in pre-1945 feminist political economy, there were also some thinkers who combined feminist ideas with other perspectives, including neomercantilism, Pan-Africanism, and anarchism.

[1] Quoted in Farnsworth 1976, 292fn1. The first English use of the term appears to have come in 1852 from Louisa McCord, an advocate of free trade in the antebellum US South, who, unlike Fourier, opposed calls for women's equality (McLeod 2011).
[2] For uses of the term "feminism" in this period, see, for example, Moynagh and Forestell 2012, xxiv.
[3] For the diversity of feminist thought in general, see Delap 2020.

## Feminism and Classical Economic Liberalism

The thinker whose ideas began this book, Adam Smith, wrote very little about the role of women or gender in economic life in *The Wealth of Nations*. For example, Smith's focus on market transactions led him to gloss over the economic importance of unpaid work in the household that was dominated by women in Britain – and elsewhere – at the time. Contemporary feminists often highlight Smith's disinterest in this economic activity by citing the following famous passage where he praised the merits of markets: "it is not from the benevolence of the butcher, the brewer, or the baker that we expect our dinner, but from their regard to their own self-interest". The fact that British dinners were usually prepared by women in an unpaid capacity is left unspoken in this sentence.[4]

Smith also did not discuss the barriers women faced to participating equally in the British market economy that he endorsed.[5] At the time Smith was writing, British women were restricted from working in many occupations and from taking up apprenticeship and educational opportunities. Even when they held paid jobs, women's wages were often significantly lower than those of men in similar kinds of work. Married women in Britain also had no property rights until 1870. In addition, Richard Olson notes that under English and Scottish common law, "women were not treated as competent to enter into contracts except in connection with household management". Discrimination was even worse in Smith's Scotland, which Olson describes as having "one of the most patriarchal cultures in Europe". As he puts it, "in Scots law, a husband could even repudiate his wife's right to purchase groceries, etc".[6]

Smith's neglect of these barriers facing women was striking given his broader emphasis in *The Wealth of Nations* on the need to promote economic "liberty" (see Chapter 2). It was also noteworthy because he had shown more interest in women's unequal status within the family and society in some earlier unpublished lectures in the early 1760s. In those lectures, Smith had argued that women's status would improve as countries became commercial societies, including with respect to their right to inherit and own property. His reasoning was that the importance of physical strength and the status of male warriors would diminish in these societies and women would have greater opportunities to accumulate

---

[4] See, for example, Folbre 2009, 59; Marçal 2016. Smith's passage is in Smith 1776, I.ii.2.
[5] See, for example, Bodkin 1999; Dimand et al. 2004; Kuiper 2006; Nyland 1993.
[6] Olson 1998, 81.

wealth.[7] With this argument, Smith challenged the idea that patriarchy was somehow inevitable. In *The Wealth of Nations*, however, Smith made little effort to contest, or even comment on, the barriers that continued to uphold patriarchy in Britain's increasingly commercialized society.

Other thinkers working within the economic liberal tradition devoted more attention to these barriers. In some cases, however, those barriers were defended for anti-feminist reasons. For example, the French popularizer of Smith's work in the early nineteenth century, Jean-Baptiste Say, explicitly supported restrictions on women's paid employment, arguing that women should focus on performing unpaid household work. Stanley Jevons (Chapter 9) held similar views later in the nineteenth century, calling for tighter controls on women's work outside the home.[8]

Other thinkers, however, combined economic liberal views with calls for women to have a more equal place in a market economy. For example, in the late eighteenth century, the pioneering English feminist Mary Wollstonecraft invoked some of Smith's ideas positively, while lamenting "the few employments open to women" (as well as their largely "menial" nature) and calling for improved educational opportunities for women to allow them to become more economically independent and gain wider job opportunities.[9] Her more conservative contemporary Priscilla Wakefield (whose grandson was Edward Wakefield, discussed in Chapter 2) called more direct attention to Smith's neglect of women in her 1798 *Reflections on the Present Condition of the Female Sex*. She highlighted how women would be able to make greater economic contributions to English society, while securing larger economic independence, if their employment and educational opportunities were widened and if they received equal pay for the same jobs as men.[10]

Some of the nineteenth-century economic liberals discussed in Chapters 2 and 3 provide further examples. In the early nineteenth century, the prominent Indian liberal Rammohun Roy (see Chapter 3) also emphasized the importance of expanding women's educational opportunities for their independence. In addition, he called for women's property rights, arguing that this would restore the "ancient rights of females" embodied in Bengali legal tradition.[11] Roy, in fact, became well known

---

[7] This line of argument was developed in more detail by Smith's student John Millar, although he warned that women's status might decline in excessively commercialized societies (Bowles 1984; Olson 1998).

[8] Dimand et al. 2004; Folbre 2009; Forget 1997; Gouverneur 2013.

[9] Quote from Wollstonecraft [1792]2004, 101. For her views on political economy, See, for example, Packham 2017; Rendall 1997.

[10] Dimand 2003; Leach and Goodman 2000.

[11] Quote in Mukherjee 1996, 63.

in British feminist circles in the 1820s. Underlying his views was a belief that both men and women were equally endowed by God with qualities for boundless improvement, qualities that were being inhibited by the low social position of women in Bengal.[12]

John Stuart Mill's famous work *Principles of Political Economy* (discussed in Chapter 2 of this book) also criticized gender inequality within the market economy, including restrictions on women's employment as well as their lower wages. In his 1869 *Subjection of Women*, Mill went further to compare women's subordinate social position to slavery, arguing that it was a product of socially constructed gender norms as well as men's use of power to deny women equal access to education, political rights, and economic independence. Mill's views were strongly influenced by his wife Harriet Taylor, who he credited with helping him to write *Principles*. In her 1851 essay *The Enfranchisement of Women*, Taylor urged gender equality in market society, arguing that "so long as competition is the general law of human life, it is tyranny to shut out one half of the competitors". Taylor also gave greater emphasis than Mill to the point that women's paid employment ensured that "the woman would be raised from the position of a servant to that of a partner" within the family.[13]

To what extent did thinkers link the feminist cause to the core international policy goal of economic liberals: free trade? An important figure who drew this connection was Harriet Martineau. Raised in the Unitarian tradition that supported women's education, Martineau was also deeply inspired by Roy, with whom she became acquainted when he visited London in 1830.[14] She took up writing after the collapse of her father's firm in the late 1820s and quickly became famous with her first major work *Illustrations of Political Economy*. Initially published as twenty-five monthly issues between 1832 and 1834, the work presented the ideas of economic liberalism through accessible stories that attracted a huge audience in Britain (with its monthly installments outselling Dickens' novels) and elsewhere.[15] Leading British politicians were soon asking her for economic advice and, when traveling in the United States in

---

[12] Zastoupil 2010, ch. 5.

[13] Taylor [1851]1868, 14, 13. For Mill's views (as well as the influence of Taylor on Mill), see Bodkin 1999; Folbre 2009, ch. 13.

[14] Chapman 1877, 179–82; Zastoupil 2010, 85–87. Roy was also cited as an inspiration by later Indian feminists in the early twentieth century such as Muthulakshmi Reddi ([1933]2012).

[15] Dimand et al. 2004. Martineau was inspired by an earlier female writer, Jane Haldimand Marcet, who had also popularized liberal political economy in her 1816 *Conversations on Political Economy* (Shackleton 1990).

the mid-1830s, she was invited to talk with President Andrew Jackson. Because of her prominence, critics of classical economic liberalism also cited her ideas, including Marx and later Keynes.[16]

In her various writings (that included many other books), Martineau emphasized that women were rational economic agents who should have the same economic opportunities as men in order to boost their independence. For this reason, she opposed the British Factory Acts of the 1840s – which limited women's working hours – for curtailing women's employment choices. She also supported efforts to boost women's access to education, to create independent property rights for married women, and to improve women's wages and working conditions.[17] In addition, Martineau called attention to the economic oppression of women in other countries, such as the United States, where they suffered from restrictions on their education and property rights, a very limited number of job opportunities, low pay, poor working conditions (particularly in the country's growing industrial mills), and slavery.[18]

Martineau went further than many other economic liberals in providing a gendered analysis of international trade policy. An example of this analysis appeared in her 1837 book *Society in America* which included a critique of US tariffs that had been designed to cultivate the growth of local manufacturing. In Martineau's view, this US trade policy had been misguided because it had caused "over-manufacture, panic, and ruin to many" with costs that were borne largely by women, who were the main employees in the factories. She explained:

In New England, there is a large class of very poor woman, - ladies; some working; some unable to work. I knew many of these; and was struck with the great number of them who assigned as the cause of their poverty the depreciation of factory stock, or the failure in other ways of factory schemes, in which their parents or other friends had, beguiled by the promises of the tariff, invested what should have been their maintenance.[19]

### Later Liberal Feminist Visions

Other feminists supported free trade because of a belief that it would curtail wars, from which they argued many women suffered enormously. Indeed, the Cobdenite equation of free trade with peace (see Chapter 2)

---

[16] Hoecker-Drysdale 2003.
[17] Dimand et al. 2004; Hoecker-Drysdale 2003, 62; Shackleton 1990, 296.
[18] Martineau 1837, 27, 73–96, 156ff.
[19] Martineau 1837, 33.

captured the imagination of many feminists well into the interwar years.[20] For example, it was strongly endorsed by the prominent Women's International League for Peace and Freedom (WILPF), which was founded in 1919 and included leading feminists from Europe, the United States, and elsewhere. In 1919, the League called for "universal free trade" and "free access to raw materials for all nations on equal terms" (as well as "a universal system of coinage and the same weights and measures in all countries"). It also insisted that tariff policies consider the needs not just of the producer but also of the "user" because "the majority of women are providers for the home".[21]

The WILPF's first president, the well-known American activist and social reformer Jane Addams, reiterated this belief in free trade in various writings, including her 1922 book *Peace and Bread in the Time of War*, which argued that "the world was faced with a choice between freedom in international commerce or international conflicts of increasing severity". She also saw free trade as a policy to ensure food availability worldwide, noting that "the nation denied the open door must suffer in its food supplies". For her peace activism, Addams won the Nobel peace prize in 1931, at which time her strong commitment to free trade remained. As she put it the next year, the "unrestricted intercourse between nations must in the long run make for better understanding and good will ... and the freedom of trade intercourse is essential to national prosperity".[22]

Addams also developed some broader arguments about international economic relations that echoed the views of others who began to reformulate economic liberalism in this period (see Chapter 14). Drawing on her experiences of social work among Chicago's urban poor beginning in the late 1880s, Addams called in her 1906 book *Newer Ideals for Peace* for public authorities to improve disadvantaged people's welfare through more activist policies than classical economic liberals had endorsed, such as old age pensions, unemployment and accident insurance, sick benefits, and strengthened labour legislation. Addams also suggested at this time that these policies be accompanied by a "new internationalism" that would involve the "displacement of the military ideals of patriotism

[20] Palen 2018. The Cobden Club did not, however, accept women as members until 1885, with the first to join being Florence Nightingale (Palen 2016, 109).

[21] WILPF 1919, 4, 3, 10, 14. See also Palen 2018, 122–32. In support of their cause, free trade advocates in the nineteenth century had also often invoked the interests of women as buyers for the household (e.g. Palen 2016, 214–15; Heaman 2017, 142–43). The WILPF included not just liberals but also some socialists; Addams even encouraged Aleksandra Kollontai (see below) to create a Russian section (Rupp 1997, 31).

[22] Quotes in Addams 1922, 88; Palen 2018, 122–23. For Addams' high international profile, see, for example, Rupp 1997, 192–93.

by those of a rising concern for human welfare" in the context of growing economic interdependence among countries.[23] In later work, she
described this as a new kind of "governmental internationalism" that
could tackle issues such as food insecurity across the globe.[24]

Addams linked this vision to feminist politics by arguing that this new
world would empower women, as citizenship became less tied to male-
dominated warfare.[25] She also suggested that women had a central role
to play in bringing it into being. At the domestic level, they needed to
push for the right to vote in order to promote a more activist economic
role for the state. She highlighted their incentive to do so because factories were increasingly taking over economic activities that women had
traditionally controlled in the household, such as "much of the brew-
ing and baking" and "practically all the spinning, dyeing, weaving, and
sewing". As these kinds of activities were "pushed out of the domestic
system into the factory system", women no longer maintained "their full
share of the world's work in the lines of production which have always
been theirs". And those women who began working as employees in the
new factories found themselves "surrounded by conditions over which
they have no control", particularly in exploitative sweatshops. If they
gained the right to vote, women could demand legislation to address
these new economic conditions. She also hoped they would promote
broader changes because "the ancient family affection, that desire to
protect and rear little children which they have expressed so long in isolation, might now be socialized and be brought to bear as a moral force
on the current industrial organization".[26]

For the same reason, Addams argued that women also had an important contribution to make at the international level to building the new
"governmental internationalism". As she put it, "the formal organization of international relations" needed to make room for "those primitive human urgings to foster life and to protect the helpless, of which
women were the earliest custodians". When calling on women's groups
to support the fight against food insecurity abroad, she also appealed
to an "instinct" which arose from the deep history of "the tribal feed-
ing of children" as well as the fact that harvest deities around the world
were "always feminine" and "that women were the first agriculturists
and were for a long time the only inventors and developers of its processes". She further noted women's enduring focus on food growing and

---

[23] Quotes from Addams, 1907a (title); 1906, 28.
[24] Addams 1915, 138. For her focus on food insecurity, see Addams 1922.
[25] Addams 1906, 208; 1915, 136.
[26] Quotes from Addams. 1906, 188; 1907b, 108.

preparation while men were fighting in World War I: "drilling soldiers and the constant reviewing of troops were seen in all the capital cities of Europe but there were also the peasant women who, all the world over, are still doing such a large part of the work connected with the growing and preparation of foods. ... the labor for bread, which to me was more basic and legitimate than war, was still going on everywhere".[27]

At the end of the war, Addams became deeply involved in trying to shape the focus of the peace talks and of the League of Nations being established. Some of her ideas were evident in the resolutions of the 1919 WILPF congress. In addition to its emphasis on free trade noted above, the WILPF urged governments to create an international organization that could make the resources of the world "available for the relief of the peoples of all countries from famine and pestilence". The congress also urged the League of Nations to commit to the "establishment of full equal suffrage and the full equality of women with men politically, socially and economically" and to adopt a "Women's Charter". The WILPF argued that the latter should include principles such as women's equal pay for equal work, equal opportunities for education and employment in all sectors, and the right of married women "to use and disposal of her own earnings and property". The WILPF also insisted that the "traffic in women, national and international, should be suppressed".[28]

The League addressed the latter, creating a 1921 International Convention for the Suppression of the Traffic in Women and Children.[29] When establishing the International Labour Organization (ILO) in 1919, the League also endorsed the "principle that men and women should receive equal remuneration for work of equal value".[30] When the ILO then took up the issue of addressing women's employment conditions, however, it backed policies such as restrictions on women's night work that proved controversial in feminist circles. Restrictions of that kind had already been endorsed by a 1906 international convention and Addams herself had supported them in the past, as did some other feminists (including many coming from a socialist tradition, as noted below).[31] But many liberal feminists objected to these restrictions on the same grounds that nineteenth-century liberal feminists had: they undermined women's right to equality in the workplace. To promote the latter, in 1929 they created a lobby group with representatives from

---

[27] Quotes from Addams, 1915, 129–30; 1922, 75–78.
[28] WILPF 1919, 1, 5, 6, 13.
[29] Berkovitch 1999, ch. 3.
[30] Quoted in Lubin and Winslow 1990, 1.
[31] See, for example, Addams 1906, 192; 1912, 12.

twenty-one countries titled Open Door International for the Economic Emancipation of the Woman Worker.[32]

Its first president was the Scottish feminist Chrystal Macmillan, who had been one of the founders of the WILPF and an advocate of the Women's Charter. After campaigning for many years against rules that kept the legal occupation closed to women, Macmillan had become one of the first practicing female lawyers in Britain in 1924 and was very critical of those who "continue to misdescribe the special regulation of the work of women as 'protection.'"[33] She highlighted how the push for greater economic equality was relevant to women across the world:

> In no country has even a beginning been made in putting women economically on a level with men. The whole law and custom of every land are such that the bulk of the national income is under the control of the male portion of the population. The vast majority of married women, although they actually handle the family income, dispense it not as a right, but merely as the agents of their husbands. In almost every country the mother of young children has a lower economic status than any other member of the community. If men's right to work is now almost universally recognised, the fact that a woman has any corresponding right is in practice constantly ignored; still more the woman's right to have equal pay for the work she does.[34]

When women's employment began to be restricted in many countries during the Great Depression, feminist support grew for these efforts to promote equality rights within the workplace.[35] It became particularly strong in Latin America, where international discussions of women's issues had been very active in settings such as the Inter-American Commission of Women (IACW), which had been created in 1928 as the world's first inter-governmental organization focused on women. Within liberal feminist circles in the region, Brazil's Bertha Lutz became the key champion of the economic equal rights agenda. Inspired by the British suffragette movement, Lutz had emerged after World War I as a leader of the Brazilian women's movement. When representing her country at the ILO's first International Labour Conference in 1919, Lutz had supported measures such as restrictions on women's night work on the grounds that they were protective of women. After she saw the Brazilian government introduce these restrictions in 1932 in ways that led to women being fired from their jobs, however, she changed her position and began to push for equal labour rights.[36]

---

[32] Ludi 2019; Rupp 1997, 139–46; Whitworth 1994; Zimmermann 2019.
[33] Quoted in Staff 2020, 49. See also Kay and Pipes 2020.
[34] Macmillan [1920]2012, 173.
[35] Whitworth 1994, 136–38.
[36] Marino 2019, 27, 97–100.

One setting where Lutz had important influence was an ILO conference in Philadelphia in 1944 that was designed to chart a course for its postwar role.[37] At the meeting, Lutz played a key role in drafting a clause declaring that "all human beings, irrespective of race, creed or sex" had "the right to pursue their material well-being" in conditions of "freedom and dignity, of economic security and equal opportunity". The Declaration also made a point of emphasizing the need to integrate this principle into international economic and financial governance: "all national and international policies and measures, in particular those of an economic and financial character, should be judged in this light and accepted only in so far as they may be held to promote and not to hinder the achievement of this fundamental objective".[38] As we shall see in Chapter 14, the ILO's point was ignored at the Bretton Woods international financial conference that took place two months later.

Although liberal feminists focused much of their attention on improving women's position in market economies, the WILPF also called in 1919 for recognition of the value of the unpaid parenting work of women, noting that "there should be adequate economic provision for the service of motherhood". They justified this provision as "both just in principle and necessary to secure status of women as free citizens" because mothers "perform a service of supreme importance to the state and have in the past been reduced to economic dependence by reason of the very service they have rendered".[39] In response to lobbying from women, the 1919 International Labour Conference supported the idea that some women workers should receive six weeks of paid benefits before and after childbirth, thereby providing an international endorsement of the principle of income support for mothers in a limited way for the first time.[40]

The WILPF's lobbying on this issue challenged the longstanding neglect of women's unpaid work in liberal economic analyses that went back to Smith's work. That neglect informed many state practices, including censuses that placed women engaged in domestic duties in a category of an "Unoccupied Class".[41] As noted below, many socialists

---

[37] For her role, see Lubin and Winslow 1990, 66–67. She also played a key role in 1945 in drafting equal rights language in the United Nations Charter (Marino 2019, ch. 8). For gender issues at the 1944 ILO conference, see also Boris 2019, 57–62.

[38] Quotes from ILO 1944, 622. Although Lutz publicly supported the anti-racist wording of the Philadelphia Declaration, Marino notes that she was privately less supportive of anti-racist politics than many other Latin American feminists at the time (Marino 2019, 211). See also Ludi 2019; Zimmermann 2019.

[39] WILPF 1919, 6, 13. Lutz also became a supporter of state-sponsored maternity benefits that were conceptualized as a social right (Marino 2019, 98, 205–6).

[40] Cobble 2018, 36–41.

[41] The quote is from an 1881 English census cited in Folbre 1991, 472.

had long challenged the liberal neglect of the economic significance of women's household work.[42] In the interwar years, the economic signifi-cance of unpaid household work finally attracted growing attention in mainstream liberal economics, with some researchers estimating that it comprised over 30 percent of the gross national product of countries such as the United States and Sweden.[43] Particularly important was the work of Margaret Reid, a professor of economics in Iowa whose 1934 book *Economics of Household Production* (that was based on her PhD dissertation from the University of Chicago) criticized economists for focusing only "on that part of our economic system which is organized on a price basis" while ignoring the fact that "[t]he household is our most important economic institution ... more workers are engaged in it than in any other single industry".[44]

## The Emergence of Socialist Feminism

Within the feminist movement, liberals met strong criticism from social-ists of both a Marxist and non-Marxist persuasion. While liberal femi-nists sought to improve women's position in a liberal market economy, socialist feminists saw the latter as a source of woman's oppression. An important early version of this line of argument was advanced in a lengthy appeal (over two hundred pages) published in 1825 by two Irish thinkers, William Thompson and Anna Wheeler, who were promi-nent in emerging socialist circles at the time. Like many liberal femi-nists, they criticized the "unequal legal and unequal moral restraints" that prevented women from voting, accessing education, choosing an occupation, owning and inheriting property, and holding an equal place in marriage. Even if these restraints were removed, however, Thompson and Wheeler argued that women would remain in a subordinate place if society remained based on the principle of "individual competition". Their reasoning was that women's "permanent inferiority of strength, and occasional loss of time in gestation and rearing infants" would inevi-tably render women less successful "in the race of the competition for wealth". To achieve true gender equality, they argued for the creation of cooperative socialist communities in which children would be raised collectively, traditional marriage structures would be transcended, and

---

[42] Others discussed elsewhere in this book also criticized this neglect in liberal econom-ics, such as John Ruskin (discussed in the previous chapter) (Albritton and Jonsson 2016, 29).

[43] Jefferson and King 2001.

[44] Reid 1934, v.

wealth would be shared among all members, with "individual property and competition for ever excluded".[45]

Although Thompson and Wheeler did not focus on international economic relations, they did place this socialist feminist critique in an international frame, calling on women in all countries to unite: "women, in whatever country ye breathe – wherever ye breathe, degraded, – awake!"[46] Another early socialist feminist thinker with this kind of vision of international solidarity was Flora Tristan, who knew Wheeler and became prominent within French socialist circles that included Fourier in the 1830s and early 1840s. Tristan was particularly concerned about the oppression of working-class women both in the workplace and in the home. In her best-known book *The Workers' Union* (1843), Tristan called – before Marx and Engels – for an international union of all working men and women to overthrow their capitalist bosses and to create cooperative communities in which gender equality prevailed and childcare was shared by the community.[47]

Not all early socialists were strongly devoted to the cause of greater gender equality. For example, the mid-nineteenth-century French socialist Pierre-Joseph Proudhon insisted on male domination in the household and notoriously argued that women needed to choose between being a "housewife or harlot".[48] In the late nineteenth and early twentieth centuries, many other socialists remained wedded to the idea of the patriarchal family and were wary of women's growing work outside the home, not least because of the competition it posed to male workers.[49] Reactionary views towards women were also held by some prominent Marxist politicians such as Marx's son-in-law Paul Lafargue, who is described by Patricia Hilden as sharing the "notoriously backward Proudhonist view of women's proper place".[50]

Marx himself also did not write extensively or systemically about gender issues. Although he echoed Fourier's view that the degree of women's emancipation reflected the progress of a society, his primary interest was the class struggle and emancipation of workers.[51] One year after Marx's death in 1883, Engels justified this focus in his *The Origins of the*

---

[45] Quotes from Thompson and Wheeler, 1825, x, 199. Although Thompson was the formal author, he noted that the ideas had been developed jointly with Wheeler. As a result, the two are often listed as co-authors for this publication.
[46] Thompson and Wheeler, 1825, 187.
[47] Talbot 1991; Blomberg 1998.
[48] Quoted in Stuart 1996, 64. See also Folbre 2009, 176.
[49] See, for example, Hilden 1987; Kealey 1984; Lavrin 1989.
[50] Hilden 1987, 294.
[51] See, for example, Brown 2013; Folbre 2009, ch. 15; Tronto 2015.

*Family, Private Property and the State*, which drew on some of Marx's notes. In that work, Engels linked women's oppression to their subordination within the bourgeois nuclear family, which he argued was a product of the rise of capitalism and private property. He called attention to the unpaid labour of women, describing them as an exploited proletariat within the bourgeois family. But Engels did not think this proletariat could become a self-conscious class capable of revolutionary leadership. Instead, he argued that women's emancipation would come only from a broad socialist revolution that abolished private property and the bourgeois family as the core economic unit of society, while promoting female wage work outside the home, socialized child rearing and domestic work, and free choice marriage. In other words, the class struggle and worker-led revolution were preconditions for gender equality.[52]

This Marxist perspective was advanced further and placed more in the context of international action by the German thinker Clara Zetkin, whose ideas about women became very influential among German Social Democrats before 1914. Like Engels, Zetkin argued that "the emancipation of women, together with that of all humanity, will take place only with the emancipation of labor from capital". But she gave greater emphasis to the importance of women in the anti-capitalist struggle, noting their growing employment in industry and arguing that the proletariat "cannot fight its economic and political battles without the participation of its women". To give women a stronger voice, Zetkin supported the movement for women's suffrage, although she also emphasized that it was "dominated by class contradictions and class struggle" and that "there cannot be a unified struggle for the entire sex".[53] Zetkin also stressed the need for socialist women to organize internationally, helping to launch the first International Women's Day in 1911. In contrast to Addams and Macmillan, however, she was not interested in lobbying the League of Nations. Instead, after she left Germany's Social Democrats and joined the communist cause in 1917, she assumed the leadership of the Comintern's International Women's Secretariat that was established in 1920.[54]

The most prominent feminist in the Soviet Union's policymaking circles during the early post-revolutionary years, Aleksandra Kollontai, shared many of Zetkin's views. Indeed, she played a key role in ensuring that the Comintern recognized International Women's Day as an official

---

[52] See, for example, Molyneux 1981; Pankhurst 1982; Tronto 2015.

[53] Quotes from Boxer 2007, 131; Zetkin [1907]2012, 140, 139. Her colleague Rosa Luxemburg ([1912]2004) shared this view, although she did not focus on gender issues in most of her writing.

[54] See, for example, Edwards 2016, 91; Pankhurst 1982.

communist festival in 1922.[55] Earlier in 1919, Kollontai put forward a resolution to the Comintern's first congress arguing that "the final victory of the world proletariat and the final abolition of the capitalist system, can be ensured only through the common joint struggle of working men and women". She highlighted a number of reasons why it was so important for the Comintern to attract "working women" worldwide to its cause:

The enormous increase in female labour in all branches of the economy; the fact that at least half of the wealth in the world is produced by female labour; in addition, the important part, recognized by all, which women workers play in the construction of the new communist living conditions, in the reform of family life and in the realization of a socialist, community education for children, the goal of which will be to turn out hard-working citizens, imbued with the spirit of solidarity, for the Council republic.[56]

Kollontai was also actively involved in debates about the status of women within the Soviet Union. Before the revolution, she had echoed Engels' emphasis on paid work and the socialization of domestic labour as keys to women's emancipation. She had also critiqued traditional marriage structures, developing what Marilyn Boxer calls "one of the most radical critiques of women's roles in family and sexuality of her era".[57] After the 1917 revolution, she promoted these goals, but also became increasingly critical of government policy as it shifted in different directions. She was particularly vocal in her opposition to a new government family code of 1925, which claimed to assist women by strengthening private alimony payments from men instead of by expanding public support. At this time, the Soviet leadership began to promote much more conservative views about the importance of women's traditional roles in the household.[58]

Another feminist who became involved in the politics of the Comintern was Williama Burroughs, an American who participated in a Comintern meeting in 1928. In her speech to the Comintern, she criticized US and European communist parties for not devoting enough attention to anti-colonial struggles in Africa and the Caribbean. An acquaintance of George Padmore, she helped to create the International Trade Union Committee of Negro Workers (see Chapter 7), and she put particular emphasis on the task of organizing female workers of African descent in the United States and Caribbean. She had in mind not just industrial

[55] Edwards 2016, 91.
[56] Kollantai [1919]2012, 340.
[57] Boxer 2007, 137–38.
[58] Farnsworth 1976; Pankhurst 1982.

workers but also the larger number of women employed as domestic help and in agricultural labour. She was critical of communists and their unions not just for neglecting these workers but also for discriminating against them. In her view, communists also needed to recognize that these workers were concerned with not just higher wages but also broader issues such as improved education, health, sanitation, and housing.[59]

## Interwar Socialist Feminism Beyond the Comintern

While figures such as Zetkin, Kollontai, and Burroughs became involved with the Comintern in the 1920s, other socialists pursued feminist goals through other channels. For example, one of the most prominent leaders of the Indian women's movement, Kamaladevi Chattopadhyaya, challenged women's economic subordination through the All India Women's Conference (created in 1927) and other institutions associated with the Indian nationalist movement in which she held prominent positions. Kamaladevi was drawn to socialist and Marxist ideas when she was imprisoned various times for her prominent role in the civil disobedience campaign against British imperial rule that Gandhi led in the early 1930s. She came to see imperialism as a product of capitalism's need for new markets and investment locations, and argued that it exploited the Indian masses with the help of "Indian allies, such as the princes, landlords, capitalists, middlemen, money-lenders".[60] An extensive world traveler, Kamaladevi also took a global view of the phenomenon, condemning not just European imperialism but also its American and Japanese variants.[61]

In her 1939 work *The Awakening of Indian Women*, Kamaladevi followed other Indian nationalists in criticizing the British for their "merciless destruction of Indian industries" and forcing India "into becoming more and more a cheap granary for supplying raw products to British industries, and a ready market for British manufacturers". But she added a gendered analysis, noting that India's deindustrialization had forced people into farming where the "ownership of land is mainly in male hands". She also argued that women were poorly served by the colonial educational system and were "degraded" by imperialism's "passion for militarism and conquests" in which "warfare comes to be regarded as a male

---

[59] Makalani 2016.
[60] Chattopadhyaya and others 1939, 38. This 1939 book included chapters by some other authors. All quotes come from the chapters she wrote. For her life, see Nanda 2002. I have followed the practice of Nanda (and others) in using the name "Kamaladevi" when discussing her.
[61] See, for example, Brijbhushan 1976, 99–100; Chattopadhyaya 1939; Nanda 2002, 91.

virtue". Kamaladevi invoked a better pre-colonial past: "Before Imperialism laid its dead hand upon our brave ancestors, women did enjoy a great measure of freedom and contributed not a little to the building-up of a fine culture. But a class-dominated society and the crushing heel of Imperialism slowly enslaved them – rich and poor alike".[62] These arguments directly challenged British views – including those in feminist circles – that colonialism was a progressive force for Indian women. Indeed, Kamaladevi was critical more generally of Western-dominated international women's groups that failed to condemn imperialism, including a 1939 meeting of the International Alliance of Women in Copenhagen that she left because so many of its attendees "could not think of Eastern people except as primitive and backward needing the protective wing of some European power or other".[63] When she traveled to the United States later that same year, her criticism of racist worldviews extended to American segregationist policies.[64]

To end the subordination of Indian women, Kamaladevi argued that they needed to join the anti-imperialist nationalist movement but she also insisted that the movement needed to be committed to gender equality. In the early 1930s, she challenged Gandhi's initial reluctance to see women in a front-line role in the civil disobedience campaign and she worked to ensure the nationalist movement endorsed equal rights for women.[65] She also highlighted the need for women to be "economically independent" and for the women's movement to go beyond the agenda of "bourgeois women" to include issues of concern to "those 90% who toil and labour in green fields and dark factories", such as equal pay, maternity benefits and other social benefits, and improvements in working conditions.[66] In her 1944 presidential address to the All India Women's Conference, she also emphasized the need to value household work, noting that "the housewife expends more energy and time and skill in the production of commodities than the unionised, legally protected worker, for her hours are unlimited and her tools countless".[67]

Some prominent Latin American women drawn to socialism also pursued feminist goals in distinct settings. One example was Peru's Magda Portal, who pushed for women's emancipation in the household and broader society through her involvement from the late 1920s onwards

---

[62] Quotes from Chattopadhyaya and others 1939, 24, 25, 3, 4.
[63] Quote from a document jointly authored by Kamaladevi and Malmi Sukthankar, in Barbieri 2008, 12.
[64] Slate 2012, 1, 138.
[65] Nanda 2002, 38–39, 48–50.
[66] Quotes from Chattopadhyaya and others 1939, 2, 7, 35.
[67] Quoted in Devenish 2017, 359. See also Nanda 2002, 38.

with a left-wing anti-imperialist party, the Alianza Popular Revolucionaria Americana (see Chapter 13). The highest ranking and best-known
female official in any political party in Latin America during the interwar
years, Portal became inspired by Kollontai's ideas in the late 1920s after
taking refuge in Mexico, where Kollontai had just completed a diplo-
matic posting. Portal subsequently also became very interested in Flora
Tristan's ideas, not least because Tristan had had a Peruvian father and
had traveled to Peru in 1833, after which she wrote about oppression
in the country, including that of women. Although Portal insisted that
class divisions were more important than those of gender, she lamented
in 1940 the sexism of her colleagues and emphasized that the "day
when woman will take her place alongside man in complete equality and
mutual respect, the most transcendent revolution of all time will have
been accomplished".[68] Like Kollontai and Tristan, Portal believed that
gender equality could not emerge without a socialist revolution and she
was sceptical of bourgeois-led women's movements.[69]

Another important figure in Latin America – and a friend of Portal's –
was Paulina Luisi. After becoming Uruguay's first female doctor before
World War I, Luisi emerged as what Katherine Marino calls "the recognized 'mother' of Latin American feminism" during the interwar years.[70]
An admirer of Addams, Luisi initially embraced liberal feminism and even
attended the founding meeting of Macmillan's Open Door International in
1929. But after a coup in 1933 in her country, Luisi's politics increasingly
moved left into the socialist camp as she became very concerned about the
rise of fascism. In 1934, she helped to organize an important World Congress of Women against War and Fascism in Paris that mobilized over one
thousand delegates around a feminist agenda that was not just anti-fascist
but also anti-imperialist and anti-racist. Like other Latin American feminist socialists at this time, Luisi increasingly saw the international promotion of women's rights – including equal economic rights – as central to the
fight against fascism in a context where Adolf Hitler and Benito Mussolini
were dramatically scaling back women's rights in countries they ruled.[71]
In this context, Latin American socialist feminists found a common cause
with more liberal feminists in the region such as Bertha Lutz.

During World War II, Luisi also shared Lutz's interest in trying to
incorporate feminist goals into the plans being developed for the postwar
international economic order. She urged US authorities in May 1943 to

---

[68] Quote in Weaver 2019, 9.
[69] García-Bryce 2014.
[70] Quote from Marino 2019, 8. For her friendship with Portal, see p. 91.
[71] Marino 2019, 20, 78, 128–29, 143–44, 168–69.

ensure that any postwar multilateral economic institution being created explicitly included women's rights because the war was being fought "with the effort and sacrifice of *both men and women*".[72] Luisi had quite ambitious ideas about how such an institution needed to be able to, in Marino's words, "regulate trade, control world production and allow for equitable distribution of primary materials and food supplies". The push by Luisi and Lutz for women's rights to be incorporated into postwar international economic planning was shared by many other Latin American feminists who had unanimously endorsed the idea at a meeting of the IACW in late 1942. These attendees had also called for women to be included in every government's delegation to postwar planning conferences to help realize this outcome as well as to promote pacifist values more generally. At a subsequent April 1944 meeting of the IACW in Washington, Marino notes that Latin American feminists also "connected their hopes for women's rights with desires for equitable trade policies, protective tariffs to secure fair commodity prices, and a multilateral international body to enforce such provisions".[73]

As noted earlier, some socialist women were more wary of this kind of equal rights agenda in the economic field at this time. For them, it risked undermining labour laws that gave special protection to female workers. Indeed, during the interwar years, many women – both socialists and non-socialists – were engaged actively in debates about the ILO's role in supporting international labour standards that backed these kinds of laws, such as bans on night work for women.[74] Some used the ILO forum to pressure their own governments, such as Tanaka Tana, who told ILO delegates in 1919 of the terrible working conditions in the textile mills of her country, Japan, as a way of building support for such a ban at home. Her description of the "misuse of women, physically and mentally, to swell the capitalist's purse" attracted worldwide attention and embarrassed Japanese officials into supporting a gradual phase-in of such a law.[75] Some women also pushed for more ambitious labour protections. For example, at the 1919 International Congress of Working Women (which brought together trade union women and their supporters), Czech delegate Marie Majerová highlighted "the endless labors of the domestic slave" and called for laws that would extend limits on women's working hours to domestic household work.[76]

---

[72] Quoted in Marino 2019, 190.
[73] Quotes from Marino 2019, 189, 190. See also pp. 180–81.
[74] See, for example, Boris 2019, ch. 1; Cobble 2015; Whitworth 1994, ch. 5; Zimmermann 2019.
[75] Quoted in Cobble 2015, 3. For the working conditions, see Tsurumi 1990.
[76] Quote in Vapnek 2014, 167.

## Beyond the Liberal-vs.-Socialist Debate

Although liberal and socialist ideas had a prominent place in the history of feminist thought about political economy before 1945, some proponents of other perspectives also deserve attention. One was Henry Carey (Chapter 4), who linked his neomercantilist worldview to the cause of promoting greater gender equality. When critiquing the social costs of free trade, Carey argued that women suffered the most because they were often employed in factories exposed to global competitive pressures that generated terrible working conditions, low wages, and unstable employment. In countries where local manufacturing was shut down by foreign competition, he also argued that women had few other employment opportunities: "Unfit to dig the earth, they find themselves driven from the light labor of conversion, in every country subject to the system [of free trade] ... What, then, remains to them? In millions of cases, little else than prostitution". In addition, when free trade undermined the health of local soils, Carey argued that male farmers often emigrated to other countries, while women remained stuck in place. He further suggested that women lost out when free trade drove small proprietors from the land.[77]

For Carey, trade protectionism would end these costs and promote greater gender equality by creating a more diversified economy in which women had greater employment opportunities. When appealing to "advocates of women's rights", he put the case as follows: "the road towards elevation of the [female] sex, lies in the direction of that varied industry which makes demand for all the distinctive qualities of woman". A more diversified economy, in turn, would boost equality within the household: "Brain then taking the place of mere muscle, the weak woman finds herself becoming more and more the equal of the man who is strong of arm – passing by slow degrees, from the condition of man's slave towards that of his companion and his friend". He suggested that these trends would boost national wealth and productivity in ways that served neomercantilist goals in a kind of virtuous cycle: "The more perfect the diversification of employments, the greater, therefore, must be the tendency to equality between the sexes. ... The greater the tendency towards equality, the more continuous and rapid becomes the motion of society, and the greater the power of accumulation".[78]

Carey also suggested that the advancement of the position of women in one country via neomercantilist policies would help promote the same

---

[77] Quote from Carey 1859, 377. See also pp. 368–85.
[78] Quotes from Carey 1859, 470, 369, 53.

trend in other countries: "Were the labor of the English people more productive, English women could make more demand for the products of the skill and taste of the women of France; and were the American women enabled to find, in the making of cloth, a demand for their peculiar powers, they could become better customers for the taste and skill of the women of both France and England". When free trade resulted in British manufacturers outcompeting their foreign counterparts, the opposite result unfolded: "What ... is the object of this competition? That of preventing the women of India, of Ireland, and of America, from finding purchasers for their taste or talent, their labor, whether physical or mental. The English woman is thus degraded to the condition of a mere instrument for crushing her fellow-women throughout the world".[79]

Amy Ashwood Garvey provides another example of a thinker who linked the cause of promoting gender equality in an international context to a perspective beyond economic liberalism and socialism. Born in Jamaica, Ashwood Garvey emerged as a key figure within the Pan-African movement that is discussed in the next chapter of this book. Her initial role involved helping Marcus Garvey to found one of the key bodies of the movement in 1914: the Universal Negro Improvement Association (UNIA). She then married Garvey in 1919, but the two quickly separated, in part because she opposed his conservative views that married women should focus on household duties. Adam Ewing and Ronald Stephens note that "Garvey and his lieutenants embraced a proudly masculinist, and often starkly misogynistic, vision of gender roles".[80] Ashwood Garvey challenged these views, advancing what Nydia Swaby calls a "Pan-African feminist" position.[81] To support this cause, she established a "Ladies Division" in the UNIA with female leadership that focused attention on the issues facing women in the Pan-African movement.[82]

After her work with the UNIA, Ashwood Garvey subsequently travelled extensively and became a prominent figure in Pan-African and anti-imperialist circles in London in the 1930s, working closely with George Padmore and C. L. R. James (see Chapter 7).[83] In 1939, she returned

---

[79] Quotes from Carey 1859, 383, 379–80.
[80] Ewing and Stephens 2019, 8.
[81] Swaby 2011, 2.
[82] Reddock 2014; Sherwood 2003; Shilliam 2021b; Swaby 2011.
[83] Matera 2015, 104–11; Reddock 2014. In these London circles during the 1930s, see also the role of another Jamaican woman, Una Marson, who also worked briefly in the League of Nations in 1935 and then as a secretary to Haile Selassie (Matera 2015, 121–42; Umoren 2018).

to Jamaica and became very involved in its politics, promoting women's education and improved wages and working conditions for female domestic workers. She also lobbied Eleanor Roosevelt to include women in a US wartime program to assist the American economy through the recruitment of Caribbean workers. Although some Jamaicans worried that the exportation of women to the United States would represent a new kind of exploitation of the country, Garvey argued that they would gain beneficial money and skills. In April 1944, just a few months before the Bretton Woods conference, she outlined plans (ultimately unsuccessful) to publish a magazine to "bring together the women, especially those of the darker races, so that they might work for the betterment of all". As she put it, "There must be a revolution among women. They must realize their importance in the post-war world ... Women of the world must unite".[84] As noted above (and discussed in Chapter 14), the Bretton Woods planners showed little interest in these issues.

One final example comes from China. He-Yin Zhen is known as "one of the founders of Chinese feminism" because of her writings in 1907–8 in a journal of the Women's Rights Recovery Association that she founded while living in Japan.[85] Her feminism was distinctive from that of others discussed in this chapter because of its association with the anarchist tradition that was mentioned briefly in Chapter 8's discussion of Peter Kropotkin's thought. He-Yin was very interested in global economic transformations in her day, particularly the worldwide growth of industrial capitalism. She noted that growing imports of machine-made textiles and the establishment of modern textile factories in coastal China were undermining her country's traditional home-based handicraft spinning and weaving that were dominated by women working in conditions of "free or voluntary employment". With their livelihood destroyed, she highlighted how many women were forced to become wage labourers in factories with terrible working conditions (or to become domestic servants, concubines, or prostitutes). Because of China's low wages, He-Yin Zhen anticipated further growth of factories of this kind in which women would be employed as "the slaves of capitalists".[86]

He-Yin Zhen was very critical of earlier Chinese advocates of women's rights such as Liang Qichao (see Chapter 5) for ignoring this plight of Chinese women. A decade earlier, Liang had called for improved female education in order to enable women to take on a more productive paid work in ways that contributed to his neomercantilist goal of boosting

---

[84] Quoted in Swaby 2011, 70. See also Baptiste 2003; Matera 2015, 108; Sherwood 2003.
[85] Zarrow 1988, 811. See also Liu et al. 2013a, b.
[86] Quotes from He-Yin Zhen [1907a]2013, 77, 81.

China's wealth and power.[87] He-Yin Zhen argued, however, that this goal simply "forces people into bitter lives" associated with "the system of buying and selling labor power". While women had controlled their own production in home-based weaving and spinning, they were now being used *as instruments of wealth accumulation*.[88] Noting the trend of rising female paid labour in Japan, the United States, and European countries, she did not think these countries should be seen as models in the way that people such as Liang (who also translated Mill's 1869 *Subjection of Women*) believed. He-Yin Zhen also rejected the neomercantilist goal of strengthening China's military power, arguing that "military buildup and warfare harm women" and that "the very origin of inequality between men and women lies in militarism".[89]

He-Yin Zhen's ideas also departed from socialists and Marxists, who blamed capitalism for women's subordination. She argued that the oppression of women in China, including the commodification of their bodies, had much deeper roots in older structures of inequality as well as in Confucian scholarship. As an anarchist, she also rejected the belief in state control of the economy. Indeed, the bylaws of her society explicitly "prohibited supporting governments".[90] Instead, she called for "an economic revolution", the goal of which would be "to overthrow the system of private property and to replace it with communal property, meanwhile abandoning all monies and currencies". In this new world, gender equality could be realized as "everyone, whether man or woman, would labor equally" and "everyone would be independent".[91]

## Conclusion

Many issues raised in contemporary feminist IPE literature also interested thinkers in the pre-1945 years. Although not always describing themselves as feminists, these thinkers were interested in challenging practices and structures that upheld patriarchy in order to end women's subordination within the world economy of their era. They called attention to discrimination against women in areas such as property and voting rights, wage levels, access to employment, and education, as well as

---

[87] See, for example, Liu et al. 2013a, b. The idea that a country's wealth and power could be augmented through female work in industry was a common theme of neomercantilist literature including that of Hamilton ([1791]1964, 131) and List ([1841]1909a, 161).

[88] Quotes from He-Yin Zhen [1907a]2013, 82, 78.

[89] Quotes from He-Yin Zhen [1907b]2013, 170, 178. For Liang's translation, see Liu et al. 2013b, 36–37.

[90] Quoted in Zarrow 1988, 800.

[91] Quotes from He-Yin Zhen [1907c]2013, 103; [1907a]2013, 91.

to oppressive working conditions that many women experienced in paid employment and to the trafficking of women. Thinkers also highlighted the significance of women's unpaid work as well as the broader unequal status of women within households. They further highlighted how economic trends influenced women differently than men, and how multilateral institutions might support feminist goals. In these ways, these thinkers brought attention to distinctive ways in which women participated in the world economy and the significance of gender identities and norms to its dynamics (as well as to the theorizing about it). Many of them also placed a high value on the cultivation of international solidarity among women, and many drew inspiration from each other's ideas.

There were also important disagreements among these thinkers. Some insisted on equal treatment for women in the workplace, while others favoured measures to address distinctive issues facing female workers. Some called for monetary compensation for women's unpaid work, while others favoured its socialization (via the state or in a community context). Some argued that women's broader unequal position in the household could be addressed only by dissolving traditional nuclear family structures, while others hoped simply to boost women's position within the latter. Thinkers also held different views about the desirability of government economic activism at the domestic and international levels and even whether governments should be supported at all. In their international advice, thinkers also disagreed about whether free trade served women's interests and about whether gender equality was best promoted through the League of Nations or the Comintern. Some were also more committed to anti-imperialism than others. More generally, there were quite diverse views on the question of whether capitalist societies could be reformed to serve the cause of gender equality. Many of these issues continue to be debated in contemporary feminist IPE scholarship.

# 11    Pan-African Responses to a Racialized World Economy

This chapter examines some key figures associated with the Pan-African movement who are rarely mentioned in IPE textbooks but who developed innovative ideas about the politics of the world economy that were influential in many parts of the world in the early twentieth century. The Pan-African movement has already been briefly noted in the previous chapter's discussion of Amy Ashwood Garvey and Chapter 7's analysis of George Padmore and C. L. R. James. Its formal origins are usually dated to a 1900 Pan-African Conference in London that called for an end to the oppression and exploitation of Africans and the African diaspora across the world.[1] In their final statement addressed to "the Nations of the World", delegates from Africa, Britain, North America, and the Caribbean argued that the problem of racism was the central one facing the world at the time: "The problem of the twentieth century is the problem of the colour-line, the question as to how far differences of race – which show themselves chiefly in the colour of the skin and the texture of the hair – will hereafter be made the basis of denying to over half the world the right of sharing to their utmost ability the opportunities and privileges of modern civilization".[2]

The racism highlighted by the Pan-African movement pervaded many political economy structures and texts in the pre-1945 era, as noted in various places in previous chapters.[3] The Pan-African thinkers discussed in this chapter sought to challenge it by cultivating a transnational form of economic solidarity among Africans and the African diaspora in order to end their subordination within the world economy.[4] The best-known

---

[1] From some precursors, see Esedebe 1994, 7–8.
[2] Quotes in Langley 1979, 738.
[3] See also Hobson 2012.
[4] Previous chapters have noted other thinkers beyond the Pan-African movement who challenged racist hierarchies in various ways, including: Naoroji (Chapter 3; he was also involved in the organization of the first Pan-African Conference in 1900; Patel 2020, 228); Mariátegui (Chapter 7); Paul (Chapter 7); Gregg (Chapter 9); Luisi, Burroughs, and Kamaladevi(Chapter 10); and Víctor Raúl Haya de la Torre (Chapter 13). Other

popularizer of this "economic Pan-Africanism" was the Jamaican-born activist Marcus Garvey, whose ideas attracted an enormous number of supporters across the world in the early 1920s.[5] But Garvey's version of economic Pan-Africanism was also contested by others in ways that revealed how this perspective – like all the others discussed in this book – had considerable diversity within it.

## Marcus Garvey's Economic Pan-Africanism

After leaving school at the age of fourteen, Garvey became increasingly politically active in Jamaica before travelling to Europe and Central America between 1910 and 1914. When he returned to Jamaica, he established the Universal Negro Improvement Association (UNIA) with Amy Ashwood (see previous chapter) and then built it as a transnational movement after moving to New York in 1916. By the early 1920s, the UNIA had millions of members across the world, including not just in the United States and Caribbean but also elsewhere in the Americas, in Africa, in Europe, and even in far away Australia as. Even his critics such as James acknowledged that he "created for the first time a feeling of international solidarity among Africans and people of African descent". As James put it in 1938, "there has never been a Negro movement anywhere like the Garvey Movement, and few movements in any country can be compared to it in growth and intensity".[6]

Garvey described the ambition for the UNIA in the following way in 1920: "We are endeavoring to unite Negros everywhere, and for what? For the purpose of building up a powerful nation on the continent of Africa, a nation in the near future boasting as a first-rate power ... We are endeavoring to perform the function of government for our race".[7] As Erik McDuffie notes, the UNIA was seen by Garvey and others as a kind of "provisional government-in-exile committed to building self-reliant black institutions, an independent Africa, and a global black empire capable of protecting the rights and dignity of African-descended people everywhere".[8] In keeping with this vision, the UNIA created an anthem and flag, and its first international convention in 1920 endorsed

---

thinkers discussed in this volume can also be mentioned, such as Jane Addams and the members of the WILPF (1919, 15) who condemned "discrimination against human beings on account of race or colour".

[5] Quote from Stein 1986, 110.
[6] James [1938]2012, 94, 92. For Garvey's life and the UNIA's history, see, for example, McDuffie 2016; Stein 1986.
[7] Hill 1984, 23–24.
[8] McDuffie 2016, 147. See also Ewing 2014; Shilliam 2006.

a "Declaration of the Rights of the Negro Peoples of the World" that, among other things, condemned colonialism and called for "the freedom of Africa for the Negro people of the world".[9]

In his conception of the UNIA's role, Garvey placed high priority on the task of cultivating economic power for the Pan-African community. He noted how Bismarck had turned Germany into a powerful state by focusing on this strategy: "Commerce and industry were the forces that pushed the great German Empire to the front ... Develop yourselves into a commercial and industrial people, and you will have laid the foundation for racial greatness". He also invoked the fact that Japan's growing commercial and industrial power had enabled it to become a world power, defeating the Russian empire in 1905. He drew the following lesson from this experience in 1920: "Not until the Negroes of the world on the battle plains of Africa teach some nation as the Japanese taught the Russian will they stop burning and lynching you in all parts of the world".[10]

Garvey insisted that the goal of cultivating economic strength was more important than ever after World War I because the leading powers were now developing plans for "industrial and commercial expansion and conquest". As he put it, "England is preparing for a great commercial warfare; so is America, Japan, France, Germany and the other nations. The next twenty-five year[s] will be a period of keen competition among people. It will be an age of survival of the fittest". If others were making these preparations, Garvey insisted that "so must the Negro be prepared to play". Embracing social Darwinist ideas of the time, he portrayed this world of commercial warfare in racialized terms: "I can see that everyone is looking out for himself where the question of race comes in. The white race is looking out for the white race; the yellow race is looking out for the yellow race or Asiatic race. The time has come when the Negro should look out for himself and let the others look out for themselves. This is the new doctrine today".[11]

With his focus on promoting the wealth and power of the Pan-African community in order to build up a future African state, Garvey was advancing a perspective with some similarities to neomercantilism, but of a kind that was applied to a diasporic community in support of a state that was still to be created. He hoped the UNIA could play the kind of activist economic role that states played in places such as Germany and Japan in supporting the growth of local firms. As he put it: "If we are

[9] UNIA 1920.
[10] Quotes from Hill 1983a, 352–53; 1984, 24.
[11] Quotes from Hill 1983a, 351–52; 1983b, 92.

... to become a great national force, we must start business enterprises of our own".[12]

His major economic initiative was the creation of a UNIA-run shipping company in 1919 called the Black Star Line that was to operate between the United States, the Caribbean, and Africa. In addition to providing better routes and services for members of the Pan-African community, this shipping line was designed to foster greater economic self-reliance by reducing their dependence on existing shipping lines and by bolstering trade and other connections among themselves. In an era when a merchant marine was a key attribute of state power, the Black Star Line would also bolster the Pan-African community's economic power and broader sense of common identity in ways that worked towards the longer-term goal of building a powerful independent African state. As Robbie Shilliam notes, "[I]t was through the UNIA's shipping company – the *Black Star Line* – that Garvey sought to concretely establish commercial and industrial links between the Black Diaspora and the African continent that would build the 'sinews of power' even in the absence of sovereign territory".[13]

Garvey called on Africans and the African diaspora to buy shares in the Black Star Line, depicting the company as "the property of the Negro race".[14] Many responded to Garvey's call. Adam Ewing describes the appeal of Garvey's vision to the investors:

By purchasing shares at $5 apiece, black men and women in Africa and the Americas were buying ownership in a collective project that would ultimately comprise a fleet of black-owned ships, carrying raw materials and goods manufactured in black-owned factories, sold in black-owned stores, underwritten by black-owned banks. The idea of the Black Star Line, a shining symbol of emerging New Negro industrial potential, captured the imagination of peoples of African descent like few projects before or since. By 1920, seemingly 'unlimited amount[s] of money' arrived daily at Liberty Hall.[15]

The reaction to the voyage of the first ship in the Black Star Line in 1919 was also enthusiastic. Huge crowds met the ship in the places where it landed in the Caribbean, and the Cuban president even held a banquet for the crew.[16]

Garvey's goal of creating "business enterprises of our own" was not limited to the shipping sector. He also sought to cultivate industrial

---

[12] Hill 1983a, 352.
[13] Shilliam 2006, 397. See also Bandele 2008.
[14] Quoted in Ewing 2014, 82
[15] Ewing 2014, 82.
[16] Bandele 2008, 111; Ewing 2014, 88.

power by establishing another UNIA-run company: the Negro Factories Corporation. Here is how he outlined his goals in this economic sector:

In these factories we must manufacture boats, clothing, and all the necessaries of life, those things that the people need, not only our people in America, the West Indies and Africa, but the people of China, of India, of South and Central America, and even the white man. He has for hundreds of years made a market for his goods among Negroes and alien races; therefore, Negroes have the same right to make a market among white people...When we can as a race settle down to business with honesty of purpose, we will be on the way to the founding of a permanent and strong position among the nations and races of the world.[17]

Garvey's economic initiatives drew some inspiration from the African American thinker and political leader Booker T. Washington, who had insisted in an 1895 speech that "no race that has anything to contribute to the markets of the world is long in any degree ostracized".[18] Garvey also shared with Washington the idea that the African diaspora could support the economic development of Africa through the provision of technical and educational assistance.[19] In discussing this topic, the UNIA constitution employed a similar civilizational discourse as European imperialists, noting that it hoped "to assist in civilizing the backward tribes of Africa".[20]

Garvey was also interested in the earlier ideas of Edward Blyden. Born in the Danish West Indies, Blyden had moved to Liberia in 1850 and emerged as a prominent critic of European theories of racial superiority. His work attracted attention in Africa as well as across Europe and North America in the late nineteenth and early twentieth centuries. Blyden emphasized that Africa had been "the cradle of civilization" and that Africans had been held back economically not by any inferiority but by circumstances such as the slave trade. He also highlighted – as Garvey later did – Africans' contribution to Britain's industrialization: "The rapid growth and unparalleled prosperity of Lancashire are, in part, owing to the cotton supply of the Southern States, which could not have risen to such importance without the labour of the African".[21] Like Garvey, Blyden had also been interested in the role that the African

---

[17] Quoted in Bandele 2008, 94.
[18] Quoted in Prasch 2008, 320. For his influence on Garvey, see Derrick 2008, 84; Ewing 2014, 42.
[19] Esedebe 1994, 56–57; Ewing 2014, 83–84; Langley 1973, 33.
[20] Quoted in Bandele 2008, 95.
[21] Blyden quotes from Blyden [1887]1888, 134, 37. For Garvey's similar point, see Esedebe 1994, 80. As noted in Chapter 7, Eric Williams (1944) later developed a broader argument about the importance of slavery and the slave trade to Britain's industrialization.

diaspora could play in helping to promote the economic development of African states. He even insisted to an African American audience in the early 1860s that "we must build ships and navigate them" as part of helping to "build up negro states".[22]

Blyden's arguments were also interesting because he emphasized the need for Africans to follow an economic path that was compatible with their distinct "personality". As he put it in 1908, "the political economy of the white man is not our political economy".[23] But Blyden's conceptualization of this political economy differed from Garvey's. Whereas Garvey sought to build an African state that could compete with, and match, the industrial power of European countries, Blyden suggested that the continent should be "largely an agricultural" place, with the "Northern races" taking "the raw materials from Africa" in exchange for manufactured goods. He argued that Africans were less materialistic, competitive, and individualistic than Europeans, and praised how "the African, in the simplicity and purity of rural enterprises, will be able to cultivate those spiritual elements in humanity which are suppressed, silent and inactive under the pressure and exigencies of material progress".[24]

Before creating the UNIA, Garvey had also read Joseph Casely Hayford's 1911 book *Ethiopia Unbound: Studies in Race Emancipation*. From the British colony of the Gold Coast and influenced by Blyden, Casely Hayford wrote about the "African nationality" and lamented how Africans around the world were pressed into "the service of the Caucasian" and victimized by economic "exploitation". Like Garvey, he also went beyond Blyden in arguing that "race emancipation" required the pursuit of "industrial training" and he praised Japan's successful cultivation of wealth and power while preserving its culture. Hayford subsequently helped to create the National Congress of British West Africa, which, among other things, supported initiatives to create economic self-reliance among Africans and to challenge British economic power in the region. At its first meeting in Accra in 1920, the Congress – with Casely Hayford as its vice-president – supported the Black Star Line.[25]

Garvey was also familiar with an effort by a Gold Coast businessman, Alfred Sam, in 1914–15 to create a steamship line to bolster Africa's "economic independence" with African American support.[26] Sam's initiative had attracted the attention of allies of Blyden such as the Sierra

[22] Quotes from Blyden 1862, 75–76.
[23] Quotes in Frenkel 1974, 283; Lynch 1971, 122.
[24] Quotes from Blyden 1888, 126–27.
[25] Quotes from Casely Hayford 1911, 167–68, 170. See also Langley 1973, 129.
[26] Quoted in Langley 1973, 43.

Leonian clergyman James Johnson, who had been a prominent critic of
European colonialism since the late nineteenth century and who had
attended the 1900 Pan-African conference. When Sam's ship arrived
in Sierra Leone in 1914, Johnson formally welcomed it with comments
that were similar to the logic Garvey would use to explain his initiative
a few years later: "With steamships of our own, traversing the ocean to
and fro between West Africa, America and England, in the interest of
commerce, we shall in respect of carrying power, be in the great measure
commercially independent".[27]

Garvey's economic Pan-Africanism thus built upon the ideas of a
number of other thinkers. But he consolidated these ideas in creative
ways that generated enormous interest among Africans and the African
diaspora in the early 1920s. Despite the widespread support for Garveyism in this period, however, the results of its economic initiatives were
disappointing. Particularly discouraging was the bankruptcy of the Black
Star Line by 1922, a development that was caused partly by internal mis-
management but also by the hostility of some US officials. After Garvey
was convicted of mail fraud in 1923, his imprisonment undermined
the UNIA, as did the fact that he was deported to Jamaica after being
released from jail in 1927.

## Du Bois' Different Ideas

Although Garveyism was the most politically prominent version of economic Pan-Africanism that emerged in this period, it was not the only
one. Alongside the UNIA conventions after World War I, a number of
other "Pan-African Congresses" took place in 1919, 1921, 1923, and
1927 that promoted somewhat different ideas. The leading figure behind
these meetings was the prominent African American intellectual W. E.
B. Du Bois, who had attended the first Pan-African conference in 1900
and who had drafted its famous statement that "the problem of the twentieth century is the problem of the colour-line".[28]

Like Garvey, Du Bois was very interested in economic issues. But he
came to the subject with much more scholarly training than Garvey,
including a Harvard PhD that had analyzed the history of the slave
trade and previous graduate study at the University of Berlin with
famous political economists such as Gustav Schmoller (see Chapter
4). After starting an academic career, Du Bois turned in 1910 to work
for the newly created National Association for the Advancement of

[27] Quoted in Stein 1986, 110–11, 52–53. See also Ayandele 1970, 193–95, 308.
[28] Quoted in Langley 1979, 738.

Colored People (NAACP). At the end of World War I, Du Bois developed some ideas that were similar to those of Garvey about the need for "a new African World State, a Black Africa" that would be supported by the African diaspora, who could furnish "technical experts, leaders of thought, and missionaries of culture for their backward brethren in the new Africa". Earlier, at the turn of the century, Du Bois had also explored the idea of a "development program" for the Congo to be organized by African Americans working with Congolese and West Indians.[29]

Despite these similarities with Garvey, Du Bois emerged as a very strong critic of Garvey in 1920–21. While supporting the general idea of creating a Pan-African shipping company, Du Bois was critical of Garvey's poor management of the Black Star Line. At a more theoretical level, he also did not share Garvey's social Darwinist worldview and was more sympathetic to socialist ideas than Garvey was. Reflecting this latter orientation, he envisioned a new African state (that was to be built initially around the nucleus of ex-German colonies) following "newer ideals of industrial democracy, avoiding private land monopoly and poverty, and promoting co-operation in production and the socialization of income".[30]

Du Bois was also less insistent than Garvey on the need for immediate African political independence. When discussing his proposed African state, he argued that "no one would expect this new state to be independent and self-governing from the start". Du Bois suggested instead that it be subject to some form of initial "international control" via a commission that would include both "white men" and "educated and trained men of Negro blood". He was also more open than Garvey to the idea that the new state could use capital "attracted from the white world", as long as it received "the same modest profits as legitimate home industry offers".[31] At the time of the 1919 Paris peace conference, the first Pan-African Congress also called for the League of Nations to play the role of supervising African colonies. Under its proposal, the League would encourage growing self-government and improved living standards, including through the monitoring of labour conditions and the regulation of "the system of concessions" in order "to prevent the exploitation of the natives and the exhaustion of the natural wealth of the country".[32]

---

[29] Du Bois quotes from Du Bois [1920]1969, 65, 70; Langley 1973, 59. For Du Bois' training, see Prasch 2008.
[30] Du Bois [1920]1969, 71. See also Contee 1970, 221–23; Bandele 2008, 98; Langley 1973, 69; Vitalis 2015.
[31] Quotes from Du Bois [1920]1969, 68, 70, 72.
[32] Quoted in Langley 1973, 65. See also Esedebe 1994, 65–66.

As Du Bois put it in May 1919, the League was "absolutely necessary to the salvation of the Negro race".[33]

Du Bois also developed much more detailed ideas about how the Pan-African movement's promotion of racial equality – alongside that of other anti-racist movements – would help the world community as a whole. His case was summarized in the 1921 Pan-African Congress' manifesto, which argued that "the absolute equality of races, physical, political and social, is the founding stone of World Peace and human advancement". The document went on to criticize the complicity of "white labour" in what it called "the outrageously unjust distribution of world income between the dominant and suppressed peoples, – in the rape of land and raw material, the monopoly of technique and culture". It made the following case:

Unconsciously and consciously, carelessly and deliberately the vast power of the white labour vote in modern democracies has been cajoled and flattered into imperialistic schemes to enslave and debauch black, brown and yellow labour and, with fatal retribution, are themselves to-day bound and gagged and rendered impotent by the resulting monopoly of the world's raw material in the hands of a dominant, cruel and irresponsible few.[34]

These arguments drew on an innovative analysis of imperialism and war that Du Bois published in a 1915 article titled "The African Roots of War". One year before Lenin, Dubois attributed World War I to economic causes associated with inter-imperial rivalries. He argued that imperial expansion and conflict had been promoted partly by European capitalists who sought new profits from the exploitation of African resources and labour at a time when white labour at home was successfully demanding higher wages and better working conditions. Du Bois also emphasized that imperialism was backed by those same white workers who shared in its economic benefits: "Never before was the average citizen of England, France, and Germany so rich, with such splendid prospects of greater riches. Whence comes this new wealth and on what does its accumulation depend? It comes primarily from the darker nations of the world – Asia and Africa, South and Central America, the West Indies and the islands of the South Seas".[35]

In contrast to many European critics of imperialism, Du Bois highlighted the centrality of racism to the phenomenon.[36] He noted the long

---

[33] Quoted in Getachew 2019, 68.
[34] Quotes in Langley 1973, 376, 378.
[35] Du Bois 1915, 709.
[36] Some European critics did discuss the central role of racism in imperialism (e.g. Hilferding [1910]1981, ch. 22; Robertson 1899, 190, 202). For the acceptance of scientific racism by many British anti-imperialists at this time, see Schneer (1999).

history of racism with its origins in the slave trade when "the world began to invest in color prejudice" and which had "left the continent in precisely that state of helplessness which invites aggression and exploitation". In the late nineteenth and early twentieth centuries, racism had then justified imperial expansion and reduced domestic class conflict within imperial powers by encouraging white European workers to join in the exploitation of the rest of the world. He suggested that racism was further reinforced at this time by European capitalists who attempted to resist the demands of white workers by invoking the threat of "competition by colored labor", such as warnings "to send English capital to China and Mexico ... [and] to hire Negro laborers in America". Rising racism then interacted with economic pressures to encourage conflict and war:

We must fight the Chinese, the laborer argues, or the Chinese will take our bread and butter. We must keep Negroes in their places, or Negroes will take our jobs. All over the world there leaps to articulate speech and ready action that singular assumption that if white men do not throttle colored men, then China, India, and Africa will do to Europe what Europe has done and seeks to do to them.[37]

According to Du Bois' 1915 analysis, lasting world peace could be achieved only by eliminating the global inequalities and "racial prejudice" that sustained imperialism and war. He was concerned not just about imperial rivalries triggering future wars between the leading powers. He also warned that "war will come from the revolutionary revolt of the lowest workers" as the "costs of armament" made it "more difficult to fulfill the promises of industrial democracy in advanced countries". Even more important, however, was a third source of conflict that would result from the fact that "the colored peoples will not always submit passively to foreign domination". This, he argued, would have the most serious consequences: "the War of the Color Line will outdo in savage inhumanity any war this world has yet seen. For colored folk have much to remember and they will not forget". He concluded: "We shall not drive war from this world until we treat them as free and equal citizens in a world-democracy of all races and nations".[38] This link between the Pan-African cause and world peace was reiterated by the second Pan-African Congress in 1921, which noted that a future "great black African State" would be "founded in Peace and Good Will" in order to be "a part of a great society of peoples in which it takes its place with others as

---

[37] Quotes from Du Bois 1915, 708, 711–12.
[38] Quotes from Du Bois 1915, 712–14. See also Du Bois [1920]1969, 49. Like many others of his time, Du Bois' optimism about global cooperation waned in the 1930s. As noted at the end of the next chapter, he also became increasingly interested during that decade in Japan's challenge to Western powers.

co-rulers of the world". The Congress added that this future state would also be committed to "freedom of trade".[39]

## Harrison's More Radical Pan-Africanism

Another critic of Garvey with interesting ideas was Hubert Harrison. Born in the Danish West Indies (like Blyden), in 1900 at the age of seventeen Harrison migrated to New York, where he was distressed by the greater racial oppression he encountered there. He was soon drawn to socialist politics because of its commitment, as he put it in 1911, "to put an end to the exploitation of one group by another, whether that group be social, economic or racial". In 1915, however, he left the Socialist Party, disillusioned by its limited efforts to oppose racism, a task that he now prioritized above the class struggle. As he put it in 1919, "the international Fact to which Negros in America are now reacting is not the exploitation of laborers by capitalists; but the social, political and economic subjection of colored peoples by white".[40]

Because he saw Du Bois' NAACP as too elitist and conservative, in 1917 he created a new organization (The Liberty League) and a new newspaper (*The Voice*) that promoted many of the ideas that Garvey subsequently popularized. In 1920, Harrison became editor of UNIA's leading publication, *Negro World*, and Jeffrey Perry notes that he "proceeded to reshape it into the most powerful organ of Black race consciousness in the world".[41] But Harrison also quickly became sceptical of Garvey. Like Du Bois, he supported the idea of the Black Star Line but was very critical of Garvey's management of it. In 1922, Harrison left his editorial post and argued in the next year that Garvey's conviction had been a fair trial. While praising the broader economic Pan-African vision of the UNIA, he suggested that "Garvey has a great talent for lying" and that the Black Star Line was "designed as a money-getter for Garvey".[42]

Harrison was also critical of Garvey's view that the African diaspora should assume a lead role in promoting Africa's liberation. This criticism echoed that of figures in West Africa.[43] Harrison argued that Garvey "knew next to nothing of Africa" and that African Americans start learning from Africans rather than the other way around.[44] As he put it in 1918,

---

[39] Quoted in Langley 1973, 376.
[40] Quotes in Adi 2013, 8; Harrison 2001, 103.
[41] Perry 2001, 24.
[42] Harrison 2001, 198, 197. See also Perry 2009, 17, 294–96. Some years later, Padmore ([1931]1971, 125) was also very critical of Garvey's management of Black Star Line.
[43] See, for example, Langley 1973, 99; Shilliam 2006.
[44] Quote from Harrison 2001, 197. See also 188–90, 196–98, 210–12, 325.

let us American Negroes go to Africa, live among the natives and LEARN WHAT THEY HAVE TO TEACH US (for they have much to teach us). ... Let us learn to know Africa and Africans so well that every educated Negro will be able at a glance to put his hands on the map of Africa and tell where to find the Jolofs, Ekois, Mandingoes, Yorubas, Bechuanas or Basutos and can tell something of their marriage customs, their property laws, their agriculture and systems of worship. For, not until we can do this will it be seemly for us to pretend to be anxious about their political welfare.[45]

Harrison also used his own studies of Africa to forcefully reject the idea that Africans needed "civilizing". As he put it, "If by civilization we mean a stable society which supports itself and maintains a system of government and laws, industry and commerce, then the Hausas and Mandingos, the people of Ashanti and Dahomey, and the Yorubas of the Gold Coast had and have all these, and they are consequently civilized. So were the Zulus and Bechuanas, the Swazis and Mashonas of South Africa as well as the Baganda people of Uganda". He saw the "civilizing" mission of colonial power as a cover for economic interests: "The real civilization meant by most whites who talk of civilizing African is the system which produces profits by taking land from under the feet of the workers, producing a propertyless, landless proletarian class which must either work (for wages) or starve".[46]

Like Du Bois, Harrison was also more committed to a wider antiracist internationalism than Garvey was. Although Garvey expressed solidarity with Japan and the Indian nationalist movement, his energies were squarely focused on the Pan-African movement and the UNIA. Harrison had more ambitious ideas of building solidarity with groups around the world who were trying to "take their destinies out of the hands of the white lords of misrule". In 1921, he called for "a Colored International" that would be "worldwide in scope" and "frankly antiimperialistic". As he put it,

it should include representatives and spokesmen from the oppressed peoples of India, Egypt, China, West and South Africa, and West Indies, Hawaii, Philippines, Afghanistan, Algeria, and Morocco. It should be made up of those who realize that capitalist imperialism which mercilessly exploits the darker races for its own financial purposes is the enemy which we must combine to fight with arms as varied as those by which it is fighting to destroy our manhood, independence and self-respect.[47]

Harrison's reference to the common enemy of "capitalist imperialism" highlighted one further difference between his views and Garvey's: his

---

[45] Harrison 2001, 212.
[46] Harrison 2001, 220, 221.
[47] Quotes from Harrison 2001, 217, 223, 226.

emphasis on the role of capitalism in generating racial inequality and conflict. He called for a "stark internationalism of clear vision which sees that capitalism means conflict of races and nations, and that war and oppression of the weak spring from the same economic motive – which is at the very root of capitalist culture". Harrison's views were closer to those of Du Bois in this sense and he also shared the latter's interest in linking the Pan-African cause to the cosmopolitan goal of global peace. Harrison, however, placed more emphasis on an underconsumptionist explanation of imperialism and inter-imperialist conflict than did Du Bois:

> every nation whose industrial system is organized on a capitalist basis must produce a mass of surplus products over and above, not the need, but the purchasing power of the nation's producers. ... Hence the need for foreign markets, for fields of exploitations and "spheres of influence" in "undeveloped" countries whose virgin resources are exploited in their turn after the capitalist fashion. But since every industrial nation is seeking the same outlet for its products clashes are inevitable ... hence the exploitation of white men in Europe and America becomes the reason for the exploitation of black and brown and yellow men in Africa and Asia. Just as long as black men are exploited by white men in Africa, so long must white men cut each other's throats over that exploitation.[48]

In challenging racialized capitalist imperialism, Harrison was willing to consider alliances with white workers: "The international of the darker races must avail itself of whatever help it can get from those groups within the white race which are seeking to destroy the capitalist international of race prejudice and exploitation which is known as bourgeois 'democracy' at home and colonial imperialism abroad". But he differed from Du Bois in his unwillingness to work with the League of Nations, which he saw as a tool of white capitalists: "The object of the capitalist international is to unify and standardize the exploitation of black, brown and yellow peoples in such a way that the danger to the exploiting groups of cutting each other's throats over the spoils may be reduced to a minimum. Hence the various agreements, mandates and spheres of influence. Hence the League of Nations, which is notoriously not a league of the white masses, but of their gold-brained governors".[49]

Despite his radical views, Harrison also refused to work with the Comintern for the same reason he had broken with the Socialist Party: he thought that it prioritized class over racial solidarity.[50] Harrison's criticism of the Comintern anticipated that of Padmore and James after

---

[48] Quotes from Harrison 2001, 226–27. See also pp. 206, 221–22. For the link to global peace, see, for example, p. 203.
[49] Quotes from Harrison 2001, 227.
[50] See, for example, Harrison 2001, 223, 228.

the early 1930s (see Chapter 7). Indeed, Harrison's radical kind of Pan-Africanism bore some similarities to the version later promoted by those two Caribbean thinkers who emerged as leading Pan-African figures in the 1930s. If Harrison had not died in 1927 in surgery, Padmore and James may well have found common cause with him.

Interestingly, they did begin working with Ashwood Garvey as well as with Du Bois, whose views were moving in a more radical direction in the early 1930s.[51] But the ongoing divisions in the Pan-African movement were evident in their unwillingness to work with Marcus Garvey, despite the fact that the latter also moved to London in 1935. Indeed, they even heckled Garvey for his conservatism at London's Hyde Park corner at the time of Caribbean political unrest in 1937.[52] In his 1938 work *A History of Negro Revolt* (see Chapter 7 of this book), James acknowledged Garvey's remarkable popularity in the early 1920s, but criticized his ideas as "pitiable rubbish" and argued that "his movement was in many respects absurd and in others thoroughly dishonest. It has resulted in a widespread disillusionment".[53] Garvey died in relative obscurity soon after in 1940.

## Conclusion

Economic Pan-Africanism was an innovative perspective that attracted considerable support after World War I in many parts of the world. It sought to cultivate a transnational form of economic solidarity among Africans and the African diaspora in order to end their subordination within the world economy. Its advocates highlighted that racism directed against Africans and the African diaspora was a pervasive feature of the world economy of their era. Indeed, this racism could be found not just among prominent thinkers in regions of the world that participated actively in driving the African slave trade and/or in the colonization of Africa, but also in other places.[54]

Marcus Garvey's ideas about economic Pan-Africanism were the most influential, but other thinkers advanced alternative versions that highlighted the diversity within this perspective during the interwar years. Garvey's vision was a kind of diasporic neomercantilist one of cultivating the wealth and power of the pan-African community. Du Bois and

[51] For their cooperation, see Hooker 1967, 413; Schwartz 2003. For Du Bois' shifting views, see Getachew 2019, 68; Robinson 1983, 194–208, 228–40.
[52] Schwartz 2003, 140, 150fn13.
[53] James [1938]2012, 92, 94.
[54] See, for example, the views of China's Liang Qichao (Pusey 1983, 117–18; Liang [1903]1989, 91) and Kang Youwei (Hsiao 1975, 445–46, 472–73).

Harrison shared this goal but were also more interested than Garvey in linking Pan-Africanism to wider anti-racist internationalism and the cosmopolitan goal of world peace. They were also more critical of capitalism and each developed important (but somewhat different) explanations of how it was connected to imperialism, war, and racism. Du Bois also did not share Garvey's social Darwinist worldview and was less insistent on immediate African independence after World War I, while being more willing than Harrison to engage with the League of Nations. Harrison's views were also distinctive in his greater scepticism of the African diaspora's potential leadership role in Africa, including the idea that it had a "civilizing" role to play vis-à-vis Africans.

# 12   Religious and Civilizational Political Economies of Pan-Islamism and Pan-Asianism

Pan-Africanism was not the only "Pan" movement in the pre-1945 era to develop innovative analyses of the politics of the world economy. This chapter examines the important, but quite different, ideas of some thinkers associated with the Pan-Islamic and Pan-Asian movements in this period. These figures also called for new kinds of economic solidarity among transnational communities that were designed to promote those communities' interests and values within the world economy. But they were focused on transnational communities conceptualized around religious (Pan-Islamism) and civilizational (Pan-Asianism) identities rather than around the kind of identity that inspired the Pan-African movement.[1]

Religious and civilizational perspectives receive little attention in summaries of competing worldviews within contemporary IPE texts, but they had a high profile in pre-1945 discussions of international economic relations and the world economy in many parts of the world (and continue to be important politically today)[2]. Previous chapters have already provided many examples of thinkers linking religious values and/or conceptions of "civilization" to the perspectives they were promoting. The Pan-Islamic and Pan-Asian thinkers discussed in this chapter placed these issues at the center of their worldview. Focusing on the distinctive transnational community whose interests and values they were each promoting, these thinkers developed unique perspectives and normative projects that attracted considerable attention in their respective political contexts.

## Economic Pan-Islamism

The Pan-Islamic movement emerged in the late nineteenth century and quickly gained considerable support among Muslims in many places

---

[1] Some Pan-Islamic thinkers also invoked civilizational discourse, seeing themselves as defending a longstanding Islamic civilization.

[2] For the enduring influence of the two identities discussed in this chapter, see, for example, Lee 2020; Rethel 2019.

across the world. Its influence also soon attracted the attention of outside observers. For example, in his famous 1914 article on ultra-imperialism (see Chapter 6), Karl Kautsky urged his readers to recognize the rise of "the Pan-Islamic movement in the Near East and North Africa" as a key political development that "threatens not just one or other of the imperialist States, but all of them together".[3] As noted in Chapter 7, the leadership of the Soviet Union also felt sufficiently threatened by the movement's popularity in central Asia that it secured a Comintern resolution in 1920 calling on communists everywhere "to struggle against Pan-Islamism". That same chapter described how the Comintern resolution also had political reverberations in other places such as the Dutch East Indies.

Although Islam had long been a highly cosmopolitan religion, scholars note that the novelty of Pan-Islamism in this period was its emphasis on the need for *political* solidarity among Muslims across the world.[4] Among proponents of this perspective, some were also interested in the cultivation of a new kind of Pan-Islamic *economic* solidarity. They included Jamal al-Din al-Afghani, one of the best-known of the early advocates of Pan-Islamism.

*Early Versions*

Born in Iran, al-Afghani first became a strong critic of European imperialism when he studied in India and witnessed British oppression of Muslims there in the wake of the 1857 Indian rebellion. His concern for the Islamic world only grew after Russia attacked the Ottoman Empire in 1877–78 and the French and British occupied Tunisia and Egypt, respectively, in 1881–82. In a widely read periodical he published in Paris in the early 1880s, al-Afghani began to call for Muslim unity to resist European imperialism. He also directly challenged European thinkers who attacked Islam at this time, including Ernest Renan, with whom he directly debated in 1883 in what Panjay Mishra describes as "the first major public debate between a Muslim and a European intellectual".[5]

Al-Afghani's criticism of European imperialism included economic issues. In the late 1870s, for example, he argued that the British constructed railroads and telegraph lines in India "only in order to drain the substance of our wealth and facilitate the means of trade for the

---

[3] Kautsky [1914] 1970, 45.
[4] See, for example, Aydin 2017; Landau 1990.
[5] Mishra 2012, 100. See also pp. 54–8, 102; Aydin 2007, 51, 62; 2017, 52–53; Hourani 1983, 114–15.

inhabitants of the British Isles and extend their sphere of riches".[6] After returning to Iran in 1886, he also criticized European investment in that country and helped mobilize opposition to a foreign tobacco concession given to some British investors by the Iranian government. To challenge European imperialism, al-Afghani argued that the Islamic world needed to collectively embrace economic modernization in order to catch up to Europe's economic progress and power.[7]

Al-Afghani's call for the Islamic world to strengthen its collective economic power bore some similarities to Marcus Garvey's later ideas about boosting the economic power of the transnational Pan-African community. But al-Afghani did not propose the kinds of non-state economic initiatives to meet that goal that Garvey pursued. Instead, he travelled across the Islamic world trying to find a government leader who was willing to mobilize the transnational Islamic community around his goals. Like many other Pan-Islamic thinkers, al-Afghani became particularly interested in the role that the Ottoman sultan, Abdulhamid II, might play in leading the Pan-Islamic movement in this direction.[8] The Ottoman Empire's constitution of 1876 had described the sultan, who came to power that year, as "the Protector of the Muslim religion", and the empire itself was the largest independent Muslim-majority state at the time, housing about 20 percent of the world's Muslims.[9]

During his rule, which lasted until 1909, Abdulhamid II had to be cautious about endorsing the strong anti-imperialism of Pan-Islamists such as al-Afghani because he needed the support of Britain (in whose empire half of all Muslims lived) against the Russian threat he faced. But he did hire al-Afghani briefly in the 1890s and was interested in the Pan-Islamic cause, not least because it helped to bolster his domestic legitimacy and to create potential leverage over European powers who ruled large Muslim populations.[10] The sultan was also very interested in the study of political economy.[11]

In the economic realm, the sultan's most important Pan-Islamic initiative was building a railway that connected Damascus to Mecca and Medina, thereby facilitating pilgrimages to these holy cities. Announced in 1900, the sultan described the Hejaz railway as a "sacred line" that

[6] Quoted in Mishra 2012, 59.
[7] Kilinçoğlu 2015, 91; Mishra 2012, 110.
[8] Landau 1990, 16–18; Mishra, 2012, 88, 102. For the wider interest at this time, see Aydin 2007, 33; 2016, 123.
[9] Quoted in Landau 1990, 11. Statistic from Aydin 2016, 137.
[10] Aydin 2017, 82–90, 97–98; Hanioğlu 2011, 27; Landau 1990, 37–39, 56; Mishra 2012, 90; Özyüksel 2014.
[11] See, for example, Kilinçoğlu 2015, 2, 32.

would be a joint economic project of Muslims worldwide.[12] While most railways being built in the Ottoman Empire at the time were financed and operated by foreigners, this one was to be run by the Ottoman government, built entirely by Muslims, and financed with both official Ottoman funds and voluntary donations from Muslims around the world. It would thus demonstrate the collective economic power and solidarity of the Islamic world in ways that served its interests (as well as some specific Ottoman strategic goals in the region).[13]

European governments were very sceptical of the initiative and they actively discouraged the solicitation of donations to support it in the territories they controlled. But the initiative proved very popular across the Islamic world. As one journalist noted at the time of its announcement, the sultan "became at one shot the most popular man of the Islamic world, and hero of the day". Encouraged by religious groups, donations arrived from places as diverse as Morocco, Russia, China, India, Indonesia, and the Caribbean. By the time the project had been completed in 1908, donations had financed almost one-third of the railway project, with 9.5% of them originating outside of the Ottoman Empire.[14]

In the wake of this success, Pan-Islamists proposed other collective economic projects to promote the interests of the Islamic world. For example, in a speech in Cairo in 1907, a Crimean Tartar journalist, Ismail Gasprinskii, called for the creation of a "general Muslim congress" to address the Islamic world's economic weakness, such as the lack of Muslim-owned steamship companies and banks.[15] Building on Gasprinskii's ideas, an Egyptian journalist in 1913 called for more Muslim-owned shipping and transport companies and an Islamic bank to help fund commercial and industrial operations as well as the Ottoman state. He also called for a boycott campaign European imports alongside very active promotion of consumption of Muslim-produced goods. The latter idea was endorsed at the outset of World War I by the Ottoman government, which called on "all the People of Islam" to "buy nothing" of the goods of "infidels" as well to stop "the giving of the taxes to the infidels who have usurped the rule over the Islamic countries and who are hostile to the assembly of Muslims".[16]

After the defeat of the Ottoman Empire during the war, many Muslims around the world looked to the Kemalists who fought for Turkish

[12] Quoted in Ozyüksel 2014, 39.
[13] Ozyüksel 2014, 43, 60–62, 69–70.
[14] Quote from Özyüksel 2014, 60. See also pp. 69–70, 75,79, 93–94.
[15] Kramer 1986, 39–40.
[16] Quotes in Landau 1990, 351, 356. For the journalist's proposals, see Kramer 1986, 52–53.

independence to lead the Pan-Islamic community. Even the Comintern's 1920 condemnation of Pan-Islamism drew this link, warning communists that the movement would strengthen "Turkish" imperialism.[17] But Pan-Islamists were deeply disappointed in 1924 when Kemal Atatürk abolished the caliphate and embraced a secular and nationalist path of economic modernization. Many elites in Muslim-dominated countries then followed Atatürk's example. Some of those who continued to emphasize the political importance of Islam, such as the prominent anti-imperialist Indonesian politician Sukarno, also did so within a nationalist framework rather than a transnationalist Pan-Islamic one.[18]

In this context, the cause of Pan-Islamism endured but without clear leadership. Pan-Islamic congresses were held in 1926 and 1931, but did not leave much of a legacy.[19] Without strong state support, Pan-Islamic thinkers shifted to focus – like the Pan-African movement – on non-state means by which to promote their cause. The key figure to promote this strategy was Sayyid Abul A'la Mawdudi, who emerged as a key Pan-Islamic thinker in India in the 1930s and who pioneered a movement for what he called "Islamic Economics".[20]

### Mawdudi's Islamic Economics

Born to a middle-class family, Mawdudi received an Islamic education and then studied Western literature before pursuing a career in journalism in the 1920s and then becoming a writer. Like many other Indian Muslims, he was deeply disappointed by Atatürk's abandonment of the caliphate in 1924. He then became increasingly concerned about the future of Islam in India, particularly as he worried that the Indian

---

[17] Quoted in d'Encausse and Schram,1969, 153. See also Tan Malaka's comments in 1922 (McVey 1965, 161).

[18] See, for example, Aydin 2017, 131. For the impact of Atatürk's move, see Landau 1990, ch. 4.

[19] These congresses did not address economic issues in much detail, although the 1931 congress called for the advancement of "the economic development of the Muslims" and the creation of Muslim-financed agricultural bank (quoted in Kramer 1986, 186; see also Landau 1990, 242).

[20] Mawdudi [1941]2011, 12. Spellings of his name vary considerably; I have followed Jackson's (2011) spelling. A similar idea emerged within Indonesia's Sareket Islam movement that was discussed in Chapter 7. After expelling communists in the early 1920s, it became a formal political party in 1923 whose leader at the time, H.O.S. Tjokroaminoto, supported Pan-Islamism and attended the 1926 World Islam Congress in Mecca (McVey 1965, 420fn23). Inspired by Gandhi's idea of *swadeshi*, the party committed to building a Islam-inspired society in Indonesia that was independent of Dutch colonial structures and that would strengthen the connection between Muslims' daily activities and religious duties (Formichi 2012, 63).

National Congress was becoming increasingly dominated by Hindus.[21] While some Indian Muslims called for a future Islamic state in South Asia, Mawdudi began arguing in the early 1930s that Muslims could better defend themselves by embracing a cultural revival that prioritized a comprehensive Islamic way of life. In 1941, he created an Islamic political party dedicated to this ideal.[22]

His ideas about this Islamic way of life covered many topics, including the role of women, who he insisted should not participate in politics or paid employment outside the home.[23] Because of the growing importance of economics to daily life, Mawdudi became increasingly interested in developing a distinctive comprehensive Islamic perspective on the subject. We have seen in Chapters 3 and 7 how some earlier Muslim thinkers had argued that Islamic values were compatible with perspectives such as economic liberalism (Hassuna D'Ghies, Ahmed Cevdet Pasha) or Marxism (Tan Malaka). Mawdudi's contribution was to suggest that Islam could form the basis of an *alternative* to existing economic perspectives. He proposed a new kind of economic solidarity among Muslims worldwide that would be based on their common adherence to this new approach to economics founded on Islamic values. His ideas on this subject served as a key foundation for the Islamic economics movement that subsequently grew in influence in many parts of the Islamic world.

Mawdudi outlined his economic vision for the first time in detail in a 1941 lecture titled "Mankind's economic problems and their Islamic solutions" given at India's Aligarh Muslim University soon after creating his new Islamic political party. In that lecture, Mawdudi was very critical of how countries across the world were engaged in what he called a system of "global antagonistic competition". In his view, that system arose partly from a moral failure of excessive selfishness (particularly among the economic elite) but also from large inequalities within countries. He suggested that the latter prevented low-income citizens from purchasing all that their country produced, leading to a search for export markets and foreign investment locations where higher profits could be made. That trend encouraged imperialism, protectionism, and war as well as intensified international economic rivalries (that only worsened inequality within each country, as wages were kept low for competitive reasons). In his view, "economic struggle" within this "satanic system" had become so tough "that all of life's other issues have been rendered

---

[21] Aydin 2017, 153.
[22] See, for example, Jackson 2011; Kuran 1997; 2004, ch. 4.
[23] Jackson 2011, 133–36, 145.

almost meaningless and futile". It had also "given rise to a small group of exploitative people that includes bankers, brokers and the heads of industrial and commercial cartels and monopolies" who "so dominated the world's economic resources that the whole of humanity today appears to be helpless before it".[24]

Mawdudi argued that Islamic Economics was the only solution to this "satanic economic order" which had "adversely affected the world's moral outlook, its political systems and legal codes". This approach to economics, he argued, endorsed private property, market-based economies, and people's freedom to strive for their own livelihood. He also noted: "Islam has removed restrictions of the tax on the inland transportation of trade goods and duties on imports and exports in order to facilitate the free exchange of consumer goods". While endorsing these liberal policies, Mawdudi also argued that his proposed economic system would be distinctive in requiring people to reform their "conduct and mentality" in order to act according to broader Islamic norms of economic behaviour that prioritized morality over excessive selfishness. As he put it, "the starting point of economic problems is selfishness that transgresses the boundaries of moderation".[25] He also insisted that the state needed to redistribute wealth through inheritance laws and economic support for poorer people. It should also ban "all interest-based transactions", a measure that he argued "blunted the sharp edges of the tools through which a capitalist goes on multiplying his wealth and grabbing economic resources from others". More generally, Mawdudi argued that the state needed to outlaw economic activities that led to moral degradation such as "bribery, theft, gambling, speculation, betting, all fraudulent deals, hoarding, monopolies and cartels". He also noted his disapproval of "professions like the sex trade, music, dance, etc. as a means of livelihood".[26]

Mawdudi distinguished his Islamic Economics not just from economic liberalism but also from communism. In his view, "communism's fundamental mistake is that it takes the economic issue as the core factor in human life" instead of moral and spiritual issues. He was also very sceptical of central planning, which he argued would create a new exploitative and tyrannical ruling elite with all a country's resources at its disposal. Even if state planners had good intentions, he argued that "a group of humans, however intelligent, well-meaning and well-qualified,

[24] Quotes from Mawdudi [1941]2011, 13–14.
[25] Quotes from Mawdudi [1941]2011, 14, 22, 18, 9. Other Pan-Islamic thinkers were less keen on free trade than Mawdudi, including India's Mushir Hosain Kidwai (1912, 77–8) whose work influenced the Indonesian political leader H.O.S. Tjokroaminoto.
[26] Mawdudi [1941]2011, 19, 20, 18.

cannot be so knowledgeable and *omniscient* that they can correctly assess the intrinsic qualities and inborn faculties of countless millions of their fellow humans, and then chart out for each of them a perfect course for their growth and development". As a result, he argued that a central planner would inevitably make mistakes and undermine individual "freedom" and "human civilization's diversity", while turning society into a "lifeless monotony".[27]

Mawdudi emphasized that his proposed economic system rested on people's embrace of Islamic religious beliefs: "one would be grossly mistaken if one thinks that this system can function independently of the whole body of Islamic beliefs, moral values and social norms". Crucial to the success of Islamic Economics, thus, was the promotion of Islam as a belief system. He described the latter goal in very ambitious terms in 1939: "the truth is that Islam is not the name of a 'Religion', nor is 'Muslim' the title of a 'Nation'. In reality Islam is a revolutionary ideology and programme which seeks to alter the social order of the whole world and rebuild it in conformity with its own tenets and ideals".[28]

Mawdudi argued that these global ambitions for Islam were necessary for two reasons. One was "self-defense". As he put it, "no state can put her ideology into full operation until the same ideology comes into force in the neighbouring states". The second was the cosmopolitan orientation of Islam itself. As he put it, "Islam has no vested interest in promoting the cause of this or that Nation. The hegemony of this or that State on the face of this earth is irrelevant to Islam. The sole interest of Islam is the welfare of mankind".[29]

## Pan-Asian Civilizational Political Economy

Like Pan-Islamism, the roots of Pan-Asianism can be found in the late nineteenth century. Although the term "Pan-Asianism" did not become popular in Asia until the early twentieth century, there were earlier precursors of this perspective. For example, in 1881, Japan's Fukuzawa Yukichi (see Chapter 5) called on Asian countries to join together to resist European and American power. By 1885, however, Fukuzawa had abandoned this idea, arguing that "Japan is located in the eastern extremities of Asia, but the spirit of her people have already moved away from the old conventions of Asia to the Western civilization".[30] Around

---

[27] Quotes from Mawdudi [1941]2011, 16–17.
[28] Quotes from Mawdudi [1941]2011, 22; [1939]1976, 5.
[29] Quotes from Mawdudi [1939]1976, 23, 6.
[30] Fukuzawa [1885]1997, 352.

the turn of the century, some other Asian thinkers were drawn to the notion of anti-imperialist Asian cooperation, including, briefly, China's Zheng Guanying and Liang Qichao (see Chapter 5).[31]

The idea of Asian cooperation gained much greater support in the wake of Japan's military defeat of Russia in 1905, which inspired anti-imperialists across Asia (as well as those elsewhere such as Marcus Garvey, as noted in Chapter 11).[32] The phrase "Pan-Asianism" soon began to be widely used across the continent.[33] Although it was often used in racialized ways, it also became associated with a discourse of civilizational difference. To many Pan-Asianists, Asia needed to contest Western power by drawing on its own distinctive civilizational traditions. Earlier Asian thinkers such as Fukuzawa had embraced the European idea of civilization as a universal concept to which all societies could aspire. But that idea lost support when the expansion of imperialism in the late nineteenth century both raised new questions about the civilized nature of European societies and was accompanied by heightened European discourses of civilizational and racial superiority. Reacting to these developments, Asian thinkers increasingly endorsed the idea of civilizational difference, while challenging European ideas that Asian civilization was inferior.[34]

### Sun's Pan-Asianism

Some thinkers who endorsed this Pan-Asian civilizational discourse were interested in the international dimensions of political economy. The most important of them was the Chinese thinker and political leader Sun Yat-sen, whose neomercantilist ideas were discussed in Chapter 5. Alongside his advocacy of neomercantilism, Sun had a longstanding interest in Pan-Asianism. His interest in the topic may initially have been piqued in the early 1880s when he was student in Hawaii at a time when its king Kalākaua called for "a league of the countries of the East" to oppose European power.[35] After settling in Japan in 1897, Sun also became acquainted with Japanese advocates of Pan-Asianism and his interest in this perspective was bolstered by his support for the Filipino independence struggle at the turn of the century.[36] Sun's expressions

---

[31] Hwang 2016, 110; Schmid 2002, 88; Wu 2010, 80–84.
[32] Although many anti-imperialists outside Japan were inspired by its victory, prominent Japanese critics of imperialism opposed the war, such as Kōtoku Shūsui (discussed in Chapter 7) (Tierney 2015, 83–86).
[33] See, for example, Hwang 2016, 79; Smith 2019.
[34] Aydin 2007; Mark 2006.
[35] Quoted in Gonschor 2016, 324.
[36] See, for example, Jansen 1967, 68–74; Wilbur 1976, 17–18.

of support for Pan-Asianism grew after this time, with his most famous statement coming in a high-profile speech he made in late 1924 in the Japanese city of Kobe (just before his death the next year).

In that speech, Sun was highly critical of Western expressions of civilizational superiority. As he put it, "the Westerners consider themselves as the only ones possessed and worthy of true culture and civilization; other peoples with any culture or independent ideas are considered as Barbarians in revolt against Civilization". In his view, this view neglected that Asia was the "the cradle of the world's oldest civilization" and that Asian civilization was superior to that of the West. To be sure, he acknowledged that "during the last several hundred years, the material civilization of Europe has reached its height while Oriental civilization has remained stagnant" and that "outwardly, Europe is superior to Asia". But he argued that the materialistic focus of European civilization was associated with a "cult of force" which had been "repeatedly employed by the Western peoples to oppress Asia". He noted: "To oppress others with the cult of force, in the language of the Ancients, is the rule of Might … The rule of Might has always been looked down upon by the Orient". He added: "Since the development of European materialistic civilization and the cult of Might, the morality of the world has been on the decline".[37]

By contrast, he argued that Asian civilization was "superior to the rule of Might" with its "fundamental characteristics" being "benevolence, justice and morality". He argued: "This civilization makes people respect, not fear, it. Such a civilization is, in the language of the Ancients, the rule of Right or the Kingly Way". In his view, the "Pan-Asian" movement arose out of the distinction between these two kinds of civilization:

what is the problem that underlies Pan-Asianism, the Principle of Greater Asia, which we are discussing here to-day? Briefly, it is a cultural problem, a problem of comparison and conflict between the Oriental and Occidental culture and civilization. Oriental civilization is the rule of Right; Occidental civilization is the rule of Might. The rule of Right respects benevolence and virtue, while the rule of Might only respects force and utilitarianism. The rule of Right always influences people with justice and reason, while the rule of Might always oppresses people with brute force and military measures.[38]

Sun did not see this civilizational contrast in essentialist terms as a permanent condition arising from factors such as race or climate. He noted, for example, that Asian civilizational culture had influenced countries beyond its region (including even Great Britain and America, where, he

---

[37] Quotes from Sun [1924]2011, 81, 78, 81.
[38] Quotes from Sun [1924]2011, 81–83.

argued, "there are people who advocate the principles of benevolence and justice"). He also argued that post-revolutionary Russia – which he considered a European country – had endorsed the "rule of Right" with the consequence that "she joins with the Orient and separates from the West".[39] Sun's idea that Asia's "rule of Right" could find support among all peoples and races was also emphasized in another prominent lecture he gave earlier in the same year in China: "the war of the future will be between might and right. ... Throughout the world white and yellow defenders of right will unite against white and yellow defenders of might".[40]

In this war, Sun argued that Pan-Asianism had a key role to play. In his words, it would address the problems of "how to terminate the sufferings of the Asiatic peoples and how to resist the aggression of the powerful European countries". As he put it, "only by the unification of all the peoples in Asia on the foundation of benevolence and virtue can they become strong and powerful". Sun outlined a strategy in which all Asian countries should "learn science from Europe for our industrial development and the improvement of our armaments, not, however, with a view to oppressing or destroying other countries and peoples as the Europeans have done, but purely for our self-defense".[41] In other words, he hoped Asian countries would collectively pursue the kind of neomercantilist goals that Sun recommended for China alone in other writings.

Sun anticipated that this collective effort might be assisted by specific forms of economic cooperation among Asian countries. He provided no details about this issue in his 1924 speech, but at earlier moments he had invoked Pan-Asian ideals when trying to secure Japanese financial support for Chinese economic development, including for the railway projects he promoted when he was briefly in the Chinese government after the 1911 revolution. As he put it in a 1913 speech to Chinese students in Japan, "were China and Japan to cooperate in their development then our power would be greatly expanded and we could easily create a Great Asia revitalizing the past glories of history. We could bring peace to the world, bring *datong* to humanity with rights of equality and freedom for all".[42]

---

[39] Quotes from Sun [1924]2011, 84. This argument was ironic given that the Comintern condemned the "Pan-Asian movement" for reinforcing "Japanese imperialism" at the same 1920 meeting that it criticized "Pan-Islamism" (quoted in d'Encausse and Schram, 1969, 153). For Comintern's wariness of Pan-Asianism, see McVey 1965, 223–24.

[40] Sun 1928, 20.

[41] Quotes from Sun [1924]2011, 84, 83.

[42] Quoted in Smith 2019, 595.

When calling for Asian countries to boost their power through economic development, Sun argued that it was particularly important for them to match European military strength because force might be needed to secure Asia's independence and end European privileges in the region. As an example, he cited Japan's 1905 military victory over Russia and the fact that it had given "a new hope to all Asiatic peoples". Sun deemed the use of force to be compatible with a "rule of Right" because it was correcting the injustice of European imperialism. As he put it, "Pan-Asianism is based on the rule of Right, and justifies the avenging of the wrongs done to others ... we advocate the avenging of the wrong done to those in revolt against the civilisation of the rule of Might, with the aim of seeking a civilisation of peace and equality and the emancipation of all races". Sun emphasized the benefits of Pan-Asian cooperation in this struggle: "Should all Asiatic peoples thus unite together and present a united front against the Occidentals, they will win the final victory".[43]

With these arguments, Sun fused his neomercantilist ideas with Pan-Asianism and a long-term vision in which the world was governed by "the rule of Right". The latter was rooted firmly in the Confucian intellectual tradition. Well-known ancient Confucian thinkers such as Mencius had argued that social orders needed to be based on power derived from virtue rather than the amoral exercise of brute force.[44] Sun's invocation of a future "*datong*" also drew inspiration from the Confucian classic *Book of Rites*. These aspects of Sun's Pan-Asian arguments might have appealed to his Japanese audience, who shared this Confucian intellectual heritage. In the very final lines of his 1924 speech, Sun appealed directly to them, suggesting that their country had an important choice to make about whether to join the West or an anti-imperialist, Pan-Asian united front:

Japan to-day has become acquainted with the Western civilization of the rule of Might, but retains the characteristics of the Oriental civilization of the rule of Right. Now the question remains whether Japan will be the hawk of the Western civilization of the rule of Might, or the tower of strength of the Orient. This is the choice which lies before the people of Japan.[45]

Harold Schiffrin notes that Sun's speech was met with enthusiastic shouts of "Banzai" from his Japanese audience.[46] Despite Sun's opposition to Japanese imperialism (and imperialism of any kind), his ideas

---

[43] Quotes from Sun [1924]2011, 79, 85, 84.
[44] See, for example, Cohen 1974, 91–92.
[45] Sun [1924]2011, 85.
[46] Schiffrin 1980, 265. Brown (2011, 78) also notes that "the speech received wide coverage in Japan at the time", although some Japanese newspapers reporting on the speech "redacted Sun's closing challenge to Japan".

were later invoked in the 1930s and early 1940s by Japanese officials to justify their military expansion in East Asia and their creation of the Japanese-led regional economic bloc, the Greater East Asia Co-Prosperity Sphere (see the next chapter).[47] As part of their use of wider Pan-Asian discourse, Japanese authorities depicted the Co-Prosperity Sphere as a new "moral bloc" in contrast to the "egotistical", "power-oriented blocs" led by Western states.[48] When announcing its creation in 1940, Japan's foreign minister even declared Japan's mission to be "the promulgation of the 'Kingly Way' to the world".[49] The head of the Chinese collaborationist government in Nanjing, Wang Jingwei, also used the 1924 speech of Sun – with whom he had been close – to justify his willingness to work with Japan.[50]

### Invoking the Tributary System

One further aspect of Sun's Pan-Asianism deserves attention. When discussing the "rule of Right", Sun invoked China's historical tributary system as a model. Here is how he described that system:

between 500 and 2000 years ago, there was a period of a thousand years when China was supreme in the world. Her status in the world then was similar to that of Great Britain and America to-day. What was the situation of the weaker nations toward China then? They respected China as their superior and sent annual tribute by their own will, regarding it as honour to be allowed to do so. They wanted, of their own free will, to be dependencies of China. Those countries which sent tribute to China were not only situated in Asia but in distant Europe as well. ... It was not the rule of her Might that forced the weaker nations to send tribute to China. It was the influence of her rule of Right.[51]

Historians debate the extent to which the tributary system ever influenced the foreign economic policy of China and other East Asian states historically.[52] But at the level of ideas, it certainly represented a unique model for governing inter-state economic relations that was well known within the East Asian region. Even Japan, which refused to participate in China's tributary system during the Tokugawa era, had sought to create an alternative Japan-centered tributary order with its close neighbors during that time.[53]

---

[47] Linebarger 1937, 198; Bergère 1994, 411; Brown 2011. For Sun's opposition to Japan's annexation of Korea, see Smith 2019, 598; Sun 1928, 132.
[48] Quoted in Mimura 2011, 7.
[49] Quoted in Duus 1996, 59.
[50] Brown 2011, 76; Schiffrin 1980, 265.
[51] Sun [1924]2011, 81–82. See also Sun 1928, 67.
[52] See, for example, Kang 2010; Park 2017.
[53] Kazui and Videen 1982; Laver 2011; Toby 1984; Walker 2001.

In its ideal form, the tributary system involved a set of bilateral trade relations between China and other various tributary states under which the former granted specific trade privileges to the latter in return for their expression of respect and subordination to the Chinese emperor through offerings of tribute. Within this system, the Chinese emperor was seen as the son of heaven and the leader of a superior Chinese civilization whose culture could gradually diffuse to the tributary states within a universal moral order. Despite the clear hierarchy of the system, Chinese leadership was expected to respect the independence of tributary states and promote peaceful and cooperative relationships in which trade was non-exploitative, mutually beneficial, and serving higher principles of "right".

By the time of Sun's 1924 speech, the idea of the tributary system had long been abandoned by China and other East Asian elites in favour of European models of international relations. But it had informed Chinese debates in the nineteenth century about how to respond to foreign economic demands. For example, according to John Fairbank, it helped to explain why Chinese officials acquiesced to foreign demands for trade opening with remarkably little controversy in the wake of the First Opium War. Chinese officials saw their agreement to the new tariff regime and creation of treaty ports as compatible with tributary notions of using trade privileges to serve foreign policy goals. The new treaty provisions, in other words, represented continuity with past practices for them rather than any radical new arrangement. As Fairbank puts it, "The outward show of tribute was gone, but the spirit remained".[54]

Even prominent Chinese reformers at the time of the First Opium War, such as Wei Yuan, were wedded to the tributary model. As noted in Chapter 5, Wei urged Chinese authorities to respond to the foreign threat by cultivating the empire's wealth and power through greater foreign commerce, strengthened naval power, and imports of foreign knowledge and skills. But his advice did not reflect his embrace of European and American practices, which he deemed immoral. Instead, Wei sought to expand commerce and naval power as a way of strengthening China's traditional tributary relations in maritime Asia in the face of the encroachment of Europe and the United States. In his view, the tributary system was needed to restore regional peace, harmony, and mutually

---

[54] Fairbank [1953]1964, 105. See also Fairbank 1968, 260–63; Motono 2000, 7. Not until Chinese nationalist worldviews became more prominent in the early twentieth century did a Chinese narrative about the humiliating "unequal treaties" begin to become prominent (Wang 2005).

beneficial trade, all of which he argued had been disrupted by violent and unvirtuous practices of Europe and the United States.[55]

The tributary model also informed debates elsewhere in East Asia in the nineteenth century. For example, Korean opponents of foreign pressure for economic opening in the 1870s such as Lee Hang-ro (see Chapter 8) argued that China's tributary system offered their country a better kind of international order than the Western-led one that Japan and other Asian countries were embracing at the time. According to Lee, the former was a "civilized" system governed by ethical principles, while the latter was characterized by conflict, war, and immoral struggles for power and wealth that were more suitable for "beasts" than civilized humans.[56] Korean conservatives also emphasized how the tributary system preserved Korea's autonomy in ways that served the country well. More generally, these figures considered Chinese neo-Confucian ideals to be the standard of "civilization" rather than the ideas and practices of Westerners who they viewed as "bandits" and "barbarians".[57]

Sun's suggestion that the tributary system represented a model for international economic governance that was superior to the Western "rule of Might" echoed these earlier views. His interest in the tributary system was longstanding, dating back to his earliest writings about political economy in 1894 when he had argued that the boosting of China's wealth and power would help "to maintain our tributary states".[58] By the early 1920s, China had lost those states, but Sun suggested in his 1924 speech that the tributary system could serve as an inspiration for those seeking to build Pan-Asian economic solidarity on the basis of civilizational values that differed from those of Europe. Like his argument about those values deriving from a Confucian "rule of Right", however, Sun's invocation of the tributary system as a model was one likely to resonate much more in East Asia than other parts of the continent.

## Conclusion

The Pan-Islamic and Pan-Asian thinkers described in this chapter developed ideas about the politics of the world economy that were distinctive from those of other perspectives examined in this book. In the Pan-Islamic

[55] Leonard 1984.
[56] Quotes in McNamara 1996, 55; Chey and Helleiner 2018, 204.
[57] Chey and Helleiner 2017, 203. Some Korean conservatives showed an interest in Pan-Asian ideas in the 1890s, but Japan's subsequent colonization of their country then undermined this interest (Schmid 2002, 88–100).
[58] Quoted in Wei et al. 1994, 13.

case, they called for new kinds of economic solidarity among a transnational Islamic community that could promote its interests and values within the world economy. Their proposals ranged from al-Afghani's calls for the collective economic modernization of the Islamic world to the endorsement of specific joint economic projects such as Abdulhamid II's railroad to Mawdudi's focus on the need for all Muslims to embrace a new kind of Islamic Economics. By contrast, Sun's Pan-Asianism was focused on the interests and values of a transnational community that he conceptualized in civilizational terms. He argued that Asian countries' interests and values could be promoted by development-oriented economic cooperation among themselves, their collective pursuit of neo-mercantilist goals, and an alternative tributary model of international economic governance centered on the principle of the "rule of Right".

In these ways, these Pan-Islamic and Pan-Asian thinkers insisted that religious values and civilizational discourse needed to be front and center in discussions of political economy. Their ideas also challenged the universalism of some Western perspectives on this subject. Interestingly, they sometimes did so by proposing alternative universal visions of political economy, such as Mawdudi's idea that Islamic Economics should spread globally and Sun's hope that the "rule of Right" would triumph across the world.[59] This ambitious focus had some parallels to thinkers in the Pan-African movement who linked their cause to a wider anti-racist internationalism. Indeed, Du Bois became interested in the Pan-Asian cause during the 1930s when Japanese authorities actively cultivated his support for their often-racialized version of it.[60] Some in Garvey's UNIA also praised Sun's 1924 Kobe speech, drawing parallels between its vision and that of Garvey (who hoped Japan would support the UNIA initiatives).[61] There were also links between Pan-Islamists and the Pan-Asian movement in the pre-1945 era.[62]

The Pan-African, Pan-Islamic, and Pan-Asian movements were not the only "Pan" movements in the pre-1945 era. There were others, some of which also generated important economic initiatives. For example, a prominent Egyptian supporter of Pan-Arabism, Muhammad Tal'at Harb, created the first bank financed and managed exclusively by Egyptians in 1920, which soon expanded to other Arab countries in order

---

[59] Aydin (2007) also emphasizes the universalism of Pan-Asianism and Pan-Islamism.

[60] Lee 2015. As far back as his famous 1915 analysis of imperialism, Du Bois had been interested in how "Japan does not dream of a world governed mainly by white men" (Du Bois 1915, 710).

[61] Ewing 2014, 130. For Garvey's hopes about Japan, see Bandele 2008, 97; Ewing 2014, 133.

[62] Koyagi 2013; Kramer 1986, ch. 13.

to became what Eric Davis calls "the first Arab multinational corporation". Under Harb's leadership, this Bank Misr promoted industrialization, challenged European firms, and was associated more generally with
anti-imperialism and Arab interests throughout the region.[63] In the early
twentieth century, supporters of the Pan-Slavic movement also fostered
economic self-help among Slavic groups across the Austro-Hungarian
and Russian empires, and advanced proposals for a common bank as
well as railroad to connect Slavic capitals.[64] One more example comes
from a Latin American movement that became associated with an
innovative regionalist vision of political economy that is discussed in
the next chapter.

[63] Quote from Davis 1983, 4. See also Davis 1983, ch. 4; Jakes 2020, 237–39; Tignor
    1977.
[64] Kubu et al. 2006.

# 13 Distinctive Visions of Economic Regionalism for East Asia, Europe, and the Americas

Previous chapters have noted in passing how proponents of various perspectives were sometimes supportive of regional economic integration. Chapter 2 described how some European economic liberals in the mid-nineteenth century supported the creation of regional monetary unions such as the Latin Monetary Union and Scandinavian Monetary Union. Chapters 4 and 5 mentioned List's and Bunge's endorsement of regional free trade arrangements as a way to boost subordinate states' collective wealth and power vis-à-vis dominant powers. In the Marxist camp, Chapter 7 noted Sano Manabu's call for a regional "socialist league" in East Asia. Chapter 12 also highlighted how Sun's Pan-Asian ideas were invoked by Japanese authorities involved in creating a regional economic bloc in East Asia during the early 1940s.

This chapter explores the issue of economic regionalism in more depth, focusing on some distinctive perspectives that were centrally focused on this issue during the interwar years and early 1940s. I begin by examining in greater detail the ideas associated with the creation of Japan's Greater East Asia Co-Prosperity Sphere, particularly those of Akamatsu Kaname, who developed an innovative "Wild Geese Flying Pattern theory" of regional economic integration. I then turn to some German thinkers in the 1930s, who developed prominent ideas about new forms of European economic regionalism in the context of their country's growing domination of the continent. The final example comes from Latin America, where the Peruvian political leader Víctor Raúl Haya de la Torre developed innovative visions of what he called "Indoamerican economic nationalism" and "democratic Interamericanism without empire".

## Visions of a Greater East Asia Co-Prosperity Sphere

In August 1940, Japan's foreign minister Matsuoka Yōsuke declared the objective of creating a Greater East Asia Co-Prosperity Sphere (GEACS). The announcement came a few months after Germany had defeated

France and the Netherlands, and it was designed to discourage Germany from taking over their East Asian colonial possessions. Although the idea emerged from this specific political context, Jeremy Yellen notes: "By July 1941, the Co-Prosperity Sphere had become in Japan the central goal of national policy, a goal that dominated discourse until the war's end in 1945". Yellen also highlights how the precise ideational content of the GEACS was vague: "The Co-Prosperity Sphere was a moving target – a shifting, mutable, and contested notion, one that meant different things to different people at different times".[1] Indeed, Japanese officials and scholars could not even agree on its geography, with some arguing that it should include places such as India, Australia, and eastern Siberia and others preferring a narrower spatial conception.[2]

Despite the imprecise content of the GEACS, most visions of it were influenced by some core general ideas. One was the Japanese notion of *hakkō ichiu* ("universal brotherhood"), an idea that resonated with a Japanese audience but was poorly understood outside of the country.[3] Another was Pan-Asianism, which included not just Sun's vision of Asia's moral civilizational tradition but also more racialized discourses that challenged "the White man's mastery over all of the Orient".[4] The importance of that challenge was also highlighted in a "Greater East Asia Joint Declaration" that was announced by Japan and a number of other Asian countries in November 1943 and that appeared to compete with the Anglo-American Atlantic Charter of August 1941 (discussed in the next chapter). Dubbed the Pacific Charter by the Japanese media, this document committed signatories not just to "enhance the culture and civilization of Greater East Asia" but also to "work for the abolition of racial discriminations".[5] The latter commitment was absent from the Atlantic Charter.

Visions of the GEACS were also informed by criticisms of economic liberalism. Its supporters highlighted how the liberal international economic order had collapsed during the 1930s, with even Britain and the United States creating preferential economic blocs to defend their interests. In this context, advocates of the GEACS argued that Japan needed to create its own "pan-regional economy" in order to protect access to foreign markets and resources that were key to its economy

---

[1] Quotes from Yellen 2019, 4, 208. See also Duus 1996, 69–70.
[2] Yellen 2019, 83.
[3] Quoted in Yellen 2019, 95.
[4] Quote from Matsuoka in 1941, and quoted in Yellen 2019, 37. For Pan-Asian discourses in the GEACS, see also Mimura 2011; Aydin 2007, ch. 7.
[5] Quoted in Yellen 2019, 158.

and military.[6] This East Asian economic bloc was also usually concep-tualized in relatively autarkic terms. Indeed, one Japanese cabinet paper produced just after the December 1941 attack on Pearl Harbor even referred to the "Greater East Asia Co-Prosperity Sphere autarkic sys-tem". Other visions, however, were less firm on this point, such as the Pacific Charter, which supported "the opening of resources throughout the world".[7]

Visions of the intra-regional organization of the GEACS also usu-ally rejected economic liberal principles. Instead of highlighting the benefits of free markets and intra-regional free trade, they anticipated "co-prosperity" among member countries being generated by state-led economic development policies.[8] This developmental orientation of the idea of co-prosperity was also differentiated from past practices in the region of powers such as the United States and Britain who, according to the Pacific Charter, had "indulged in insatiable aggression and exploi-tation". By contrast, the Charter's signatories committed to "construct an order of common prosperity and well-being based upon justice" and "to accelerate their economic development through close cooperation upon a basis of reciprocity and to promote thereby the general prosper-ity of their region". As Matsuoka put it in early 1941, "my *motto* for the establishment of the Greater East Asian Co-Prosperity Sphere. ... is no conquest, no oppression, no exploitation".[9]

There were, of course, large gaps between these ideas and the real-ity of Japanese policy in East Asia. Because of their experience with Japanese rule, Filipinos mocked Japan's idea of co-prosperity as "prosperity-*ko*" or "me-first prosperity". A Japanese "navy brain trust" even acknowledged in October 1941 that "the reality is that Japanese occupation brings not 'prosperity' but 'poverty'".[10] Commitments to abolish racial discrimination were also contradicted by Japanese mili-tary memos at the time that described the Japanese as "master peoples" and that advised them to maintain the "purity of the blood".[11] More generally, lofty Japanese rhetoric was hard to square with the fact that, as Yellen notes, "Japanese wartime rule was brutal, oppressive, and domineering".[12]

---

[6] Quoted in Yellen 2019, 86. See also pp. 12, 30, 39; Duus 1996, 66–67; Mimura 2011.
[7] Quotes in Yellen 2019, 80, 158. For the role of autarkic goals, see also Barnhart 1987, ch. 1; Mulder 2022, 249–58.
[8] See, for example, Duus 1996; Yellen 2019, 87.
[9] Quotes in Yellen 2019, 157–58, 62.
[10] Quotes in Yellen 2019, 210, 78.
[11] Quoted in Peattie 1984, 125.
[12] Yellen 2019, 6.

Contradictions also abounded with respect to the Pacific Charter's idea that East Asian countries committed to "respecting one another's sovereignty and independence". The Charter did not mention Japan's longstanding colonies of Korea, Taiwan, and Karafuto, none of which was invited to send representatives to the 1943 conference that produced it. Also not invited were representatives of places under Japanese control at the time such as Malaya, Singapore, French Indochina, and the Dutch East Indies. Even among the invited countries – the Chinese Nanjing regime, Manchukuo, Thailand, India, the Philippines, and Burma – independence was often more nominal than real. It was hardly surprising, then, that Japan's Pan-Asian rhetoric provoked criticism from people such as India's Benoy Kumar Sarkar (see Chapter 5), who argued in 1943 that the GEACS "may turn out to be a Japanification of East Asia" rather than "a genuine Asia for Asians".[13]

While the content of the GEACS was vague and easily criticized, some ideas about East Asian economic regionalism promoted at this time were more sophisticated. Particularly interesting was the "Wild Geese Flying Pattern theory" (*Gankou Keitai Ron*) developed by the Japanese economist Akamatsu Kaname.[14] The son of a poor rice retailer, Akamatsu became a university lecturer at Nagoya Higher Commercial School in 1921 and then at Tokyo University of Economics in 1939. Developed in the 1930s and early 1940s, his theory focused on how countries could follow Japan's example of catching up economically to Europe and the United States by using international trade. Akamatsu argued that trade opening would encourage the growth of specific local industries in three stages: "import, production, and export".[15] In the first stage, imports of a new foreign consumer good would undermine domestic handicraft production, but also encourage the introduction of new knowledge and consumer tastes. New foreign knowledge (and machinery) would then generate an expansion of local production of the consumer good to meet the new patterns of local demand, thereby gradually displacing the imports. Finally, as production ramped up, these new local producers would begin exporting the goods back to advanced industrial economies.

This sequential pattern of import–production–export in a specific industry was also related by Akamatsu to the wider international relocation of industries. As less advanced economies expanded their production of consumer goods, more advanced economies would shift out of those

---

[13] Sarkar 1943a, 303.

[14] Quote from Ohtsuki 2017a, 117.

[15] Quoted in Ohtsuki 2011, 304. For other analyses of Akamatsu's ideas, see Ohtsuki 2017a, b; Korhonen 1994; Schröppel and Nakajima 2003; Kasahara 2019.

sectors into more complex industrial activities. These more complex industries would subsequently be shed to the less advanced economies by the same process unfolding at the next level of sophistication, prompting the lead economies to advance technologically into new sectors. In this way, all countries would advance economically in a complementary and interdependent manner that Akamatsu saw as resembling a pattern of flying geese. In his theory, the most advanced economies of Europe and the United States were the lead geese, followed by Japan, whose industrialization, in turn, would help foster industrialization in the rest of Asia.[16]

Akamatsu's theory offered an innovative vision of the benefits of international economic interdependence. It also had a strong neomercantilist orientation. Akamatsu saw states playing an important role in facilitating the dynamic processes associated with the flying geese formation. As he put it in 1943, a country's industrialization would be fostered by an activist "national economic policy", including moderate forms of protectionism.[17] Akamatsu himself later acknowledged some similarities between his ideas and those of List.[18] After initially being interested in Marxism, Akamatsu had been drawn to the ideas of the German historical school (see Chapter 4) in his initial university studies and had even pursued further study in Germany between 1924 and 1926.[19]

According to Pekka Korhonen, Akatmatsu's theory became "part of Japanese war propaganda aimed at nations of the Greater East Asia Coprosperity Sphere".[20] Its importance in this respect should not be overstated given that the GEACS's meaning was so vague and contested. Akamatsu's flying geese theory also fit awkwardly with more autarkic visions of the GEACS because it emphasized that Japan and the rest of East Asia were engaged in active trade with countries beyond the region (with Europe and the United States as lead geese). But it is easy to see how Akamatsu's theory was useful for the Japanese government's propaganda, since it offered a sophisticated justification of the idea of "co-prosperity" by highlighting how trade between industrial Japan and the rest of East Asia was mutually beneficial rather than exploitative. Even if Japan had a privileged position in a hierarchical division of labour

---

[16] Akamatsu also suggested that the flying geese metaphor applied to the sequential rising and falling of imports, production, and exports within a single industry in each country, a pattern that he argued resembled overlapping Vs of flying geese.

[17] Quoted in Schröppel and Nakajima 2003, 213.

[18] Akamatsu 1962, 207n1.

[19] Kasahara 2019, 13, 26; Korhonen 1994; Ohtsuki 2017a, 119; Schröppel and Nakajima 2003, 205.

[20] Korhonen 1994, 94.

in the region, the flying geese theory offered the prospect of upward mobility for all. Indeed, Akamatsu even emphasized that follower geese could become lead ones over time. Akamatsu's vision of independent but regionally complementary neomercantilist policies also respected the sovereignty of East Asian countries and was compatible with the developmentalist orientation of many advocates of the GEACS.

Akamastu himself supported the idea of the GEACS. Tadashi Ohtsuki shows that he was already expressing support for "Japanese colonial expansion, and totalitarianism" in the late 1930s.[21] At that time, he also published scholarly work that depicted colonial wars as a mechanism by which economic depressions at the bottom of Kondratieff long waves could be overcome by generating new markets, spending, and armament production.[22] In 1942, he wrote that the GEACS was "close to being gloriously achieved by the Imperial Military. ... But we still lack India, Australia and the Chiang Kai-shek government in Burma. ... To gain these areas we take both military and economic war yet further". At this time, he also repeated some of the wider justifications for the GEACS, including noting that "the new idea of the emancipation of the Great East Asia from colonization, the foundation of Asia for the Asian peoples ... and the new world order without any exploitation has been settled on the basis of the essential trend of Asia centring in Japan".[23] Akamatsu also became directly involved in the Japanese war effort after the military administration took control of a university institute whose research he directed in early 1942 and then sent him to Singapore, where the Japanese military command in Southeast Asia was headquartered, to lead a research group on that region.[24]

### German Designs for Europe's Economy

Other examples of distinctive non-liberal regional economic visions in the 1930s and early 1940s emerged from Nazi Germany. These visions initially emerged from the economic shock of the Great Depression when the country suspended external debt payments and imposed exchange controls and higher tariffs. While some Germans advocated a turn to autarky in this context (see Chapter 8), others recognized Germany's enduring need for international trade, including imports of

---

[21] Ohtsuki 2017a, 124.
[22] Ohtsuki 2011, 308; Tausch 2016. "Kondratieff long waves" are roughly fifty year economic cycles, each of which includes an economic upswing followed by a downswing, that were hypothesized by the Russian economist Nikolai Kondratieff in the 1920s.
[23] Quotes in Ohtsuki 2017a, 125, 126.
[24] Ohtsuki 2017a, 127; 2017b, 148–50.

raw materials. But their focus shifted from engaging with the Anglo-American world that had dominated German foreign economic policy in the 1920s to the cultivation of new economic partners, particularly in Southeast Europe. New economic ties with countries in that region were facilitated not through free trade but rather through various non-liberal bilateral mechanisms that fostered what Ted Fertik has called "managed" economic flows instead of the "free flows" of a liberal order.[25]

After the Nazis came to power in 1933, this new approach was consolidated and expanded, particularly by Hjalmar Schacht, who was president of Germany's central bank (the Reichsbank) from 1933 to 1939 and economics minister from 1934 to 1937. In 1934, Schacht introduced a "New Plan" that tightened the country's exchange controls in ways that gave the government enormous power over the country's external trade. That power was reinforced by the expansion of bilateral clearing and payment arrangements that encouraged barter and through which officials managed the prices and quantities of bilateral trade. By 1938, over half of Germany's external trade was covered by over two dozen of these arrangements and the country's trade had shifted dramatically towards Southeast Europe, with the latter exporting resources in return for Germany's manufactured goods.[26]

This Schachtian system of managed bilateralism was defended by its architect on the grounds that economic liberalism had become outdated. As he put it in 1938, "the world has become too small, people and goods are crowding in on each other so much, that a self-steering economy in the sense of the automatism of the gold standard or the theory of free trade is no longer possible".[27] He also echoed wider Nazi criticisms of the Anglo-American dominated international economic order of the 1920s which was seen to have subordinated and exploited Germany, including via international loans and debt.[28] But the main goal of Schacht's plan was an immediate practical one of supporting Germany's rearmament and Adolf Hitler's quest for international power and domination. The tight foreign exchange controls enabled the German state to reward domestic sectors that supported rearmament, while minimizing the risk of balance of payments problems. The bilateral trade arrangements could also be used politically to cultivate allies abroad as well as to deepen their economic dependence on Germany.[29]

[25] Fertik 2018, 203. See also Hirschman 1945; Link 2020, ch. 4; Woolf 1968.
[26] James 2001, 142–43; Neal 1979, 391; Tooze 2006.
[27] Quoted in James 2001, 141.
[28] Frieden 2006, 198–206; Tooze, 2006.
[29] See, for example, Fertik 2018; James 2001,144–45; Hirschman 1945; Link 2020, ch. 4.

Hitler soon began to use not just bilateral agreements but also military force to forge a new European regional economy – or what he called a wider "living space" (*Lebensraum*) for the German people.[30] After Germany's initial military victories in Europe in 1939–40, the country's new economic minister, Walther Funk, outlined an official Nazi vision for the organization of that regional economy. Published in July 1940, Funk's "New Order" in Europe centered on more multilateral principles than the many bilateral arrangements Germany had put in place in the previous decade. Funk suggested that trade imbalances in German-controlled Europe would be covered by a multilateral clearing system supported by fixed exchange rates. In a speech the next month, he emphasized how this new system would foster regional economic integration and a more efficient division of labour: "Europe's unbearable economic atomisation and chaos has to be ended. It is economic madness if every country, no matter how small, tries to produce everything from trouser buttons to locomotives and if it fosters dwarf-industries for this purpose, which have no right to exist and can only be kept alive with subsidies, import restrictions, or excessive tariffs".[31]

Funk's multilateral vision was not a liberal one. Based on the German currency, the multilateral clearing system would be actively managed by the Reichsbank rather than by the automatic principles of the gold standard. As Raimund Bauer puts it, the German goals were "to establish a monetary long-term alternative to the liberal gold standard and to enable the *Reich* to orchestrate the European economies systematically". Funk also did not back regional free trade. Instead, the European division of labour would continue to be determined by German wartime planning and needs. In general, the goal of regional integration was to serve German power. As Funk put it in internal discussions at the time: "Germany now possesses the political power in Europe to reorganise the economy according to its needs. ... The economies of the other European countries have to adapt to our needs".[32]

This vision of multilateralism was, in other words, a fascist one both in its economic endorsement of planning and in the political sense that served the goals of Germany's conquest and dominance of the rest of Europe.[33] While the GEACS' Pacific Charter paid lip service to ending

---

[30] Quote in Tooze 2006, 8.
[31] Quoted in Bauer 2015, 102. See also Faudot 2022; Gross 2017.
[32] Quotes from Bauer 2015, 196–97, 101. See also p. 105.
[33] Around the time that Funk announced his New Order, more ambitious versions of fascist multilateralism were also circulating in German policymaking circles, including some that called for a new European central bank and regionwide industrial policy (Gross 2017, 295–96; Mazower 1996, 37). Earlier in 1934, Italy's Giuseppe de

racial discrimination, Hitler overtly promoted his ideology of German racial superiority in the context of what he and other Nazis saw as a social Darwinian struggle among races. In Mark Mazower's words, the objective was the "economic subordination of the lesser races of Europe to the Nordic-Germanic Volk. ... ultimately, race was to be the genuine 'organizing' principle for the continent". Indeed, Hitler asserted in August 1941 that "Europe is not a geographical entity. It is a racial entity".[34]

While Funk called for economic multilateralism within German-controlled Europe, he noted that the continent's trade with the rest of the world would be governed by Schachtian bilateral means (or what he called "government agreements reached by using the German instruments of power").[35] Hitler himself was drawn to a relatively autarkic vision of the German-controlled economic space (and his interest in military expansion was associated with this vision). As he put it in September 1941, "Europe will cover its entire demand for raw materials itself and have its own export market in the Russian space, so that we will no longer need the rest of world trade".[36] But Funk made a point of noting in July 1940 that Germany's economic bloc would continue to pursue trade with the outside world in order to ensure a rising standard of living.[37]

Funk's views on this topic were similar to those of Nazi theorist Friedrich Zimmermann, whose autarkic views in the early 1930s were discussed in Chapter 8. In the late 1930s, Zimmermann emerged as what Joshua Derman calls the "the preeminent theorist" of the idea of a "great-space economy" (*Grossraumwirtschaft*). That idea was frequently invoked by Funk and other Nazis in the early 1940s to legitimate German hegemony over Europe. Indeed, Derman notes that "throughout the Third Reich, and especially during the early years of the Second

---

Michelis had also proposed extending fascist economic ideas to the global level through the creation of a global institution to coordinate tasks such as colonial administration, international public works, the provision of credit to farmers and small business, and the organization of the world's resources (Steffek 2015).

[34] Quotes from Mazower 1996, 44.

[35] Quoted in Bauer 2016, 109.

[36] Quoted in Derman 2021, 768fn62. For Hitler's interest in what Mulder (2022, 227) calls "autarkic expansion", particularly after Italy faced widespread economic sanctions for its 1935 invasion of Ethiopia, see Mulder 2022, 242–49. For earlier German visions of autarky associated with visions of imperial expansion at the turn of the century and during World War I, see Helleiner 2021b, 940–41; Mulder 2022, 59–60. See also the discussion in Chapter 8 of this book of Fichte's earlier endorsement in 1800 of forceable annexation of neighbouring territories to create "natural frontiers" compatible with autarkic needs.

[37] Derman 2021.

World War, the vision of a 'world economy of great spaces' played a major role, arguably the predominant one, in the regime's articulation of its foreign-policy goals".[38]

Zimmerman had first discussed this idea in the early 1930s when he had flirted with autarkism. At that time, despite his advocacy of autarkic goals, Zimmerman recognized the country's enduring need for some raw material imports to maintain its standard of living. These imports, he argued, could come from Southeast Europe, which he suggested could be part of a "great-space economy" with Germany, paralleling the emergence of economic blocs in other parts of the world.[39] He then elaborated on this idea in a 1939 book titled *Turning Point of World Economy* that he finished just before the outbreak of the world war. The book attracted attention not just in Nazi circles but also among scholars elsewhere.

In it, Zimmermann argued that the British-led world economy of the nineteenth century which had been based on free trade had undermined itself by fostering the industrialization of competitors to Britain and by encouraging vast zones of environmentally unsustainable monoculture commodity production to serve the industrial core.[40] In the context of subsequent geopolitical uncertainty and the growing instability of markets, states had responded in the 1930s with autarkic policies. But those policies, too, were deemed unsustainable by Zimmermann because modern technology required larger markets than national ones. As a compromise, nation-states had begun during the 1930s to construct regional economic blocs – or "great-space economies" – which allowed for larger markets but still reduced vulnerabilities to the world economy as a whole. Zimmermann referred to this as a "third way" that he argued was "nothing other than the Hegelian synthesis between the thesis of the generally free world economy and the antithesis of autarky".[41]

He pointed to the emergence of seven such economic spaces, each led by a powerful state (Britain, France, Germany, Italy, the United States, Japan, and the Soviet Union). But he insisted that these spaces could not be run as empires because "no future development can any longer be based on domination, but rather, as is the case for all bloc formations in the world, only on the free and equal consolidation of all individual parts to a community, or better yet, an association".[42] He suggested further

---

[38]  Derman 2021, 759, 780. See also Bauer 2016, 137.
[39]  Quote in Derman 2021, 762.
[40]  Zimmermann cited Jacks' 1939 environment analysis discussed in Chapter 9 (Derman 2021, 765fn41).
[41]  Quoted in Derman 2021, 774.
[42]  Quote in Derman 2021, 766.

that these regional economic blocs, while largely self-sufficient, would still need to trade with each other. In addition to securing resources they did not have, each bloc would need to exchange specialty high-value consumer goods in order to foster higher standards of living. More generally, Zimmermann argued that a world economy organized around these blocs promised "the possibilities of future economic cooperation among the great nations of the Earth". As a result of this cooperation, he anticipated that "it is not a unified world culture and world civilization that emerges but a manageable coexistence of different great and unique cultures in a world community".[43]

At the time of writing his book, Zimmermann was not working for the German government, but he later acknowledged that the work was partly propaganda for Nazis. Indeed, the contrast between his vision and the brutality, violence, and racism of Nazi rule in Europe was striking. As Derman notes, the propaganda value of Zimmermann's theory of "great spaces" was not just that it "served to normalize a global order based on violence and the subordination of weaker nations" but also that it might assuage "neutral countries about the limits of German ambitions" by promising future "coexistence and economic cooperation between the 'great spaces' of the world".[44] To boost the propaganda appeal of his ideas beyond Germany, Zimmermann also insisted in some lectures in 1943 that the idea of "great-space economies" was not a Nazi one, but one pioneered by Britain with its trade agreements in the early 1930s and increasingly a global consensus around which the postwar world economic order could be organized.[45]

## Haya's Anti-Imperialist Economic Regionalism

A final example of a distinctive vision of economic regionalism emerging in the interwar years and the early 1940s comes from Peru's Víctor Raúl Haya de la Torre. Like Mariátegui (see Chapter 7) with whom he was well acquainted, Haya was on the Peruvian political left. After being sent into exile for his political activities in 1923, Haya travelled through Panama and Cuba to Mexico, during which time he became shocked at what he called the "imperialist danger of the United States" in the region. The experience led him in 1924 to create a pan–Latin American movement called the Alianza Popular Revolucionaria Americana (APRA) that was dedicated to fostering the unity of Latin America to

---

[43] Quotes in Derman 2021, 764, 767–68.
[44] Derman 2021, 780.
[45] Derman 2021, 774.

fight against "Yankee Imperialism" in the region.[46] APRA-related political parties were subsequently created in many Latin American countries
(including in Peru in 1928 with the help of Magda Portal whose views
were discussed in Chapter 10) and Haya quickly became a very well-
known figure across the region.

Haya outlined his views about political economy in a number of places,
including a book titled *Antiimperialism and the APRA* that was published
in 1935 (although it had been written seven years earlier). In that book
and elsewhere, Haya was particularly critical of growing US investments
in Latin America, which he argued were a "more advanced, better hid-
den, but no less dangerous" form of imperialism than formal military
intervention.[47] These investments, he argued, were introducing a dis-
torted form of capitalism to the region, one which was "dependent" and
served the "necessities of imperialist capitalism". In his view, this economic form of imperialism in the region was an "exploiting" and "con-
quering" force that used "wealth to subjugate our peoples as nations and
our workers as exploited classes". In addition to these economic problems, he worried about the threat of US military intervention to defend
growing US investments as well as the emergence of local "political oli-
garchies" who were "subject to the orders of the White House, itself the
political organ of Wall Street".[48]

In these circumstances, Haya called for a broad coalition of peasants,
workers, and the middle class to push for the establishment of "anti-
imperialist" governments across Latin America. Within each country,
he suggested that these governments pursue a kind of "state capitalism"
dedicated to industrialization via a "plan of economic progress". But
he also recommended that they cooperate regionally to create common
market and especially to regulate foreign capital. The latter was a particularly innovative idea. As he put it, what was needed was "the formation of a bloc of economic defense for Latin America, a union which by
the unity of leadership could fix uniform conditions for the necessary
invasion of North American capital in our countries".[49]

Haya acknowledged that foreign capital was "necessary to countries
of elemental economic development such as ours", but he insisted that
Latin America needed "good relations with foreign capital, without
falling into dependence upon it, defending the equilibrium of our own
economy and making foreign capital a cooperator in national economic

[46] Quotes in Helleiner and Rosales 2017, 669.
[47] Quoted in Einaudi 1966, 46.
[48] Quotes in Helleiner and Rosales 2017, 672.
[49] Quotes in Helleiner and Rosales 2017, 672–73, 675.

development". He argued that Latin American governments needed to set conditions for foreign capital's entry into the region, including blocking it in specific sectors. In his view, their efforts required regional cooperation that both boosted their collective bargaining power vis-à-vis foreign capital and prevented one government's regulations from simply diverting foreign money to other countries. As he put it, they needed to avoid situations in which, "if a country imposes conditions, there are nineteen others which give free passage".[50]

To be successful, Haya argued that this project needed to be supported by a regional "consciousness" that would "go beyond the limited and localist, false patriotism of the spokesmen of chauvinism, and will include the twenty countries which form our great nation". He referred to this as a kind of "Indoamerican economic nationalism" that needed to be cultivated "among the masses". This idea would, he argued, "bring to our peoples that conviction that the wealth which imperialism exploits is ours and that that same wealth must be converted into our best defense" and demonstrate that "the boycott and passive or active resistance will be used against imperialism".[51]

Haya chose the term "Indoamerican economic nationalism" to emphasize the Indigenous roots of Latin American societies. To reinforce this point, APRA songs and cheers included Quechua battle cries, and APRA cells were named after Inkan emperors. Haya had been interested since his youth in Peru's Inkan history and he was also influenced by the emergence of a wider *Indigenismo* movement in Latin American intellectual circles at this time (that also inspired Mariátegui). Haya justified his concept of Indoamerican economic nationalism in a following way:

It cannot be denied that our continent, in spite of its cities and sporadic white islands is, in quantity and quality a mixture of Indian and white, and to a lesser degree, of Indian and Negro ... But it is not the numbers, the census data, the statistical index, that supports Indoamericanism as a name and as an idea. It is something much deeper and more telluric, more concealed and living: It is in our spirit and our culture that there flourishes a reserve of strength emanating from the remote ancestry of the old races in these ancient lands ... The Indian is within us.[52]

This line of argument represented a strong rejection of the traditional focus of Latin American elites on the region's European links. It was part of Haya's deeper critique of Eurocentric thought and its universal

---

[50] Quotes in Helleiner and Rosales 2017, 673; Alexander 1973, 180.
[51] Quotes in Helleiner and Rosales 2017, 675.
[52] Alexander 1973, 352.

claims as well as of discourses of European civilizational superiority (that were common among Latin American elites). Inspired by Einstein's theory of relativity and new anthropological literature emphasizing cultural relativism, Haya argued that the peoples of different continents developed distinctive worldviews that derived from their particular "historical space-time". As he put it, "the so-called historic laws and their universal application must be conditional upon the relativity of the viewpoint. Therefore, the history of the world, seen from the Indoamerican historical space-time will never be the same as that seen by a philosopher from the European historical space-time".[53]

For this reason, Haya strongly critiqued the "mental colonialism" of people in Latin American who followed European doctrines, including many Marxists who were "unthinking repeaters of an imported creed". As he put it, "we do not need to go to Europe to ask advice or to receive lessons in struggling". Although he endorsed a long-term socialist future, he insisted that APRA "has not submitted to, nor is it ever going to submit to the Third, to the Second, or whatever other political International with European headquarters; and it thus defines its status as an Indoamerican nationalist and anti-imperialist movement". Even Mariátegui, who also distanced himself from the Comintern and developed a distinctive Latin American version of Marxism, earned Haya's criticism as a "Europeanizer". Haya was also critical of Leninist theory for depicting imperialism as the highest stage of capitalism when it was associated with what he called "the first stage of the modern capitalist age" in Latin America.[54]

At the same time that Haya insisted on a Latin American worldview, he committed APRA to work towards "the solidarity of all the oppressed people and classes of the world". He also drew strong inspiration from a non–Latin American thinker, Sun Yat-sen, whom he praised as "one of the most illustrious creative spirits of our times". He applauded Sun's commitment to building a broad-based anti-imperialist movement, and compared APRA to the political party that Sun had created, the Guomindang. Haya also shared Sun's commitment to regulating foreign capital in support of state-led industrialization as well as his interest in a long-term future that transcended inter-state struggles for wealth and power. On the latter point, Haya noted: "Even when we give full play to make-believe and imagine that we [Indoamerica] shall come to form a group of capitalist powers rivaling the present empires in Europe, North America, and Asia, such an ingenious and complacent thesis

---

[53] Quotes in Helleiner and Rosales 2017, 671.
[54] Quotes in Helleiner and Rosales 2017, 670–71, 685, 671.

would present the tragic perspective of new competition and incessant and ruinous struggle".[55]

In the late 1930s and early 1940s, Haya's ideas underwent an important transformation as he began to embrace the idea of the wider conception of anti-imperialist economic regionalism in the Americas as a whole. This shift in his thought was prompted by US president Franklin Roosevelt's Good Neighbor policy towards Latin America. That policy not only renounced military intervention in the region but also began in the late 1930s to extend public economic assistance to Latin American governments in order to support their state-led development and industrialization policies. As part of this new policy, top US officials also denounced past US economic imperialism and praised how publicly managed capital flows to the region would serve Latin America's development goals better than the old "imperialist" flows of the past.[56] Before an audience in Haya's Peru in 1943, US vice-president Henry Wallace even spoke directly to the kind of *Indigenismo* ideology that interested Haya, praising the Inkans for inventing the concept of social justice in the Americas.[57]

In this new political context, Haya suggested as early as 1938 that the Good Neighbor policy had led to "the reduction of the imperialist tension in Indoamerica" and was "worthy of support". Haya's new willingness to work with US authorities was also fostered by his belief that they had a central role to play in a global fight against fascists and the racism of the Nazis. In April 1940, he warned that a Nazi military victory would "not only bring economic hegemony, the exploitation, and subjugation of peoples because of their poverty and weakness, but enslavement because they are 'inferior' and not Ayrans". Indeed, he made the following warning: "If the European Jews – so many of whom are so blonde and so white – have been persecuted because their race is not pure, what can be expected by the Indoamerican Indians and mestizos who constitute eighty-five percent of the population of our vast continent".[58]

At this time, Haya began to support ambitious ideas to build what he called in 1941 a kind of *"democratic Inter Americanism without empire"*. He distinguished this from the Pan-American cause that US policymakers had promoted since the late nineteenth century because the latter was associated with "imperialist expansionism". He called at this time for

---

[55] Quotes from Alexander 1973, 97, 119, 156–57.
[56] Quoted in Helleiner 2014, 66. See Chapters 1–3 of that book for this shift in US foreign policy.
[57] Pike 1986, 203–4.
[58] Quotes from Alexander 1973, 247–48, 302–3.

economic coordination and planning via an "Inter American grand economic congress" as well as the creation of an "Inter American Export-Import Bank" to engage in public lending and other activities that supported "productive investment", exchange rate stability, "economic improvement for workers", and inter-American commerce, including by fostering an "Inter American customs union". When proposing these initiatives, he insisted on the need to "avoid all the excesses of the economic hegemony of the most powerful, making the capital invested in each country a factor of cooperation with the state, and an instrument of progress, and not one of oppression or exploitation".[59]

Some of these proposals were similar to ones that Latin American officials had been promoting in inter-American meetings since the early 1930s, such as the creation of an Inter-American Bank (IAB). After the outbreak of World War II in 1939, US officials also backed the negotiation of a convention for an IAB that was completed in the spring of 1940 (although US Congress never ratified it). German discussions of a New Order in Europe in mid-1940 then prompted US officials to embrace even more ambitious efforts to expand public lending to Latin America and foster inter-American commerce. These new American policies largely reflected its strategic and economic concerns in the Latin American region in the new wartime context. But the fact that American officials endorsed a form of regionalism in which governments assumed an activist economic role also reflected an ideational shift that will be discussed in the next chapter: the growing prominence of the perspective of "embedded liberalism" in US policymaking circles.[60]

## Conclusion

During the interwar years and the early 1940s, a number of perspectives on economic regionalism emerged in East Asia, Europe, and the Americas that were distinctive from earlier ideas of this kind. In East Asia, Japanese officials and thinkers offered visions of a Greater East Asian Co-Prosperity Sphere, of which Akamatsu's flying geese theory was the most sophisticated. In Europe, a number of German thinkers developed new conceptions of a reorganized European economic space, ranging from Schacht's bilateral clearing and payment arrangements to Funk's New Order and Zimmermann's "great-space economy". In the Americas, Haya advanced an Indoamerican anti-imperialism that led him to

---

[59] Quotes from Alexander 1973, 294, 329–30.
[60] For the history in this paragraph, see Helleiner 2014.

endorse a new kind of "Indoeconomic economic nationalism" and then a wider "democratic Inter Americanism without empire".

Each of these perspectives envisioned forms of economic regionalism that were not based on economic liberal principles. They endorsed distinct kinds of inter-state economic relations, such as Akamatsu's conception of regionally complementary neomercantilism in a hierarchical division of labour, Schacht's system of bilateral "managed flows", Funk's fascist multilateral vision of regional economic planning, and Haya's coordinated regulation of foreign capital as well as his later proposals for activist regional multilateral institutions. Many were also linked to regional identities that invoked ideas of race and/or civilization, including Japan's Pan-Asianism, Hitler's conception of Europe as a racial entity, and Haya's notion of Indoamericanism. As we have seen, thinkers also outlined distinctive ideas about how regionalism would fit into a wider world economic order. While some anticipated quite autarkic regional economies, Akamatsu's flying geese theory depicted the East Asian region embedded within a wider global economy in which European countries and the United States remained the technological leaders. Zimmermann also advocated for a postwar world in which many "great-space economies" co-existed cooperatively and traded resources and high-value consumer products among each other.

The idea that the future world economy might be organized around regional economic blocs reached its highpoint in 1940–41. That was the moment when Germany's New Order and Japan's GEACS were announced and ambitious proposals for strengthened inter-American economic cooperation were advanced. After the United States entered World War II in December 1941, however, American officials and many others among the United Nations alliance began to outline a quite different vision of an integrated world economy centered around global multilateral principles and institutions. Their influential ideas are the subject of the next chapter.

*Part III*

Ending at a Beginning

# 14 The Embedded Liberalism of Bretton Woods

There is one final perspective that deserves attention in this analysis of pre-1945 thought: embedded liberalism. In contrast to many of the perspectives described in the second part of this book, this one is well known to contemporary IPE scholars and students because it informed the famous 1944 Bretton Woods conference. The conference helped to create the postwar international economic order by endorsing the creation of the International Monetary Fund (IMF) and International Bank for Reconstruction and Development (IBRD, later called the World Bank). In a widely cited 1982 article, John Ruggie coined the term "embedded liberalism" to describe the common vision of the Anglo-American officials leading the Bretton Woods negotiations.[1] These officials reformulated classical economic liberalism in innovative ways to create this new version of economic liberal thought. Like classical economic liberals, they endorsed the overall goals of boosting global prosperity, international peace, and individual freedom. But they argued that these goals were best met with a new kind of institutionalized liberal multilateralism that would make an open world economy compatible with various kinds of active public management of the economy.

Ruggie detailed how the embedded liberal perspective was developed by Anglo-American policymakers during the Bretton Woods negotiations as a way of accommodating the new interest across Western Europe and North America in governmental support for domestic social security and activist macroeconomic management in the wake of the Great Depression. This chapter highlights how the roots of embedded liberalism can also be found in earlier efforts to reformulate the international side of classical economic liberal thought. In addition, it shows how the

---

[1] The phrase "embedded liberalism" is sometimes used generally to refer to a preference for a mixed domestic economy of regulated capitalism, but Ruggie (1982) himself emphasized that he intended it to describe a normative framework for *international* economic governance. As Seabrooke and Young (2017, 17) note, Ruggie's article has become one of the most widely cited publications in the contemporary IPE field.

Anglo-American architects of Bretton Woods sought support for their new vision of global economic governance well beyond Western Europe and North America by partially accommodating the Soviet Union's commitment to central planning as well as neomercantilist ideas popular in many less industrialized regions. The final section of the chapter highlights one further issue that is often overlooked in analyses of Bretton Woods: how advocates of embedded liberalism in the negotiations engaged very little with the perspectives discussed in the second part of this volume.

## Reformulating Classical Economic Liberalism

The embedded liberalism of Bretton Woods built upon efforts to reformulate the international dimension of economic liberal thought in the early twentieth century. A prominent example can be found in the writings of John Hobson. Hobson is best known among contemporary IPE scholars for his 1902 book on imperialism that was discussed in Chapter 6. But he was subsequently also important for developing what David Long calls a "new liberal internationalism" that represented "a stage between classical and 'embedded' liberalism".[2]

Although Hobson was inspired by Cobden's views, his views went beyond those of his British predecessor in two ways that anticipated the embedded liberalism of Bretton Woods. First, he was more willing to endorse state activism in the economy. Hobson argued that the liberal push for free markets had initially bolstered individual freedom and helped small producers, but it increasingly simply protected the wealth and privilege of powerful industrial trusts and financiers. In this context, what was needed, he argued, was a more active state that provided for the welfare of citizens and made powerful firms better serve societal needs.

Second, during World War I, Hobson began to call for a new kind of "international government" to support multilateral economic cooperation. In his view, this "international government" could play a useful role in facilitating the settlement of economic disputes among countries as well as in supporting and supervising growing "scientific and expert co-operation" in "utilitarian" areas such as "postal and telegraphic services", "transport and communication", and "the standardization of money, weights, and measures".[3] Hobson also suggested that international government could promote peace through the collective

---

[2] Long 1996, 2. The first quote is from the title of Long's book.
[3] Quotes from Hobson 1915, 112, 116–17.

application of an "economic boycott" against aggressors.[4] This idea contrasted particularly sharply with Cobden's views. While Cobden hoped economic interdependence would eliminate war, Hobson (and other liberals at this time) began to see the threat of excluding countries from the world economy as a way to preserve peace.[5]

Hobson argued further that international government could help "to remove all commercial restrictions which impair the freedom of economic intercourse between nations". To prevent inter-imperialist wars, he argued that it was necessary to secure not just free trade but also "economic liberty and equality ... for the capital, enterprise, and the labour, which are required to do the work of development in all the backward countries of the earth". Hobson proposed the creation of new "International Commissions" to uphold this kind of "economic liberty" in independent countries, while suggesting that international conventions among imperial powers could perform this role in colonies. Although Hobson is known as a critic of imperialism, the latter provides a reminder that he was in fact a liberal imperialist who endorsed colonial rule as long as it met certain conditions, such as improving "the character" of the colonized and securing "the safety and progress of the civilization of the world".[6] He argued that one sign of the latter would be adherence to an international convention of this kind.

A final economic role for international government was to "better develop and appropriate the natural and human resources of the earth". In the "backward" areas of the world, he argued that this task could no longer be left to unregulated "private companies, with armed forces of their own...enslaving or killing off the native populations, as in San Thomé or Putumayo, and using up the rich natural resources of the country in a brief era of reckless waste". He suggested instead that the task of development be "conducted on a basis of pacific co-operation between the business groups in the respective countries under the joint control of their Governments". His proposed International Commissions could also control trade and "exercise a supervising authority over the loans and investments made by financiers to the Governments or private persons in these backward countries, and over the methods of business exploitation employed by the agents of the investing companies".[7]

Hobson was not the only liberal thinker to begin to endorse new kinds of economic activism and multilateral economic cooperation. Some of his

---

[4] Hobson 1915, ch. 7.
[5] For the broader new interest in liberal circles at this time in this idea, see Mulder 2022.
[6] Quotes from Hobson 1915, 135; 1916, 121–22, 133–34; 1902, 232.
[7] Quotes from Hobson 1915, 118; 1916, 127–28, 134.

ideas found a parallel in those of Jane Addams discussed in Chapter 10 (as well as of the socialist Leonard Woolf, a leading thinker with the British Labour party, in his widely read 1916 work *International Government* which was also cited by Addams).[8] Liberal interest in multilateral economic cooperation intensified after World War I with the creation of the League of Nations. Drawing on the experience of inter-Allied coordination of supplies and shipping during the wartime, some even called for an international economic institution that could take on economic planning roles.[9] Many non-Marxist socialists were also attracted to this idea, including Woolf as well as the French head of the new International Labour Organization, Albert Thomas, who promoted common international labour standards and internationally coordinated public works programs to address unemployment.[10]

The League did take on some important international economic roles in its early years. In addition to encouraging free trade and the restoration of the international gold standard, it promoted what Hobson had called various "utilitarian" forms of economic cooperation. The League was also empowered to implement collective economic sanctions and it endorsed the transformation of the ex-colonies of defeated powers into mandates that were governed by specific states according to international rules. Echoing Hobson's earlier ideas in the more limited context of the mandates, those rules included securing "equal opportunities for the trade and commerce of other Members of the League" and supporting "the well-being and development" of people in the mandate territories. The League also took on the supervision of economic and financial reforms in debtor countries such as Austria as part of encouraging new foreign private lending to them.[11]

More ambitious ideas about international economic cooperation soon emerged from liberal circles during, and in the wake of, the Great Depression of the early 1930s. As noted in Chapter 8, that economic catastrophe led to the unravelling of the liberal world economy with debt defaults, rising trade protectionism, the collapse of the gold standard, and the introduction of controls on cross-border financial flows. At the domestic level, governments across the world responded to the crisis with economic activist policies that were anathema to those trained in a classical economic liberal tradition. In this context, some economic

---

[8] For Woolf's ideas, see Reader 2019. For Addams' citation, see Addams 1922, 199.
[9] Martin 2022, 56; Trentmann 2008, 267–70.
[10] Martin 2016, 27; 2022, 132. For Woolf, see Reader 2019; Trentmann 2008, 263.
[11] Quotes from Article 22 of the League of Nations convenant. For economic supervision, see Clavin 2013, 25–33; Martin 2022, ch. 2; Pauly 1997.

liberals began to endorse bolder kinds of intergovernmental economic cooperation, including Hobson, who called for international redistributive policies and coordinated policies to boost wages and public spending as ways to address what he perceived as a global underconsumption problem.[12]

One of the many figures developing innovative ideas about multilateral economic cooperation at this time was the Indian economist Jehangir Coyajee in his 1932 book *The World Economic Depression* (which drew on his experience of representing India at the League and that was dedicated to Albert Thomas). Although trained in the economic liberal tradition at Cambridge, Coyajee had already shown his willingness to depart from liberal orthodoxy in the early 1920s when he backed infant-industry protectionism for India and invoked the neomercantilist ideas of List and Ranade. His 1932 book had a different focus, emphasizing the need to address the Depression by combining domestic economic planning with new kinds of economic internationalism such as "international industrial agreements", a "planned gold standard", and cooperation relating to "the control and utilization of raw materials" and "foreign investment and loans".[13] Acknowledging that his vision of a new international economic order was not fully developed, he noted: "we are still awaiting the advent of some outstanding economist who will perform the same service for this new aspect of Economics that was rendered to Competitive Economics by Adam Smith".[14]

## Anglo-American Embedded Liberalism

That service was soon provided by the two leading economists involved in the Bretton Woods negotiations: John Maynard Keynes from Britain and Harry Dexter White from the United States. Their planning for the postwar international economic order was informed by the Atlantic Charter of August 1941, which was the first official statement by the US and British governments of their collective vision of a postwar world. This document endorsed the liberal goal of rebuilding a worldwide open trading system. Influential figures at the time such as longstanding US Secretary of State Cordell Hull – nicknamed "Tennessee Cobden" by some – emphasized the liberal case that free trade would lay the foundation for postwar prosperity, peace, and freedom.[15] In the eyes of many

---

[12] Long 1996; Matsunaga 2021.
[13] Coyajee 1932, iii, 59, 5.
[14] Coyajee 1932, 95.
[15] Quote from Palen 2018, 123. See also Wollner 2017.

liberals, these rationales for free trade had been reinforced by the 1930s experience when protectionist policies appeared to contribute to the economic depression, international political tension, and eroding individual liberty. What was needed now, they argued, was a strong multilateral institutional framework to support and protect open trade.

At the same time, the Atlantic Charter also endorsed government economic activism with its commitment "to bring about the fullest collaboration between all nations in the economic field, with the object of securing for all improved labor standards, economic advancement, and social security". This wording had been drafted by the British Labour politician Ernest Bevin, who blamed the rise of fascism and war on economic insecurity, and who argued that postwar peace could be achieved only if people across the world were guaranteed "security against poverty, care in sickness and trouble, protection against injury, provision for old age". Since the autumn of 1940, he had argued that international cooperation designed to serve these goals would need to involve "directed planning of the use of international resources and capital".[16]

US president Franklin Roosevelt had liked Bevin's draft wording because he thought it resonated with his own commitment to "freedom from want" which he had outlined in his high-profile "Four Freedoms" speech of January 1941. In that speech, Roosevelt had defined this goal as securing "to every nation a healthy peacetime life for its inhabitants – everywhere in the world". Roosevelt's idea internationalized his New Deal philosophy that had prioritized the provision of greater economic security to individuals as the basis of a more stable political order. At the time he was writing the speech, Roosevelt had been following British debates in which Bevin and others had been arguing that the promise of minimum standards for things such as housing, food, education, and medical care needed to be part of the overall plan for defeating Hitler. Roosevelt's idea of "freedom from want" was also included in the Atlantic Charter, which assured that "all the men in all the lands may live out their lives in freedom from fear and want".[17]

The economic content of the Atlantic Charter established the broad context for the embedded liberal philosophy of the early plans of Keynes and White for Bretton Woods. Their plans sought to build a new kind of multilateral institutional framework that would promote an open trading order but in a way that was compatible with government economic activism aimed at providing "freedom from want" and "improved labor standards, economic advancement, and social security". They and other

---

[16] Quotes in Helleiner 2014, 210–11.
[17] Quotes in Helleiner 2014, 120.

Anglo-American policymakers saw this framework as serving the broad liberal goals of promoting global prosperity, international peace, and individual freedom. In this new embedded liberal vision, the meaning of "individual freedom" was wider than many nineteenth-century liberal conceptions with its inclusion of the positive "freedom from want".

Keynes' importance to the Bretton Woods negotiations stemmed from the fact that he was an advisor to the British Treasury and the most famous economist in the world. His 1936 *General Theory of Employment, Interest and Money* had revolutionized liberal economics with its theoretical justification of domestic activist macroeconomic policy to support full employment. He now saw an opportunity to reform the international side of economic liberalism by building a new kind of open multilateral economic order that was compatible with such policies. In so doing, he rejected his earlier advocacy of national economic self-sufficiency in 1933 (discussed in Chapter 8) and returned to his earlier and longstanding belief in free trade.

Keynes outlined some initial ideas on this topic in late 1940 when he was asked to develop a radio broadcast to counter German propaganda surrounding Funk's New Order proposal for European countries (discussed in Chapter 13). He surprised his colleagues by noting that Funk's idea of multilateral clearing had some merit: "much of what Dr. Funk offers is, taken at its face value, excellent". Its main drawback, Keynes argued, was that it would be administered as "tyranny" in the service of German economic interests and war aims instead of serving "the general advantage".[18] He set about developing an "international clearing union" that would serve liberal goals instead. He also insisted at this time that Bevin's ideas about prioritizing "social security" needed to be at the centre of British plans for the postwar international economic order.[19]

While British planning was led by Keynes, the American plans for Bretton Woods were developed by White, who was much less well known. After earning his PhD in economics in 1930, White had joined the US Treasury in 1934 and had risen to become its top official for international issues. White shared with Keynes the goal of constructing a new kind of multilateral economic order that would combine trade openness with support for government economic activism. His commitment to government economic activism was linked to his strong support for the values of the New Deal. Several years before Keynes' *General Theory*, he had published innovative ideas about activist counter-cyclical

[18] Quoted in Helleiner 2019b, 1132fn6. See Faudot (2022) for Keynes' interest in German clearing initiatives and ideas.
[19] Helleiner 2014, 209.

fiscal policies to boost employment. His interest in an open international trading order had also been more consistent than that of Keynes. When the latter had briefly endorsed national self-sufficiency at the height of the Great Depression, White had rejected the idea, noting the need to preserve the economic gains from trade as well as the "stabilizing influences" of international economic relations.[20]

White completed his initial detailed plans in early 1942, soon after the United States entered the war. He described them ambitiously as proposals for a "New Deal in international economics" that were designed to facilitate "the attainment of the economic objectives of the Atlantic charter". He also highlighted the link between his proposals and "the ideal of freedom for which most of the peoples are fighting the aggressor nations", noting that the "people of the Anti-Axis powers … must be assured that something will be done in the sphere of international economic relations that is new, that is powerful enough and comprehensive enough to give expectation of successfully filling a world need".[21]

The plans of Keynes and White differed in many specifics and, not surprisingly, the final Bretton Woods agreements looked much closer to White's because of the dominant power of the United States at the time. But those final agreements also embodied very clearly the new embedded liberal perspective that they shared and that was influential in wider Anglo-American policymaking circles at the time. To begin with, the agreements established a new kind of institutionalized liberal multilateralism in the economic realm with the creation of two publicly owned and managed international financial institutions. The IBRD was designed to facilitate foreign loans and investments to support reconstruction and development, while the IMF was empowered to make short-term loans to governments for balance of payments support. The Fund's articles of agreement also outlined a set of legal commitments that member states had to uphold in their monetary and financial relations with other countries. Those commitments created a new kind of multilateral constitution for the international monetary and financial system, one that the Bretton Woods architects hoped would have global reach.

These two institutions were designed to foster a more open world economy, with a particular emphasis on the growth of international trade. Because the Bretton Woods conference was focused on monetary and financial issues, it did not create rules for open trade directly. Its

---

[20] Quote in Rees 1973, 39.
[21] Quotes in Helleiner 2014, 121; Horsefield 1969, 38.

delegates anticipated that a follow-up conference would take up the task by creating an international trade organization. But the IMF and IBRD were designed to promote open trade in various indirect ways. In the IMF's case, its rules prohibited members from restricting payments for trade transactions and required them to peg their currencies to the US dollar (which in turn was pegged to gold) in order to prevent the kinds of competitive depreciations that had disrupted trade in the 1930s. The IMF's lending would also help countries experiencing external payment deficits to avoid the use of foreign exchange restrictions, which hampered the growth of world trade. Through its role in facilitating long-term foreign loans and investment, the IBRD was also meant "to promote the long-range balanced growth of international trade and the maintenance of equilibrium in balances of payments".[22]

In keeping with the new embedded liberal philosophy, the new Bretton Woods institutions were also designed to ensure that a more open world economy would be compatible with government economic activism. For example, when faced with balance of payments deficits, national governments would now have more policy autonomy than they had under the pre-1931 gold standard because they could draw on IMF funds. The IMF rules also bolstered their overall policy autonomy by allowing them to control all capital movements in any circumstance and to adjust their exchange rate pegs if they faced a "fundamental disequilibrium". The IMF and IBRD were also given the capacity to engage in active public management of the international economy as a whole through their public lending and IMF's mandate to "promote international monetary cooperation".[23]

Anglo-American officials highlighted how these institutions' activities and rules were meant to serve broader liberal goals. For example, in an important speech at the start of the conference, US Treasury Secretary Henry Morgenthau emphasized how Bretton Woods would foster international peace by constraining "economic aggression" that had "no other offspring than war". He also highlighted to the delegates how the Bretton Woods agreements were meant to promote global prosperity: "Prosperity, like peace, is indivisible. We cannot afford to have it scattered here or there among the fortunate or to enjoy it at the expense of others. Poverty, wherever it exists, is menacing to us all and undermines the well-being of each of us". Morgenthau further linked Bretton Woods to the strengthening of individual freedom:

[22] Quote from the Articles of Agreement of the International Bank for Reconstruction and Development, Article 1(iiii).

[23] Quotes from Articles of Agreement of the IMF Article IV, Section 5(a); Article 1(i).

We are to concern ourselves here with essential steps in the creation of a dynamic world economy in which the people of every nation will be able to realize their potentialities in peace; will be able, through their industry, their inventiveness, their thrift, to raise their own standards of living and enjoy, increasingly, the fruits of material progress on an earth infinitely blessed with natural riches. This is the indispensable cornerstone of freedom and security. All else must be built upon this. For freedom of opportunity is the foundation for all other freedoms.[24]

## Reactions to the New Embedded Liberalism

The reformulation of economic liberalism in this new embedded liberal perspective did not appeal to all liberals. Some opposed both the new institutionalized economic multilateralism and the new support for active public management of the economy. Inspired by classical economic liberalism, these figures called for a return to the pre-1930s world of an international gold standard, free trade, and free capital movements. In place of the Bretton Woods effort to build an ambitious new multilateral framework for global economic governance, they backed a "key currency" proposal to rebuild international trade and private financial flows through the restoration of dollar–sterling convertibility supported by a US bilateral loan to Britain.[25]

A more innovative line of liberal criticism came from "neoliberals" led by the Austrian thinker Friedrich Hayek. Hayek was more willing to agree with embedded liberals that new multilateral economic institutions were needed to protect an open world economy. But he strongly opposed the embedded liberal idea that active public management of the economy should be accommodated and supported. In his view, economic planning of all kinds would generate economic inefficiencies and erode individual freedom in ways that led to a "road to serfdom".[26] Hayek argued that efforts to extend economic planning to the international level risked being particularly tyrannical and were likely to generate international political tension. What was needed at the international level, Hayek argued, was an authority whose role was limited to maintaining free trade and enforcing other rules needed for a market-based world economy. As he put it, "the powers which such an authority would need are mainly of a negative kind: it must above all be able to say 'no' to all sorts of restrictive measures".[27]

Although the new embedded liberalism did not win over all economic liberals, it appealed to many in Western Europe and North America

---

[24] Quotes from US State Department 1948, 80–81.
[25] Helleiner 1994, ch. 2.
[26] Quote from the title of Hayek 1944. See also Slodobian 2018, ch. 3.
[27] Hayek 1944, 172.

as well as some figures further left on the political spectrum in those regions, including some socialists and labour leaders such as Bevin. Of course, many on the left preferred much more ambitious commitments to government economic activism. As noted above, Bevin wanted to see "directed planning of the use of international resources and capital". The prominent British socialist Barbara Wootton also wanted Keynes' clearing union proposal to take on more ambitious roles of global economic planning and she called for a supranational federal entity that could promote international redistribution and set global standards vis-à-vis issues such as food, clothing, education, housing, and employment.[28]

Another important socialist thinker at this time who favoured more ambitious kinds of government economic activism was Karl Polanyi, whose 1944 book *The Great Transformation* helped to inspired Ruggie's concept of "embedded liberalism". Published in the United States, that book argued that the classical economic liberal goal of building an economic order around self-regulating markets had inevitably provoked a social backlash that culminated in the unravelling of the liberal world economy during the 1930s. Polanyi argued that the postwar world economy should be organized instead around twin principles of "economic collaboration of governments *and* the liberty to organize national life at will" in order to allow government to build economies that were more "embedded in social relations".[29] Ruggie argued Polanyi's general vision bore some similarities to that of Keynes and White, but Polanyi himself thought the American-led postwar plans went too far in trying to promote liberal economic values instead of the socialist ones he preferred.[30]

In addition to appealing to those favouring new forms of government economic activism in Western Europe and North America, embedded liberals hoped their new vision of global economic governance would gain support beyond those regions. For example, US officials made clear that they wanted their wartime ally, the Soviet Union, which participated in the Bretton Woods negotiations, to join the system being created. As Morgenthau put it after the conference, "I am firmly convinced that capitalist and socialist societies can coexist, as long as neither resorts to destructive practices and as long as both abide by the rules of international economic fair play".[31] In this sense, the embedded liberalism of Bretton Woods embodied a remarkably wide conception of the kinds of economic activism that were compatible with the open world economy it

[28] Rosenboim 2016.
[29] Polanyi 1944, 254, 57.
[30] Dale 2016.
[31] Morgenthau 1945, 191. See also Pechatnov 2017; Ruggie 1982, 392fn41.

endorsed. Those kinds included not just the new commitments in Western Europe and North America to social security and activist macroeconomic management, but also Stalin's heavy-handed state economic control that extended to the country's external trade. Indeed, the head of the Soviet delegation at the Bretton Woods conference, Mikhail Stepanov, reminded delegates at the conference of the distinctive nature of the Soviet commitment to open trade, noting that in his country "foreign trade is conducted by the State".[32]

While accommodating the Soviet Union's economic policies, Anglo-American embedded liberals also sought to encase them within a broader multilateral framework devoted to liberal goals. After all, governments that joined the Bretton Woods system had to accept some constraints on their behaviour that were embodied within the IMF's rules. Those rules, in turn, served the broader liberal objectives of promoting global prosperity, international peace, and individual freedom. Although the Soviet delegation to the Bretton Woods conference supported the final agreements, it recognized that membership in the IMF would impose new constraints on Soviet policies and Stalin soon decided in 1946 not to join the Bretton Woods system when political relations with the West began to deteriorate after the war.[33]

American policymakers also highlighted how they saw the Bretton Woods framework as compatible with neomercantilist policies in less industrialized countries.[34] Many of them, including White, had been deeply involved in efforts to support state-led economic development strategies in Latin America since the late 1930s in the context of Roosevelt's Good Neighbor Policy (see Chapter 13). Drawing on that experience, they now highlighted how these strategies would be supported by the IBRD's mobilization of foreign capital and the IMF's endorsement of capital controls and exchange-rate adjustments as well as its provision of short-term loans for balance of payment support. At the same time, US officials sought – once again – to encase these strategies within a broader multilateral order committed to liberal goals. Neomercantilist goals of maximizing state wealth and power would be tamed by countries' participation in a system of institutionalized multilateralism aimed at promoting global prosperity, international peace, and individual freedom.[35]

The fact that the Bretton Woods agreements accommodated and offered some support for state-led development strategies helps to explain why they were backed by so many officials from less industrialized parts

[32] Department of State 1948, 1208.
[33] Pechatnov 2017.
[34] British officials were less supportive and interested (Helleiner 2014, ch. 8).
[35] Helleiner 2014.

of the world, such as Latin America, China, India, Eastern Europe, and Africa. Particularly important were Latin American governments, which made up almost half of those represented at Bretton Woods and whose officials had been pressing for international support of their economic development since the early 1930s, including with innovative proposals for an Inter-American Bank (as noted in Chapter 13). White was deeply involved in the efforts to create such a bank in 1939–40 and his early drafts of the IMF and IBRD drew inspiration from that experience as well as from other discussions with Latin American officials that he had been having since the late 1930s. The head of the Chinese delegation also used his opening statement at the conference to remind the delegates of Sun Yat-sen's 1920 book that proposed a multilateral financial institution to support China's state-led development (see Chapter 5). Indeed, both Chinese and American observers commented on the compatibility of the Bretton Woods framework with this idea of Sun's, and prominent American supporters of the creation of an international development institution at the time cited Sun's 1920 work as an inspiration.[36]

The endorsement of Bretton Woods by policymakers from these places did not necessarily mean an embrace of embedded liberalism. Many officials were interested simply in gaining access to IBRD funds to support their state-led industrialization strategies without buying into the broader goals of the Bretton Woods system as a whole. Some neomercantilist thinkers in poorer parts of the world were also deeply sceptical of the Anglo-American postwar planning process altogether, despite the efforts of its advocates to emphasize its compatibility with their policy preferences. For example, India's Benoy Kumar Sarkar (see Chapter 5) saw the Atlantic Charter as a tool for "Anglo-American world-domination" that was not much different than the German plans for a New Order in the sense that "both these Anglo-American and Germanic orders are nothing but forms of imperialism and slavification, pure and undefiled".[37]

One final issue needs to be discussed about the place of less industrialized regions of the world in the vision of embedded liberals: how did those thinkers view imperialism? Like their classical liberal predecessors, the Anglo-American embedded liberals at Bretton Woods were split on the issue. On the one hand, White and some other American embedded liberals were very critical of imperialism, including that of their own country in the past. On the other, Keynes followed many other British

---

[36] Helleiner 2014, 186–200. Chinese officials also lobbied Germany in mid-1940 to include Sun's ideas about international development assistance for China in German plans for a new international economic order at the time (Kirby 1984, 250).

[37] Sarkar 1943b, 183–84.

liberals in endorsing the British Empire. Like Hobson, he favoured reforms to colonial economic policies to make them more supportive of economic development, but he did not question imperialism itself. In Robert Skidelsky's words, "he assumed the Empire as a fact of life and never showed the slightest interest in discarding it".[38]

At the Bretton Woods conference itself, the American delegation debated internally about whether they should express their opposition to colonial rule by insisting on the creation of separate quotas in the IMF for colonies (or including a provision to allow countries' quotas to be divided up when colonies became independent). After much debate, they decided not to raise the issue in order to avoid a major political row with Britain and other European powers at the conference. White's early plans had also allowed the IMF to liquidate blocked sterling balances held by colonies in Britain. This idea was reiterated at the 1944 conference by delegates from India, one of only two colonies represented at the conference (the other was Philippines). But this proposal met strong British opposition and was dropped, thereby ensuring that the intra-imperial financial relations of European empires were insulated from the multilateralism of Bretton Woods.[39]

### Silences of Bretton Woods

Although Anglo-American embedded liberals at Bretton Woods tried to accommodate the central planning of the Soviet Union and neomercantilist ideas in less industrialized regions, they did little to engage with the perspectives discussed in the second part of this book. Given that the central goal of embedded liberals was to rebuild an open world economy, the neglect of autarkist perspectives was hardly surprising. Embedded liberals believed strongly that autarkism had been discredited by the economic and political traumas of the 1930s. This view was widely shared beyond Anglo-American policymaking circles. As the leader of the French delegation Pierre Mendès-France put it at the end of the 1944 conference, his government was "opposed to autarchy" and "to all techniques consistent with the preparation, the continuation or the liquidation of a war, but inconceivable in a world guided by fraternal cooperation of all people of good will".[40]

Environmentalist views also drew little attention from the Anglo-American policymakers at Bretton Woods whose focus was on promoting economic growth and industrialization without much concern for

[38] Skidelsky 1983, 91.
[39] Helleiner 2014, 184–85, 221–22.
[40] Department of State 1948, 1115.

environmental constraints. As Morgenthau put it in his opening speech to the conference (quoted above), the meeting's goal was to enable people of every nation to enjoy "the fruits of material progress on an earth *infinitely* blessed with natural riches".[41] Keynes, too, emphasized the need to "develop the resources and productive capacity of the world" without repeating the kind of "Ruskinian" lamentation he had briefly expressed in 1933 about the need to preserve "the unappropriated splendours of nature" (see Chapter 8).[42]

This lack of engagement with environmentalist thought was striking in light of its profile in both Britiain and the United States at this time. In Britain, for example, Eve Balfour's environmentalist advice for postwar economic planning outlined in her 1943 book *The Living Soil* (see Chapter 9) received significant attention during the spring of 1944 when the final preparations for Bretton Woods were taking place.[43] In the United States, Lewis Mumford's *The Condition of Man* was published in the same year as Bretton Woods and included his environmentalist warning that "a final destruction" of civilization would result from a postwar order centered about the goal of deepening international economic integration (see Chapter 9). Polanyi's 1944 book, too, included environmental warnings about how unregulated markets resulted in "landscapes defiled, rivers polluted ... [and] the power to produce food and raw materials destroyed".[44] One month before the conference began, Roosevelt was also being lobbied by prominent environmentalists to hold a world conference on conservation issues, an idea to which he appeared quite sympathetic.[45] Further, the final report of the 1943 United Nations conference on food and agriculture held in Hot Springs, Virginia, highlighted the need to address environmental problems ranging from soil erosion and water conservation to the protection of forests and wildlife across the globe.[46]

Feminist perspectives also received little attention within the embedded liberal discourse of the Bretton Woods architects. Gender inequality and the gendered division of labour in the world economy were on full display at the Bretton Woods meeting, which included only two women as official delegates but was supported by a large secretarial staff of

---

[41] US State Department 1948, 80; emphasis added.

[42] The first Keynes quote comes from Helleiner 2014, 220; the other comes from Chapter 8 of this book. The description of Keynes' 1933 critique as "Ruskinian" comes from Skidelsky 1992, 478.

[43] Gill 2010, 103–6; 2018, 196. For the US movement, see Beeman 1995.

[44] Polanyi 1944, 73. Polanyi was not included in Chapter 9 because his comments on environmental issues were quite brief.

[45] Jundt 2014; McCormick 1989, 25.

[46] US State Department 1943. Figures in the British organic movement did not, however, think the conference went far enough (Conford 1998, 205).

254    The Embedded Liberalism of Bretton Woods

around 200 women. One journalist noted of the latter: "They work on a 24-hour basis – three shifts. Without them, there'd be no conference".[47] The official transcripts of the meeting include no criticism or comment on this gendered division of labour from the delegates, many of whom may simply have seen it to be a natural one. At the end of the conference, the patriarchal perspectives of some delegates were displayed in an unofficial proposal written anonymously in the hotel bar for a new institution called the "International Ballyhoo Fun", which required countries to make part of their initial contributions in "gold blondes or their equivalents" and the remainder in "brunettes".[48]

As in the case of environmentalism, the limited attention to feminist perspectives at Bretton Woods was noteworthy in light of the history examined in this volume. Chapter 10 highlighted a rich history of feminist analyses in political economy that predated the conference as well as efforts to promote gender equality within discussions about postwar international planning at the time. The latter included not just Amy Ashwood Garvey's 1944 call for women of the world to unite but also the active efforts of Latin American feminists such as Bertha Lutz and Paulina Luisi to ensure that postwar multilateral economic institutions explicitly incorporated women's rights into their mandates. As noted in Chapter 10, Lutz's efforts resulted in the ILO's endorsement two months before the Bretton Woods conference of the right of "all human beings, irrespective of race, creed or sex", to pursue their "material well-being" in conditions of "equal opportunity". The ILO's statement even insisted that "all national and international policies and measures, *in particular those of an economic and financial character*, should be judged in this light and accepted only in so far as they may be held to promote and not to hinder the achievement of this fundamental objective".[49] Despite this (and Roosevelt's strong support for the ILO's declaration), the Bretton Woods architects made little effort to judge how their international financial proposals might promote gender equality.[50]

As noted in Chapter 10, to avoid this kind of outcome, Latin American feminists had pushed for women to be included in their governments' delegations to postwar planning conferences. In the case of Bretton Woods, these calls were ignored. US women's groups were more

---

[47] Quote from a radio broadcast by the Colombia Broadcasting Service on the conference in Morgenthau 1944a, 248.
[48] Quotes in Conway 2014, 257.
[49] ILO 1944, 622; emphasis added.
[50] As a result of the content of Bretton Woods and other postwar planning conferences, Latin American feminists such as Luisi and Magda Portal had become deeply pessimistic about the postwar world by late 1944 (Marino 2019, 190–91).

successful in lobbying for a woman to be on the US delegation to the Bretton Woods conference: Mabel Newcomer, an economics professor at Vassar College (and past teacher of Morgenthau's daughter).[51] In the formal conference discussion, however, Newcomer did not promote an equal economic rights agenda of the kind that Lutz had endorsed. Indeed, many women close to the Roosevelt administration – including Eleanor Roosevelt – worried that the promotion of this kind of agenda might undermine labour legislation designed to protect women.[52]

What about the ideas of the Pan-African movement? At the time of Bretton Woods, they remained influential in Africa and among the African diaspora, as was evident by a high-profile Pan-African Congress held in Manchester in 1945 (in which figures such as Ashwood Garvey, Du Bois, and Padmore were prominently involved).[53] But they received little attention in embedded liberal circles at Bretton Woods. Aside from the white-run South African government, the only African governments represented at the conference were those from Egypt, Ethiopia, and Liberia, and none of their representatives raised issues of racial inequality or oppression in their formal contributions to the meeting. Members of the African diaspora also were not represented in any other delegation.

More generally, issues of race and racial discrimination were not much discussed at the Bretton Woods conference (and they were not mentioned in the Atlantic Charter, as noted in the previous chapter). Once again, the absence of serious engagement with these issues was striking in light of the ILO conference's insistence two months earlier that international economic and financial policies should be judged with the goal of enabling "all human beings, irrespective of race" to pursue their "material well-being" in conditions of "equal opportunity". To be sure, at the end of the conference, Brazil's Artur de Souza Costa argued that Bretton Woods' success provided "evidence that human solidarity is not a result of racial unity". He added: "Against the Nazi claim that a supposed racial superiority gives the right to rule the world, Bretton Woods offers a way for the guidance of human destinies through the development of human brotherhood.[54] But these statements sat awkwardly alongside the racist views that were sometimes expressed in private correspondence by Anglo-American officials involved in postwar planning.[55]

---

[51] Conway 2014, 209; Vassar Historian (n.d.). The only other official female delegate at the conference was Russia's L. J. Gouseva, about whom little is known.
[52] See, for example, Marino 2019, 172–77, 180, 199, 203–6; Helleiner 2022.
[53] See, for example, Esedebe 1994.
[54] US State Department 1948, 1120. Many on the Latin American left at the time emphasized anti-racist principles in the Allied struggle against the Axis powers (Marino 2019).
[55] See, for example, Conway 2014, 146; O'Sullivan 2008, xviii, 138–39, 178.

The architects of Bretton Woods also showed little interest in Pan-Islamic economic thought, such as the "Islamic economics" that Mawdudi had begun to promote at this very time. When choosing the speaker's list for the closing ceremonies, US policymakers briefly considered whether they should be including a representative from one of the "Moslem states" at the conference, but the idea was not implemented.[56] Even if it had been, it is unlikely that Pan-Islamist ideas would have been mentioned since delegates from Muslim-majority countries such as Iran, Iraq, Syria, and Egypt did not raise them at other moments during the conference. Indeed, the potential relevance of religion to issues of political economy in general received little attention at Bretton Woods (in contrast to Polanyi's 1944 book, in which his advocacy of "embeddedness" ended with a discussion of the importance of religious teachings).[57] There were occasional references to God by European and American delegates, but the conference discussion was almost entirely conducted on secular terms.[58] Neither of the two leading architects of the embedded liberalism of Bretton Woods – Keynes and White – held strong religious beliefs.[59]

It is hardly surprising that Pan-Asian ideas also had no place at Bretton Woods given their centrality to the Japanese war effort at the time. As noted above, Sun Yat-sen's thought was praised by the Chinese delegation to the conference (and by some American thinkers at the time), but the focus was on his ideas about international development cooperation rather than his Pan-Asianism. Interestingly, Keynes did refer to Asia's contribution to civilization in his final speech at the conference, but he put it in the context of a more universal conception of civilization. In his words, Bretton Woods was designed to help "in bringing back to a life of peace and abundant fruitfulness those great European and Asiatic parents of civilization to which all the world owes so much of what is honorable and grand in the heritage of mankind".[60]

The concept of "civilization" was also occasionally invoked in Anglo-American policy circles at this time in opposition to the practices of the Nazis. For example, US officials at Bretton Woods argued that the Nazis aimed to "rid this world of civilization as you and I know it" and wondered how Germany (and other defeated powers) "should be brought back into the fold of civilized countries".[61] In this context, the concept

---

[56] Quote from Morgenthau 1944b, 277.
[57] For Polanyi, see Polanyi 1944, 258.
[58] For these references, see, for example, US State Department 1948, 74, 110.
[59] See, for example, Kirshner 2015, 402; Schuler and Rosenberg 2012a, n4.
[60] US State Department 1948, 1217.
[61] Quotes from Fred Vinson (US State Department 1948, 1203) and Ansel Luxford (Schuler and Rosenberg 2012b, 432).

of civilization seemed to refer to the values of liberal democratic societies in general, without reference to any specific region of the world.[62]
In contrast to earlier liberal discourse (including that of Hobson), the
dichotomy of civilized/uncivilized also no longer referred to a distinction
between societies in the context of a stadial theory of economic development. To the extent that stadial theory endured in liberal discourse, it
was being reborn in the language of "development" at this time.

Finally, ideas of economic regionalism did not have much place in
the embedded liberalism of Bretton Woods. The latter was a universalist vision that sought to bring all sovereign states under a single system
of global economic governance. This vision challenged the predictions
(noted in the previous chapter) of thinkers such as Zimmermann that the
postwar world would be organized around large economic regions. Zimmermann was not the only one to make that prediction. In 1943, Benoy
Kumar Sarkar predicted a postwar "polycentric world-economy" organized around seven "zones of 'economic regionalism'", each of which
would trade with the others to some extent and be led by a dominant
power.[63] Hayek's 1944 *The Road to Serfdom* called for a kind of global
economic governance that would also allow regional cooperation among
countries "which are more similar in their civilization, outlook, and standards".[64] In writings since the late 1930s (though not his 1944 book),
Polanyi also had been interested in a world of somewhat autarkic regional
economic orders – what he called "tame empires" – that would enable
greater institutional and cultural diversity than the American plans for
the postwar world. The latter, he worried, were trying to restore the
pre-1914 liberal world economic order and its accompanying "enforced
uniformity" on a global basis.[65]

## Conclusion

This book began by analyzing the perspective of classical economic liberalism pioneered by Adam Smith. At the very end of the period covered
in this text, embedded liberals reformulated that perspective by endorsing new ways to pursue the liberal goals of boosting global prosperity,

---

[62] Polanyi (1944, 3) also began his 1944 book by noting that "nineteenth-century civilization has collapsed", by which he meant liberal civilization.

[63] Sarkar 1943a, 319. Although Sarkar's prediction sounds similar to Zimmermann's, he
was very critical of German plans for a New Order, arguing that they were designed to
serve German racial domination and to perpetuate "the agrarian character of the backward and politically subject nations" (p. 95).

[64] Hayek 1944, 176.

[65] Quoted in Dale 2016, 410.

international peace, and individual freedom. Building on the ideas of thinkers earlier in the century, they used the Bretton Woods negotiations to construct a new kind of institutionalized multilateralism that could foster an open world economy compatible with various kinds of active public management of the economy. This new perspective – as well as the reactions it provoked in some liberal circles – contributed further to the diversity within the liberal camp that was noted in Chapters 2 and 3.

The embedded liberalism at Bretton Woods appealed not just to many economic liberals but also to some socialists in Western Europe and North America. Its Anglo-American advocates at the 1944 conference also sought to accommodate the Soviet Union's commitment to central planning as well as neomercantilist views prominent in many less industrialized regions. At the same time, those advocates made much less effort to engage with the perspectives discussed in the second part of this volume. The latter silences of Bretton Woods are usually ignored in IPE textbooks and even specialist literature examining the conference. By contrast, the wider history examined in this volume encourages a focus on them. It highlights how these perspectives had considerable support in many parts of the world during the years leading up to the conference and even at the time of the conference itself. The limited attention they received at Bretton Woods was a reflection not of their absence from intellectual debates at the time but rather of the specific political priorities of those who pioneered embedded liberalism.

In this way, the pre-1945 intellectual history told in the previous chapters of this book is important even for teachers and students whose IPE courses begin with Bretton Woods. For them, it sheds new light on the priorities of those who constructed the postwar international economic order. It reminds us not just of the voices that were around the table at the conference but also of those that were uninvited and went unheard. Both left enduring legacies in the post-1945 era. To be sure, the former were initially much more important than the latter in shaping the evolution of the international economic order after World War II. But many perspectives that were marginalized at Bretton Woods subsequently became much more influential. The content of those perspectives will be better understood with more knowledge of their intellectual roots in the pre-1945 years. Students will only gain that knowledge, however, once the deep intellectual history of IPE is presented in a wider way than is currently the norm in the textbooks of the field.

# 15   The Case for a Wider History

This book encourages scholars and students of IPE to recognize the deep intellectual roots of their field in the pre-1945 period, dating back to the late eighteenth century. I have also tried to show how this history can be told in a wider way than the conventional approach. It was not just well-studied figures from Europe and the United States who developed important and influential ideas about this subject during this period. Other thinkers did too, including many from other parts of the world. Debates also went well beyond the divisions between economic liberals, neomercantilists, and Marxists that are highlighted in the field's textbooks. In this brief concluding chapter, I highlight some benefits of embracing this wider view of the deep history of IPE (beyond the fact that it sheds new light on the Bretton Woods conference, as noted in Chapter 14).

## Towards a More Comprehensive History

The most obvious and important benefit is that this wider view provides a more comprehensive history of the pre-1945 roots of IPE (though the history I have analysed is still very far from comprehensive). To begin with, the wider geographical scope highlights many contributions that were made to debates by thinkers from beyond Europe and the United States. Although these thinkers are overlooked in most existing IPE textbooks, their contributions were interesting and important. Building on the discussion of the previous chapters, we can classify these contributions into four broad categories.

The first involved creative adaptations of the three orthodoxies emanating from Europe and the United States. Adaptations of foreign ideas are often overlooked by historians of ideas, but they deserve recognition as important intellectual innovations. As Cornel Ban puts it, thinkers engaged in this activity serve both as "translators" of economic scripts that are prominent abroad and as producers of innovative "hybrids" of those scripts.[1] Chapters 3, 5, and 7 highlighted many translators of this kind who developed hybrids of economic liberalism, neomercantilism, and Marxist thought emanating from Europe (in the cases of economic liberalism and Marxism) as well as the United States (in the case of neomercantilism). The content of these hybrids varied enormously, but they all emerged from the common goal of "localizing" foreign ideas to better fit their specific contexts and experiences.[2]

The second kind of contribution involved the independent development of perspectives whose content paralleled that of the three well-studied orthodoxies of Europe and the United States. This phenomenon was most pronounced in the case of neomercantilist thought, where important versions of this perspective emerged in East Asia and elsewhere from local roots (Chapter 5).[3] Chapter 3 also noted how ideas with similarities to some aspects of European economic liberalism were advanced by eighteenth-century Chinese thinkers such as Chen Hongmou without knowledge of the former. That chapter further described how thinkers in the Ottoman Empire, Japan, and China claimed pre-Smithian roots of economic liberalism in their regions. Marxists around the world were much more inclined to accept their perspective's European origins, but Chapter 7 did call attention to the development of a Marxist theory of imperialism by Japan's Kōtoku Shūsui that predated the better known analyses of this issue by figures such as Lenin and Luxemburg.

A third kind of contribution involved the development of perspectives that were quite different in content from economic liberalism, neomercantilism, or Marxism. As noted in Chapter 8, one such perspective was autarkism, which emerged independently in a number of places outside Europe and the United States.[4] Others included the environmentalist ideas of Sada Kaiseki and Radhakamal Mukerjee (Chapter 9) and the feminist thought of Kamaladevi Chattopadhyaya, Paulina Liusi, Bertha Lutz, and He-Yin Zhen. Further examples included the innovative vision of economic Pan-Africanism advanced by Jamaica's Marcus and Amy Ashwood Garvey (Chapters 10 and 11),[5] as well as the economic Pan-Islamism of a number of thinkers, and Sun Yat-sen's promotion of older East Asian tributary norms as a model for economic governance

---

[1] Ban 2016, 5. See also Hall 1989; Todd 2015, 236.

[2] For the conception of "localization", see Acharya 2004.

[3] Other examples beyond East Asia are analysed in Helleiner 2021a.

[4] Some non-European autarkists also embraced European versions of this ideology, such as Francia and Paul, who drew on Rousseau and Fichte's thoughts, respectively.

[5] I highlight in Chapter 11 how Marcus Garvey's ideas can conceptualized as a kind of "diasporic neomercantilism", but it was so different from conventional neomercantilist ideas that I have placed it in this third category of contributions.

(Chapter 12). Two more cases involved the unique conceptions of economic regionalism put forward by Akamatsu Kaname and Víctor Raúl Haya de la Torre (Chapter 13). None of these perspectives makes much of an appearance, if any, in textbook accounts of IPE's deep history, but they represented important contributions to debates in various contexts in the pre-1945 era.

The final kind of contribution was that thinkers from beyond Europe and the United States sometimes influenced their European and American counterparts. In some cases, these influences came before Smith's time and in a rather general way, as in the case of François Quesnay's use of Chinese intellectual tradition (Chapter 3) or Englebert Kaempfer's engagement with Japanese ideas (Chapter 8). But there were also many more direct impacts that came in the post-Smithian period, such as the attention given in European liberal circles to the ideas of Olaudah Equiano, Rammohun Roy, Hassuna D'Ghies, Dadabhai Naoroji, and John Rae (Chapters 3 and 5). Syme's Australian neomercantilist ideas also attracted attention in Europe and the United States, while Naoroji's critical economic analysis of British imperialism was taken up by the prominent British Marxist Henry Hyndman and perhaps even Marx himself (Chapter 6).[6] European Marxist debates were also informed by the ideas of other non-Europeans such as C. L. R. James, Tan Malaka, George Padmore, and M. N. Roy (Chapter 7). Among environmentalists, Radhakamal Mukerjee's work influenced Richard Gregg (who also drew heavily on Gandhi's ideas) and Lewis Mumford. British feminists such as Harriet Martineau were inspired by Rammohun Roy's ideas, and Brazil's Bertha Lutz influenced the ILO's Philadelphia Declaration of 1944 (Chapter 10). Garvey's ideas also gained a large following among the African American community in the United States in the 1920s (Chapter 11). In addition, some embedded liberals in the United States at the time of Bretton Woods drew inspiration from Sun Yat-sen's ideas about international development cooperation as well as from Latin American proposals on this same topic in the 1930s (Chapter 14).

In these four ways, thinkers beyond Europe and the United States made important contributions to debates about the international dimensions of political economy in the pre-1945 period. But it is not just the wider geographical scope of this book's analysis that provides a more comprehensive history of the pre-1945 roots of IPE. Equally important is its efforts to demonstrate that the *content* of debates was wider than the textbook depiction of a three-way dispute between advocates

---

[6] Naoroji's ideas also attracted the attention of American anti-imperialists at the turn of the century (Patel 2020, 230–33).

of economic liberalism, neomercantilism, and Marxism. To be sure, disagreements between supporters of these three perspectives were an important part of the intellectual landscape during the period being studied. But this book has highlighted two important limitations with that conventional focus.

First, common depictions of pre-1945 debates overlook the fact that there were interesting and important divisions that existed *within* each of the three orthodoxies. I do not have space here to summarize all these internal divisions, but some issues that generated debate within all three perspectives can be noted briefly. One concerned the economic foundations of international peace. Among economic liberals, the link between free trade and peace drawn by Richard Cobden was quite different from that advanced by Adam Smith (Chapter 2) or from the case for collective "economic boycotts" made by John Hobson (Chapter 14). Among neomercantilists, Henry Carey, Friedrich List, and Mihail Manoilescu each put forward quite different reasons why trade protectionism might generate peace over the long term, while other neomercantilists saw inter-state rivalry and conflict as a more permanent condition (Chapter 4). Leading Marxists such as Karl Kautsky and Vladimir Lenin were also bitterly divided on the question of the relationship between capitalism and war (Chapter 6).

Some other disagreements cut across all three perspectives in fascinating ways. For example, one of the most important phenomena shaping the world economy in this era – imperialism – found supporters and opponents among advocates of each of these three perspectives.[7] The same was true of the goal of gender equality.[8] A common split also existed within all three perspectives regarding the desirability of strong multilateral economic institutions.[9] At a more theoretical level,

[7] As noted in Chapters 2, 3, and 14, liberals who endorsed various kinds of imperialism included Crummell, Hobson, Keynes, Mill, and R. Roy, while others were more critical of it (although sometimes with inconsistencies), such as Calvo, Cobden, Guzman, Smith, and White. Still others changed their minds on the issue over time, such as D'Ghies (Chapters 2, 3, and 14). Among neomercantilists, the pro-imperialist stance of Ashley, Liang, List, and Schmoller was not shared by Carey and Sun (Chapters 4, 5, and 12). The anti-imperialist stance of many Marxists contrasted with its endorsement by some others such as Ballod, Bernstein, Takahashi, and even Marx himself in some writings (Chapters 6 and 7).

[8] Alongside many supporters from all three camps noted in Chapter 10, that chapter also noted opponents of feminism such as Jevons and Say in the liberal camp and Marxists such as Lafargue. For opposition in the neomercantilist camp, see, for example, the views of Schmoller (Helleiner 2021a, 81).

[9] The support of economic liberals such as Hayek, Hobson, Keynes, and White contrasted with the view of most nineteenth-century economic liberals as well as Calvo's emphasis on the primacy of domestic law and sovereignty (Chapters 2, 3, 14). Neomercantilists such as List, Manoilescu, and Sun advanced innovative ideas about multilateral

a fascinating cross-cutting debate existed on the question of whether political economy could generate universal truths with relevance across the entire world or not.[10] When featuring these kinds of disagreements, this book has sought to bring to light a number of thinkers whose important ideas are overlooked in conventional histories of IPE's pre-1945 roots.

The second limitation of the conventional focus on a three-way debate is that it ignores many other perspectives that were prominent in discussions of the international dimensions of political economy during the period examined in this book. The entire second section of the book was devoted to the study of these other perspectives (as well as divisions that existed within many of them), namely autarkism, environmentalism, feminism, Pan-Africanism, Pan-Islamism, Pan-Asianism, and various visions of economic regionalism. Although their content sometimes overlapped that of the three orthodoxies, these perspectives raised issues and perspectives that were quite distinctive from those identified in the usual textbook accounts of pre-1945 debates between economic liberalism, neomercantilism, and Marxism.

The study of these other perspectives is important for more than just gaining a fuller picture of the range of debate about the international dimensions of political economy in the pre-1945 era. It also highlights how debates had much wider boundaries in this earlier era than is usually understood. When textbooks focus on the debate between the three orthodoxies, they rarely say much about topics that were at the center of concern for advocates of these other perspectives, such as national self-sufficiency, environmental degradation, gender inequality, racism, religious and civilizational values, and economic regionalism. Although some of these topics were discussed by advocates of the three orthodoxies, none was at the center of their three-way debate.

---

economic institutions, but their enthusiasm was not shared by other neomercantilists such as Carey (Chapters 4 and 5). In the Marxist camp, Ballod's vision of future autarkic socialist national economies was also very different from that of many Marxists who anticipated a more integrated socialist global economy, some of whom discussed proposals for multilateral economic institutions such as the Comintern in 1920 and Hilferding (Chapter 6).

[10] Economic liberals such as Cobden, Smith, and Taguchi saw their ideas as having universal relevance, whereas Bagehot, D'Ghies, and Innis emphasized the need to modify economic liberal principles to fit local circumstances (Chapters 2 and 3). In the neomercantilist camp, the same split existed between Carey's universal aspirations for his theory and Ranade's insistence on the need for nationally distinctive approaches to political economy (Chapters 4 and 5). Among Marxists, many Europeans saw their ideology as a universal science, while others outside Europe emphasized the importance of tailoring it to their countries or regions, such as Mao, Mariátegui, Sano, and Takahashi (Chapters 6 and 7).

## Some Broader Benefits

In addition to contributing to historical understanding, this wider approach to the study of IPE's pre-1945 roots may help to strengthen recent efforts to build more "global conversations" among contemporary IPE scholars. These efforts have been driven by frustrations with the domination of the IPE field today by scholars from Europe and the United States. The cultivation of wider conversations that are more inclusive of IPE scholars from all parts of the world parallels similar initiatives in the field of international relations to build a more "global IR".[11] The history told in this volume can support this goal of building a more "global IPE" in both a general and a specific manner.[12]

At a general level, it may provide an inspiration by highlighting that "global conversations" are nothing new among thinkers interested in the international dimensions of political economy. This volume has shown that pre-1945 debates on this topic were never just among thinkers from Europe and the United States. As noted above, ideas flowed from Europe and the United States to the rest of the world as well as in the other direction. They also circulated widely within and between regions outside Europe and the United States as evidenced by the embrace of Calvo's doctrine across Latin America (Chapter 3), the flow of neomercantilist ideas within East Asia (Chapter 5), the popularity of Garvey's ideas in Africa (and elsewhere) and his learning from Africans such as Casely Hayford (Chapter 11), the international diffusion of Pan-Islamic and Pan-Asian thought (Chapter 12), and the support for Haya's APRA movement across Latin America as well as Haya's own interest in Sun's ideas (Chapter 13).

These kinds of extensive and multidirectional international flows of ideas serve as a precedent for contemporary initiatives aiming to build more "global conversations" in the IPE field. To be sure, some historical figures promoted their ideas internationally with little effort to listen to foreign voices. But others were more interested in widening their horizons by learning from abroad. The latter included some thinkers in Europe and the United States who engaged with ideas and thinkers from other parts of the world in ways that anticipated the aspirations of their contemporary counterparts who are advocating greater "global conversations" today.

The history told in this book can also support the strengthening of global conversations in a more specific way by fostering greater mutual understanding among scholars across the world. Contemporary IPE

---

[11] For "global IR", see Acharya and Buzan 2020. For references to "global conversation", see, for example, Blyth 2009; Chin, Pearson, and Wang 2014; Deciancio and Quiliconi 2020; Tussie and Riggirozzi 2015.

[12] For this phrase, see Helleiner and Rosales 2017; Tussie and Changas-Bastos 2022.

scholars from outside Europe and the United States often draw on historical intellectual traditions from their country or region that are not familiar
to scholars elsewhere. For example, the prominent Argentine IPE scholar
Diana Tussie has noted that Haya de la Torre and Mariátegui were
key "forerunners of Latin American IPE", but these two thinkers rarely
appear in IPE textbooks produced in Europe and the United States.[13]
The same is true of tributary conceptions of international economic relations that are invoked by contemporary Chinese IPE scholars or of Innis'
staples approach that is often cited by Canadian IPE scholars.[14] More
productive global conversations will result if wider histories of the field's
deep roots can build familiarity with historical thinkers and ideas such as
these from beyond Europe and the United States. Put simply, initiatives
to build a more "global IPE" will be more fruitful if they are built on a
more globally oriented foundation of the deep history of the field.[15]

Improving understanding of the global nature of IPE's deep history
of ideas will also help to provincialize well-studied pre-1945 analyses of
European and American thinkers.[16] Many of the ways that contemporary
IPE scholars think about their subject have roots in these analyses that
reflected historical experiences of their authors. The study of how international dimensions of political economy were conceptualized elsewhere
can help reveal some of the idiosyncratic nature of those experiences
and the ideas that emerged from them. Indeed, many historical thinkers
examined in this book from beyond Europe and the United States raised
this issue explicitly. Their point is one echoed by more contemporary
IPE scholars such as Robert Cox, who has noted that "you look upon the
world from a certain place in it". Cox highlights how these geographically situated world views often have deep historical foundations because
of what he calls "the impact of the *longue durée* in shaping mentalities".[17]

Alongside strengthening global conversations, this volume's wider
approach to analyzing the deep history of IPE can contribute to contemporary IPE scholarship in two further ways. One is to improve analyses of contemporary political discourse. The ideas of historical thinkers
influence not just the work of IPE scholars, but also public debate. In
some cases, the influence is not explicit, as in the case of the "madmen
in authority" who hear "voices in the air" that Keynes referred to in
the passage quoted at the start of this book. But many contemporary

---

[13] Tussie 2020, 95.
[14] See, for example, Chin, Pearson, and Wang 2014; Cox 1995.
[15] See also Cox 2009, 324.
[16] See more generally Chakrabarty 2000.
[17] Cox 2009, 321, 324.

politicians and policymakers also directly cite specific pre-1945 thinkers as sources of inspiration. While some of these thinkers are featured in existing IPE textbooks, others are not, including many figures outside Europe and the United States.

A few contemporary examples of the latter figures being invoked can highlight this point. In 2016, China's president Xi Jinping claimed that the Chinese Communist Party was fulfilling Sun Yat-sen's dream of boosting China's position in the world economy.[18] At the start of the COVID-19 pandemic, there were calls within India's ruling party for a return to "*swadeshi* economics" of the kind promoted by pre-1945 Indian thinkers.[19] In Peru, the president elected in 2021, Pedro Castillo, cited Mariátegui's thought as an inspiration.[20] Mawdudi's ideas have been a touchstone for the Islamic Economics movement that is politically prominent in some Muslim-majority countries. Policy debates about East Asian economic regionalism often make reference to Akamatsu's flying geese model. The Calvo doctrine continues to be invoked in international legal circles across the world.

The ideas of these various historical thinkers from outside Europe and the United States receive very little attention in existing IPE textbooks. By bringing them more centrally into the story of IPE's deep history, this volume can improve understanding of contemporary political discourse when references are made to them. The same purpose is served by widening the history of thought to include thinkers from within Europe and the United States who are often less well known. For example, when Donald Trump was campaigning for the US presidency in 2016, he and his supporters suggested they were resurrecting the neomercantilist stance of the older US Republican party.[21] As noted in Chapter 3, that stance was inspired by the ideas of Carey, a figure whose distinctive strand of neomercantilism is rarely discussed in IPE textbooks.

The final way in which wider analyses of IPE's historical roots can contribute to contemporary IPE scholarship relates to current initiatives to broaden the focus of the field. Those involved in such initiatives may find useful insights in this wider history. For example, scholars calling for more study of the significance of religious and civilizational values in IPE can find many precedents in the pre-1945 era.[22] Those interested in analyzing emerging post-neoliberal forms of economic regionalism may

---

[18]  Helleiner 2021a, 352.
[19]  Chari 2020.
[20]  Ayala 2021.
[21]  Helleiner 2021a, 353–54.
[22]  See, for example, Lee 2020; Rethel 2019.

also be interested in the ideas that drove regional economic integration during the interwar years and early 1940s.[23] The deep history of autarkic thought discussed in Chapter 8 can also be useful for those researching the growing contemporary interest in ideas of greater national economic self-sufficiency as well as broader deglobalization trends.[24]

This wider history may also be useful for recent literature calling for more attention to be devoted in IPE scholarship to the study of gender, the environment, colonialism, race, and Eurocentrism. This volume shows how each of these topics was extensively discussed in pre-1945 analyses. Those historical analyses may prove relevant for those seeking to address these relative "blind spots" in the current field.[25] Some IPE scholars working on these topics do already cite this earlier intellectual history, such as feminist scholarship that highlights pre-1945 debates about the political economy of gender inequality.[26] But others show less awareness of it.

Take, for example, contemporary efforts to bring environmentalist perspectives more centrally into the contemporary field of IPE. Many of these efforts make little reference to the relevance of pre-1945 environmentalist analyses. To be sure, these earlier discussions were less focused on some environmental topics that have a high priority today, such as climate change (although that phenomenon was understood already in this earlier period, as noted in Chapter 9). But they did address many others that remain important and for which earlier analyses are relevant. Indeed, some of these topics are ones that are relatively neglected in current environmentalist IPE scholarship despite their enduring importance, such as soil erosion and exhaustion.[27] Chapter 9 also highlighted a diversity of environmentalist approaches that is not always matched in environmentalist IPE literature today.

Contemporary "decolonial" scholarship can also draw some inspiration from pre-1945 writings about issues of colonialism, racism, and Eurocentrism. Scholars working in the decolonial tradition highlight and challenge the enduring legacies of European colonialism – including its Eurocentric and racist worldviews – in shaping structures and knowledge in the world economy. Decolonial scholarship has engaged more than much environmentalist IPE scholarship with pre-1945 political economy texts. One goal has been to show (as does this volume) that many historical works of European political economy were infused with Eurocentric and

---

[23] For a discussion of new forms of regionalism, see, for example, Nemiña and Tussie 2021.
[24] Helleiner 2021b.
[25] Quote comes from the title of Best et al. 2021. Even critics of the idea of "blind spots" agree that many of these topics are "understudied" in the field (Hall 2021, 1).
[26] For example, see Whitworth 1994.
[27] For the enduring importance of this issue, see Handelsman 2021.

racist attitudes which accompanied the era of European colonialism.[28] But decolonial scholars have also highlighted pre-1945 thinkers who analyzed colonialism from a critical standpoint and who challenged racism and Eurocentrism in ways that overlap with decolonial efforts today.[29]

This volume also provides many examples of these latter figures. For example, as noted above, there were opponents of imperialism in all of the three orthodoxies discussed in the first part of the book. Many advocates of other perspectives discussed in the rest of the volume also advanced various anti-imperialist position.[30] In addition, this book has highlighted many thinkers who critiqued racialized hierarchies within the world economy.[31] Others challenged Eurocentric views more broadly. For example, Blyden, Marcus Garvey, and Williams critiqued Eurocentric narratives about the sources of Europe's wealth by emphasizing the key contributions made to it by Africans and the African diaspora (Chapters 7 and 11). Naoroji's drain theory challenged British imperial discourse about the causes of Indian poverty by calling attention to the ways Britain extracted resources from its South Asian colony (Chapter 3). Mukerjee highlighted how lifestyles in industrialized countries were environmentally unstable and maintained only because people in those countries drew parasitically on resources from other parts of the world (Chapter 9). Others such as Carey and Harrison critiqued Eurocentric civilizational discourses that supported imperialism (Chapters 4 and 11), while Ranade directly confronted Eurocentric assumptions that justified the subordinate place of tropical regions in the international division of labour (Chapter 5). Both Haya and Mariátegui also rejected ideas of European civilizational superiority, while James and M. N. Roy undermined Eurocentric perspectives among Marxists that downplayed the importance of the revolutionary agency of the colonized.

More generally, many thinkers in the pre-1945 years also challenged Eurocentric narratives that assumed European knowledge to be a standard for the rest of the world. In some cases, these thinkers advanced

---

[28] See, for example, Blaney and Inayatullah 2021; Hobson 2013; Ince 2018; Shilliam 2021a.

[29] For some recent examples, see Bhambra's (2021) citing of Naoroji's work or Narayan's (2017) invocation of Du Bois.

[30] See, for example, Kropotkin, Gandhi, Sekyi, Chen, Aydemir (Chapter 8); Humboldt, Black Elk, Mukerjee, Gregg (Chapter 9); Burroughs, Kamaladevi, Portal, Luisi, Ashwood Garvey (Chapter 10); Garvey, Du Bois, Harrison (Chapter 11); al-Afghani, Mawdudi (Chapter 12); Haya (Chapter 13); and White (Chapter 14).

[31] See, for example, Equiano, Naoroji (Chapter 3); James, Mariátegui, Padmore, Takahashi, Williams (Chapter 7); Paul (Chapter 8); Gregg (Chapter 9); Ashwood Garvey, Burroughs, Kamaladevi, Luisi, (Chapter 10); and Du Bois, Marcus Garvey, Harrison, and other thinkers who influenced, or were associated, with the Pan-African movement (Chapter 11).

counter-universalistic claims for their ideas, such as Mawdudi's global ambitions for Islamic economics or Sun's hope that the Asian "rule of Right" would triumph across the world (Chapter 12). In other cases, however, critiques of Eurocentrism were accompanied by broader attacks on universalist knowledge claims, such as Ranade's appeal to a "law of Relativity and Correspondence" (Chapter 5) or Haya de la Torre's thesis that ideas about political economy emerged from distinct regional "historical space-times" (Chapter 13). These relativist positions came closer to the approach of many contemporary decolonial scholars. They also bore some similarity to the views of some advocates of "global conversations" in IPE, such as Mark Blyth, who (echoing Cox's comment noted above) has argued that "where you sit determines what you think about IPE".[32]

In short, many issues that appear new to IPE scholarship in the contemporary era look less novel when viewed in the context of its deep intellectual history. Rather than reinvent the wheel, IPE scholars can learn from thinkers in earlier times. Susan Strange made this general case well in one of her more famous essays: "If ... we need better 'tools of analysis,' it is not because we will be able to dig up golden nuggets with them. Those nuggets – the great truths about human society and human endeavor – were all discovered long ago. What we need are constant reminders so that we do not forget them".[33] What needs reminding in this context is that the deep history of IPE involved much more than just thinkers from Europe and the United States and much more than a debate between just economic liberals, neomercantilists, and Marxists.

## Why the Narrow Approach?

Given these benefits of adopting a wider approach to IPE's deep history, why has the narrower one been so popular? Future historians of the field's post-1970 development may be able to provide a detailed answer to this question. But as closing comments to this volume, I can offer a few potential hypotheses. The attention devoted to historical thinkers from just Europe and the United States has no doubt been partly a product of the fact that the study of the history of political economy more generally often has this narrow geographical focus. It is also probably significant to the story that the formal field of IPE was heavily shaped since its origins in the early 1970s by scholars from Europe and the United States, where this narrow focus is often more pronounced.[34]

---

[32] Blyth 2009, 3. See also Cox 2009, 321; Deciancio and Quiliconi 2020.
[33] Strange 1982, 493.
[34] For this influence, see Cohen 2008.

The emphasis placed on a trilateral debate between the three orthodox-ies is less easy to explain. It appeared in some influential early works in IPE in the early 1970s and was then popularized in leading IPE textbooks that began to be published in the 1980s.[35] This depiction of the histori-cal foundation of debate in the field clearly resonated with scholars in the 1970s and 1980s given the political salience of economic liberal, neomer-cantilist, and Marxist perspectives in the politics of the world economy of that era. But why was there not more attention paid to the history of the various perspectives discussed in the second section of this volume?

In cases such as autarkism, Pan-Asianism, and interwar regionalist visions, their marginalization was understandable because these perspec-tives had, by the 1970s and 1980s, lost the influence they had in the pre-1945 years. But that explanation is less relevant to environmentalism, feminism, Pan-Islamism, and Pan-Africanism, each of which remained influential in various places, and even gained popularity in some cases, during the very period that the formal field of IPE was growing. The neglect of these perspectives – and their pre-1945 history – in IPE text-books may have reflected the specific concerns of those who pioneered the formal field of IPE as well as their judgments about which perspec-tives were most influential in the politics of the world economy at the time.[36] It may also have been reinforced by the absence of attention to these perspectives (and the issues they raised) at the Bretton Woods con-ference, whose status as a foundational moment in many IPE textbooks and courses helped to shape the agenda of the field.

To explain the enduring focus on the historical trilateral debate in more recent textbooks, those same explanations may still be relevant. But this narrow focus may also be a product of a kind of intellectual path dependence in the field. Indeed, even when textbooks have begun to recognize other perspectives in contemporary IPE scholarship (such as feminist, environmentalist, or decolonial ones), their discussion of the pre-1945 history of the field usually remains the same. These perspec-tives are often portrayed as "new" to the field rather than ones with a long history. I hope this book helps to challenge that path dependence and to encourage more interest in the fascinating nature of the field's deep and global roots in the pre-1945 era.

[35] See especially Gilpin 1987, ch. 2 (titled 'Three Ideologies of Political Economy").
[36] Not all of the pioneers of the formal field of IPE ignored these ideologies in the 1970s and 1980s. For example, Strange (1974) wrote a sympathetic review of one of the key environmentalist texts of that era, E. F. Schumacher's *Small Is Beautiful*. In her edited book *Paths to IPE*, Strange (1984) also included a chapter on an "ecological approach" to IPE by Denis Pirages. But I have not seen any place where Strange showed an interest in deeper pre-1945 roots of environmentalist perspectives.

# Works Cited

Accominotti, Olivier and Marc Flandreau. 2008. Bilateral treaties and the most-favored-nation clause. *World Politics* 60(2): 147–88.

Acharya, Amitav. 2004. How ideas spread: Whose norms matter? Norms localization and institutional change in Asian regionalism. *International Organization* 58(2): 239–75.

Acharya, Amitav and Barry Buzan. 2020. *The Making of Global International Relations*. Cambridge: Cambridge University Press.

Adams, John. 1971. The institutional economics of Mahadev Govind Ranade. *Journal of Economic Issues* 5(2): 80–92.

Addams, Jane. 1906. *Newer Ideals of Peace*. New York: MacMillan.

Addams, Jane. 1907a. The new internationalism. In National Arbitration and Peace Congress, *Proceedings*, 213–16. https://digital.janeaddams.ramapo.edu/items/show/5954. Accessed April 12, 2022.

Addams, Jane. 1907b. Newer ideals of peace. *National Arbitration and Peace Congress, Proceedings*, 106–10. https://digital.janeaddams.ramapo.edu/items/show/5953. Accessed April 12, 2022.

Addams, Jane. 1912. The new party. *The American Magazine* 74(1): 12–14.

Addams, Jane. 1915. Women and internationalism. In Jane Addams, Emily Balch, and Alice Hamilton, eds., *Women at the Hague*, 124–41. New York: Macmillan.

Addams, Jane. 1922. *Peace and Bread in Time of War*. New York: Macmillan.

Adi, Hakim. 2013. *Pan-Africanism and Communism*. Trenton: African World Press.

Akamatsu, Kaname. 1962. A historical pattern of economic growth in developing countries. *The Developing Economies* 1(1): 3–25.

Albritton, Vicky and Fredrik Albritton Jonsson. 2016. *Green Victorians*. Chicago: University of Chicago Press.

Alexander, Robert, ed. 1973. *Aprismo: The Ideas and Doctrines of Víctor Raúl Haya de la Torre*. Kent, OH: The Kent State University Press.

Ambirajan, S. 1978. *Classical Political Economy and British Policy in India*. Cambridge: Cambridge University Press.

Anderson, Benedict. 2005. *Under Three Flags*. London: Verso.

Anscombe, Frederick. 2010. Islam and the age of Ottoman reform. *Past and Present* 208(1): 159–89.

Ashley, William. 1904. *The Tariff Problem*. London: P. S. King and Son.

Ashworth, Lucian. 2019. How should we approach the history of international thought? In Brian Schmidt and Nicolas Guilhot, eds., *Historiographical*

*Investigations in International Relations*, 79–96. Cham, Switzerland: Palgrave Macmillan.

Ayala, Adrián. 2021. Castillo de gira por cinco días y aquí todo está de cabeza. *El Perfil*. September 18. https://elperfil.pe/politica/castillo-de-gira-por-cinco-dias-y-aqui-todo-esta-de-cabeza/. Accessed April 13, 2022.

Ayandele, Emmanuel. 1970. *Holy Johnson*. London: Frank Cass and Co.

Aydin, Cemil. 2007. *The Politics of Anti-Westernism in Asia*. New York: Columbia University Press.

Aydin, Cemil. 2016. The emergence of transnational Muslim thought, 1774–1914. In Jens Hanssen and Max Weiss, eds., *Arabic Thought beyond the Liberal Age*, 121–41. Cambridge: Cambridge University Press.

Aydin, Cemil. 2017. *The Idea of the Muslim World*. Cambridge, MA: Harvard University Press.

Bacon, Jules. 2019. Settler colonialism as eco-social structure and the production of colonial ecological violence. *Environmental Sociology* 5(1): 59–69.

Bagehot, Walter. [1876]1885. *The Postulates of English Political Economy*. New York: G. P. Putnam's Sons.

Balabkins, Nicholas. 1973. Carl Ballod. *Journal of Baltic Studies* 4(2): 113–26.

Balfour, Eve. [1943]1975. *The Living Soil*. London: Faber and Faber.

Ban, Cornel. 2016. *Ruling Ideas*. New York: Oxford University Press.

Bandele, Ramla. 2008. *Black Star*. Urbana: University of Illinois Press.

Baptiste, Fitzroy Andre. 2003. Amy Ashwood Garvey and Afro-West Indian labor in the United States emergency farm and war industries' programs of World War II, 1943–1945. *Ìrìnkèrindò: A Journal of African Migration* 2: 94–131.

Barbieri, Julie Laut. 2008. *Kamaladevi Chattopadhyaya, Anti-Imperialist and Women's Rights Activist, 1939–41*. MA Thesis, Department of History, Miami University.

Barlas, Dilek. 1998. *Étatism and Diplomacy in Turkey*. Leiden: Brill.

Barnhart, Michael. 1987. *Japan Prepares for Total War*. Ithaca: Cornell University Press.

Bauer, Raimund. 2016. *A "New Order": National Socialist Notions of Europe and Their Implementation during the Second World War*. PhD diss., Loughborough University.

Bayly, Christopher. 2012. *Rediscovering Liberties*. Cambridge: Cambridge University Press.

Beeman, Randal. 1995. Friends of the Land and the rise of environmentalism, 1940–1954. *Journal of Agricultural and Environmental Ethics* 8(1): 1–16.

Bergère, Marie-Claire. 1994. *Sun Yat-sen*. Translated by Janet Lloyd. Stanford: Stanford University Press.

Berkovitch, Nitza. 1999. *From Motherhood to Citizenship*. Baltimore: John Hopkins University Press.

Best, Jacqueline, Colin Hay, Genevieve Lebaron, and Daniel Mugge. 2021. Seeing and not seeing like a political economist: The historicity of contemporary political economy and its blind spots. *New Political Economy* 26(2): 217–28.

Bhagwati, Jagdish and Douglas Irwin. 1987. The return of the reciprocitarians: US trade policy today. *The World Economy* 10(2): 109–30.

Bhambra, Gurminder. 2021. Colonial global economy. *Review of International Political Economy* 28(2): 307–22.

Blacker, Carmen. 1964. *The Japanese Enlightenment*. Cambridge: Cambridge University Press.

Blaney, David and Naeem Inayatullah. 2021. *Within, Against, and Beyond Liberalism*. New York: Rowman and Littlefield.

Blomberg, Gisela. 1998. Flora Tristan: A predecessor of Marx and Engels. *Nature Society and Thought* 11(19): 5–16

Blyden, Edward. 1862. *Liberia's Offering*. New York: John Gray.

Blyden, Edward. [1887]1888. *Christianity, Islam and the Negro Race*. 2nd ed. London: Whittingham and Co.

Blyth, Mark. 2009. Introduction. In Mark Blyth, ed., *Routledge Handbook of IPE*, 243–65. London: Routledge.

Bodkin, Ronald. 1999. Women's agency in classical economic thought: Adam Smith, Harriet Taylor Mill and J. S. Mill. *Feminist Economics* 5(1): 45–60.

Boris, Eileen. 2019. *Making the Woman Worker*. Oxford: Oxford University Press.

Borokh, Olga. 2013. Chinese tradition meets Western economics: Tang Qingzeng and his legacy. In Ying Ma and Hans-Michael Trautwein, eds., *Thoughts on Economic Development in China*, 136–57. London: Routledge.

Borrows, John. 2018. Earth-Bound: Indigenous resurgence and environmental reconciliation. In Michael Asch, James Tully, and John Borrows, eds., *Resurgence and Reconciliation*, 49–81. Toronto: University of Toronto Press.

Bowles, Paul. 1984. John Millar, the four-stages theory, and women's position in society. *History of Political Economy* 16(4): 619–38.

Boxer, Marilyn. 2007. Rethinking the socialist construction and international career of the concept "bourgeois feminism". *American Historical Review* 112(1): 131–58.

Brading, David. 1991. *The First America*. Cambridge: Cambridge University Press.

Bramwell, Anna. 1989. *Ecology in the 20th Century*. New Haven: Yale University Press.

Brijbhushan, Jamila. 1976. *Kamaladevi Chattopadhyaya*. New Delhi: Abhinav Publications.

Brown, Heather. 2013. *Marx on Gender and the Family: A Critical Study*. Chicago: Haymarket.

Brown, Roger. 2011. Sun Yat-sen: "Pan-Asianism", 1924. In Sven Saaler and Christopher Szpilman, eds., *Pan-Asianism: A Documentary History, Vol. 2, 1920–Present*, 75–78. Boulder, CO: Rowman and Littlefield.

Brown, Sidney Devere. 1962. Ōkubo Toshimichi. *Journal of Asian Studies* 21(2): 183–97.

Buchanan, Isaac. 1864. *The Relations of the Industry of Canada with the Mother Country and the United States*. Edited by Henry Morgan. Montreal: John Lovell.

Cain, Peter. 1979. Capitalism, war and internationalism in the thought of Richard Cobden. *British Journal of International Studies* 5(3): 229–47.

Callicott, J. Baird. 2018. Black Elk, 1862–1950. In Joy Palmer Cooper and David Cooper, eds., *Key Thinkers on the Environment*, 146–51. London, Routledge.

Carey, Henry. [1847]1889. *The Past, the Present and the Future*. Philadelphia: Henry Carey Baird.

Carey, Henry. 1858a. *Principles of Social Sciences, Vol. 1*. Philadelphia: J. B. Lippincott and Company.

Carey, Henry. 1858b. *Principles of Social Sciences, Vol. 2*. Philadelphia: J. B. Lippincott and Company.

Carey, Henry. 1859. *Principles of Social Sciences, Vol. 3*. Philadelphia: J. B. Lippincott and Company.

Carlander, Jay R. and W. Elliot Brownlee. 2006. Antebellum Southern political economists and the problem of slavery. *American Nineteenth Century History* 7(3): 389–416.

Casely Hayford, J. E. 1911. *Ethiopia Unbound*. London: C. M. Phillips.

Chakrabarty, Dipesh. 2000. *Provincializing Europe*. Princeton: Princeton University Press.

Chandra, Bipan. 1965. Indian nationalists and the drain, 1880–1905. *Indian Economic and Social History Review* 2(2): 103–144.

Chapman, Maria Weston. 1877. *Memorials of Harriet Martineau*. Boston: James R. Osgood and Company.

Chari, Seshadri. 2020. Modi's idea of self-reliant India same as Gandhi's. *The Print*, May 15, 2020. https://theprint.in/opinion/modis-idea-of-self-reliant-india-same-as-gandhis/421820/. Accessed April 13, 2022.

Charnovitz, Steve. 1991. Exploring the environmental exceptions in GATT Article XX. *Journal of World Trade* 25(5): 37–55.

Chatterjee, Partha. 2012. *The Black Hole of Empire*. Princeton: Princeton University Press.

Chattopadhyaya, Kamaladevi. 1939. *Uncle Sam's Empire*. Bombay: Padma Publications.

Chattopadhyaya, Kamaladevi and others. 1939. *The Awakening of Indian Women*. Madras: Everymans Press.

Chen, Huan-Chang. 1911. *The Economic Principles of Confucius and His School*. New York: Faculty of Political Science, Columba University.

Chen, Songchuan. 2012. An information war waged by merchants and missionaries at Canton. *Modern Asian Studies* 46(6): 1705–35.

Cheng, Enfu and Jun Yang. 2020. The Chinese revolution and the Communist International. *Third World Quarterly* 41(8): 1338–52.

Chey, Hyoung-kyu and Eric Helleiner. 2018. Civilisational values and political economy beyond the West. *Contemporary Politics* 24(2): 191–209.

Chin, Gregory, Margaret Pearson, and Wang Yong, eds. 2014. IPE in China: The global conversation. *Review of IPE* 20(6): 1145–1299.

Chiu, Y. Stephen and Ryh-song Yeh. 1999. Adam Smith versus Sima Qian: Comment on the Tao of Markets. *Pacific Economic Review* 4(1): 79–84.

Chowduri, Satyabrata Rai. 2007. *Leftism in India, 1917–1947*. Basingstoke: Palgrave Macmillan.

Chung, Chai-sik. 1995. *A Korean Confucian Encounter with the Modern World*. Korea Research Monograph 20. Berkeley: Institute of East Asian Studies, University of California, Berkeley.

Clavin, Patricia. 2013. *Securing the World Economy*. Oxford: Oxford University Press.

Clift, Ben, Peter Marcus Kristensen, and Ben Rosamond. 2022. Remembering and forgetting IPE. *Review of International Political Economy* 29(2): 339–70.

Cobble, Dorothy Sue. 2004. A higher "standard of life" for the world: U.S. labor women's reform Internationalism and the legacies of 1919. *The Journal of American History* 100(4): 1052–85.

Cobble, Dorothy Sue. 2015. Who speaks for workers? Japan and the 1919 ILO debates over rights and global labor standards. *International Labor and Working-Class History* 87: 1–22.

Cobble, Dorothy Sue. 2018. The other ILO founders: 1919 and its legacies. In Eileen Boris, Dorothea Hoehtker, and Susan Zimmermann, eds., *Women's ILO*, 27–49. Leiden: Brill.

Cobden, Richard. 1903. *Speeches on Free Trade*. London: MacMillan and Co.

Cohen, Benjamin. 2008. *International Political Economy*. Princeton: Princeton University Press.

Cohen, Paul. 1974. *Between Tradition and Modernity*. Cambridge, MA: Harvard University Press.

Colás, Alejandro. 1994. Putting cosmopolitanism into practice. *Millennium* 23(3): 513–34.

Coller, Ian. 2015. African liberalism in the age of empire? Hassuna D'Ghies and liberal constitutionalism in North Africa, 1822–1835. *Modern Intellectual History* 12(3): 529–53.

Coller, Ian. 2016. Ottomans on the move: Hassuna D'Ghies and the "New Ottomanism" of the 1830s. In Maurizio Isabella and Konstantina Zanou, eds., *Mediterranean Diasporas*, 97–115. London: Bloomsbury.

Communist International. 1920. *The Capitalist World and the Communist International, Manifesto of the Second Congress of the Communist International*. Moscow: Publishing Office Third Communist International.

Conford, Philip. 1998. A forum for organic husbandry: The "New English Weekly" and agricultural policy, 1939–1949. *The Agricultural History Review* 46(2): 197–210.

Conford, Philip. 2001. *The Origins of the Organic Movement*. Edinburgh: Floris Books.

Conkin, Paul. 1980. *Prophets of Prosperity*. Bloomington: Indiana University Press.

Contee, Clarence Garner. 1970. *W. E. B. Du Bois and African Nationalism, 1914–1945*. PhD diss., Department of History, American University.

Conway, Ed. 2014. *The Summit*. London: Little, Brown and Co.

Cooper, Thomas. 1835. Slavery. *The Southern Literary Journal and Magazine of Arts* 1(3): 188–93.

Cot, Annie. 2014. Jeremy Bentham's Spanish American utopia. In José Luís Cardoso, Maria Cristina Marcuzzo, and María Eugenia Romero Sotelo, eds., *Economic Development and Global Crises*, 34–52. London: Routledge.

Coutinho, Maurício C. 2016 Silva Lisboa on free trade and slave labor. In Alexandre Mendes Cunha and Carlos Eduardo Suprinyak, eds., *The Political Economy of Latin American Independence*, 58–80. New York: Routledge.

Coyajee, J. C. 1932. *The World Economic Depression*. Madras: The Huxley Press.

Cox, Robert. 1995. Civilizations: Encounters and transformations. *Studies in Political Economy* 47(1): 7–32.

Cox, Robert. 2009. The "British School" in the global context. *New Political Economy* 14(3): 315–28.

Crawcour, Sydney. 1997. *Kōgyō iken*: Maeda Masana and his view of Meiji economic development. *Journal of Japanese Studies* 23(1): 69–104.

Cribb, Robert. 1985. The Indonesian Marxist tradition. In Colin Mackerras and Nick Knight, eds., *Marxism in Asia*, 251–72. London: Croom Held.

Crummell, Alex. [1855]1862. The duty of a rising Christian state. In Alex Crummell, ed., *The Future of Africa*, 57–102. 2nd ed. New York: Charles Scribner.

Crummell, Alex. [1870]1892. Our national mistakes and the remedy for them. In Alex Crummell, ed., *Africa and America*, 167–98. Springfield, MA: Willey and Co.

Dale, Gareth. 2016. In search of Karl Polanyi's international relations theory. *Review of International Studies* 42(3): 401–24.

David, Heather and Zoe Todd. 2017. On the importance of a date, or decolonizing the Anthropocene. *ACME: An International Journal for Critical Geographies* 16(4): 761–80.

Davis, Eric. 1983. *Challenging Colonialism, 1920–1941*. Princeton: Princeton University Press.

Davis, Teresa. 2018. *America for Humanity*. PhD diss., Department of History, Princeton University.

Davis, Teresa. 2021. The Ricardian state: Carlos Calvo and Latin America's ambivalent origin story for the age of decolonization. *Journal of the History of International Law* 23(1): 32–51.

Dawson, Frank. 1981. Contributions of lesser developed nations to international law: The Latin American experience. *Case Western Reserve Journal of International Law* 13(1): 37–81.

Deciancio, Melisa and Cintia Quiliconi. 2020. Widening the "global conversation". *All Azimuth* 9(2): 249–66.

De Mallie, Raymond, ed. 1984. *The Sixth Grandfather*. Lincoln: University of Nebraska Press.

Delap, Lucy. 2020. *Feminism: A Global History*. Chicago: University of Chicago Press.

d'Encausse, Hélène Carrrère and Stuart R. Schram. 1969. *Marxism and Asia*. London: Penguin Press.

Derman, Joshua. 2021. Prophet of a partitioned world: Ferdinand Fried, "great spaces", and the dialectics of deglobalization, 1929–1950. *Modern Intellectual History* 18(3): 757–81.

Derrick, Jonathan. 2008. *Africa's "Agitators"*. New York: Columbia University Press.

Devenish, Annie. 2017. Creativity as Freedom. In Ellen Carol Dubois and Vinay Lal, eds., *A Passionate Life*, 351–74. New Delhi: Zubaan.

Dimand, Robert. 2003. An eighteenth century English feminist response to political economy: Priscilla Wakefield's *Reflections* (1798). In Robert Dimand and Chris Nyland, eds., *The Status of Women in Classical Economic Thought*, 194–205. Cheltenham: Edward Elgar.

Dimand, Robert, Evelyn Forget, and Chris Nyland. 2004. Gender in classical economics. *Journal of Economic Perspectives* 18(1): 229–40.

Dohan, Michael. 1976. The economic origins of Soviet autarky 1927/8–1934. *Slavic Review* 35(4): 603–35.

Du Bois, W. E. Burghardt. 1915. The African roots of War. *The Atlantic* (May): 707–14.

Du Bois, W. E. Burghardt. [1920]1969. *Darkwater*. New York: Schocken.

Dunstan, Helen. 1996. *Conflicting Counsels to Confuse the Age*. Ann Arbor: Center for Chinese Studies, University of Michigan.

Duus, Peter. 1996. Imperialism without colonies: The vision of a Greater East Asia Co-Prosperity Sphere. *Diplomacy and Statecraft* 7(1): 54–72.

Earle, Edward. 1986. Adam Smith, Alexander Hamilton, Friedrich List. In Edward Earle, ed., *The Makers of Modern Strategy*, 117–54. Princeton: Princeton University Press.

Edwards, Louise. 2016. International Women's Day in China: Feminism meets militarised nationalism and competing political party programs. *Asian Studies Review* 40(1): 89–105.

Edwards, Paul. [1969]2001. Introduction to the life of Olaudah Equiano. In Olaudah Equiano, ed., *The Interesting Narrative of the Life of Olaudah Equiano or Gustavus Vassa, The African, Written by Himself*, 302–38. New York: W. W. Norton and Co.

Einaudi, Luigi. 1966. *Marxism in Latin America: From Aprismo to Fidelismo*. PhD diss., Harvard University.

Elder, William. 1880. *A Memoir of Henry C. Carey*. Philadelphia: Henry Carey Baird.

Equiano, Olaudah. [1798] 2001. *The Interesting Narrative of the Life of Olaudah Equiano or Gustavus Vassa, The African, Written by Himself*. New York: W. W. Norton and Co.

Esedebe, P. Olisanwuche. 1994. *Pan-Africanism*. 2nd ed. Washington: Howard University Press.

Ewing, Adam. 2014. *The Age of Garvey*. Princeton: Princeton University Press.

Ewing, Adam and Ronald Stephens. 2019. Introduction. In Ronald Stephens and Adam Ewing, eds., *Global Garveyism*, 1–14. Gainesville: University Press of Florida.

Fairbank, John King. [1953]1964. *Trade and Diplomacy on the China Coast*. Cambridge, MA: Harvard University Press.

Fairbank, John King, ed. 1968. *The Chinese World Order*. Cambridge, MA: Harvard University Press.

Falkner, Robert. 2021. *Environmentalism and Global International Society*. Cambridge: Cambridge University Press.

Farnsworth, Beatrice Brodsky. 1976. Bolshevism, the woman question, and Aleksandra Kollontai. *The American Historical Review* 81(2): 292–316.

Faudot, Adrien. 2022. The dual context of Keynes' International Clearing Union. *The European Journal of the History of Economic Thought* 29(2): 349–68.

Fertik, Edward. 2018. *Steel and Sovereignty: The United States, Nationalism, and the Transformation of World Order, 1898–1941*. PhD diss., Department of History, Yale University.

Folbre, Nancy. 1991. The unproductive housewife: Her evolution in nineteenth-century economic thought. *Signs* 16(3): 463–84.

Folbre, Nancy. 2009. *Greed, Lust and Gender*. Oxford: Oxford University Press.

Forget, Evelyn. 1997. The market for virtue: Jean-Baptiste Say on women in the economy and society. *Feminist Economics* 3(1): 95–111.

Forman-Barzilai, Fonna. 2000. Adam Smith as a globalization theorist. *Critical Review* 14(4): 391–419.

Formichi, Chiara. 2012. *Islam and the Making of the Nation*. Leiden: KITLV Press.

Foster, John Bellamy. 2000. *Marx's Ecology*. New York: Monthly Review Press.

Fowkes, Ben and Bülent Gökay. 2009. Unholy alliance: Muslims and communists. An introduction. *Journal of Communist Studies and Transition Politics* 25(1): 1–31.

Frenkel, M. Yu. 1974. Edward Blyden and the concept of African personality. *African Affairs* 73(292): 277–89.

Frieden, Jeffry. 2006. *Global Capitalism*. New York: W. W. Norton and Co.

Fukuzawa, Yukichi. [1875]2009. *An Outline of a Theory of Civilization*. Translated by David Silworth and G. Cameron Hurst III. New York: Columbia University Press.

Fukuzawa, Yukichi. [1885]1997. Good-bye Asia. In David Lu, ed., *Japan: A Documentary History*, Vol. 2, 351–53. London: Routledge.

Gabrahiwot Baykadagn. [1924]1995. *State and Economy of Early Twentieth-Century Ethiopia*. Translated and introduced by Tenkir Bonger. London: Karnak House.

Gallarotti, Guilio. 1992. *The Anatomy of an International Monetary Regime*. Oxford: Oxford University Press.

Gandhi, Mohandas. 1971. *The Collected Works of Mahatma Gandhi, Vol. 28*. New Delhi: Government of India.

Gandhi, Mohandas. 1997. *Hind Swaraj and Other Writings*. Edited by Anthony Parel. Cambridge: Cambridge University Press.

Ganguli, Birendranath. 1965. *Dadabhai Naoroji and the Drain Theory*. London: Asia Publishing.

Ganguli, Birendranath. 1977. *Indian Economic Thought*. New Delhi: Tata Graw-Hill Publishing Co.

García-Bryce, Iñigo. 2014. Transnational activist: Magda Portal and the American Popular Revolutionary Alliance (APRA), 1926–1950. *The Americas* 70(4): 677–706.

Geddes, Patrick. 1884. *John Ruskin, Economist*. Edinburgh: William Brown.

Germain, Randall. 2021. Nearly modern IPE? *Review of International Studies* 47(4): 528–48.

Gerth, Karl. 2003. *China Made*. Cambridge, MA: Harvard University Asia Center.

Getachew, Adom. 2019. *Worldmaking after Empire*. Princeton: Princeton University Press.

Gill, Erin. 2010. *Lady Eve Balfour and the British Organic Food and Farming Movement*. PhD diss., Department of History and Welsh History, Aberystwyth University.

Gill, Erin. 2018. Eve Balfour, 1898–1990. In Joy Palmer Cooper and David Cooper, eds., *Key Thinkers on the Environment*, 194–99. London: Routledge.

Gilpin, Robert. 1987. *The Political Economy of International Relations*. Princeton: Princeton University Press.

Goebel, Michael. 2014. Geopolitics, transnational solidarity or diaspora nationalism? The global career of M. N. Roy, 1915–1930. *European Review of History* 21(4): 485–99.

Gökalp, Ziya. 1959. *Turkish Nationalism and Western Civilization*. Translated and edited by Niyazi Berkes. New York: Columbia University Press.

Gonschor, Lorenz. 2016. *"A Power in the World": The Hawaiian Kingdom as a Model of Hybrid Statecraft in Oceania and a Progenitor of Pan-Oceanianism*. PhD diss., Department of Political Science, University of Hawai'i.

Goodman, Grant. 2005. Dutch learning. In Wm. Theodore de Bary, Carol Gluck, and Arthur Tiedemann, eds., *Sources of Japanese Tradition, 2nd ed., Vol. 2: 1600–2000*, 361–89. New York: Columbia University Press.

Gootenberg, Paul. 1989. *Between Silver and Guano*. Princeton: Princeton University Press

Gootenberg, Paul. 1993. *Imagining Development*. Berkeley: University of California Press.

Goswami, Manu. 2004. *Producing India*. Chicago: University of Chicago Press.

Goswami, Manu. 2012. Imaginary futures and colonial internationalisms. *American Historical Review* 117(5): 1461–85.

Gouverneur, Virginie. 2013. Mill versus Jevons on traditional sexual division of labour: Is gender equality efficient? *The European Journal of the History of Economic Thought* 20(5): 741–775.

Gramlich-Oka, Bettina. 2006. *Thinking Like a Man*. Leiden: Brill.

Gregg, Richard. 1928. *Economics of Khaddar*. Madras: S. Ganesan.

Gregg, Richard. 1935. *The Power of Non-Violence*. London: George Routledge and Sons.

Gregg, Richard. [1936]1974. Voluntary simplicity. *Manas* 27(36): 1–5 (reprinted from original published in *Visva-Bharati Quarterly*).

Gregor, A. James. 2000. *A Place in the Sun*. Boulder, CO: Westeview.

Gregor, A. James and Maria Hsia Chang. 1989. The thought of Sun Yat-sen in comparative perspective. In Chu-yuan Cheng, ed., *Sun Yat-sen's Doctrine in the Modern World*, 103–37. Boulder, CO: Westview.

Groenewegen, Peter. 1977. Introduction. In P. D. Groenewegen, ed., *The Economics of A. R. J. Turgot*, ix–xxvi. The Hague: Martinus Nijhoff.

Gross, Stephen. 2017. Gold, debt and the quest for monetary order: The Nazi campaign to integrate Europe in 1940. *Contemporary European History* 26(2): 287–309.

Grove, Richard. 1995. *Green Imperialism*. Cambridge: Cambridge University Press.

Guettel, Jens-Uwe. 2012. The myth of the pro-colonialist SPD. *Central European History* 45(3): 452–84.

Guha, Ramachandra. 2000. *Environmentalism: A Global History*. New York: Longman.

Guha, Ramachandra and Joan Martínez-Alier. 1997. *Varieties of Environmentalism*. London: Routledge.

Gülap, Haldun. 1998. The eurocentrism of dependency theory and the question of "authenticity": A view from Turkey. *Third World Quarterly* 19(5): 951–61.

Gunn, Jeffrey. 2010. Creating a paradox: Quobna Ottobah Cugoano and the slave trade's violation of the principles of Christianity, reason and property ownership. *Journal of World History* 21(4): 629–56.

Gupta, Shanti. 1968. *The Economic Philosophy of Mahatma Gandhi*. Delhi: Ashok Publishing House.

Hale, Charles. 1968. *Mexican Liberalism in the Age of Mora, 1821–1853*. New Haven: Yale University Press.

Hall, Derek. 2021. On blind spots in (international) political economy. *Review of International Political Economy*.

Hall, Peter, ed. 1989. *The Political Power of Economic Ideas*. Princeton: Princeton University Press.

Halsey, Stephen. 2015. *Quest for Power*. Cambridge, MA: Harvard University Press.

Hamilton, Alexander. [1791]1964. Report on manufactures. In Jacob Cooke, ed., *The Reports of Alexander Hamilton*, 115–205. New York: Harper and Row.

Handelsman, Jo. 2021. *A World Without Soil*. New Haven: Yale University Press.

Hanioğlu, M. Şükrü. 2011. *Atatürk*. Princeton: Princeton University Press.

Harlen, Christine. 1999. A reappraisal of classical economic liberalism and economic nationalism. *International Studies Quarterly* 43(4): 733–44.

Harrison, Hubert. 2001. *A Hubert Harrison Reader*. Edited by Jeffrey Perry. Middletown, CT: Wesleyan University Press.

Harrison, Peter. 2011. Adam Smith and the history of the invisible hand. *Journal of the History of Ideas* 72(1): 29–49.

Hayek, Friedrich. 1944. *The Road to Serfdom*. London: George Routledge and Sons.

He-Yin, Zhen. [1907a]2013. On the question of women's labor. In Lydia Liu, Rebecca Karl, and Dorothy Ko, eds., *The Birth of Chinese Feminism*, 72–91. New York: Columbia University Press.

He-Yin, Zhen. [1907b]2013. On feminist anti-militarism. In Lydia Liu, Rebecca Karl, and Dorothy Ko, eds., *The Birth of Chinese Feminism*, 169–78. New York: Columbia University Press.

He-Yin, Zhen. [1907c]2013. Economic revolution and women's revolution. In Lydia Liu, Rebecca Karl, and Dorothy Ko, eds., *The Birth of Chinese Feminism*, 92–104. New York: Columbia University Press.

Heaman, Elsbeth. 2017. *Tax, Order and Good Government*. Montreal: McGill-Queen's University Press.

Helleiner, Eric. 1994. *States and the Reemergence of Global Finance*. Ithaca: Cornell University Press.

Helleiner, Eric. 2002. Economic nationalism as a challenge to neoliberalism? *International Studies Quarterly* 46(3): 307–29.

Helleiner, Eric. 2003. *The Making of National Money*. Ithaca: Cornell University Press.

Helleiner, Eric. 2014. *Forgotten Foundations of Bretton Woods*. Ithaca: Cornell University Press.

Helleiner, Eric. 2019a. Conservative economic nationalism and the National Policy: Rae, Buchanan and Early Canadian Protectionist thought. *Canadian Journal of Political Science* 52(3): 521–38.

Helleiner, Eric. 2019b. The life and times of embedded liberalism. *Review of International Political Economy* 26(6): 1112–36.

Helleiner, Eric. 2021a. *The Neomercantilists*. Ithaca: Cornell University Press.

Helleiner, Eric. 2021b. The return of national self-sufficiency? Excavating autarkist thought in IPE for a de-globalizing era. *International Studies Review* 23(3): 933–57.

Helleiner, Eric. 2022. Silences of Bretton Woods: Gender inequality, racial discrimination, and environmental degradation. *Review of International Political Economy*. https://doi.org/10.1080/09692290.2022.2144408

Helleiner, Eric and Antulio Rosales. 2017. Towards Global IPE: The neglected significance of the Haya-Mariátegui debate. *International Studies Review* 19(4): 667–91.

Herres, Jürgen. 2015. Rhineland radical and the "48ers". In Terrell Carver and James Farr, eds., *The Cambridge Companion to The Communist Manifesto*, 15–31. Cambridge: Cambridge University Press.

Hilden, Patricia. 1987. Re-writing the history of socialism: Working women and the Parti Ouvier Francais. *European History Quarterly* 17(3): 285–306.

Hilferding, Rudolph. [1910]1981. *Finance Capital.* Translated by T. B. Bottomore. London: Routledge and Kegan Paul.

Hill, Robert, ed. 1983a. *The Marcus Garvey and Universal Negro Improvement Association Papers, Vol. 1.* Berkeley: University of California Press.

Hill, Robert, ed. 1983b. *The Marcus Garvey and Universal Negro Improvement Association Papers, Vol. 2.* Berkeley: University of California Press.

Hill, Robert, ed. 1984. *The Marcus Garvey and Universal Negro Improvement Association Papers, Vol. 3.* Berkeley: University of California Press.

Hiroshi, Mitani. 2006. *Escape from Impasse.* Translated by David Noble. Tokyo: International House of Japan.

Hirschman, Albert. 1945. *National Power and the Structure of Foreign Trade.* Berkeley: University of California Press.

Hirschman, Albert. 1977. *The Passions and the Interests.* Princeton: Princeton University Press.

Hobson, John. 1902. *Imperialism: A Study.* New York: James Pott and Company.

Hobson, John. 1915. *Towards International Government.* London: George Allen and Unwin.

Hobson, John. 1916. *The New Protectionism.* New York: G. P. Putnam's Sons.

Hobson, John M. 2012. *The Eurocentric Conception of World Politics.* Cambridge: Cambridge University Press.

Hobson, John M. 2013. Part 1: Revealing the Eurocentric foundations of IPE. *Review of International Political Economy* 20(5): 1024–54.

Hobson, John M. 2019. What's a stake in doing (critical) IR/IPE historiography? The imperative of critical historiography. In Brian Schmidt and Nicolas Guilhot, eds., *Historiographical Investigations in International Relations,* 149–70. Cham, Switzerland: Palgrave Macmillan.

Hobson, John M. 2020. *Multicultural Origins of the Global Economy.* Cambridge: Cambridge University Press.

Hoecker-Drysdale, Susan. 2003. Harriet Martineau. In George Ritzer, ed., *The Blackwell Companion to Major Classical Social Theories,* 41–68. Oxford: Blackwell.

Høgsbjerg, Christian. 2014. *C. L. R. James in Imperial Britain.* Durham: Duke University Press.

Høgsbjerg, Christian. 2017. Introduction. In C. L. R. James and Christian Høgsbjerg, eds., *World Revolution, 1917–1936,* 1–57. Durham: Duke University Press.

Hont, Istvan. 2005. *Jealousy of Trade.* Cambridge, MA: Belknap Press of Harvard University Press.

Hooker, James. 1967. *Black Revolutionary.* London: Frederick Praeger.

Hopkins, A. G. 1995. The "New International Economic Order" in the nineteenth century: Britain's first development plan for Africa. In Robin Law, ed., *From Slave Trade to "Legitimate" Commerce,* 240–64. Cambridge: Cambridge University Press.

Horsefield, J. K. 1969. *The International Monetary Fund, 1945–65, Vol. 3.* Washington: International Monetary Fund.

Horton, James Africanus. [1868]1969. *West African Countries and Peoples.* Edinburgh, Edinburgh University Press.

Hoston, Germaine. 1983. Tenkō: Marxism and the national question in prewar Japan. *Polity* 16(1): 96–118.

Hoston, Germaine. 1984. Marxism and Japanese expansionism: Takahashi Kamekichi and the theory of "petty imperialism". *The Journal of Japanese Studies* 10(1): 1–30.

Hoston, Germaine. 1986. *Marxism and the Crisis of Development in Prewar Japan.* Princeton: Princeton University Press.

Hoston, Germaine. 1994. *The State, Identity and the National Question in China and Japan.* Princeton: Princeton University Press.

Hourani, Albert. 1983. *Arabic Thought in the Liberal Age, 1798–1939.* Cambridge: Cambridge University Press.

Howe, Anthony. 1990. Bimetallism, c. 1880–1898: A controversy re-opened? *The English Historical Review* 105(415): 377–91.

Hsiao, Kung-chuan. 1975. *A Modern China and a New World.* Seattle: University of Washington Press.

Hu, Jichuang. 1988. *A Concise History of Chinese Economic Thought.* Beijing: Foreign Languages Press.

Hudis, Peter. 2018. Non-linear pathways to social transformation: Rosa Luxemburg and the post-colonial condition. *New Formations* 94: 62–81.

Hveem, Helge. 2009. Pluralist IPE: A view from outside the "schools". *New Political Economy* 14(3): 367–76.

Hwang, Kyung Moon. 2016. *Rationalizing Korea.* Oakland: University of California Press.

Imlay, Talbot. 2016. Socialist internationalism after 1914. In Glenda Sluga and Patricia Clavin, eds., *Internationalisms.* Cambridge: Cambridge University Press.

Ince, Onur. 2018. *Colonial Capitalism and the Dilemmas of Liberalism.* Oxford: Oxford University Press.

Ince, Onur. 2021. Adam Smith, settler colonialism, and limits of liberal anti-imperialism. *Journal of Politics* 83(3): 1080–96.

Innis, Harold. [1929]1956. The teaching of economic history in Canada. In H. Innis and Mary Q. Innis, eds., *Essays in Canadian Economic History*, 3–16. Toronto: University of Toronto Press.

International Labour Office (ILO). 1944. *International Labour Conference, Twenty-Sixth Session, Philadelphia, 1944, Record of Proceedings.* Montreal: International Labour Office.

Irwin, Douglas. 1996. *Against the Tide.* Princeton: Princeton University Press.

Irwin, Douglas. 2017. *Clashing over Commerce.* Chicago: University of Chicago Press.

Iwata, Masakazu. 1964. *Ōkubo Toshimichi.* Berkeley: University of California Press.

Jacks, Graham Vernon and R. O. Whyte. 1939. *The Rape of the Earth.* London: Faber and Faber.

Jackson, Roy. 2011. *Mawlana Mawdudi and Political Islam.* London: Routledge.

Jacobsen, Nils. 2005. Liberalismo tropical: The career of an European economic doctrine in nineteenth-century Latin America. In Valpy FitzGerald and Rosemary Thorpe, eds., *Economic Doctrines in Latin America*, 115–141. London: Palgrave Macmillan.

Jacobsen, Stefan Gaarsmand. 2013. Physiocracy and the Chinese model. In Ying Ma and Hans-Michael Trautwein, eds., *Thoughts on Economic Development in China*, 12–34. London, Routledge.

Jakes, Aaron. 2020. *Egypt's Occupation*. Stanford: Standford University Press.

James, C. L. R. [1937]2017. *World Revolution, 1917–1936*. Edited by Christian Høgsbjerg. Durham: Duke University Press.

James, C. L. R. [1938]1989. *The Black Jacobins*. 2nd ed., revised. New York: Vintage Books.

James, C. L. R. [1938]2012. *A History of Pan-African Revolt*. Oakland, CA: PM Press.

James, Harold. 2001. *The End of Globalization*. Cambridge, MA: Harvard University Press.

James, Leslie. 2015. *George Padmore and Decolonization from Below*. Basingstoke: Palgrave Macmillan.

Jansen, Marius. 1967. *The Japanese and Sun Yat-sen*. Cambridge, MA: Harvard University Press.

Jarvis, Helen. 1987. Tan Malaka: Revolutionary or renegade? *Bulletin of Concerned Asian Scholars* 19(1): 41–55.

Jedlicki, Jerzy. 1999. *A Suburb of Europe*. Budapest: Central European University Press.

Jefferson, Therese and John King. 2001. "Never intended to be a theory about everything": Domestic labour in neoclassical and Marxian economics. *Feminist Economics* 7(3): 71–101.

Jevons, W. Stanley. 1865. *The Coal Question*. London: Macmillan and Co.

Jiang, Yihua. 2012. A brief history of Chinese socialist thought in the past century. *Journal of Modern Chinese History* 6(2): 147–63.

Jonsson, Fredrik Albritton, 2010. Rival ecologies of global commerce: Adam Smith and the natural historians. *The American Historical Review* 115(5): 1342–63.

Jonsson, Fredrik Albritton. 2013. *Enlightenment's Frontier*. New Haven: Yale University Press.

Jonsson, Fredrik Albritton. 2014. Adam Smith in the forest. In Susan Hecht, Kathleen Morrison, and Christine Padoch, eds., *The Social Lives of Forests*, 45–54. Chicago: University of Chicago Press.

Jonsson, Fredrik Albritton. 2020. The coal question before Jevons. *The Historical Journal* 63(1): 107–26.

Jundt, Thomas. 2014. Dueling visions for the postwar world: The UN and UNESCO 1949 conferences on resources and nature, and the origins of environmentalism. *Journal of American History* 101(1): 44–70.

Kaempfer, Engelbert. [1692]1906. *The History of Japan, Vol. 3*. Translated by J. G. Scheuchzer. Glasgow: James MacLehose and Sons.

Kang, David. 2010. *East Asia before the West*. New York: Columbia University Press.

Kasahara, Shigehisa. 2019. *A Critical Evaluation of the Flying Geese Paradigm*. PhD diss., Erasmus University Rotterdam.

Kautsky, Karl. [1914]1970. Ultra-imperialism. *New Left Review* 59(1): 41–46.

Kay, Helen and Rose Pipes. 2020. Chrystal Macmillan, Scottish campaigner for women's equality through legal reform. *Women's History Review* 29(4): 716–36.

Kazui, Tashiro and Susan Downing Videen. 1982. Foreign relations during the Edo period: Sakoku reexamined. *Journal of Japanese Studies* 8(2): 283–306.

Kealey, Linda. 1984. Canadian socialism and the woman question, 1900–1914. *Labour* 13: 77–100.

Kellogg, Laura Cornelius. [1912]2011. Industrial organization for the Indian. In David Martínez, ed., *The American Indian Intellectual Tradition*, 156–65. Ithaca: Cornell University Press.

Keynes, John Maynard. [1933]1982. National self-sufficiency. In Donald Moggridge, ed., *The Collected Writings of J. M. Keynes, Vol. 21*, 233–46. Cambridge: Cambridge University Press.

Keynes, John Maynard. 1936. *The General Theory of Employment, Interest and Money*. London: Macmillan.

Khuri-Makdisi, Ilham. 2010. *The Eastern Mediterranean and the Making of Global Radicalism, 1860–1914*. Berkeley: University of California Press.

Kidwai, S. Mushir Hosain. 1912. *Islam and Socialism*. London: Luzac and Co.

Kilinçoğlu, Deniz. 2015. *Economics and Capitalism in the Ottoman Empire*. London: Routledge.

Kilinçoğlu, Deniz. 2017. Islamic economics in the late Ottoman Empire. *European Journal of the History of Economic Thought* 24(3): 528–554.

Kindleberger, Charles. 1975. The rise of free trade in Western Europe, 1820–1875. *Journal of Economic History* 35(1): 20–55.

Kirby, William. 1984. *Germany and Republican China*. Stanford: Stanford University Press.

Kirshner, Jonathan. 2015. Keynes's early beliefs and why they still matter. *Challenge* 58(5): 398–412.

Kollantai, Aleksandra. [1919]2012. Resolution on the role of working women. In Nancy Forestell and Maureen Moynagh, eds. *Documenting First Wave Feminisms, Vol. 1*, 340. Toronto: University of Toronto Press.

Korhonen, Pekka. 1994. The theory of the flying geese pattern of development and its interpretations. *Journal of Peace Research* 31(1): 93–108.

Kosek, Joseph Kip. 2005. Richard Gregg, Mohandas Gandhi, and the strategy of nonviolence. *The Journal of American History* 91(4): 1318–48.

Kōtuku, Shūsui. [1901]2015. Imperialism. In Robert Thomas Tierney, ed., *Monster of the Twentieth Century*, 133–208. Berkeley: University of California Press.

Koyagi, Mikiya. 2013. The Hajj by Japanese Muslims in the interwar period. *Journal of World History* 24(4): 849–76.

Kramer, Martin. 1986. *Islam Assembled*. New York: Columbia University Press.

Kropotkin, Petr. [1892]1906. *The Conquest of Bread*. London: Chapman and Hall.

Kropotkin, Petr. [1898]1901. *Fields, Factories and Workshops*. New York: G.P. Putnam's Sons.

Kubu, Eduard, Jiri Novotny, and Jiri Sousa. 2006. Slavism in national Czech enterprises in the first half of the twentieth century. In Helga Schultz and Eduard Kubu, eds., *History and Culture of Economic Nationalism in East Central Europe*, 185–206. Berlin: Berliner Wissenschafts-Verlag.

Kuiper, Edith. 2006. Adam Smith and his feminist contemporaries. In Leonidas Montes and Eric Schliesser, eds., *New Voices on Adam Smith*, 40–60. London: Routledge.

Kumar, Ashutosh. 1992. Marx and Engels on India. *The Indian Journal of Political Science* 53(4): 492–504.

Kumarappa, Joseph. 1945. *Economy of Permanence*. Rajghat, Varanasi: Savra-Seva-Sangh-Prakashan.

Kuran, Timur. 1997. The genesis of Islamic economics: A chapter in the politics of Muslim identity. *Social Research* 64(2): 301–38.

Kuran, Timur. 2004. *Islam and Mammon*. Princeton: Princeton University Press.

Landau, Jacob. 1990. *The Politics of Pan-Islam*. Oxford: Clarendon Press.

Langley, J. Ayodele. 1973. *Pan-Africanism and Nationalism in West Africa, 1900–1945*. Oxford: Clarendon Press.

Langley, J. Ayodele. 1979. Introduction. In J. Ayo Langley, ed., *Ideologies of Liberation in Black Africa*, 1856–1970. London: Rex Collings.

Larrain, Jorge. 1991. Classical political economists and Marx on colonialism and "backward" nations. *World Development* 19(2/3): 225–43.

Laver, Michael. 2011. *The Sakoku Edicts and the Politics of Tokugawa Hegemony*. Amherst, New York: Cambria Press.

Lavrin, Asunción. 1989. Women, labor, and the left: Argentina and Chile, 1890–1925. *Journal of Women's History* 1(2): 88–116.

Lazer, David. 1999. The free trade epidemic of the 1860s and other outbreaks of economic discrimination. *World Politics* 51(4): 447–83.

Leach, Camilla and Joyce Goodman. 2000. Educating the women of the nation: Priscilla Wakefield and the construction of a national identity, 1798. *Quaker Studies* 5(2): 165–82.

Leddy, Lianne. 2017. Intersections of Indigenous and environmental history in Canada. *Canadian Historical Review* 98(1): 83–95.

Lee, Seok-Won. 2015. The paradox of racial liberation: W. E. B. Du Bois and Pan-Asianism in wartime Japan, 1931–1945. *Inter-Asian Cultural Studies* 16(4): 515–30.

Lee, Yong Wook. 2020. Performing civilisational narratives in East Asia: Asian values, multiple modernities, and the politics of economic development. *Review of International Studies* 46(4): 456–76

Lenin, Vladimir [1916]1970. *Imperialism*. Moscow: Progress Publishers.

Leonard, Jane. 1984. *Wei Yuan and China's Rediscovery of the Maritime World*. Cambridge, MA: Council on East Asian Studies, Harvard University Press.

Leopold, David. 2015. Marx, Engels and other socialisms. In Terrell Carver and James Farr, eds., *The Cambridge Companion to The Communist Manifesto*, 32–49. Cambridge: Cambridge University Press.

Liang, Qichao. [1903]1989. The power and threat of America. In R. David Arkush and Leo O. Lee, trans. and eds., *Land without Ghosts*, 84–95. Berkeley: University of California Press.

Linebarger, Paul. 1937. *The Political Doctrines of Sun Yat-sen*. Baltimore: The Johns Hopkins Press.

Link, Stefan. 2018. How might 21st-century de-globalization unfold? Some historical reflections. *New Global Studies* 12(3): 343–65.

Link, Stefan. 2020. *Forging Global Fordism*. Princeton: Princeton University Press.

List, Friedrich. [1837]1983. *The Natural System of Political Economy*. Translated and edited by W. O. Henderson. New York: Routledge.

List, Friedrich. [1841]1909a. *The National System of Political Economy*. Translated by Sampson S. Lloyd. London: Longmans, Green and Co.

List, Friedrich. [1841]1909b. Introduction to The National System of Political Economy. In Margaret Hirst, ed., *The Life of Friedrich List*, 287–318. London: Smith, Elder and Co.

Liu, Glory. 2018. "The apostle of free trade": Adam Smith and the nineteenth-century trade debates. *History of European Ideas* 44(2): 210–23.

Liu, Lydia, Rebecca Karl, and Dorothy Ko. 2013a. Introduction. In Lydia Liu, Rebecca Karl, and Dorothy Ko, eds., *The Birth of Chinese Feminism*, 1–26. New York: Columbia University Press.

Liu, Lydia, Rebecca Karl, and Dorothy Ko. 2013b. The historical context. In Lydia Liu, Rebecca Karl, and Dorothy Ko, eds., *The Birth of Chinese Feminism*, 27–48. New York: Columbia University Press.

Liu, Qunyi. 2016. Yan Fu and Kaiping mines: The meaning of economic liberalism in early modern China. In Gilles Campagnolo, ed., *Liberalism and Chinese Economic Development*, 49–62. New York: Routledge.

Long, David. 1996. *Towards a New Liberal Internationalism*. Cambridge: Cambridge University Press.

Lubin, Carol Riegelman and Anne Winslow. 1990. *Social Justice for Women*. Durham: Duke University Press.

Ludi, Regula. 2019. Setting new standards: International feminism and the League of Nations' Inquiry into the Status of Women. *Journal of Women's History* 31(1): 12–36.

Lutz, Jessie Gregory. 2008. *Opening China*. Grand Rapids, MI: William B. Eerdmans.

Luxemburg, Rosa. [1912]2004. Women's suffrage and class struggle. In Peter Hudis and Kevin Anderson, eds., *The Rosa Luxemburg Reader*, 237–41. New York: Monthly Review Press.

Luxemburg, Rosa. [1913]1963. *The Accumulation of Capital*. Translated by Agnes Schwarzschild. London: Routledge and Kegan Paul.

Lynch, Hollis, ed. 1971. *Black Spokesman*. London: Frank Cass and Co.

Lynch, John. 2006. *Simón Bolívar*. New Haven: Yale University Press.

Macmillan, Chrystal. [1920]2012. The future of the international women suffrage alliance. In Nancy Forestell and Maureen Moynagh, eds., *Documenting First Wave Feminisms, Vol. 1*, 172–76. Toronto: University of Toronto Press.

Magnusson, Lars. 1994. *Mercantilism*. London: Routledge.

Makalani, Minkah. 2011. *In the Cause of Freedom*. Chapel Hill: University of North Carolina Press.

Makalani, Minkah. 2016. An apparatus for Negro women: Black women's organizing, communism and the institutional spaces of radical Pan-African thought. *Women, Gender, and Families of Color* 4(2): 250–73.

Manoilescu, Mihail. 1931. *The Theory of Protection and International Trade*. London: P. S. King and Son.

Manjapra, Kris. 2014. *Age of Entanglement*. Cambridge, MA: Harvard University Press.

Mantena, Karuna. 2010. *Alibis of Empire*. Princeton: Princeton University Press.

Marçal, Katrine. 2016. *Who Cooked Adam Smith's Dinner?* Translated by Saskia Vogel. London: Pegasus Books.

Marcon, Federico. 2015. *The Knowledge of Nature and the Nature of Knowledge in Early Modern Japan*. Chicago: University of Chicago Press.

Marino, Katherine. 2019. *Feminism for the Americas*. Chapel Hill: University of North Carolina Press.

Mark, Ethan. 2006. "Asia's" transwar lineage. *Journal of Asian Studies* 65(3): 461–93.

Marsh, George. 1864. *Man and Nature*. London: Sampson, Low, Son and Marston.

Marshall, Byron. 1967. *Capitalism and Nationalism in Prewar Japan*. Stanford: Stanford University Press.

Marsot, Afaf Lutfi Al-Sayyid. 1984. *Egypt in the Reign of Muhammad Ali*. Cambridge: Cambridge University Press.

Martin, Jamie. 2016. Experts of the World Economy. PhD diss., Harvard University, Graduate School of Arts and Sciences.

Martin, Jamie. 2022. *The Meddlers*. Cambridge, MA: Harvard University Press.

Martineau, Harriet. 1837. *Society in America, Vol. 2*. Paris: Baudry's European Library.

Marx, Karl. [1857–61] 1973. *Grundisse*. Translated with a forward by Martin Nicolaus. London: Penguin

Marx, Karl. [1867]1976. *Capital, Vol. 1*. New York: Vintage.

Marx, Karl. 2019. *Karl Marx, The Political Writings, Vol. 2, Surveys from Exile*. New York: Verso Books.

Marx, Karl and Friedrich Engels. [1848]2004. *The Communist Manifesto*. Translated and edited by L. M. Findlay. Peterborough: Broadview.

Masani, R. P. 1939. *Dadabhai Naoroji*. London: George Allen and Unwin.

Matera, Marc. 2015. *Black London*. Oakland: University of California Press.

Matsunaga, Tomoari. 2021. The paradoxical coexistence between free trade ideology and economic nationalism within left liberals in Britain. *History of European Ideas* 47(7): 1150–68.

Mawdudi, Abul A'la. [1939]1976. *Jihad in Islam*. Lahore: Islamic Publications,

Mawdudi, Abul A'la. [1941]2011. Mankind's economic problems and their Islamic solutions. In Abul A'la Mawdudi and Khurshid Ahmad, eds., *First Principles of Islamic Economics*. Translated by Ahmad Imam Shafaq Hashemi, 2–23. Markfield, UK: The Islamic Foundation.

Mazlish, Bruce. 2001. Civilization in a historical and global perspective. *International Sociology* 16(3): 293–300.

Mazower, Mark. 1996. Hitler's New Order, 1939–45. *Diplomacy and Statecraft* 7(1): 29–53.

McCormick, John. 1989. *The Global Environmental Movement*. London: Belhaven Press.

McDuffie, Erik. 2016. The diasporic journeys of Louise Little. *Women, Gender and Families of Color* 4(2): 146–70.

McLellan, David. 1977. *Karl Marx*. Frogmore, UK: Paladin.

McLeod, Cindy. 2011. *Louisa S. McCord and the "Feminist" Debate*. PhD diss., Program of Interdisciplinary Humanities, Florida State University.

Mcmullen, James. 2021. Twenty-first-century ecology lessons from seventeenth-century Japan: Climate change, deforestation, and moral regeneration. *Japan Forum* 33(1): 424–44.

McNamara, Dennis. 1996. *Trade and Transformation in Korea, 1876–1945*. Boulder, CO: Westview.

McVey, Ruth. 1965. *The Rise of Indonesian Communism*. Ithaca: Cornell University Press.

Meardon, Stephen. 2008. From religious revivals to tariff rancor. *History of Political Economy* 40(5): 265–98.

Mehrotra, S. R. and Dinyar Patel, eds. 2016. *Dadabhai Naoroji: Selected Private Papers*. Oxford: Oxford University Press.

Mendes Cunha, Alexandre and Carlos Eduardo Suprinyak. 2017. Political economy and Latin American independence from the nineteenth to the twentieth century. In Alexandre Mendes Cunha and Carlos Eduardo Suprinyak, eds., *The Political Economy of Latin American Independence*, 7–31. New York: Routledge.

Merricks. Linda. 1996a. Frederick Soddy: Scientist, economist and environmentalist. An examination of his politics. *Capitalism, Nature, Socialism* 7(4): 59–78.

Merricks, Linda. 1996b. *The World Made New*. Oxford: Oxford University Press.

Mervart, David. 2009. A closed country in the open seas: Engelbert Kaempfer's Japanese solution for European modernity's predicament. *History of European Ideas* 35(3): 321–29.

Mervart, David. 2015. The republic of letters comes to Nagasaki: Record of a translator's struggle. *Transcultural Studies* 6(2): 8–36.

Metzler, Mark and Gregory Smits. 2010. Introduction. In Bettina Gramlich-Oka and Gregory Smits, eds., *Economic Thought in Early Modern Japan*, 1–19. Leiden: Brill.

Mill, John Stuart. [1871]1965. *Principles of Political Economy*. New York: Augustus Kelley.

Millar, Ashley. 2017. *A Singular Case*. Montreal: McGill-Queen's University Press.

Mimura, Janis. 2011. Japan's new order and Greater East Asia Co-Prosperity Sphere: Planning for empire. *The Asia-Pacific Journal* 9(49)(3): 1–12.

Mishra, Panjay. 2012. *From the Ruins of Empire*. New York: Farrar, Straus and Giroux.

Molyneux, Maxine. 1981. Socialist societies old and new: Progress towards women's emancipation? *Feminist Review* 8(1): 1–34.

Morgenthau, Henry. 1944a. *Morgenthau Diary, Book 755*, The Papers of Henry Morgenthau Jr, 1866–1960, Franklin D. Roosevelt Library, Hyde Park (NY), United States.

Morgenthau, Henry. 1944b. *Morgenthau Diary, Book 756*, The Papers of Henry Morgenthau Jr, 1866–1960, Franklin D. Roosevelt Library, Hyde Park (NY), United States.

Morgenthau, Henry. 1945. Bretton Woods and international cooperation. *Foreign Affairs* 23(2): 182–94.

Morris, Marcus. 2014. From anti-colonialism to anti-imperialism: The evolution of H. M. Hyndman's critique of empire, c 1875–1905. *Historical Research* 87(236): 293–314.

Morris-Suzuki, Tessa. 1989. *A History of Japanese Economic Thought*. London: Routledge.

Morrison, James. 2012. Before hegemony: Adam Smith, American independence and the origins of the first era of globalization. *International Organization* 66(3): 395–428.

Motono, Eiichi. 2000. *Conflict and Cooperation in Sino-British Business, 1860–1911*. New York: St. Martin's Press.

Moynagh, Maureen and Nancy Forestell. 2012. General introduction. In Nancy Forestell and Maureen Moynagh, eds., *Documenting First Wave Feminisms*, Vol. 1, xxi–xxv. Toronto: University of Toronto Press.

Mrázek, Rudolf. 1972. Tan Malaka: A political personality's structure of experience. *Indonesia* 14: 1–48.

Mt.Pleasant, Jane and Robert Burt. 2010. Estimating productivity of traditional Iroquoian cropping systems from field experiments and historical literature. *Journal of Ethnobiology* 30(1) 52–79.

Mukerjee, Radhakamal. 1916. *The Foundations of Indian Economics*. London: Longmans, Green and Co.

Mukerjee, Radhakamal. 1934. The broken balance of population, land and water. In J. Krishnamurty, ed., *Towards Development Economics*, 159–66. New Delhi: Oxford University Press.

Mukerjee, Radhakamal. 1938. *The Regional Balance of Man*. Madras, University of Madras.

Mukherjee, Soumyen. 1996. Raja Rammohun Roy and the status of women in Bengal in the nineteenth century. *Sydney Studies in Society and Culture* 13: 41–65.

Mulder, Nicholas. 2022. *The Economic Weapon*. New Haven: Yale University Press.

Mumford, Lewis. 1934. *Technics and Civilization*. New York: Harcourt Brace and Company.

Mumford, Lewis. 1938. *The Culture of Cities*. New York: Harcourt Brace and Company.

Mumford, Lewis. 1941. *Faith for Living*. London: Secker and Warburg.

Mumford, Lewis. 1944. *The Condition of Man*. New York: Harcourt, Brace and Co.

Murphy, Craig. 1994. *International Organization and Industrial Change*. Oxford: Oxford University Press.

Muthu, Sarkar. 2008. Adam Smith's critique of international trading companies. *Political Theory* 36(2): 185–212.

Najita, Tetsuo. 1987. *Visions of Virtue in Tokugawa Japan*. Chicago: University of Chicago Press.

Nakai, Kate Wildman. 1988. *Shogunal Politics*. Cambridge: Council on East Asian Studies, Harvard University.

Nakhimovsky, Isaac. 2011. *The Closed Commercial State*. Princeton: Princeton University Press.

Nanda, Reena. 2002. *Kamaladevi Chattopadhyaya*. New Delhi: Oxford University Press.

Naoroji, Dadabhai. 1887. *Essays, Speeches, Addresses and Writings*. Edited by Chunilal Lallubhai Parekh. Bombay: Caxton Printing Works.

Narayan, John. 2017. The wages of whiteness in the absence of wages: racial capitalism, reactionary intercommunalism and the rise of Trumpism. *Third World Quarterly* 38(11): 2482–2500.

Neal, Larry. 1979. The economics and finance of bilateral clearing agreements: Germany, 1934–8. *The Economic History Review* 32(3): 391–404.

Neill, R. 1972. *A New Theory of Value: The Canadian Economics of H. A. Innis*. Toronto: University of Toronto Press.

Nemiña, Pablo and Diana Tussie. 2021. Post hegemonic policies in South America. *Sul Global* 2(2): 18–37.

Nguyen, Me and Benoit Malbranque. 2014. Le Chinois de Turgot. May 25 www.institutcoppet.org/les-chinois-de-turgot/. Accessed April 30, 2022.

Nicholls, David. 1996. *From Dessalines to Duvalier*. New Brunswick, NJ: Rutgers University Press.

Nolan, Mark C. 2013. *The Political and Economic Context of Keynes's 1933 Finlay Lecture*. DBA Thesis, University College Cork.

Noonan, Murray. 2017. *Marxist Theories of Imperialism*. London: I. B. Tauris.

Norman, Jesse. 2018. *Adam Smith*. New York: Basic Books.

North, Robert and Xenia Eudin. 1963. *M. N. Roy's Mission to China*. Berkeley: University of California Press.

Notehelfer, Fred. 1971. *Kōtoku Shūsui*. Cambridge: Cambridge University Press.

Nyland, Chris. 1993. Adam Smith, stage theory, and the status of women. *History of Political Economy* 25(4): 617–40.

O'Brien, Robert. 2021. Revisiting Rosa Luxemburg's internationalism. *Journal of International Political Theory* 17(1): 58–80.

Ohtsuki, Tadashi. 2011. The background of K. Akamatsu's *Gankou Keitai Ron* and its development: Early empirical analysis at Nagoya. In Heinz-Dieter Kurz, Tamotsu Nishizawa, and Keith Tribe, eds., *The Dissemination of Economic Ideas*, 292–314. Cheltenham: Edward Elgar.

Ohtsuki, Tadashi. 2017a. Changes in the pacifism of Akamatsu Kaname from the interwar Period to WWII. In Fabrizio Bientinesi and Rosario Patalano, eds., *Economists and War*, 117–32. London: Routledge.

Ohtsuki, Tadashi. 2017b. Economic research in national higher commercial schools in wartime Japan. In Yukihiro Ikeda and Annalisa Rosseili, eds., *War in the History of Economic Thought*, 138–56. London: Routledge.

Olson, Richard. 1998. Sex and status in Scottish Enlightenment social science: John Millar and the sociology of gender roles. *History of the Human Sciences* 11(1): 73–100.

Osterhammel, Jürgen. 2014. *The Transformation of the World*. Translated by Patrick Camiller. Princeton: Princeton University Press.

O'Sullivan. Christopher. 2008. *Sumner Welles*. New York: Columbia University Press.

Özgur, M. Erdem and Handi Genc. 2011. An Ottoman classical political economist: Sarantis Archigenes and his *Tasarrufat-i Mülkiye*. *Middle Eastern Studies* 7(2): 329–42.

Özveren, Eyüp. 2002. Ottoman economic thought and economic policy in transition. In Michalis Psalidopoulos and Marina Mata, eds., *Economic Thought and Policy in Less Developed Europe*, 129–44. London: Routledge.

Özveren, Eyüp and Erdem Özgur. 2021. The Turkish *Kadro* pIoneers of a Balkan *dependencia* in the interwar period. *The European Journal of the History of Economic Thought* 28(6): 910–39.

Özyüksel, Murat. 2014. *The Hejaz Railway and the Ottoman Empire*. Translated by Sezin Tekin. London: I. B. Tauris.

Packham, Catherine. 2017. Mary Wollstonecraft's cottage economics: Property, political economy, the European future. *ELH* 84(2): 453–74.

Padmore, George. [1931]1971. *The Life and Struggles of Negro Toilers*. Hollywood, CA: Sun Dance Press.

Padua, Jose Augusto. 2000. "Annilhating natural productions": Nature's economy, colonial crisis and the origins of Brazilian political environmentalism (1786–1810). *Environment and History* 6(3): 255–87.

Palatano, Rosario. 2016. Nation-world: autarky and geo-economics in Montchrétien's Traicté. *History of Economic Thought and Policy* 2: 87–100.

Palen, Marc-William. 2015. Free-trade ideology and transatlantic abolitionism. *Journal of the History of Economic Thought* 37(2): 291–304.

Palen, Marc-William. 2016. *The "Conspiracy" of Free Trade*. Cambridge: Cambridge University Press.

Palen, Marc-William. 2018. British free trade and the feminist vision for peace, c. 1846–1946. In David Thackeray, Richard Toye, and Andrew Thompson, eds., *Imagining Britain's Economic Future, c. 1800–1975*, 115–31. London: Palgrave MacMillan.

Palen, Marc-William. 2021. Marx and Manchester: The evolution of the socialist internationalist free-trade tradition, c.1846–1946. *The International History Review* 43(2): 381–98.

Palma, Gabriel. 2009. Why did the Latin American critical tradition in the social sciences become practically extinct? In Mark Blyth, ed., *Routledge Handbook of IPE*, 243–65. London: Routledge.

Pankhurst, Jerry. 1982. The ideology of "sex love" in postrevolutionary Russia: Lenin, Kollontai, and the politics of lifestyle liberation. *Alternative Lifestyles* 5(2): 78–100.

Parel, Anthony. 2006. *Gandhi's Philosophy and the Quest for Harmony*. Cambridge: Cambridge University Press.

Park, Saeyoung. 2017. Long live the tributary system! *Harvard Journal of Asiatic Studies* 77(1): 1–20.

Patalano, Rosario. 2016. Nation-World: Autarky and geo-economics in Montchrétien's Traicté. *History of Economic Thought and Policy* 2: 87–100.

Patel, Dinar. 2020. *Naoroji*. Cambridge, MA: Harvard University Press.

Pauly, Louis. 1997. *Who Elected the Bankers?* Ithaca: Cornell University Press.

Peattie, Mark. 1984. Japanese attitudes toward colonialism, 1895–1945. In Ramon Myers and Mark Peattie, eds., *The Japanese Colonial Empire, 1895–1945*, 80–127. Princeton: Princeton University Press.

Pechatnov, V. 2017. The Soviet Union and the Bretton Woods conference. In Giles Scott-Smith and J. Simon Rofe, eds., *Global Perspectives on the Bretton Woods Conference and the Post-War World Order*, 89–107. Cham, Switzerland: Palgrave Macmillan.

Pella Jr., John Anthony. 2015. *Africa and the Expansion of International Society: Surrendering the Savannah*. New York: Routledge.

Pearlman, Michael. 1996. *The Heroic and Creative Meaning of Socialism*. New Jersey: Humanities Press.

Perelman, Michael. 2008. Political economy and the press. *Unsettling Economics*, May 19. https://michaelperelman.wordpress.com/2008/05/19/political-economy-and-the-press-karl-marx-and-henry-carey-at-the-new-york-tribune/. Accessed April 12, 2022.

Perry, Jeffrey B. 2001. Introduction. In Hubert Harrison and Jeffrey Perry, eds., *A Hubert Harrison Reader*, 1–30. Middletown, CT: Wesleyan University Press.

Perry, Jeffrey B. 2009. *Hubert Harrison*. New York: Columbia University Press.

Phillips, Andrew. 2011 Saving civilization from empire: Belligerency, pacificism and the two faces of civilization during the Second Opium War. *European Journal of International Relations* 18(1): 5–27.

Pike, Fredrick. 1986. *The Politics of the Miraculous in Peru*. Lincoln: University of Nebraska Press.

Pitts, Jennifer. 2009. Liberalism and empire in a nineteenth-century Algerian mirror. *Modern Intellectual History* 6(2): 287–313.

Pitts, Jennifer. 2018. *Boundaries of the International*. Cambridge, MA: Harvard University Press.

Polanyi, Karl. 1944. *The Great Transformation*. Boston: Beacon.

Pradella, Lucia. 2017. Postcolonial theory and the making of the world working class. *Critical Sociology* 34(4–5): 573–86.

Prasch, Robert. 2008. W. E. B. Du Bois's contributions to US economics (1893–1910). *Du Bois Review* 5(2): 309–24.

Pusey, James Reeve. 1983. *China and Charles Darwin*. Cambridge, MA: Council on East Asian Studies, Harvard University Press.

Radkau, Joachim. 2014. *The Age of Ecology*. Translated by Patrick Camiller. Cambridge: Polity.

Rae, John. [1834]1964. *Statement of Some New Principles on the Subject of Political Economy: Exposing the Fallacies of the System of Free Trade and of Some Other Doctrines Maintained in the Wealth of Nations*. New York: Augustus Kelley.

Rambelli, Fabio. 2011. Sada Kaiseki: An alternative discourse on Buddhism, modernity, and nationalism in the early Meiji period. In Roy Starrs, ed., *Politics and Religion in Japan*, 104–42. New York: Palgrave Macmillan.

Rambelli, Fabio. 2017. Buddhism and the capitalist transformation of modern Japan. In Hanna Havnevik, Ute Hüsken, Mark Teewen, Vladimir Tikhonov, and Koen Wellens, eds., *Buddhist Modernities*, 33–50. New York: Routledge.

Ranade, Mahadev Govind. 1906. *Essays on Indian Economics*. 2nd ed. Madras: G. A. Natesan and Company.

Reader, Luke. 2019. "An alternative to imperialism": Leonard Woolf, The Labour Party and imperial internationalism, 1915–1922. *The International History Review*, 41(1): 157–77.

Reddi, Muthulakshmi. [1933]2012. Creative citizenship. In Nancy Forestell and Maureen Moynagh, eds., *Documenting First Wave Feminisms, Vol. 1*, 202–4. Toronto: University of Toronto Press.

Reddock, Rhoda. 2014. The first Mrs Garvey: Pan-Africanism and feminism in the early 20th century British colonial Caribbean. *Feminist Africa* 19: 58–77.

Rees, David. 1973. *Harry Dexter White*. New York: Coward, McCann, and Geoghegan.

Reid, Margaret. 1934. *Economics of Household Production*. New York: John Wiley and Sons.

Rethel, Lena. 2019. Corporate Islam, global capitalism and the performance of economic moralities. *New Political Economy* 24(3): 350–64.

Rendall, Jane. 1997. "The grand causes which combine to carry mankind forward": Wollstonecraft, history and revolution. *Women's Writing* 4(2): 155–72.

Ricardo, David. [1817]1908. *Principles of Political Economy and Taxation*. London: Gorge Bell and Sons.

Roberts, Luke. 1998. *Mercantilism in a Japanese Domain*. Cambridge: Cambridge University Press.

Robertson, John M. 1899. *Patriotism and Empire*. London: Grant Richards.

Robinson, Cedric. 1983. *Black Marxism*. Chapel Hill: University of North Carolina Press.

Rojas, Cristina. 2002. *Civilization and Violence*. London: University of Minnesota Press.

Rosenberg, Justin. 2020. Trotsky's error: Multiplicity and the secret origins of revolutionary Marxism. *Globalizations* 17(3): 477–97.

Rosenboim, Or. 2016. Barbara Wootton, Friedrich Hayek, and the debate on democratic federalism in the 1940s. *The International History Review* 36(5): 894–918.

Rothschild, Emma. 2001. *Economic Sentiments*. Cambridge, MA: Harvard University Press.

Rowe, William. 1993. State and market in Mid-Qing economic thought: The case of Chen Hongmou (1696–1771). *Études Chinois* 12(1): 5–39.

Rowe, William. 1997. Economics and culture in eighteenth-century China. In Kenneth Lieberthal, Shuen-fu Lin, and Ernest Young, eds., *Constructing China*, 7–23. Ann Arbor: Center for Chinese Studies, University of Michigan.

Rowe, William. 2001. *Saving the World*. Stanford: Stanford University Press.

Roy, Samaren. 1997. *M. N. Roy*. Hyderabab, India: Orient Longman.

Ruggie, John Gerard. 1982. International regimes, transactions, and change: Embedded liberalism in the postwar economic order. *International Organization* 36(2): 379–415.

Rupke, Nicolaas. 2018. Alexander von Humboldt, 1769–1859. In Joy Palmer Cooper and David Cooper, eds., *Key Thinkers on the Environment*, 76–82. London, Routledge.

Rupp, Leila. 1997. *Worlds of Women*. Princeton: Princeton University Press.

Ruskin, John. [1862]1923. "Unto This Last": Four essays on the first principles of political economy. In Humphrey Milford, ed., *The Works of Ruskin*, 11–138. London: Oxford University Press.

Sagers, John. 2006. *Origins of Japanese Wealth and Power*. New York: Palgrave MacMillan.

Saito, Kohei. 2017. *Karl Marx's Ecosocialism*. New York: Monthly Review Press.

Sally, Razeen. 1998. *Classical Liberalism and International Economic Order*. London: Routledge.

Salvatore, Ricardo. 1999. The strength of markets in Latin America's sociopolitical discourse, 1750–1850. *Latin American Perspectives* 26(1): 22–43.

Salvucci, Richard. 1996. Texas, "tyrants", and trade with Mexico. In Richard Salvucci, ed., *Latin America and the World Economy*, 60–68. Lexington, MA: D. C. Heath and Company.

Sanchez-Sibony, Oscar. 2014a. Depression Stalinism. *Kritika: Explorations in Russian and Eurasian History* 15(1): 23–49.

Sanchez-Sibony, Oscar. 2014b. *Red Globalization*. Cambridge: Cambridge University Press.

Sang-Ik, Lee. 2000. On the concepts of "New Korea" envisioned by enlightenment reformers. *Korea Journal* 40(2): 34–64.

Sarkar, Benoy Kumar. 1922. *The Futurism of Young Asia and Other Essays on the Relations between the East and the West*. Berlin: Julius Springer.

Sarkar, Benoy Kumar. [1926]1938. *The Politics of Boundaries and Tendencies in International Relations, Vol. 1*. Calcutta: N. M. Ray Chowdhury and Company.

Sarkar, Benoy. 1943a. *The Equations of World-Economy and Their Bearings on Post-War Reconstruction*. Calcutta: Chuckervertty Chatterjee and Co.

Sarkar, Benoy. 1943b. World-politics and post-war economic planning. *The Indian Journal of Political Science* 5(2): 161–90.

Schiffrin, Harold. 1980. *Sun Yat-sen*. Boston: Little, Brown, and Company.

Schmid, Andre. 2002. *Korea between Empires, 1895–1919*. New York: Colombia University Press.

Schmoller, Gustav. [1884]1910. *The Mercantile System and Its Historical Significance*. Translated by W. A. Ashley. New York: Macmillan.

Schneer, Jonathan. 1999. Anti-imperial London: The Pan-African Conference of 1900. In Felix Driver and David Gilbert, eds., *Imperial Cities*, 254–67. Manchester: Manchester University Press.

Schröppel, Christian and Nakajima Mariko. 2003. The changing interpretation of the flying geese model of economic development. *Japanstudien* 14(1): 203–36.

Schuler, Kurt and Andrew Rosenberg. 2012a. Introduction. In Kurt Schuler and Andrew Rosenberg, eds., *The Bretton Woods Transcripts*, 1–36. New York: Center for Financial Stability.

Schuler, Kurt and Andrew Rosenberg, eds. 2012b. *The Bretton Woods Transcripts*. New York: Center for Financial Stability.

Schumacher, Reinhard. 2020. Altering the pattern of trade in the *Wealth of Nations*. *Journal of the History of Economic Thought* 42(1): 19–42.

Schwartz, Benjamin. 1964. *In Search of Wealth and Power*. Cambridge, MA: Belknap Press of the Harvard University Press.

Schwarz, Bill. 2003. George Padmore. In Bill Schwarz, ed., *West Indian Intellectuals in Britain*, 132–52. Manchester: Manchester University Press.

Scott, John and Ray Bromley. 2013. *Envisioning Sociology*. Albany: State University of New York.

Seabrooke, Len and Kevin Young. 2017. The networks and niches of international political economy. *Review of International Political Economy* 24(2): 288–331.

Seishisai, Aizawa. [1825]1986. New theses. In Bob Tadashi Wakabayashi, ed., *Anti-Foreignism and Western Learning in Early-modern Japan*, 149–277. Cambridge, MA: Council on East Asian Studies, Harvard University Press.

Sekyi, Kobina. [1917]1979. The future of subject peoples. In J. Ayo Langley, ed., *Ideologies of Liberation in Black Africa, 1856–1970*, 242–51. London: Rex Collings.

Semmel, Bernard. 1993. *The Liberal Ideal and the Demons of Empire*. Baltimore: John Hopkins University Press.

Shabas, Margaret. 2005. *The Natural Origins of Economics*. Chicago: University of Chicago Press.

Shackleton, J. R. 1990. Jane Marcet and Harriet Martineau: Pioneers of economics education. *History of Education* 19(4): 283–297.

Shaev, Brian. 2018. Liberalising regional trade: Socialists and European economic integration. *Contemporary European History* 27(2): 258–79.

Shang, Yang. 2017. *The Book of Lord Shang*. Translated and edited by Yuri Pines. New York: Columbia University Press.

Sherwood, Marika. 2003. Amy Ashwood Garvey (1897–1969). In Hakim Adi and Marika Sherwood, eds., *Pan-African History*, 69–75. London: Routledge.

Shilliam, Robbie. 2006. What about Marcus Garvey? Race and the transformation of sovereignty debate. *Review of International Studies* 32(3): 379–400.

Shilliam, Robbie. 2021a. The past and present of abolition: Reassessing Adam Smith's "liberal reward of labor". *Review of International Political Economy* 28(3): 690–711.

Shilliam, Robbie. 2021b. Theorizing (with) Amy Ashwood Garvey. In Patricia Owens and Katharina Rietzler, eds., *Women's International Thought*, 158–78. Cambridge: Cambridge University Press.

Singh, Vir Bahadur. 1975. *From Naoroji to Nehru*. Delhi: Macmillan.

Singh, Sunit Sarvraj. 2018. *Echoes of Freedom: Radical Indian Thought and International Socialism, 1905–1920*. PhD diss., Divinity School, University of Chicago.

Skidelsky, Robert. 1983. *John Maynard Keynes, Vol. 1*. London: Macmillan.

Skidelsky, Robert. 1992. *John Maynard Keynes, Vol. 2*. London: Macmillan.

Slate, Nico. 2012. *Colored Cosmopolitanism*. Cambridge, MA: Harvard University Press.

Slodobian, Quinn. 2018. *Globalists*. Cambridge, MA: Harvard University Press.

Smaldone, William. 1988. Rudolf Hilferding and the theoretical foundations of German Social Democracy, 1902–33. *Central European History* 21(3): 267–99.

Smith, Adam. 1776. *An Inquiry into the Nature and Causes of the Wealth of Nations*. London: W. Strahan and T. Cadell.

Smith, Craig. 2019. Chinese Asianism in the early republic: Guomindang intellectuals and the brief internationalist turn. *Modern Asian Studies* 53(2): 582–605.

Smith, Richard. 2018. Karl Marx, 1818–1883. In Joy Palmer Cooper and David Cooper, eds., *Key Thinkers on the Environment*, 115–20. London: Routledge.

Soddy, Frederick. 1922. *Cartesian Economics*. London: Henderson.

Soddy, Frederick. 1926. *Wealth, Virtual Wealth and Debt*. New York: E. P. Dutton and Co.

Soddy, Frederick. 1934. *The Role of Money*. London: Routledge.

Sowell, David. 1996. Artisans and tariff reform. In Vincent Peloso and Barbara Tenenbaum, eds., *Liberals, Politics and Power*, 166–85. Athens: University of Georgia Press.

Spall, Richard Francis. 1988. Free trade, foreign relations, and the Anti-Corn-Law League. *International History Review* 10: 405–32.

Spengler, Joseph. 1959. John Rae on economic development. *Quarterly Journal of Economics* 73(3): 393–406.

Spenser, Daniela. 2008. Radical Mexico: Limits to the impact of Soviet Communism. *Latin American Perspectives* 35(2): 57–70.

Sperber, Jonathan. 2014. *Karl Marx*. New York: Liveright.

Staff, Michelle. 2020. Women's rights on the world stage: Feminism and internationalism in the life of Chrystal Macmillan (1872–1937). *Journal of Women's History* 32(2): 38–63.

Steffek, Jens. 2015. Fascist Internationalism. *Millennium* 44(1): 3–22.

Stein, Judith. 1986. *The World of Marcus Garvey*. Baton Rouge: Louisiana State University Press.

Strange, Susan. 1974. Review of *Small Is Beautiful. International Affairs* 50(1): 104–5.

Strange, Susan. 1982. Cave! Hic dragones: A critique of regime analysis. *International Organization* 36(2): 479–96.

Strange, Susan, ed. 1984. *Paths to International Political Economy*. London: Allen and Unwin.

Strange, Susan. 1985. International political economy: The story so far and the way ahead. In W. Ladd Hollist and F. LaMond Tullis, eds., *An International Political Economy, Vol. 1*, 13–26. London: Pinter.

Strange, Susan. 1995. Political economy and international relations. In Ken Booth and Steve Smith, eds., *International Relations Theory Today*, 154–74. Cambridge: Polity Press.

Stuart, Robert. 1996. "Calm, with a grave and serious temperament, rather male": French Marxism, gender and feminism, 1882–1905. *International Review of Social History* 41(1): 57–82.

Suganami, Hidemi. 1978. A note on the origin of the word "international". *British Journal of International Studies* 4(3): 226–32.

Sugiyama, Chūhei. 1994. *Origins of Economic Thought in Modern Japan*. London: Routledge.

Sun Yat-sen. [1920]1922. *The International Development of China*. New York: G. P. Putnam's Sons.

Sun Yat-sen. [1924]2011. Pan-Asianism. In Sven Saaler and Christopher Szpilman, eds., *Pan-Asianism: A Documentary History, Vol. 2, 1920–Present*, 78–85. Boulder, CO: Rowman and Littlefield.

Sun Yat-sen. 1928. *San Min Chu I: The Three Principles of the People*. Translated by Frank Price, edited by L. T. Chen. Shanghai: The Commercial Press.

Swaby, Nydia. 2011. *Woman Radical, Woman Intellectual, Woman Activist: The Political Life of Pan-African Feminist Amy Ashwood Garvey*. MA thesis, Sarah Lawrence College.

Szejnmann, Claus-Christian W. 2013. Nazi economic thought and rhetoric during the Weimar Republic: Capitalism and its discontents. *Politics, Religion & Ideology*, 14(3): 355–76.

Szporluk, Roman. 1988. *Communism and Nationalism*. New York: Oxford.

Ta Min. 2014. The Chinese origin of physiocratic economics. In Cheng Lin, Terry Peach, and Wang Fang, eds., *A History of Ancient Chinese Economic Thought*, 82–97. London: Routledge.

Tagher, J. 1950. Mohammad Ali jugé par lui-même ou les declarations du viceroi aux consuls et hôtes étrangers. *Chaiers d'Histoire Egyptienne* 2(1): 18–60.

Talbot, Margaret. 1991. An emancipated voice: Flora Tristan and utopian allegory. *Feminist Studies* 17(2): 219–39.

Tausch, Arno. 2016. Kaname Akamatsu: Biography and long cycles theory. In Leonid Grinin, Tessaleno Devezas, and Andrey Korotayev, eds., *Kondratiff Waves*, 65–81. Volgograd: Uchitel Publishing House.

Taylor, Harriett. [1851]1868. *Enfranchisement of Women*. New York: Office of "The Revolution".

Teichgraeber III, Richard. 1987. "Less abused than I had reason to expect": The reception of *The Wealth of Nations* in Britain, 1776–90. *Historical Journal* 30(2): 337–66.

Thompson, William and Anna Wheeler. 1825. *Appeal of One Half the Human Race, Women, Against the Pretentions of the Other Half, Men, to Retain Them in Political, and Thence in Civil and Domestic, Slavery.* London: Longman, Hurst, Rees, Orme, Brown, and Green, Paternoster-Row.

Tierney, Robert Thomas. 2015. *Monster of the Twentieth Century.* Berkeley: University of California Press.

Tignor, Robert. 1977. Bank Misr and foreign capitalism. *International Journal of Middle East Studies* 8(2): 161–81.

Tikhonov, Vladimir. 2016. Korea in the Russian and Soviet imagination, 1850s–1945. *Journal of Korean Studies* 21(2): 385–421.

Toby, Ronald. 1984. *State and Diplomacy in Early Modern Japan.* Princeton: Princeton University Press.

Todd, David. 2015. *Free Trade and Its Enemies in France, 1814–1851.* Cambridge: Cambridge University Press.

Tooze, Adam. 2006. *The Wages of Destruction.* London: Allen Lane.

Totman, Conrad. 1989. *The Green Archipelago.* Berkeley: University of California Press.

Travers, Robert. 2007. *Ideology and Empire in Eighteenth-Century India.* Cambridge: Cambridge University Press.

Trentmann, Frank. 1997. Wealth versus welfare: The British left between free trade and national political economy before the First World War. *Historical Research* 70(171): 70–98.

Trentmann, Frank. 2008. *Free Trade Nation.* Oxford: Oxford University Press.

Trescott, Paul. 2007. *Jingji Xue: The History of the Introduction of Western Economic Ideas into China, 1850–1950.* Hong Kong: The Chinese University Press.

Tronto, Joan. 2015. Hunting for women, haunted by gender: The rhetorical limits of the Manifesto. In Terrell Carver and James Farr, eds., *The Cambridge Companion to The Communist Manifesto*, 134–51. Cambridge: Cambridge University Press.

Tsurumi, E. Patricia. 1990. *Factory Girls.* Princeton: Princeton University Press.

Turner, Joyce Moore with the assistance of W. Burghardt Turner. 2005. *Caribbean Crusaders and the Harlem Renaissance.* Urbana: University of Illinois Press.

Tussie, Diana. 2020. The tailoring of IPE in Latin America. In Ernesto Vivares, ed., *The Routledge Handbook to Global Political Economy*, 92–110. London: Routledge.

Tussie, Diana and Fabricio Chagas-Bastos. 2022. Misrecognized, misfit and misperceived; Why not a Latin American school of IPE? *Review of International Political Economy* (forthcoming).

Tussie, Diana and Pia Riggirozzi. 2015. A global conversation. *Contexto Internacional* 37(3): 1041–68.

Umoren, Imaobog. 2018. *Race Women Internationalists.* Oakland: University of California Press.

United Negro Improvement Association (UNIA). 1920. *Declaration of the Rights of the Negro Peoples of the World.* New York. August 13. http://historymatters.gmu.edu/d/5122/.Accessed April 30, 2022.

US State Department. 1943. *United Nations Conference on Food and Agriculture, Hot Springs, Virginia, May 18–June 3, 1943, Final Act and Section Reports.* Washington: US Government Printing Office.

US State Department. 1948. *Proceedings of the Documents of the United Nations Monetary and Financial Conference, Bretton Woods, New Hampshire, July 1–22, 1944.* Washington: US Government Printing Office.

Vapnek, Lara. 2014. The 1919 International Congress of Working Women. *Journal of Women's History* 25(4): 160–84.

Vassar Historian. n.d. Mabel Newcomer. *Vassar Encylcopedia.* http://vcencyclopedia .vassar.edu/faculty/prominent-faculty/mabel-newcomer.html. Accessed April 30, 2022.

Vastey, Jean Louis. [1814]2014. *The Colonial System Unveiled.* Translated and edited by Chris Bongie. Liverpool: Liverpool University Press.

Vernengo, Matías. 2007. Economic ideas and policies in historical perspective: Cairú and Hamilton on trade and finance. In Estaban Pérez Caldentey and Matías Vernego, eds., *Ideas, Policies and Economic Development in the Americas,* 227–39. New York: Routledge.

Viner, Jacob. 1948. Power versus plenty as objectives of foreign policy in the seventeenth and eighteenth centuries. *World Politics* 1(1): 1–29.

Virdee, Satnam. 2017. The second sight of racialised outsiders in the imperialist core. *Third World Quarterly* 38(11): 2396–410.

von Brescius, Moritz. 2012. Connected the new world: Nets, mobility, and progress in the age of Alexander von Humboldt. *International Review for Humboldtian Studies* 13(25): 11–33.

von Liebig, Justus. 1859. *Letters on Modern Agriculture.* London: Walton and Maberly.

Von Laue, Theodore. 1951. The industrialization of Russia in the writings of Sergej Witte. *The American Slavic and East European Review* 10(3): 177–90.

van Ree, Erik. 1998. Socialism in one country: A reassessment. *Studies in East European Thought* 50(2): 77–117.

van Ree, Erik. 2010. "Socialism in one country" before Stalin: German origins. *Journal of Political Ideologies* 15(2): 143–59.

van Ree, Erik. 2019. Marx and Engels's theory of history: Making sense of the race factor. *Journal of Political Ideologies* 24(1): 54–73.

Vanden, Harry and Marc Becker, eds., 2011. José Carlos Mariátegui: An Anthology. New York: Monthly Review Press.

Vitalis, Robert. 2015. *White World Order, Black Power Politics.* Ithaca: Cornell University Press.

Voeten, Erik. 2021. *Ideology and International Institutions.* Princeton: Princeton University Press.

Von Glahn, Richard. 2016. *The Economic History of China.* Cambridge: Cambridge University Press.

Wagner, Jeffrey Paul. 1978. *Sano Manabu and the Japanese Adaptation of Socialism.* PhD diss., Department of History, University of Arizona.

Wakabayashi, Bob Tadashi. 1986. *Anti-Foreignism and Western Learning in Early-Modern Japan.* Cambridge, MA: Council on East Asian Studies, Harvard University Press.

Walker, Brett. 2001. *The Conquest of the Ainu Lands*. Berkeley: University of California Press.

Walls, Laura Dassow. 2009. *The Passage to Cosmos*. Chicago: University of Chicago Press.

Wang, Dong. 2005. *China's Unequal Treaties*. Lanham: Lexington Books.

Warde, Paul. 2018. *The Invention of Sustainability*. Cambridge: Cambridge University Press.

Watson, Mathew. 2017. Historicising Ricardo's comparative advantage theory. *New Political Economy* 22(3): 257–72.

Watts, Vanessa. 2013. Indigenous place-thought and agency amongst humans and non-humans (First Women and Sky Women go on a European world tour!). *Decolonization: Indigeneity, Education and Society* 2(1): 20–34.

Weaver, Kathleen. 2019. Flora Tristan, Precursor Lecture by Magda Portal. *Journal of International Women's Studies* 20(6): 4–22.

Weber, Heloise. 2015. Is IPE just "boring", or committed to problematic mets-theoretical assumptions? *Contexto Internacional* 37(3): 913–44.

Wei, Julie Lee, Ramon Myers, and Donald Gillin, eds. 1994. *Prescriptions for Saving China*. Translated by Julie Lee Wei, E-su Zen, and Linda Chao. Stanford: Hoover Institution Press.

Weiner, Richard. 2004. *Race, Nation and Market*. Tucson: University of Arizona Press.

Weiss, Holger. 2019. Framing Black communist labour union activism in the Atlantic world: James W. Ford and the establishment of the International Trade Union Committee of Negro Workers. *International Review of Social History* 64(2): 249–78.

Wendler, Eugen. 2015. *Friedrich List (1789–1846)*. New York: Springer.

Went, Robert. 2002. *The Enigma of Globalization*. London: Routledge.

White, Richard Alan. 1978. *Paraguay's Autonomous Revolution, 1810–1840*. Albuquerque: University of New Mexico Press.

Whitworth, Sandra. 1994. *Feminism and International Relations*. New York: St. Martins Press.

Whyte, Kyle. 2018. Settler colonialism, ecology, and environmental justice. *Environment and Society* 9(1): 125–44.

Wilbur, C. Martin. 1976. *Sun Yat-sen*. New York: Columbia University Press.

Williams, Eric. 1944. *Capitalism and Slavery*. Chapel Hill: University of North Carolina Press.

Williams, John Hoyt. 1979. *The Rise and Fall of the Paraguyan Republic, 1800–1870*. Austin: Institute of Latin American Studies, The University of Texas at Austin.

Williams, David. 2014. Adam Smith and colonialism. *Journal of International Political Theory* 10(3): 283–301.

Woolner, David. 2017. The man who wasn't there: Cordell Hull, Bretton Woods, and the creation of the GATT. In Giles Scott-Smith and J. Simon Rofe, eds., *Global Perspectives on the Bretton Woods Conference and the Post-War World Order*, 245–62. Cham, Switzerland: Palgrave Macmillan.

Wollstonecraft, Mary. [1792]2004. *A Vindication of the Rights of Women*. New York: Penguin.

Women's International League for Peace and Freedom (WILPF). 1919. *Resolutions, 2nd Congress, Zurich, 1919.* https://wilpf.org/wp-content/uploads/2012/08/WILPF_triennial_congress_1919.pdf. Accessed April 20, 2022.

Wood, James A. 2006. The Republic regenerated: French and Chilean revolutions in the imagination of Francisco Bilbao, 1842–1851. *Atlantic Studies* 3(1): 7–23.

Woolf, S. 1968. Did a fascist economic system exist? In S. J. Woolf, ed., *The Nature of Fascism*, 119–51. London: Weidenfeld and Nicolson.

Wu, Tien-wei. 1969. A review of the Wuhan debacle: The Kuomintang–Communist split of 1927. *The Journal of Asian Studies* 29(1): 125–43.

Wu, Guo. 2010. *Zheng Guanying.* Amherst, NY: Cambria Press.

Wulf, Andrea. 2015. *The Invention of Nature.* New York: Vintage Books.

Wyatt-Walter, Andrew. 1996. Adam Smith and the liberal tradition in international relations. *Review of International Studies* 22(1): 5–28.

Wylie, Raymond F. 1979. Mao Tse-tung, Ch'en Po-ta and the "Sinification" of Marxism, 1936–38. *China Quarterly* 79: 447–80.

Yan, Fu. [1902]2000. Forward to the first Chinese edition of *The Wealth of Nations*. In Cheng-chung Lai, ed. and trans., *Adam Smith Across Nations*, 27–33. Oxford: Oxford University Press.

Yellen, Jeremy. 2019. *The Greater East Asia Co-Prosperity Sphere.* Ithaca: Cornell University Press.

Young, Leslie. 1996. The Tao of markets: Sima Qian and the Invisible Hand. *Pacific Economic Review* 1(2): 137–45.

Zanasi, Margherita. 2006. *Saving the Nation.* Chicago: University of Chicago Press.

Zanasi, Margherita. 2020. *Economic Thought in Modern China.* Cambridge: Cambridge University Press.

Zarrow, Peter. 1988. He Zhen and anarcho-feminism in China. *Journal of Asian Studies* 47(4): 796–813.

Zastoupil, Lynn. 2010. *Rammohun Roy and the Making of Victorian Britain.* New York: Palgrave Macmillan.

Zetkin, Clara. [1907]2012. A resolution introduced at the International Socialist Congress. In Nancy Forestell and Maureen Moynagh, eds., *Documenting First Wave Feminisms, Vol. 1,* 137–43. Toronto: University of Toronto Press.

Zhang, Shizhi. 2021. *The Return of China: Historicising China in the Global Economy.* PhD diss., Department of Politics, Sheffield University.

Zimmermann, Susan. 2019. Equality of women's economic status? A major bone of contention in the international gender politics emerging during the interwar period. *The International History Review* 41(1): 200–27.

# Index

9 781009 337526